RAYS OF LIGHT IN A DARKENING WORLD

Daily Doses of Hope from The Book of Psalms

DR. RUSS BARKSDALE

ISBN: 978-1-953606-08-2

Published by
Engedi Publishing LLC
Austin, Texas

To Sue Barksdale
The lesser light that rules my heart

INTRODUCTION

I'm old enough to remember being in church services where no words of songs were on a big screen. We had a book of songs that we sang out of called a hymnal. During the singing part of the worship service, we'd grab one from the back of the pew in front of us and turn to the hymn number the song leader would bark out.

Through years of singing out of the hymnal, I and many others knew the page numbers of a lot of the songs: "Holy, Holy, Holy" was Hymn #1; "Great is Thy Faithfulness" was #54 (I think), & "Old Rugged Cross", #145. Many times in the Sunday evening service (yes, there was church on Sunday AND Wednesdays!), we would have a 'hymn sing' where people in the audience would call out a hymn number and we'd sing the whole service. It was fantastic!

The Book of Psalms was the song book of the ancient Hebrew people. The Hebrew title, '*Tehillim*', means 'praise songs' or 'hymns.' These were the songs of Israel. The melodies have been lost, but not the messages.

The Book of Psalms is the most powerful and rich compilation of songs, poems, and prayers on the face of the earth. You'll find raw emotions here, even calling on God to kill a personal enemy! The Book of Psalms is probably the grittiest, most gut-honest book in the Bible. Inside the Psalms you see just about every human emotional possible: praise and thanksgiving to God—certainly. But they also express their frustration and anger with God. The Psalms were written by real people who were going through real challenges and were expressing real, unfiltered emotions of joy, hope, anxiety, fear, grief, depression, loneliness, anger, resentment, sadness, shame, love wonder, and worship. That is why the Book of Psalms is probably the most read book of the Bible. God speaks to us from every part of Scripture, but sometimes it's easier to hear when we are in the Psalms!

There are 150 psalms in all. Through the years I've tried to read five psalms each morning which gets me through them completely every month. I have memorized tons of them, and they have sustained me through the trials and tragedies of my life for the last 50 years.

We know some of the writers, David is one, that God inspired to compose these songs. We know The Psalms are God's word, inspired by His Spirit for His people. We know He preserved the Psalms through the ages and they have been a source of encouragement and instruction for believers for three millennia.

I began writing these devotionals when my wife was going through chemotherapy and radiation for breast cancer. For those personal reasons and because of the increased turmoil in our world, I believe God wanted me to write this book to help others through the confusion and consternation that is a part of life. As we walk through them together this year, my prayer is that they open up to you and minister to your soul like never before.

Russ Barksdale
August 1, 2021
Arlington, Texas

INTERESTING FACTS ABOUT THE PSALMS

1. The Psalms were written over a period of about 1,000 years.

2. The Psalms are used in worship by both Jews and Christians.

3. Jesus began and ended His earthly ministry quoting the Psalms (Psalms 69:32-33 & Psalm 31:5).

4. David wrote roughly half of the 150 psalms while six other individuals are cited as authors. Almost 50 of the Psalms are anonymous.

5. The word 'selah' appears over 70 times indicating a dramatic pause.

6. The shortest chapter (Psalm 117 has two verses) and the longest chapter (Psalm 119 has 176 verses) in the Bible are found in the Psalms.

7. Jesus quoted the Psalms more than any other Old Testament writing.

TWO PATHS
January 1

"For the Lord watches over the path of the godly, but the path of the wicked leads to destruction."
Psalm 1:6

Sue and I were recently in central Oregon at a place called Smith Rock. We (I) decided that we should climb to the top of the 3,200' high ridge. There were two paths to get to the top: one path stretched around to the backside of the rock and with a longer, more sane approach to the precipice; the other, called Misery Ridge Trail (that should have been my first clue), went almost straight up with switchbacks every 3-4 feet. We (I) decided to take Misery Ridge Trail, which we found out later people have actually died on! The heat (98), the elevation, the difficulty, dehydration, our age, almost killed us—literally!

Two paths. This theme runs throughout Scripture. Adam and Eve were presented with two paths, and they chose the wrong one. Abraham chose the wrong path, then the right one. Generations later, as the Hebrews entered into the Promised Land, their leader, Joshua, challenged them to choose between Yahweh or false gods: *"Choose today whom you will serve . . . As for me and my family, we will serve the Lord"* (Joshua 14-15). For centuries after that, the prophets called people to choose the right path.

Jesus taught about the two paths: *"Enter through the narrow gate. For the gate is wide and the road broad that leads to destruction. . . . How narrow is the gate and difficult the road that leads to life, and few find it"* (Matthew 7:13-15; CSB).

Two paths. One leads to life, one leads to death. Psalm 1 is about the two paths. The last verse is the key to the entire psalm: *"For the Lord watches over the path of the godly, but the path of the wicked leads to destruction"* (v.6).

It's no accident that this psalm is the very first in the Psalter. It sets the pace and tone for the other 149 psalms. Take about five minutes and read the psalm through twice. Underline any key words that stand out to you. Write in the margins any questions you might have. This psalm is the perfect beginning for the New Year. Pray that God will cause you to fall in love with Him and His word as we walk through these psalms the next 365 days.

God, I confess I have a tendency to wander down the wrong path. I want to choose and walk the path that leads to LIFE. Draw me to Your word and down THAT path! Amen

THE FIRST PATH: BLESSED
January 2

"How happy is the one who . . ."
Psalm 1:1 (CSB)

In 2010, four of my buds and I rode our motorcycles from Arlington, Texas to Colorado Springs. From there we rode through the different mountain passes and roads. When we rode up Pike's Peak, the road stopped and we hiked up a path that took us to a lookout from this 14,000' giant of a mountain. Below we could see other mountains, the valleys, and rivers, and even the curvature of the earth! What a view—what a trip!

The Bible is clear: there are two paths humans can choose from. The first path, the path to life, is described in vv.1-3. This life path takes us on a journey that exposes us to a beautiful and majestic panorama of God's blessings that far exceed the Pike's Peak experience. Some translations begin the Psalm with "Blessed is the person who..." You might recognize the verbiage from the beginning of the Sermon on the Mount (Matthew 5-7) when Jesus began this greatest sermon ever with the words, "Blessed are the . . ."

The word '*blessed*' (Hebrew *esher*) carries the idea of being happy, joyful, and favored. The first usage of this word was to Abraham: *"I will make you into a great nation. I will bless you and make you famous, and you will be a blessing to others"* (Genesis 12:2). To Abraham, the blessing included God's favor to have a child (he and Sarah were older than dirt!) and eventually 12 great-grandsons who would become the Hebrew nation. Favor would include a measure of prosperity (though not without great trial) and a land of their own.

In His sermon, Jesus expanded the understanding of '*blessed*,' focusing on broader, more eternal themes: the blessed are those who are poor in spirit, who mourn, who are humble, etc. Their reward was greater than earthly possessions: heaven, comfort, seeing God, etc. Instead of inheriting a plot of land in the Middle East, He promised that they would inherit the entire earth as the Church advanced His gospel message.

The core meaning of '*blessed*' is the same, regardless, and it identifies the first, the best path: the path filled with joy, happiness, and the favor of God.

God, thank You for identifying the right path; the path of your favor; the path of flourishing. Enable me to walk and experience Your and Your blessing more. Amen

THE FIRST PATH: TRAP-RIDDLED
January 3

"How happy (blessed) is the one who does not walk in the advice of the wicked or stand in the pathway with sinners or sit in the company of mockers!"
Psalm 1:1 (CSB)

In 1964, my family drove to the New York World's Fair. My dad had directions from my uncle on how to get through Manhattan to their house. Somehow, we made the wrong turn coming out of the Lincoln Tunnel and ended up down at the docks during a longshoreman's strike—at night. Angry men with signs, yelling at us Okies who were as lost as a goose, was terribly unsettling. I looked over at my 11-year-old brother who was praying on his knees in the back floorboard—and decided to join him! We were definitely on the wrong path.

Our psalmist warns us that the right path, the blessed path, the path to genuine life, is littered with folks who will try to lead us astray. Remember the story of Pinocchio? Pinocchio was on the right path, the one leading to school, but he was intercepted by Honest John and his sidekick, Gideon. They convinced Pinocchio that a different path was better: "Hi-diddle-dee-dee, an actor's life for me…" This path almost led Pinocchio and his father, Geppetto, to their demise.

Notice the three deceivers listed. The first is the wicked. Most likely this refers to, not just those outside the faith, but those whose whole life is the antithesis of a godly person. Their lives are just plain evil, and they try to lure us into their evil deeds. The second is the sinner, a general reference to someone who is not a believer. We might work or go to school with them. They're nice and their lives seem fairly normal, but they don't hold biblical perspectives and values. They lure us by giving us 'worldly' wisdom and, if we're not knowledgeable, we'll take their advice and eventually suffer great harm. The third is the mocker. This is someone who mocks God and the things of God. We might come across them in our education process, particularly at the college level, or in the workplace.

We are warned over and over again about Satan's desire to lure us toward the wrong path (1 Peter 5:8, 2 Timothy 2:26, etc.), and he uses people as unwitting pawns in his game of death. The blessed person is the one who avoids the traps by being careful who we choose to walk life's path with. This new year, make an assessment of who in your life is on the right path, and stick close to them!

God, give me the insight to detect where I wander down the wrong path. Grant me wisdom to avoid worldly traps set by my Adversary. Grant me the grace and resolve to avoid them. Amen

THE FIRST PATH: A DELIGHT
January 4

"Instead, his delight is in the Lord's instruction, and he meditates on it day and night."
Psalm 1:2 (CSB)

I'm sitting here thinking about what delights me. The word *'delight'* refers to something that brings great pleasure. Take a moment and write down five delights.

Sue, my kids, 10 grandkids, family vacations, travel, and pizza. Those are some of my good delights. Unfortunately, a lot of my delights are all jacked up. The reason of course is that I'm a broken person and have been so my whole life. Once Adam and Eve decided they knew better than God, sin entered into the world (Romans 5:12), resulting in a fallen creation—and in particular, a fallen humanity. The image of God, still resident in each of us, is warped and marred. We can't blame it on A & E; we choose brokenness all the time. The result is that our desires are messed up. John Piper calls these "disordered desires."

Think about our delights and desires. God gave us a desire to love, but our brokenness causes us to love the wrong things, or love the right things too much. He gave us the desire to be loved, but we seek it in all the wrong places. He gave us a desire for sexual intimacy, but our brokenness causes us to fulfill it in harmful ways. He gave us the desire to achieve, accumulate, and influence, but in our warpedness, we end up fulfilling these desires in temporal gains. To summarize, much of our delighting is disgusting!

However, when the Spirit of God enters us at salvation, He comes in as The Great Renovator, reshaping us into the image of Jesus. Our disordered desires begin to get reordered. One of the most critical reordered desires is the hunger and desire for God and His word.

One of the genuine trademarks of being born-again is an appetite for God's word; to be delighted by it. This delight might be minuscule right now, but it can be fostered and nurtured to the point that it dominates our lives. The more we delight in God's word—thinking about it throughout our waking hours—the more blessing we experience, i.e., joy, happiness, and favor. And that's a good thing! This new year, decide to increase your daily dose of God's word. Reading five psalms a day is a good start!

God, I pray You grant me a desire for Your word. I pray that I will grow to delight in it. I pledge to get in Your word daily. Amen

THE FIRST PATH: FLOURISHING
January 5

"He is like a tree planted beside flowing streams that bears its fruit in its season and its leaf does not wither. Whatever he does prospers."

Psalm 1:3 (CSB)

Sue and I spent the first three years of our marriage and ministry in Albuquerque, N.M. Albuquerque is in a semi-arid region where it gets an average of 11 inches of rain a year (Arlington gets 40"). During the dry season, trees and bushes barely survive unless they are watered—except down on the Rio Grande River which cuts through the middle of the city. The trees and bushes by the river flourish, even when there is no rain.

The psalmist is writing in a semi-arid region as well—Israel. He's familiar with the same dynamic: trees planted along the small streams that are fed by the spring melt-off from Mount Hermon or the occasional rains, grow, flourish, and bear fruit. Those that don't, wither away.

This is a metaphor for spiritual vitality, not material accumulation. Prospering is victorious living, not wealth management. The New Testament affirms this metaphor: *"Let your roots grow down into Him, and let your lives be built on Him. Then your faith will grow strong in the truth you were taught, and you will overflow with thankfulness"* (Colossians 2:7). There are those seasons of life that leave us dry, parched, and discouraged. We can't get much flourishing from our circumstances. But if we delight in the word of God, we can get a fresh thirst-quencher just by getting into Scripture! This is another benefit of memorizing Bible verses: you have a fresh supply of flourishing any time you need one. It's kind of like one of those Camelbak water packs that you can strap on your back, that has a small tube running from the pack over your shoulder to your chest. You can sip water out of it whenever you want. Binding the Scripture around your heart is like strapping on a huge reservoir of hope and vitality for immediate access.

God wants you to flourish. He is the source of flourishing through His word and Spirit. By the way, this psalm, particularly this verse, is good to tuck into your memory (spiritual Camelbak). You'll be glad you did!

God, enable me to see that prosperity is more about victorious living than attaining wealth and comfort. Transform me into someone who has a consistent walk with You no matter the season. Amen

THE FIRST PATH: FRUIT BEARING
January 6

"He is like a tree planted beside flowing streams that bears its fruit in its season."
Psalm 1:3

If you've traveled in the Middle East, you'll know that dates (the fruit) are a staple. Dates grow on palm trees that require a fair amount of water, but ironically, cannot tolerate humidity or rain. That means they have to be planted close to sources of water. They grow as high as 100 feet and produce up to 600 pounds of fruit per year

The psalmist likely had the date tree in mind when he wrote this psalm: planted beside flowing streams, flourishing even in dry seasons. But part of the flourishing means to bear fruit. Date trees are not planted to look nice; they are planted to produce dates.

Christ-followers are to bear fruit. The New Testament speaks of two kinds of fruit: the fruit of the Spirit and the fruit of the harvest. The first is found in Galatians 5:22-23, *"But the Holy Spirit produces this kind of fruit in our lives: love, joy, peace, patience, kindness, goodness, faithfulness, gentleness, and self-control."* The deeper we sink our roots into Jesus and His word, and the more we allow the Holy Spirit in us to transform us, the more these characteristics define us.

Jesus also spoke of this in John 15:5, *"I am the vine, you are the branches; he who abides in Me and I in him, he bears much fruit, for apart from Me you can do nothing."* That word *'abide'* (Gr. *meno*) means to live and feel comfortable in. Abiding in Jesus and His word is how we produce fruit.

The second kind of fruit is the fruit of the harvest. The dates we eat are actually seeds. This is how date trees and most other plants and animals proliferate: they bear fruit/seed that becomes new life.

If we're not careful, we can make the Christ-life just about us. But the Christ-life is also about reaching others: going and telling of what Christ has done for us. Abiding in Jesus produces godly character, yes, but it also produces godly burdens. There can be no greater burden than for a lost and dying neighbor, workmate, or world. Someone said, "If we say we love God, then we must have on our hearts what God has on His heart—and God has the world on His heart" (John 3:16). Pray for God to work in your heart to bear both kinds of fruit.

Jesus, You are the vine that brings life; I am the branch that only has life as I am fully connected to You. May that be so and by Your grace, I will bear fruit: fruit of the Spirit and fruit of the harvest. Amen!

THE SECOND PATH: WRONG WAY
January 7

"The wicked are not like this."
Psalm 1:4

Feeder roads to interstate highways are one-way. To keep distracted drivers from making a fatal mistake, big red signs are posted: WRONG WAY.

After painting this glowing picture of the person on the path to a blessed life, the psalmist abruptly changes moods and blurts out: "The wicked are going the wrong way!"

We are now warned about the second path. This path is in total contrast to the first path. It is the path jam-packed with people who are heading the wrong direction. If the first path leads to life, this second path leads to death. If the first path leads to purpose and lasting impact, the second path is destined for futility and transience. If the first path is about flourishing and wholeness, the second path is about scarcity and brokenness. If the first person has the favor of God, the second person has only His condemnation.

The blessings of God are for His children. That is not to say that common grace doesn't bless the unbeliever; it does. Common grace, in contrast to saving grace, includes all undeserved blessings that humans receive from the hand of God: air, rain, sun, prosperity, health, natural talents, and so on. Those are good, but they are temporal and transient—and count for nothing in eternity.

The favor of God is for His children. This is a harsh reality. The world system insists that if there is a God, He will be benevolent to all, except for the most evil persons (Stalin, Mao, Cruella de Vil, etc.). Jesus had something else in mind. Speaking about these two paths and the people on them, He warned: *"That is the way it will be at the end of the world. The angels will come and separate the wicked people from the righteous, throwing the wicked into the fiery furnace, where there will be weeping and gnashing of teeth"* (Matthew 13:49). **YIKES!**

Remember, righteous people are not perfect people; they are people made in right standing with God through faith in His Son, Jesus. Jesus views all who refuse His authority as wicked. The psalmist put it this way: *"They are like worthless chaff, scattered by the wind. They will be condemned at the time of judgment. Sinners will have no place among the godly"* (vv.4-5). Which path are you on? Have you surrendered your life to Jesus and made Him THE authority in your life? If not, make that decision right now.

Jesus, am so overwhelmed by Your desire to bless me. I don't deserve it. I want Your favor, not Your judgment. I am trusting in You alone for that! Amen

GOD WATCH

January 8

"For the Lord watches over the path of the godly,
but the path of the wicked leads to destruction."

Psalm 1:6

Notice the phrase, *"watches over."* It's a term that any parent would recognize. When your child is playing at the park or are starting to ride a bike, you watch over them. When they begin to drive, it's difficult to watch over them because they're out on their own in a 3,000-pound death trap! That's when your prayer life goes to a whole new dimension!!

Watching over someone means to care about them with an eye for protection. Many may care about your child, but your caring involves protecting them. It's comforting to me to know God is watching over me. God watches over you.

God watches over us. That means nothing can happen to us that He hasn't already seen and permitted. He may not have caused it, but as the sovereign God, He most certainly has allowed it. The question arises: if God is watching over me with a protective eye, how is it that pain and suffering enter our lives?

Full answers are beyond this devotion, but let's glance at four:

1. Pain and suffering are in our lives because of the Fall in Genesis 3. It's not God's fault we live in a broken world. He created us with volition: a) because to be created in His image means we would have the ability to self-determine; and b) so that we could choose, or not choose, to follow and love Him. Pain and suffering are in the world because of human choices, then (Genesis.3) and now.
2. Being blessed of God has never meant total insulation from pain and suffering. Even a casual assessment of biblical characters reveals that believers have always experienced great suffering (Abraham, Joseph, Moses, David, Paul, Peter, JESUS).
3. God didn't leave us alone in our pain and suffering, He entered into it through the incarnation, God in the flesh; i.e., Jesus—and gave us The Comforter (Holy Spirit) to help us through our pain.
4. God allows pain and suffering for His greater purposes. By faith, we trust that He is sovereign and loving—and will work it out for His glory and our good (Romans 8:28).

My path, my life, is known by God. He watches over me. That is too wonderful for me to grasp.

God, thank You for Your caring and concern. I am amazed that You care as You do. To think that You watch over me with an eye for protection is beyond my ability to fully grasp. Enable me to see Your handiwork in the trials and pains of my life. I trust You. Amen

RAGE
January 9

"Why do the nations rage and the peoples plot in vain? The kings of the earth take their stand, and the rulers conspire together against the Lord and His Anointed One."

Psalm 2:1-2

Everyone is so angry nowadays: road rage where people make vulgar gestures, bang their vehicles into those who did something they didn't like, and even get into fistfights. Sadly, 37% of these incidents involve firearms and over 200 people have been killed the last few years as a result. It's disheartening to see people raging on social media, saying stuff that they would never say to someone's face. Rage is the new fashion in America.

What's crazy, is people rage against Yahweh! According to one survey, 67% of Americans blame God for their troubles. They're angry at Him because they lost their job, because they're addicted to substances, because they got divorced, because they lost a loved one—even because a car ran over their dog.

There's another reason people rage against Him: they don't want Him telling them what is right and wrong, how they are to act, or what they are to value. This started in the Garden of Eden, gathered momentum at the Tower of Babel, and continues through a sophisticated, well-developed world system that opposes God, the things of God, the people of God, and the Kingdom of God. This system insists that physicalism (if it ain't physical, it ain't real) is the only reality, empiricism (knowledge is limited to our five senses) is the only basis for knowledge, and the individual is the ultimate determiner of morality.

This world and life view excludes almost everything held in a biblical view: that God is the Creator of all that is, that He created humans to worship and love Him, that there is an Adversary who deceives and destroys, and that God is a redemptive God who enables humans to overcome the Adversary, with victory in this life and bliss in the life to come.

College professors rage against Yahweh, ridiculing students who hold a biblical view. Politicians are increasingly raging against Yahweh, making statements and passing policies that are foreign to a biblical view. Maybe you've experienced this rage among friends or acquaintances when you speak of Jesus as the only way.

Here's God's response to their raging: *"The One who rules in heaven laughs. The Lord scoffs at them"* (v.4). He will destroy them completely (v.9).

Don't cower at their rage. Yahweh will triumph! Identify with Him and you will walk in victory.

Lord, I pray for boldness as I interact with the people You have placed in my life. I want to let them know of Your great love and glory. Don't let me get overwhelmed with the chaos of this world. By Your grace, enable me to walk in victory. Amen

BETRAYAL
January 10

"So many are saying, 'God will never rescue him!' But You, O Lord, are a shield around me; You are my glory, the One who holds my head high."

Psalm 3:2-3

In my years as a pastor, I was blessed with wonderful, godly men and women who were a joy to serve with—with one exception. Decades ago, I hired a man and put a lot of trust in him. As it turned out, he was not trustworthy—the name Benedict Arnold comes to mind. It was one of the most trying leadership times of my life.

Few experiences are more devastating than betrayal, particularly if the betrayer is someone you love and care about. The deeper the relationship, the deeper the cut. Betrayal is broken trust, rejection, devaluation, pain, grief, and anger all rolled into one.

King David suffered some key betrayals, but none so hurtful as when his own son, Absalom betrayed him. You'll find the account in 2 Samuel 13-19. It is gut-wrenching to read. Events are always linked together: David sleeps with Bathsheba and kills her husband; years later, his first son, Amnon rapes his half-sister, Tamar—but David doesn't do anything about it because of his own dirty laundry; Absalom, the full brother of Tamar, takes matters into his own hands and kills Amnon; David throws Absalom out of the house; Absalom loses all respect for his dad and begins to plot against him. David has to flee his capital, Jerusalem, and hide from his own son.

That's when David wrote Psalm 3. In his pain he said, *"But You, O Lord, are a shield around me; You are my glory, the One who holds my head high. I cried out to the Lord, and He answered me from His holy mountain. I lay down and slept, yet I woke up in safety, for the Lord was watching over me"* (vv. 3-5).

David calls on God to be his Shield, his Protector. *'Glory'* is the idea of light and hope, so David is counting on God to lift the despair that weighs him down. David praises God for eventually granting him peace of heart and mind in the midst of it all.

I have been betrayed many times and have found solace in this psalm. So can you. Betrayal by a family member, friend or work associate is awful. Betrayal by a spouse—nothing worse. God will be your Protector; He will overcome your dark despair; He will lighten your load and grant you peace. Call—and keep calling on Him. He will respond.

God, people who have betrayed me are coming to mind right now. Grant me the grace to forgive those who have hurt me. I can't do it without You. Lift me up. You are my Light and Glory. Amen

FROM PRAYER TO PEACE

January 11

"Answer me when I call, O God of my righteousness! You have relieved me in my distress;
Be gracious to me and hear my prayer."

Psalm 4:1 (NASB)

I don't know about you, but there are many times I struggle with feelings of fear, anxiety, and distress. What do we do when circumstances and feelings overwhelm us? The answer is in this psalm. Most scholars believe that Psalm 3 is a companion to Psalm 4. In all likelihood, David wrote this psalm on a night that he was hiding from his son, Absalom (see January 10th). It was a dangerous time for him: on the run, camping in the open, vulnerable to attack, not knowing who he could trust. The only way he knew to deal with it was to call out to God.

Calling out to God is always our first and best move. Yet many times our mind begins to churn out man/woman-made solutions, which rarely bring much peace. Prayer must be the priority: "You can do more than pray after you have prayed but you cannot do more than pray until you have prayed." S.D. Gordon

David is desperate: *"Answer me, when I call!"* He knows his first line of defense is Yahweh. It's not that he doesn't need to set out perimeter guards to keep a lookout or keep his sword next to him. It's just that he is counting on God to work supernaturally in his circumstance. God has worked that way in the past— *"You have relieved me in my distress"*—and David is counting on God to do it again.

The Apostle Paul gave similar advice while writing from a Roman prison:

> *Don't worry about anything, but in everything, through prayer and petition with thanksgiving, present your requests to God. And the peace of God, which surpasses all understanding, will guard your hearts and minds in Christ Jesus. Philippians 4:6-7*

That word *'guard'* is interesting. It's the idea of a sentry standing watchguard over a city either at the gate or a lookout post. Imagine that, instead of a city needing protection, it's you. Wouldn't you love to have someone watching out, standing sentry over your heart and mind to guard against anxiety and fear? Who wouldn't? The Spirit will do that for you when you pray. David experienced that peace. The last verse in this psalm says, *"In peace I will lie down and sleep, for You alone, O Lord, will keep me safe"* (v.8).

What is going on in your life that is robbing you of sweet peace? Call out to Yahweh!

God, I call out to You. I pray that Your promises in Your word will be true for me as I work through these circumstances that are making me anxious and afraid. Work supernaturally in them and in my heart. Hear my cry. Amen

A GLAD HEART
January 12

"You have given me greater joy than those who have abundant harvests of grain and new wine."
Psalm 4:7

We live in a totally commercialized society. Just about everything we watch or listen to is paid for by someone who has something they want you to buy. In fact, even the programs hawk a perspective or worldview they want you to buy. The major news outlets are the worst!

The Federal Trade Commission files suits against hundreds of companies every year in an attempt to protect the consumer. A sampling:

- *Gerber Good Start* formula was supposed to keep babies from developing allergies
- *5-Hour Energy* drinks were supposed to give more jolt than coffee
- *Vitamin Water* was supposed to promote healthy joints
- *Frosted Mini Wheats* were supposed to increase children's attentiveness by 20%

Automobiles, televisions, diets, vacation spots, and gold futures are pitched to us as ways to escape the difficulties and discouragements of life.

A glad heart. That's what they're peddling, but I've learned through the years that these claims are empty. In fact, the more I buy into the thinking that material stuff gives me a glad heart, the sadder it gets! There is a law of diminishing returns at play: the more I attempt to be glad in the material, the emptier I become in my soul.

David agrees. This is a guy who had it all: complete independence, power, popularity, wealth, women—everything this world claims will make a human heart glad. But in a matter of a few days, all of that was washed down the drain as Absalom hunted him.

Crisis has a way of bringing clarity. In this calamity, David first calls out to God (v.1), he reminds himself of God's power over his enemies (vv.3-4), he reclaims his faith in God (v.5), and asserts that God is the one that brings a glad heart, regardless of circumstances (vv.6-7).

Lesson: don't get caught up in the blessing and forget the Blesser. If we make that mistake, we start hoping in IT, trusting in IT, turning to IT, counting on IT to fill our souls and make our hearts glad. IT can't do that—only HE can. Be glad in God and your heart will be glad!!

God, I realize that I tend to trust and turn to other things and people in my life to make me glad. Work in my heart to make me glad in YOU and believe YOU will make my heart glad. Amen

HELL!

January 13

"O Lord, hear me as I pray; pay attention to my groaning. Listen to my cry for help, my King and my God, for I pray to no one but You."

Psalm 5:1-2

I well remember what was called the "English Invasion" when the Animals, the Rolling Stones, and other British bands had huge hits in the U.S. in the mid-1960s. But no group was as prolific or as impactful as the Beatles, turning out more #1 hits and top 100 hits than any artists in history. One of my favorites was "*Help.*" You may remember the lyrics: "Help, I need somebody. Help, not just anybody. Help, you know I need someone. Help!"

David is making the same plea. He needs help, but not just anyone can help him in his predicament. Most scholars believe David wrote this while fleeing Absalom, maybe even the morning after he wrote Psalm 4. His enemy is powerful, popular, and persistent.

We have an adversary who is always intending to do us harm: "*Be sober-minded, be alert. Your adversary the devil is prowling around like a roaring lion, looking for anyone he can devour*" (1 Peter 5:8; CSB). He's not out to paw or toy with us—he is out to devour and destroy us. YIKES!

God has allowed Satan a considerable measure of power, so much so, that Jesus called him the '*Ruler of this world.*' He is the 2nd most powerful being on the globe. He is incredibly popular. The people of the world generally have embraced his agenda. Paul called him, the '*God of this age,*' meaning that in this era before Christ's return, Satan is THE major influence on the views, values, ideals, hopes, and opinions of the vast majority of the world's population. Philosophy, commerce, education, government, and religion have their roots in his lies and deception.

He is also persistent. Like a master chess player, he knows if he can get us to make the wrong choice in small things now, he can dominate us in big issues down the road. He knows our weaknesses and blind spots better than us and will use them to weaken and destroy us.

Fortunately, our God is bigger and badder than Satan! If you are a true believer, "*Greater is He that is in you, than he that is in the world*" (1 John 4:4). Our primary defense against Satan is praying with faith. David cries out (Hear me. Pay attention to me.) because he believes God is listening and will respond.

Do you feel as if Satan is hounding you? Attacking your marriage? Trying to steal your joy and peace? Call out to God. He's the only one who can help.

God, I do feel that Satan is hounding me. He's attacking me in many areas. I cry out to You. I need Your help. Don't let him steal my joy and peace. Come to my rescue. Amen

EACH MORNING

January 14

"Listen to my voice in the morning, Lord.
Each morning I bring my requests to You and wait expectantly."
Psalm 5:3

In college, I was exposed to a spiritual discipline called "Quiet Time." I wanted to grow closer to Jesus, so I tried to get up each morning to spend time with Him. It was quiet time, alright! In just a few minutes my head would be on my Bible, soaking it with drool.

I mentioned my difficulty to a mentor who asked what I did at nights. I told him I watched The Tonight Show (with Johnny Carson) and/or played cards until midnight or beyond. He said, "That's your problem. You know what Proverbs 32:2 says, right?" I said, "I don't have a clue." He said, "Proverbs 32:2 says, 'You can't soar with the eagles in the morning if you hoot with the owls at night.'" I thought that was a pretty amazing Bible verse—until I looked it up. There is no Proverbs 32; Proverbs only has 31 chapters!

But the principle is true and it has stuck with me for 50 years: If I want to get up and spend the first part of my day with the Lover of my soul, then I've got to make the decision to get to bed at an hour that allows me to spend ample and rich time with Jesus.

The wisest amongst us, the greatest through the centuries, including this psalm's author, David, have been those who started their day spending time with Yahweh. Mark 1:35 says this about Jesus, *"Very early in the morning, while it was still dark, He got up, went out, and made his way to a deserted place; and there He was praying."* I've always felt that if the Son of God found it necessary and helpful to get up early to spend time with the Father, so should I.

Through the years I've had folks mildly protest, "I'm a night person—that's when I get with God." This may be good, but my response has been, "When does an orchestra tune it's instruments—before or after the concert?"

If you are not spending time with Jesus each morning, I encourage you to begin the discipline immediately. It will take time to develop this good habit, but God created our brains with a neurology that grabs hold of repeated activities and makes them routine. Reading this devotional is a good start, but growing believers add extended prayer time, Bible reading, and journaling to their morning. Start with 5 minutes each day and aim at consistency. As you become consistent, add more time. We can't spend too much time with the One who loves us and gave His life for us!

God, You are worthy of being first in my life, my calendar, my day. By Your grace, enable me to establish a rich time with You each morning. Amen

CONTRAST

January 15

"For you are not a God who delights in wickedness; evil cannot dwell with You.
Lord, lead me in Your righteousness because of my adversaries;
make Your way straight before me."
Psalm 5:4,8 (CSB)

In the day of early televisions, there were 4-5 knobs on the front of the tv: channel changer, on/off/volume, vertical and horizontal hold, and contrast. The contrast knob was important because in the black and white days, the picture could look too washed out if the objects were not properly contrasted.

A good definition of contrast is: "the state of being strikingly different from something else in juxtaposition or close association." I look at pictures of me from 40 years ago and I see a great deal of contrast between my hair then and my hair now!

Our psalmist, David, is contrasting the righteous person with the unrighteous, similar to our study in Psalm 1 where the two paths were contrasted. Here David contrasts the unrighteous (wicked) with the righteous. A study in the contrast begins with the character of God.

The nature and character of God includes many attributes, including righteousness. Righteousness has to do with being, wait for it—right! Not just correct, but morally and ethically right so that who He is, what He thinks, feels, and does is absolutely right and just. Because He is righteous, He cannot and will not give a pass, entertain or ignore, anything unright or unjust: *"For you are not a God who delights in wickedness; evil cannot dwell with You"* (v.4).

This is bad news for humans because, in contrast to God's character, ours is broken, warped, and wicked. We ain't right! His righteousness won't tolerate our unrighteousness.

Notice David's request: *"Lead me in YOUR righteousness."* Brilliant! He knows he doesn't possess righteousness and looks to Yahweh to provide it. This is the good news (contrasted with the bad news) for humans: God imparts righteousness to those who seek it! He has made it clear that those who display faith in His Son and ask that Jesus' blood be applied to their wicked souls, are made righteous. At that point, righteousness changes meaning from being morally and ethically perfect, to being in right relationship and right standing with the One who is.

Are you righteous? If you are in Christ and Christ is in you, then you are. If that is not the case, you will still be held accountable for your wickedness. I'm glad I won't be!! I pray you won't be either.

God, I confess I am wicked at my core, but I ask that you apply the blood of Jesus to my soul and make me in right standing with You. Lead me to live a life that is right in Your eyes. Amen

REFUGE

January 16

"But let all who take refuge in You rejoice; let them sing joyful praises forever.
Spread Your protection over them, that all who love Your name may be filled with joy.
For You bless the godly, O Lord; You surround them with Your shield of love."

Psalm 5:11-12

We watched 'The Wizard of Oz' the other night. The wicked witch of the west scenes still scare me to death ("I'll get you my pretty--and your little dog too")!

Growing up in Oklahoma, I'm well familiar with tornadoes. Living in North Texas it's more of the same. The siren goes off and you head to a safe place: a closet, a hallway, or Auntie Em's fruit cellar.

Psalm 5 is about shelter and refuge from harm. As we've discussed, David is in harm's way and he is desperate to find refuge. As much as he needs a physical safe haven, he needs something more powerful and lasting.

It's a tough world out there. There is so much brokenness that can wreak havoc on us and those we love: broken marriages, broken homes, broken health, broken finances, broken country, broken people. It can be overwhelming and incredibly fear-producing. Where do we run for shelter and refuge? Our tendency is to shelter in the wrong places: the malls, the restaurants, the bars, the drugs, the porn, the travel, etc. We look to friends, family, social media, or even the gals on The View (groan). But the only real refuge in times of trouble is Yahweh.

We are not insulated from trouble, but His promise is that when troubles come, He can give us strength, hope, and courage to get through—along with His invaluable, abiding peace.

I have found what the psalmist said to be true in my life: when I take refuge in God, He quells the fear and fills my heart with joy, and my lips with praise. I sense more of His blessing and grace in my life. Somehow, despite the hardship and trial, I feel His presence and power. Nothing else; no one else on this planet does that. I am surrounded by His shield of love—WOW!

Are you in trouble? Run to Him. Ask Him to shelter you under His wings—and while you're there, listen to His heartbeat of love for you.

Yahweh, I do run to You. I need refuge. I need rescue. Deliver me from my enemy. Grant me grace and peace and endurance. Amen

DISCOURAGEMENT
January 17

"Have compassion on me, Lord, for I am weak. Heal me, Lord, for my bones are in agony.
I am sick at heart. How long, O Lord, until You restore me? Return, O Lord, and rescue me.
Save me because of Your unfailing love."
Psalm 6:2-4

I am extremely familiar with discouragement. More times than I can count, I have faced a challenge that ended up far short of my expectation. Sometimes the cause is I've disappointed someone, and they let me know it. Sometimes the cause has been that I've been overwhelmed with too many obligations. Fear of failure or fear of people has plunged me into discouragement multiple times. And then have been those times I let myself get too extended and I'm tired and worn out.

Some of us are easily prone to discouragement. Difficult circumstances pile on top of each other resulting in a lack of confidence or a sense of hopelessness. Our energy feels depleted and our spirit is gloomy. The root of the word discouragement is courage, right? The prefix 'dis' indicates the opposite of or the lack of something. We lack the courage, the resolution, the emotional and physical strength to push forward and overcome the challenge.

Notice the phrases David used: *"I am weak"*, *"my bones are in agony"*, *"I am sick at heart."* Sounds like he was pretty discouraged. We're not sure of the specific circumstance causing his discouragement, but there's no doubt that he was experiencing it as a result of feeling his enemies were getting the upper hand.

The prefix 'en' indicates the presence of, or the infusion of something, i.e., encouragement. Fortunately for us, God's word infuses courage where it is lacking, and this psalm has plenty of it. In his discouragement, he:

1. Asks God to have compassion on him: "I'm hurting, and I need your tender care." When discouraged, recognize it for what it is and bring it before the Lord. He knows it already, but it's important to begin a discussion about it.
2. Pleads with God to act rapidly: "I lack courage: rescue and restore me—now!" There's nothing wrong with asking God to work quickly!
3. Humbles himself before God by confessing: "I don't deserve this, but I'm counting on Your unfailing love." At this point, we must place it in His hands—and leave it there. Ultimately, we must trust that He loves us and will do what is best for His glory and our good.

Those are three pretty good steps to take when we feel discouraged. Try them out next time you feel your courage leaking.

God, thank You for how Your word brings light, perspective, and encouragement! Amen

CONTEXT
January 18

"A Shiggaion of David, which he sang to the Lord concerning the words of Cush a Benjaminite."
Superscription at the beginning of Psalm 7

When you read the Psalms, you'll notice that many of them have notes at the beginning, under the number of the psalm, but before the first verse. These are called superscriptions. Of the 150 psalms, all but 34 have some form of superscription. The contents of the superscriptions vary but fall into five broad categories: (1) identifying the author, (2) type of psalm, (3) musical notations, (4) liturgical notations and, (5) brief indications of what was going on in the author's life when the psalm was written.

The words within the superscriptions were added, sometimes by the author himself, and other times by someone else after the psalm was written. Thus, they are not inspired as are the rest of the psalms; that is, they are not Scripture. But they are somewhat reliable and give us an indication as to the setting, nature, and context of the psalm.

When the superscriptions indicate the occasion and/or purpose of the particular psalm, we are able to gain insight about the real issues facing the real people who wrote them. This particular psalm begins with the notation that it is a *shiggaion*: a plaintive song; a dirge. Other examples:

Psalm 3: A psalm of David when he fled his son, Absalom.
Psalm 13: A prayer for help in trouble.
Psalm 17: A prayer for protection against oppressors.
Psalm 21: A prayer for deliverance.
Psalm 22: A cry of anguish.

My point is that so many of the 150 poem songs were written by genuinely hurting people. When we read and contemplate them, God's Spirit uses them to touch and heal the places we're hurting. Take your time with each one—each one is a medicine for our hurting hearts and hope for struggling souls.

God, thank you for preserving these superscriptions. I pray You will use them and the words of the Psalms to draw me closer to You and strengthen me for the needs in my life. Amen

REPENTANCE
January 19

"If a person does not repent, God will sharpen His sword; He will bend and string His bow."
Psalm 7:12

As noted in the superscription that we examined yesterday, David wrote this psalm because he was being hounded and pursued by someone called Cush, from the tribe of Benjamin. Many scholars think Cush was really King Saul, and that this occurred when Saul was chasing young David around Israel trying to kill him.

As you read the psalm, you get the sense that David feels he's being unjustly treated. He calls on God to examine his motives and heart, and volunteers to be punished if he is the offender in this case. He knows God is a just God and he calls on Yahweh to render justice in this situation. On other occasions, David knew he was wrong, and we see him repenting and asking for, appealing for God's mercy.

Mercy comes after repentance. Repentance is not about feeling sorry for something we did. It is a change of mindset and behavior. When we repent, God grants forgiveness and applies mercy. When we don't, God's response is not good!

David notes that God will sharpen His sword and string up His bow, meaning that God is ready to judge the unrepentant. But God doesn't want to judge—He wants to grant mercy: *"The Lord isn't really being slow about His promise, as some people think. No, He is being patient for your sake. He does not want anyone to be destroyed, but wants everyone to repent"* (2 Peter 3:9).

Believer, is there some attitude, some action in your life that is inconsistent with the will and word of God? Repent, and avoid God's chastening instruments of discipline. If you're not a believer yet, repent of your rebellion against God's authority and avoid His destroying judgment.

Mercy comes after repentance—and God's mercies are new and glorious every morning!

God, I am so grateful that You are a merciful God. I know I need to repent of _____. I do repent and ask for Your mercy. Amen

MAJESTY
January 20

"Lord, our Lord, how magnificent is Your name throughout the earth!
You have covered the heavens with Your majesty."
Psalm 8:1 (CSB)

This is one of the most recognizable and beloved verses in all of the Psalms. In it, David magnifies the grandeur and majesty of Yahweh and His name.

A person's name gets associated with their character, their personhood, and their reputation. God and His name are synonymous. That's why, when He was giving Moses the Ten Commandments, He said: *"Do not misuse the name of the Lord your God, because the Lord will not leave anyone unpunished who misuses His name"* (Exodus 20:7). To use His name in any other form, setting, or attitude other than respect and honor is absolutely repugnant to God.

In your English Bible, when you see the word *LORD* with all caps, that means the Hebrew word used is Yahweh, which is God's personal name. He has other names and titles. For instance, in this verse, the 2nd Lord is not all caps. This Hebrew word/name is Adonai, which means "one that possesses great power and authority." But the name He guards most closely is Yahweh, which means "I AM."

Notice that Yahweh is not some distant being or inanimate force. He is a being who is personal, knowable, and relational. Sue and I might proudly show a picture of our family to someone and say, "This is our family." That doesn't mean we own them, only that we have a close, personal relationship with them. David puts it this way, "O LORD, **our** Lord."

David says about this God that His name is majestic. Majestic carries the idea of regality, loftiness, nobility, excellence, and fame. His name is so famous that it fills the earth. What does that mean? It means that when we view the beauty and splendor of this ball known as earth, it has unmistakable markings of an even more beautiful and splendorous Creator. Standing on the rim of the Grand Canyon or driving through the Colorado Rockies or watching a sunset over the ocean, something inside of us goes, "Wow! What God could do all of this? Only Yahweh!!"

How often do you pause during your waking hours and observe God's majesty on display? To do so is a form of worship. Take a moment and think of all the places you have been and pick out one or two and praise the Creator for them. Google some of the places you want to go and praise God for those as well. Let your praise for Yahweh fill and cover the earth!

Yahweh, I do praise You for _____. It displays Your power and splendor. I worship You as Creator. Amen

CREATION
January 21

"Lord, our Lord, how magnificent is Your name throughout the earth!
You have covered the heavens with Your majesty."
Psalm 8:1 (CSB)

Atheists have a lot of faith. It takes much more faith to believe the universe is without design than to believe it is designed.

Yahweh claims to be the Great Designer/Creator/Artist/Sculptor of all that is—and He claims He did it out of nothing. The term is ex nihilo: out of nothing. Matter out of no matter; something out of nothing. Trillions of stars. Billions of galaxies. Only God knows how many planets. All on display in a finely tuned system.

Lee Strobel, in his book, <u>Case for Creation</u>, sets out a scientific rationale for the universe or universes being created by intelligent design, aka, Yahweh. Many scientists subscribe to the 'Fine Tuning Theory,' that is, the universe is so finely tuned, in literally countless ways, that it must be the product of a Master Designer. For instance, if the earth were just a few thousand miles farther from or closer to the sun, it could not sustain life. If the earth tilted just a few more degrees one way or the other, it could not sustain life. For every one of these fine-tuning aspects, the odds that the solar system and universe are without design are so low, they would and should be deemed functionally and scientifically impossible. He quotes Stephen C. Meyer, Ph.D. on just one of the variables:

> Take the expansion rate of the universe, which is fine-tuned to one part in a trillion trillion trillion trillion trillion. That is, if it were changed by one part in either direction-- a little faster, a little slower--we could not have a universe that would be capable of supporting life.

Yahweh claims to be and is the Creator of all that is. And by the way, He still is creating. Astrophysicists believe a new star is born somewhere in creation every second. Incredible! He paints a new sunrise and a new sunset in innumerable places each and every day.

Superstitious? Ignorant? Nah. To think this is all happenchance is foolish and short-sighted: *"Only fools say in their hearts, 'There is no God'."* (Psalm 14:1).

All of creation has one purpose: to declare the majesty and splendor of God. If the creation is beyond our ability to grasp, how much more the Creator? If you are struggling in the grunge of life, look up, and get caught up, in the Grand Creator. Worship Him!!

Lord, our Lord, how magnificent is Your name throughout the earth! You have covered the heavens with Your majesty! Amen!!

IMAGO DEI
January 22

"When I look at the night sky and see the work of Your fingers— the moon and the stars
You set in place— what are mere mortals that You should think about them,
human beings that You should care for them? Yet You made them
only a little lower than God and crowned them with glory and honor."
Psalm 8:3-5

When I was in the Masai Mara in southern Kenya, the night sky was something I'll never forget. When they turned the camp lights out at midnight, stars and constellations filled the sky in a way I struggle to express. I've never seen so many stars! I'll never, ever forget the experience. Caught up in the vastness of the heavens, I found myself thinking about the minuscule place I had in this expansive, endless universe.

David, probably sitting under the same canopy of stars, had the same thought, *"What are mere mortals that You should think about them, human beings that You should care for them?"* Then the Spirit reminded him of his and our place in the universe: God made us just a bit lower than He is. What does that mean? After all, He is perfect, we're not. He is infinite, we're not. The contrast is pretty significant in every category.

The answer is in the Imago Dei. Imago Dei is Latin for, *"image of God,"* and it captures the concept that human beings, and humans alone, are created in the image of God. The phrase appears in other places in Scripture (Genesis 5:1, 9:6; 1 Corinthians 11:7; Colossians 3:10; James 3:9), but the most important appearance is the first one:

> *Then God said, "Let Us make human beings in Our image, to be like Us. . . ." So God created human beings in His own image. In the image of God He created them; male and female He created them. Genesis 1:26-27*

There is not a more foundational Scripture on which to build a biblical world and life view. Humans are not just the highest on the food chain. Despite what secularists believe, we are not on the tail end of an evolutionary continuum that began with microorganisms. When we first appeared, we were as we are today. We are and always will be fundamentally different and unique from all other life forms.

Realizing this uniqueness should give us a sense of great value: God made you and me more glorious than '*the moon and stars*'! Wow!! Your self-worth should shoot out the roof!

God, I can't even comprehend how valuable I am to You. Enable me to grasp the truth of this and live out of it. Amen

A LITTLE LOWER
January 23

"Yet You made them only a little lower than God."
Psalm 8:5

In the early days of Saturday Night Live, Chevy Chase would open the spoof-news segment of the show with: "Good evening. I'm Chevy Chase—and you're not!"

Yesterday we talked about how human beings are created in the image of God and in Christ we are crowned with glory and dignity. I am confounded by the Hubble spacecraft pics. To think that as glorious as the heavens are, they pale in comparison to God's greatest achievement: me! So many of us under-appreciate our value to God.

But we have another and opposite problem: we value ourselves too much. These two problems are not mutually exclusive—they are resident in each of us simultaneously. It's a part of our brokenness that we over and undervalue ourselves at the same time. Both are wrong. If I misunderstand my purpose and value, I not only suffer from low self-esteem, but I esteem myself too much!

The common word for this over-estimation is, you guessed it, pride. According to Scripture, pride is the source of all of our brokenness, problems, and grief. It started in the Garden of Eden and we keep making the same mistake: deciding we know what's best for us and for others. Like you, I can decide what is morally right in any given situation and often choose my way instead of God's. I sometimes even expect God to explain Himself to me about His activity in my life and in the world. I sometimes, knowingly or unknowingly, disapprove of His dealings, thereby inserting myself into God's position. In short, I think I'm God and I try to act so.

Well, in v. 5 God is saying, "I created You to be like Me, to know Me, and to love Me. But I'm God—and you're not!"

Although we are created and valued by God above all other creations, we cannot even imagine how much more powerful, intelligent, wise, loving, merciful, gracious, sovereign, and holy He is. We'd best leave the God role to Him. When we don't, it always leads to pain and suffering.

Is there an area of your life that you are taking on the God role? Take a moment and confess that to Him. Then strive for a truly biblical view of yourself. The result is a balanced understanding of who you are and who He is. You are crowned amongst creation—but wear it humbly.

God, I do humble myself before You. You're God, I'm not. Enable me to keep that straight. Amen

GENDER CONFUSION

January 24

"What are mere mortals that You should think about them,
human beings that You should care for them? Yet You made them
only a little lower than God and crowned them with glory and honor."

Psalm 8:3-5

There is little doubt that David wrote this psalm while reflecting on the most important and foundational Scripture:

> *Then God said, "Let Us make human beings in Our image, to be like Us. . . ." So God created human beings in His own image. In the image of God He created them; male and female He created them. Genesis 1:26-27*

Notice the language: *"male and female He created them."* In almost every case, species proliferate due to the interaction between male and female. There are some exceptions. But as we looked at yesterday, we are not like any other species; we are absolutely unique amongst all creation because we alone are created in the image of God. When God created humans, He created males and females. He wasn't ambivalent. This was consistent with the rest of the Creation account where we see God separating and making distinction in a number of ways: heaven and earth, light and dark, night and day, morning and evening, water and dry land.

There is a devious and growing insistence that humans can shift their gender based on how they feel: "Transgender is a term used to describe people whose gender identity differs from the sex they were assigned at birth" (glaad.org). While a person may be struggling with identity, sexual or otherwise, particularly in the adolescent years, there is no doubt that God's intent was and is for genders to be fixed and separate. God is not confused, nor is the Bible: every time the topic comes up, Scripture affirms Genesis 1 and 2 that marriage is between gender males and gender females, and sex is to be within that covenant relationship. Any other view is a serious break from the Bible and a result of human, fallen nature.

To be sure, because they are created in the image of Yahweh, all LGBTQ+ persons are worthy of respect and love. As we know, to love someone is not to embrace everything about them.

If you have children or grandchildren, pray daily for God to protect them from this spirit of gender confusion and God's desire for them to meet and marry a godly person of the opposite sex. Reinforce their identity in Christ, not gender. This is God's will and the way of His blessing; this is the way of hope for their future.

God, I pray for _____. Enable them to resist the worldly views on this and embrace Your view. I know this is the way of blessing. Amen

CULTURAL MANDATE

January 25

"You gave them charge of everything You made, putting all things under their authority—
the flocks and the herds and all the wild animals, the birds in the sky,
the fish in the sea, and everything that swims the ocean currents."

Psalm 8:6-8

There's no doubt that David was reflecting on Genesis 1:27-28 as he wrote this psalm. Read David's words above (Psalm 8:6-8) and notice the similarity between them and the words of Genesis 1:26, "*They will reign over the fish in the sea, the birds in the sky, the livestock, all the wild animals on the earth, and the small animals that scurry along the ground.*"

This is what is known as the 'Cultural Mandate': the divine injunction in which God, after having created the world and all that is in it, ascribes to humankind the tasks of filling, subduing, and developing its potential to create what we commonly call '*culture.*'

This mandate finds opposition from those in the radical environmental movement. To be sure, believers should be on the front line of taking care of our environment. What we do with our trash, how we recycle, what we do about our carbon footprint, etc., should be motivated by our responsibility to take care of God's creation. But we don't do it because whales or trees are equal to humans, or that this earth is all we have. We do it because God gave us this earth to care for.

This whole idea is profound when you think about it. God created human beings uniquely to be fulfilled by being industrious and creative for His glory:

> The lesson of the Cultural Mandate is that our sense of fulfillment depends on engaging in creative, constructive work. The ideal human existence is not eternal leisure or an endless vacation – or even a monastic retreat into prayer and meditation – but creative effort expended for the glory of God and the benefit of others.
>
> Nancy Searcy

While the mandate was given to all humans, only the people of God will be able to fulfill it to its fullest, that is, to the glory of God. For the believer who lacks purpose or fulfillment, the answer is right here: discover what specifically God has called and prepared you for that brings Him glory, and you satisfaction—then give yourself to it. This may include your career or may not. It certainly should include service to your church and community. It definitely includes beautifully fulfilling your role as a spouse and parent. It finds its highest expression in sharing the Good News with others.

God, enable me to find that which brings You the greatest glory and me the greatest fulfillment. Amen

HOW GREAT THOU ART
January 26

"O Lord, our Lord, your majestic name fills the earth!"
Psalm 8:9

In the 1950s-60s, almost everyone stopped what they were doing to watch a Billy Graham crusade broadcast on television. Yes, it was on a black and white tv with a screen the size of a toaster, but it was awesome to sit in our living room and watch BG preach the gospel to stadiums full of people in different spots around the globe.

One of the highlights was when George Beverly Shea stepped to the podium to sing, *How Great Thou Art.* Watch him on YouTube to hear his deep baritone voice bellowing out the song. I admit trying to mimic him while singing in the shower!

Here's the story of the song written in 1885, according to hymnologist, J. Irving Erikson:

> Carl Boberg and some friends were returning home to Mönsterås from Kronobäck, where they had participated in an afternoon service. Presently a thundercloud appeared on the horizon, and soon lightning flashed across the sky. Strong winds swept over the meadows and billowing fields of grain. The thunder pealed in loud claps. Then the rain came in cool fresh showers. In a little while, the storm was over, and a rainbow appeared. When Boberg arrived home, he opened the window and saw the bay of Mönsterås like a mirror before him… From the woods on the other side of the bay, he heard the song of a thrush… the church bells were tolling in the quiet evening. It was this series of sights, sounds, and experiences that inspired the writing of the song.

David was also captivated by Yahweh's handiwork in creation. The ancients had a far grander view of it—unencumbered by skyscrapers, highways, pollution, and urban sprawl. At night, they could see more stars than they could count. To see the glory of creation is to prompt worship for the Creator.

O Lord my God! When I in awesome wonder
consider all the works Thy hand hath made,
I see the stars, I hear the rolling thunder,
Thy power throughout the universe displayed;

Then sings my soul, my Savior God, to Thee,
how great Thou art, how great Thou art!
Then sings my soul, my Savior God, to Thee,
how great Thou art, how great Thou art!
Amen!

THE KEYS TO JOY

January 27

"I will praise You, Lord, with all my heart; I will tell of all the marvelous things You have done. I will be filled with joy because of You. I will sing praises to Your name, O Most High."

Psalm 9:1-2

As I have counseled folks through the decades, the issue that most people have dealt with is discouragement, depression, and a general lack of joy. David certainly had his valleys, but he also knew how to get out of them. In this psalm, he gives us four keys to a life of inner joy.

The first key is to recognize that Yahweh is worthy of all of our hearts. When you get up in the morning, do you seek Him with a whole heart? As you go through your day, do you desire with your whole heart to please Him? When you're in church, do you worship Him with all your heart? Someone said, **"Half a heart, is no heart."** Coaches cut players who practice or play half-heartedly. Employers fire people who work at their jobs half-heartedly. Would you expect the Creator of the Universe, the Sovereign and Majestic King of Kings, to expect anything less than a coach or an employer? No. Jesus said: *"You must love the Lord your God with all your heart, all your soul, and all your mind"* (Matthew 22:37).

This whole-heartedness must be central in our relationship with God. He keeps mentioning it all through His word. When we are confused or hurting and want God to show us His will or His way to healing, He says, *"You will seek Me and find Me when you search for Me with all your heart"* (Jeremiah 29:13).

To be sure, a perfectly whole heart is impossible this side of heaven because our hearts are so fractured, our desires so disordered. But God measures these things in terms of motivation as well as performance. Is it your desire to please Him with all your heart? Is it your desire to seek Him and His will in every area of your life? Is it your desire to love Him with all that you are?

Right now, pause and tell God that you do want to love, seek, and serve Him with a whole heart. Ask Him to clean out the parts of your heart that you have not surrendered to Him. And pray for a whole heart toward Him. This is the first step, the most important key to joy.

God, work in my heart to make it all about You; I do desire to seek You, please You, and love You with all my heart. Amen

MARVELOUS

January 28

"I will praise You, Lord, with all my heart; I will tell of all the marvelous things You have done. I will be filled with joy because of You. I will sing praises to Your name, O Most High."

Psalm 9:1-2

We saw yesterday that the first key to experiencing constant joy is to recognize that Yahweh is worthy of all of our hearts. He demands to be the center of our lives. Period. He built us in such a way that unless that God-shaped vacuum in the middle of us is filled with Him, we just won't function properly, and that dysfunctionality brings hardship, sadness, and anxiety.

The second key that David presents to us is to groom a thankful heart. He says, *"I will tell of all the marvelous things you have done."*

When I was Pastor at Rush Creek Church, I stood out on the west side of the building on our Green Oaks Campus to greet folks coming in that door. I'd say something like, "How are you this morning?" to which most would reply something like, "Good" or "Fine," or sometimes "Tired!" There was a couple that was so cute and unique by the way they responded when I said, "How are you this morning?" They'd straighten up, strut a bit, and say, "MAH-velous!"

God has certainly done MAH-velous things for you, hasn't He? It's so easy to look at the glass half empty; to focus on the stuff in our life that isn't what we want, that might be painful, or prompting fear. But this side of heaven, that's going to be life for us on a daily basis. The question is: what will we become preoccupied with?

Let's start at the top. Sometime in the past, have you recognized your sinful nature and asked God to forgive you, come into your life and save you? If you have, then the beauty, value, and permanency of that ALONE is worth being thankful for every waking moment, regardless of what else might happen. That ALONE should set our hearts singing with gratitude to this great God who looked beyond our fault and saw our need; who reached down to rescue us out of this awful sinfulness, then adopted us into His family to live forever in the light of His glorious love.

But certainly that's not all we have to be thankful for. Each breath is a gift, a favor from God. Since you began reading, you've breathed hundreds of times—and took each one for granted. Your heart has continued to beat. You can read, think, process, create, enjoy, love—and this is just the beginning of the list of reasons why we can be thankful.

Take a moment and think of five reasons to be thankful for the MAH-velous things God has done.

God, thank You for Your gifts of grace and mercy in my life. Enable me to see them more clearly and focus on them. Amen

ESSENCE
January 29

"I will praise You, Lord, with all my heart; I will tell of all the marvelous things You have done. I will be filled with joy because of You. I will sing praises to Your name, O Most High."

Psalm 9:1-2

Most people, at one time or another, struggle with discouragement, depression, and a general lack of joy. David gives us four keys to turn up the joy factor in our hearts. The first is to place Jesus at the center of our hearts; to pursue and love Him with a whole-heartedness. The second is to groom a heart of thankfulness; to focus on the MAH-velous things God has done!

Now we shift to third gear on this joy ride. Notice what David says, *"I will be filled with joy because of You."* Filled with joy because of what? Because of health? Because of family? Because of financial security? Because of friends? Because of _____?

David was filled with joy because of Yahweh. He focused on who God is, not just what He does. We all want to be appreciated for what we do. If Sue cooks a meal or runs an errand for me, she wants to know I am grateful for her acts of kindness. But if all I do is thank her for what she does, and never appreciate her for who she is, then I'm treating her as I would a servant.

When we praise someone for who they are, we focus on their character. Same with Yahweh: we focus on His character, attributes, and essence. Essence is the intrinsic nature or indispensable quality that determines who a person is by their character.

Think about who Yahweh is. When you Google His attributes, you can get a list of about 30 that define His essence. He is love, not that He is loving, but that He is love to the core of His being. He is eternal; never had a beginning and will never have an end. He is infinite; everything about Him is without limit, including His love, power, wisdom, etc. He is righteous; everything He does is 100% purely right. He is omniscient; there is nothing He doesn't know. He is holy, meaning that, although we are created in His image, He is still so completely unique and different from us or any part of His creation.

Turning our focus on who Yahweh is and praising Him for His essence, His attributes, is high praise. Try beginning your time with Him each day focusing on one of His attributes—and begin to foster a delight and a joy for who He is, not what He does.

God, enable me to value who You are, Your essence, and delight in You. Amen

SING

"I will praise You, Lord, with all my heart; I will tell of all the marvelous things You have done. I will be filled with joy because of You. I will sing praises to Your name, O Most High."

Psalm 9:1-2

Now we come to the last key that David mentions to turn up the joy in our hearts: value the privilege of singing love songs to Him.

We've all seen musicals where a couple is madly in love with each other and one or the other or both begins to sing a love song. They sound so lovely. Sometimes I sound lovely when I sing—in the shower—maybe!

David caps off his ode to joy by identifying singing as a form of worship and praise. Some of us don't sing, in church or otherwise, because we just don't have the voice for it. But God doesn't care. Recently I was sitting in front of a guy in a worship service two rows back who was singing at the top of his lungs—and he never hit a note. I know this: God would rather have that guy sing to Him with all his heart than the most amazing baritone or soprano whose heart just wasn't in it. God relishes His children singing songs of love and devotion to Him.

There is something about singing. I can read the Star-Spangled Banner, even speak it, but it doesn't move me as when I sing it. God designed the human heart to FEEL joy when we sing. Sometimes joy gives birth to singing and sometimes singing gives birth to joy. Singing and joy go together. The Bible contains over four hundred references to singing and fifty direct commands to sing. The entire Book of the Psalms is one song after another.

Did you know that God sings? Yup! Zephaniah 3:17 says, *"For the Lord your God is living among you. He is a mighty savior. He will take delight in you with gladness. With his love, he will calm all your fears. He will rejoice over you with joyful songs."*

Singing and joy go together. And when our singing is about our awesome God and His power, beauty, sovereignty, holiness, justness, righteousness, grace, mercy, and love—well, singing becomes a flowing spring of joy.

Are you struggling with joy lately? Build a playlist of great hymns and contemporary songs and listen to them as you get ready in the morning, on the way to work, during exercise, etc. I guarantee joy will increase in your heart.

God, thank you for the voice you've given me. I will use it to praise You. You're worth it! Amen

JUSTICE
January 31

"But the Lord reigns forever, executing judgment from His throne.
He will judge the world with justice and rule the nations with fairness.
The Lord is a shelter for the oppressed, a refuge in times of trouble."
Psalm 9:7-9

There is a lot of talk nowadays about social justice. To many, social justice is about equality, diversity, and inclusion. No mature believer should be against justice, equality, diversity, and inclusion. But looking under the hood reveals that the contemporary ideology of social justice does not at all line up with biblical justice. All Christians need to be aware of this.

The topic is too gargantuan to tackle in a single 450-word post, so my purpose is two-fold: to prompt believers to dig deeper into the SJ ideology and Bible to find contrasts/contradictions, and to give hope that God's justice is certain, merciful, and ultimate.

The contemporary definition of SJ is: "Deconstructing traditional systems and structures deemed to be oppressive, and redistributing power and resources from oppressors to their victims in the pursuit of equality of outcome" (Scott David Allen). If you listen closely to the language of contemporary SJ proponents, that's what you hear. What you see is a fixation on privilege, oppression, victimization, and a focus on the redistribution of wealth and power. Such an ideology finds scant basis in the Bible and offers little hope for the person or society who seeks it. Check out Russia, China, and Venezuela as recent purveyors of this ideology.

Biblical justice on the other hand is based on the moral code of the Ten Commandments and the Royal Law of Jesus; that is, loving God and loving others. Scott David Allen (<u>Why Social Justice is not Biblical Justice</u>), points out two components of biblical justice:

1. Communitive Justice: living in a way that pleases and obeys God, and loves others as themselves, including honoring them as image-bearers of Yahweh.
2. Distributive Justice: impartially rendering judgment, righting wrongs, and punishing those who break the law. Distributive justice is reserved for God and His appointees: parents, church leaders, and civil authorities.

For Christ-followers, no matter where you are on the political spectrum, know this:

1. Seeking justice for the oppressed is a matter of extending mercy, not retribution;
2. Those who subvert justice will be held accountable by The Judge;
3. Although Christ-followers should be involved in extending mercy and justice to the oppressed, this world will never achieve it fully until Jesus' return;
4. For all who feel they have been treated unjustly, the remedy is to seek shelter and mercy from the only One who can actually give it.

God, empty me of hateful, vengeful emotions and fill me with Your Spirit of love and mercy. Amen

YHWH

"Those who know Your name trust in You, for You,
O Lord, do not abandon those who search for You."
Psalm 9:10

Recently I was taking an Uber home from the airport. As is my custom, I began to ask questions of the driver to get into a gospel conversation. He was a Muslim from Bethlehem and now a U.S. citizen. During the discussion, he made the claim that all religions worship the same God. He insisted that people may call this God by different names (Allah, Krishna, etc.), but they all refer to the same God. We had a lively and good-natured conversation that could have lasted as long as a trip from DFW to Houston, not DFW to Arlington!

The fallacies of his argument were many: with Islam and the Koran, there is no Trinity, Jesus is not God, there is no need for the atonement for sin, the story of the crucifixion/resurrection is a myth, there is no assurance of salvation but only the hope that at the end of your life, you've been good enough to make it, etc. In terms of values, plans, activity, essence, it is obvious there is no way his and mine are the same God.

But let's focus on the one in our text. David references the name of God: *"Those who know Your name trust in You, for You, O LORD"*. The name of David's God is YHWH. Because the Hebrew language does not contain vowels, oral tradition developed millennia ago added markings in between the consonants to help with pronunciation. Thus, YHWH is pronounced *Yahweh*. As mentioned before, YHWH/Yahweh is God's personal name, roughly meaning, "I AM." Jesus' name in Hebrew, Yeshua, is a conjunction of two Hebrew words meaning, *"Yahweh saves."*

Allah, on the other hand, is the generic Arabic word for God, meaning deity. In Hebrew, the common word for a god is '*el*' and is usually used to describe false gods. Many Christian Arabs (yes, there are millions) use the word Allah because that's the Arabic word for El. El is also used in other names/titles of Yahweh, such as Elohim, *"Creator God,"* or El Shaddai, *"God Almighty."*

The point is that the generic **word** for God in Arabic, Allah, does not equate to the personal **name** of God in Hebrew, YHWH. Furthermore, the Koran and the Bible depict two separate and distinct entities; they share almost nothing in kind.

The God of the Bible, YHWH, is not aloof and disinterested in the affairs of your life. He is deeply and personally involved. That's why David admonishes us to trust in Him and seek after Him. As we do, we can count on the fact that He will not abandon us in our troubles: *"If God is for us, who can be against us?"* (Romans 8:31).

Yahweh, I look to You as my Creator and Sovereign. I trust You to come alongside me as I walk through my day. Amen

DISAPPOINTMENT

February 2

"O LORD, why do You stand so far away?
Why do You hide when I am in trouble?"

Psalm 10:1

Do you ever feel as if God is distant and aloof—particularly in times of trouble? I remember calling on a dear friend who had just been diagnosed with a terrible, life-ending disease. He was struggling to feel and sense God's presence when he needed it the most.

There are times, even for the mature believer, when God seems distant. Some refer to this as "The dark night of the soul," a phrase traced back to St. John of the Cross, a 16th-century mystic. Generally, it refers to feeling out of touch with God, even betrayed by Him. It can last a few days or much, much longer. To be certain, God has promised in His word that He will be with us no matter what, but at times it doesn't feel as if He's keeping His word. To have faith is to have expectations, right? And when those expectations are not met, disappointment follows.

I love this about Scripture in general and the Psalms in particular: there is no effort to hide the flaws, weaknesses, and doubts of the people on its pages. This psalmist is disappointed in God.

Two brief insights. One, it's ok to be disappointed with God. Sounds odd, right? But you will find this expression by God's people all through the Bible: Moses in the wilderness, David as he was hunted, Elijah running from Jezebel, etc. I'm not saying there's a reason to be disappointed, only that as a part of our fallen, human condition it naturally shows up in all relationships, even the one with God.

Here's the point: this mysterious relationship between the Divine and depraved can handle it. Healthy relationships can handle real emotions. If you're in Christ and Christ is in you, this relationship can handle your honest expressions and gut-level feelings. God knows them already, and because of God's great love for you, He welcomes the dialogue.

So 'let it go' and get gut honest with God. But get gut honest with yourself as well. God's not the problem. He hasn't moved away from you. You're allowing circumstances and emotions to create the distance. The only way to lessen the gap is to purposely, persistently draw close to Him by faith through prayer and His word.

The second insight: although I have been disappointed **WITH** God, I have come to believe there is no reason to ever be disappointed **IN** God. My perception is rarely 20-20, so I continue to trust **IN** Him—seeking His presence and calling for Him to draw near. And He does.

God, thank You for being the God who never changes and is always there for me. Help me to believe it. Amen

PERCEPTION
February 3

"O LORD, why do You stand so far away?
Why do You hide when I am in trouble?"
Psalm 10:1

In our increasingly secular culture, there is the notion that the individual is the ultimate decider of truth; of what is. Of course, this is lunacy—everyone cannot be right at the same time. I can't be right in saying you don't have a nose, if, in fact, you have a nose. I can't say you are wrong, just because you disagree with me on something until first it has been proved by rationale or evidence that I am indeed right.

I can't remember the first time I heard the phrase, "Perception is reality," but as it became a more popular aphorism, I had this instinctive resistance to the truthfulness of it. One blogger went so far as to put it this way:

> Each individual has his or her own **perception** of **reality**. The implication is that because each of us perceives the world through our own eyes, **reality** itself changes from person to person. While it's true that everyone perceives **reality** differently, **reality** could care less about our **perceptions**.

Fortunately, the Ultimate Reality, Yahweh, does care about our perceptions, opinions, and feelings. That's why His followers pray, appeal, and cry out to Him: we believe He cares.

Certainly, the psalmist believed that. He had a perception that God was disinterested in his reality. But nothing could be farther from the truth. His perception was definitely not reality.

Our tendency is to judge reality based on our feelings, on circumstances, even on a measure of presenting evidence. All of those may be important, but they should not be the final determination of what is real; what is right; what is true.

Truth is, God insists all the way through His word that He is interested in the nitty-gritty of our lives. Jesus said, "*What is the price of five sparrows—two copper coins? Yet God does not forget a single one of them. And the very hairs on your head are all numbered. So don't be afraid; you are more valuable to God than a whole flock of sparrows*" (Luke 12:6-7). And He insists He is not distant: "*I will never abandon you*" (Hebrews 13:5).

Don't look to your feelings or circumstances to define reality. Look to Him and His word and BELIEVE He cares for you.

LORD, by faith, I will accept and believe that you are intimately concerned about me and my circumstances. Thank you for Your care. Amen

BUSTED!

February 4

"Why do the wicked get away with despising God?
They think, 'God will never call us to account.'"

Psalm 10:13

When I was in 4th grade, I made a particularly large haul of Halloween candy in my burlap sack (!). We had been told the day before to only bring one piece of candy to eat at lunch. I, however, showed up with a number of Tootsie Rolls (the small, cigarette-sized ones) in my pocket because they wouldn't melt. The first bathroom break I stuffed 3-4 in my mouth. I overestimated my ability to get them chewed and swallowed in the required time. When I walked out, I kept my mouth closed, thinking I could pull it off. Mrs. Long, way too smart for me, bent over and proceeded to squeeze my cheeks. When she did, a dark stream oozed out of my mouth onto the floor. BUSTED!

The psalmist has been complaining that God is aloof and distant in times of trouble, particularly when the trouble is caused by the wicked. The wicked persist in their dark deeds because they think they'll get away with their rebellion against God and His moral code.

Recent events in our country have prompted true believers along the political spectrum to cry out: "God, aren't You seeing this? How can you let them get away with this?" To be sure, there are plenty of truly wicked people along that spectrum, from deep blue to deep red. But the question stands: "How long will You let this go on?" If ever Romans 1 had application to a generation, it is now: *"They know the truth about God because he has made it obvious to them. For ever since the world was created, people have seen the earth and sky. Through everything God made, they can clearly see his invisible qualities—his eternal power and divine nature. So they have no excuse for not knowing God. They know God's justice requires that those who do these things deserve to die, yet they do them anyway. Worse yet, they encourage others to do them, too"* (Romans 1:19-20,32).

Look at our passage again, *"They think, 'God will never call us to account.'"* Like a 4th-grade punk's attempt to avoid accountability, those who ignore and resist God and His moral law, encoded into them at conception, will be dealt with on **HIS** timetable. Then, it won't be some harmless chocolate extracted from them, but horrible, eternal pain and suffering. BUSTED!

In the meantime, we are to accept and live by faith in this one truth, expressed at the conclusion of the psalm: *"The Lord is king forever and ever! The godless nations will vanish from the land"* (v.16). America will be judged just as the nations before her have been. God is still on His throne. Be faithful. Be steadfast. Keep looking to the Eastern Sky: our Redemption is coming!

God, enable me to walk uprightly and leave the judging to You. Amen

ALIGNMENT
February 5

"Lord, you have heard the desire of the humble;
You will strengthen their hearts. You will listen carefully."
Psalm 10:17 (CSB)

My four-year-old granddaughter has a way about her that can be frustrating to a parent or grandparent: she is certain that she is always right! Of course, she can't be because she doesn't have all the knowledge, wisdom, and insight to make that determination. But oh, does she ever insist that she is!!

Our culture is addicted to a self-validation need that causes us to desperately seek the affirmation and valuation of others. One of the byproducts of that is the idea that "My perception, my opinion, is just as valid as yours," regardless of any basis in fact or truth. We have become a country of 350 million realities. This narcissism is incredibly unhealthy. It keeps the individual stuck in their misperceptions and keeps them from aligning with true realities.

The need for alignment is critical; alignment to what is, what is true, what is real. The psalmist comes to that. After complaining that God was distant (v. 1), he confesses: *"Lord, you have heard the desire of the humble; You will strengthen their hearts. You will listen carefully"* (v.17).

God is the Ultimate Reality. His word reveals "reality on the ground", i.e., what is real and true in this world. I can ignore it at my peril or align with it to my delight (Psalm 1).

Are you feeling empty? Worthless? Unloved? Demeaned? Fearful? Anxious? Depressed? Alone? Abandoned by God? Discover what God says about the issue. Type in your browser: "What does the Bible say about _____." Then study, maybe even memorize the word of God to get the perspective of God. Accept His word as reality and align your mind with it. Your feelings will eventually follow: *"Don't copy the behavior and customs of this world, but let God transform you into a new person by changing the way you think. Then you will learn to know God's will for you, which is good and pleasing and perfect"* (Romans 12:2).

God, I am struggling with a perception that is not healthy; not Yours. By Your grace, align my perception with Yours. Amen

TESTING

February 6

"The Lord tests the righteous and the wicked."
Psalm 11:5 (NASB)

One of the most picturesque bridges in the world is the Golden Gate Bridge in San Francisco. Completed in 1937, it was the longest and tallest suspension bridge in the world at the time. Civil engineers routinely test the various stress points of the structure to make sure it can hold the 39 million cars and trucks that cross it annually.

Testing is about discovery and God is certainly in the testing business. Of course, He doesn't need to discover anything—He is all-knowing and all-wise. He tests us so that we will do the discovering, discovering where our passions are focused and where our faith really lies—so that we can repent, refocus, and be remade into the image of Jesus.

It's tempting for believers to assume that because we have been made in right standing with God (righteous) through faith in Christ, that we get to avoid the tests and trials of life. In fact, there is a whole multibillion-dollar industry of false teachers who have gained incredible wealth making promises of health and prosperity to folks who are desperate enough to believe it—and pay for it. However, a fair examination of Scripture reveals a legacy of testing and trial experienced by saints too long to recount here (e.g., Joseph, Moses, Elijah, Jeremiah, the Disciples, Paul, Stephen). And then there is Jesus, who was tortured and tested severely, even to death.

God tests us. One of the purposes is to reveal where our passions and faith rest. If someone's passion is focused on earthly pursuits, when that pursuit is threatened or removed, then fear, emptiness, and panic ensue. If faith is focused on finances, the significant loss of money will crush the person; if focused on health, the same occurs with the diagnosis of a serious or life-threatening illness.

When Sue was diagnosed with breast cancer, our faith and passions were tested severely. Fortunately, we had been preparing for the test most of our adult lives: daily time with Jesus and His word, memorizing Scripture, building strong community, and fostering effective prayer lives. The test has been difficult, and we are discovering flaws in our faith. Those flaws become obvious when fear and anxiety creep in. But the discovery has prompted us to reinforce what we know is true and double down on the attitudes and actions that strengthen faith.

God didn't cause her cancer, but in His sovereign love, He is revealing to us where our faith is weak, and by His Spirit, enabling us to grow in our faith. Growth rarely comes easily.

God, open my eyes to see where my passions are misdirected and my faith is underdeveloped. By your grace, enable me to respond to the tests by faith. Amen

REFINING
February 7

"The Lord tests the righteous and the wicked."
Psalm 11:5 (NASB)

On January 24, 1848, James Marshall was supervising the construction of a sawmill on the American River in northern California, when he went for a walk along a tributary known as Sutter Creek. He noticed some shiny pieces of metal and put 10-12 nuggets in his hat. Within a year, over 100,000 gold diggers arrived looking for fame and fortune. Precious metals are rarely found in the bottom of a creek. They have to be mined out of rock or lead and come with varying degrees of impurity. The process of purification is fairly simple: heat is applied to the ore melting it, causing the less heavy impurities to float to the top where they can be skimmed off.

Yesterday we discussed the fact that God tests us so that we can discover where our passions are focused and where our faith really lies. Another and associated purpose of testing is to refine our character.

God's ultimate goal for you and me as believers is not to make us happy (sorry!). It's not to make us healthy, wealthy, and wise. It is singular: *"For those whom He foreknew, He also predestined to become conformed to the image of His Son"* (Romans 8:29). To put it bluntly, God is all about us becoming more like Jesus.

Everything about me is impure: thoughts, desires, motives, words, actions—I don't look, sound, or act like Jesus in too many ways. BUT, when I surrendered my life to Him and placed my trust in Him, His Spirit invaded me and His primary job is to bring glory to the Father by transforming me into the likeness of Jesus, i.e., His character. A life lived like Jesus is the ultimate, abundant good on this earth.

Testing is what produces the heat and there's nothing like heat to bring out the impurities: illness, grief, loss of job/income, struggling marriage, family conflict, etc. When the heat is on, know that God is orchestrating (not necessarily causing) the test for your good and His glory.

We can complain or comply. We can resist or embrace. We can get discouraged or get joyful: *"We can rejoice, too, when we run into problems and trials, for we know that they help us develop endurance. And endurance develops strength of character, and character strengthens our confident hope of salvation. And this hope will not lead to disappointment. For we know how dearly God loves us, because he has given us the Holy Spirit to fill our hearts with his love"* (Romans 5:3-5). There's that pleasure-pain connection again. No pain—no gain.

God, teach me to respond to trials in faith and trust that the heat will purify me—for my good and Your glory. Amen

THE SMILE
February 8

"The Lord tests the righteous and the wicked. Upon the wicked He will rain snares; Fire and brimstone and burning wind will be the portion of their cup. For the Lord is righteous, He loves righteousness; The upright will behold His face."
Psalm 11:5-7 (NASB)

We've spent the last two days discussing God's testing of believers. But the Bible also says that God will test the wicked as well. The scripture uses the word '*wicked*' to denote the ungodly person; the person who disregards God and His moral code—and is proud of it. Whereas God tests the believer to reveal areas that need purifying, God tests the wicked to reveal their rebellion and guilt. Instead of responding positively to the revelations of impurity and turn to God, the wicked harden their hearts and push away from God.

The psalmist doesn't pull any punches. All the way through the Bible, the concept of an eternally wicked place for wicked people is undeniable. Some post-moderns find an eternal punishment incongruent with the love and compassion displayed by Jesus on the pages of the gospel. But Jesus' own teachings refute that explicitly: *"And do not fear those who kill the body but cannot kill the soul. Rather fear him who can destroy both soul and body in hell"* (Matthew 10:28). *"Then he will also say to those on the left, 'Depart from me, you who are cursed, into the eternal fire prepared for the devil and his angels! And they will go away into eternal punishment, but the righteous into eternal life"* (Matthew 25:41, 46). *"And if your hand causes you to fall away, cut it off. It is better for you to enter life maimed than to have two hands and go to hell, the unquenchable fire"* (Mark 9:43). *"And in Hades, being in torment, he lifted up his eyes and saw Abraham far off and Lazarus at his side"* (Luke 16:23). *"The one who believes in the Son has eternal life, but the one who rejects the Son will not see life; instead, the wrath of God remains on him"* (John 3:36). It's an understatement that when the wicked are tested before the Judge, they will see only His righteous frown.

BUT, we who are in Christ, never see God frown like that at us. We may get a stern look when we disobey, but like a loving Father, He looks at us with a grace and mercy that is unfathomable. This is so important when we go through trials. We can sense His presence and love for us. **During trials and testing, there is intimacy with Him that is rarely experienced at any other time.**

In a test? Heat high? Look to heaven and see His smile for you, His precious child.

God, I am so grateful to know I will not, by your grace, be tested as the wicked are. Enable me to sense Your pleasure. Amen

WORDS
February 9

"The words of the Lord are pure words,
like silver refined in an earthen furnace, purified seven times."
Psalm 12:6 (CSB)

Have you ever known someone who said nice things about you to your face, but then not-so-nice things behind your back? Or someone who said they would do such-and-such, but then never followed through? You just couldn't count on their words to be reliable and trustworthy?

David, the author of this psalm, was complaining about just that. We're not sure who he was talking about, but many scholars think it was King Saul at a time when David was in Saul's court but was the object of scorn and jealousy. In the first five verses, he talks about people who speak unreliable words: flattery, deceit, and lies—and how disappointing and hurtful it is.

But then in v.6, David writes a clear and compelling statement about the reliability and rock-solid truthfulness of God's words. He uses the precious metal of silver to signal the value of God's word and purity, to signal its flawlessness. In fact, David uses the metaphor of silver being heated up to remove the impurities, not once, not twice, but seven times. Seven, of course, is the perfection number.

Since the Garden of Eden ("Did God *really* say…? Genesis 3), Satan and his allies have been assaulting the word of God. They know if they can get people to doubt God's word, their chances of ruining someone's life are greatly enhanced. Yet, despite the attacks from skeptics and secularists, the Bible stands as the unadulterated, inerrant word of God. I love how secularists in cosmology or archeology will ridicule something in the Bible, only to affirm it years or decades later. Time Magazine (!) published an article a few decades ago after doing thorough research on its veracity:

> After more than two centuries of facing the heaviest guns that could be brought to bear, the Bible has survived – and is perhaps the better for the siege. Even on the critics' own terms – historical fact – the Scriptures seem more acceptable now than when the rationalists began the attack.

God's word is true. It is absolutely reliable. Build your life on it.

God, grant me a hunger for Your word and enable me to build my life on it. Amen

VICTORY
February 10

"But I have trusted in your faithful love; my heart will rejoice in your deliverance.
I will sing to the Lord because he has treated me generously."
Psalm 13:5-6 (CSB)

This psalm is so me.

David begins it by complaining, *"O Lord, how long will You forget me? Forever? How long will You look the other way?"* (v.1). It is so easy for me to complain to God about something that is just not right. It could be a health situation, a financial situation, my marriage—but something is amiss, frustrating, or worse. I pray. I lay it before Him. But it seems He is not listening.

My complaining reveals the fact that I don't think He's doing a good job at running the universe; that not responding to me the way I want when I want is a poor reflection on His performance! What arrogance and ingratitude.

But eventually I come around, as does David. He gathers up his faith, stops complaining, and recalls God's faithfulness and goodness in his life: *"I HAVE trusted in Your lovingkindness; You HAVE dealt bountifully with me"* (v.5).

And then by faith, he begins to sing: *"My heart WILL rejoice in Your salvation; I WILL sing to the LORD; You HAVE been good to me"* (v.6).

This is where the victory begins. For almost 50 years people have asked me how they can overcome being overwhelmed; how to defeat discouragement, dejection, and hopelessness.

I tell them the same thing that I tell myself: victory begins by recognizing and articulating the grace and goodness of God in your life.

There's an old hymn that goes like this:

> *When upon life's billows you are tempest-tossed,*
> *When you are discouraged, thinking all is lost,*
> *Count your many blessings, name them one by one,*
> *And it will surprise you what the Lord has done.*

Victory in the tough battles of life begins with recalling the grace and mercy of God. If that's not enough, nothing else will be. Take time to write down ten blessings in your life and see what difference it makes in your soul. Begin with your undeserved, unmerited salvation.

God, thank You for all the many blessings You have bestowed on me. I love You! Amen

LOVE SONGS
February 11

"I will sing to the Lord because He has treated me generously."
Psalm 13:5-6 (CSB)

When Sue and I moved to Albuquerque, N.M. at the beginning of our marriage and ministry, Steve and Melissa took us in and treated us like family. We didn't have kids yet, so we got to watch and learn from them on how to be great parents. It served us well when our own started arriving a few months later. One of their children was particularly strong-willed.

Steve would say, "Son, don't do that!" And the son would reply defiantly, "I **WILL!!**"

David declares that he **WILL** sing to the LORD. For him, it wasn't an option. His relationship with Yahweh compelled him to sing songs of praise, adoration, and thanksgiving to his great God. We don't really know what kind of voice David had. He could have had a beautiful voice or a dreadful one—or somewhere in between. It doesn't matter. If your heart is in tune—then it doesn't matter if your voice is. The point is to sing to Him. We are admonished all through Scripture to lift our voices and SING! It's not a suggestion; it is a directive to all subjects of The King of Kings; a privilege for all who know, love, and worship Yahweh.

Being on a stage in front of 1000s of Sunday morning attendees, I've always been baffled by observing the non-participation of many who just stand there like totem poles, not participating vocally with those around them in corporate worship of our great God. What a missed opportunity; what a waste of the chance to be blessed.

Just recently (again), I was standing in the congregation during worship lifting my voice in praise. There was a young man a few rows back who was singin' it loud and singin' it proud! He didn't hit a single note! I wanted to cry— not because of the quality of his voice, but because of the love in his heart for his Jesus who had rescued and redeemed him. He was singing as if it was a love song. It was love that compelled him to overcome his timidity and lack of vocal talent.

David says that emotions won't deter him; circumstances won't dissuade him. He **WILL** sing to the Lord. Why? Because God has been so gracious and merciful to him.

Sing love songs to the One who loves you and gave His life for you. Don't hold back. Sing it loud and sing it proud. He's worthy of that—and more.

God, I pledge to overcome my discomfort and sing love songs to You—because You set aside Your comfort for me. Amen.

THE FOOL

February 12

"Only fools say in their hearts, 'There is no God.'"
Psalm 14:1

A good friend of mine tells the story of a lady in our church who was 9 months pregnant. She called him one Wednesday night saying, "I can't get hold of Jeff at the church." This was before cell phones. She continued in a panic, "My water has broken and I'm about to deliver this baby. Help me!" He hopped in his car, drove 100 mph to her house about 5 miles away, rushed in the house yelling, "Patti, Patti! Where are you? Are you OK?" Just then Patti came around the corner and yelled, "April Fools!"

April Fools jokes can be funny—and usually fun. But it's no laughing matter to be called a fool by God Himself. God's Holy Spirit prompts David to begin the psalm with a declaration that seems particularly harsh: "Only a fool would think, 'There is no God.'"

The English word *'fool'* can be applied to someone who has been punked, like my friend, or someone who has been fooled because they didn't have the mental acuity to recognize a ruse when they should have. But the Hebrew word for *fool* (*nabal*) refers to someone who is morally insensitive and corrupt. The rest of David's psalm expands on that understanding: *"They are corrupt, and their actions are evil; not one of them does good!"*

There is no way to soften this accusation: those who refuse to believe God exists, even though presented with overwhelming evidence, are morally corrupt in God's eyes. It's not about their intellectual prowess; it's about their moral incompetence.

> *For God's wrath is revealed from heaven against all godlessness and unrighteousness of people who by their unrighteousness suppress the truth, since what can be known about God is evident among them, because God has shown it to them. For His invisible attributes, that is, His eternal power and divine nature, have been clearly seen since the creation of the world, being understood through what He has made. As a result, people are without excuse. Claiming to be wise, they became fools* (Romans 1:18-20; 22; CSB).

All humans are innately fools and morally corrupt in God's eyes. Wisdom begins with the acknowledgment that Yahweh, the Creator of all that is, exists. It should lead us to declare our own moral bankruptcy and ask for God's mercy and grace through Jesus Christ.

If you haven't acknowledged your own foolishness before God, do so this very minute. His wrath awaits those who refuse.

God, thank You for providing a way to avoid Your wrath and the consequence of my moral wickedness. I place my faith in Jesus to make me right with You. Amen

CHRISTIAN ATHEISTS
February 13

"Only fools say in their hearts, 'There is no God.'"
Psalm 14:1

Christian atheist—a contradiction of major proportion, right?

Yet in America, there are thousands, if not millions of men and women who claim to be Christ-followers (and maybe are) but act in everyday life as if they don't really believe in God. They get up in the morning, get dressed, eat breakfast, and head to work without any notable desire to spend time with their Creator and Redeemer. They roll through the day, busy with tasks, and projects, calls, and emails, but rarely pausing to converse with the Lover of their souls. They commute home, eat dinner, get through the evening with the fam without talking about how they saw the hand of God at work in their lives. They hit the pillow with thoughts of tomorrow's challenges without worshipping God for His today provisions.

They are functional atheists.

When challenges come, they may throw up a foxhole prayer, but usually, they turn to their screens or books or alcohol or friends or food or shopping or pursuits to deliver them. Oh— they'll show up at church on Sundays for an hour. They'll profess to be believers. But they act like atheists the other 167 hours of the week.

To be sure, even the best and most mature believers can slide in that direction at times. But that's why we foster the spiritual disciplines in our lives to help keep us tethered close to Him. I've found that daily Bible reading and daily prayer, as close to first thing in the morning as I can get them, help me focus on my relationship with Jesus and keep it vibrant and fulfilling. It sets my day off rightly and enhances my sensitivity to His will, His grace, and His presence during my day.

An atheist doesn't **believe** God exists. Let's not be the kind of believer that **acts** as if He doesn't exist. Draw close to Him and make Him the center of your life.

God, I ask Your forgiveness for the times I go about my day as if You don't exist. Draw me closer to You, I pray. Amen

INTIMACY
February 14

"Who may worship in Your sanctuary, Lord?
Who may enter your presence on Your holy hill?"

Psalm 15:1

Sue and I normally keep our front door locked. If a friend is coming over, many times we'll just unlock the door and tell them to come on in when they get there. But if a stranger approaches the door, we won't give them that kind of access.

So it is with God. The intimacy of the relationship determines the appropriateness of access. David asks a very important question: who has access to an intimate relationship with Yahweh?

It is interesting that he uses anthropomorphic language to describe this: *"Who may enter Your presence?"* Since God is omnipresent (His divine presence is not limited by time or space, i.e., He's everywhere all the time), the idea of entering into God's presence is expressed by using anthropomorphic language: figures of speech to represent God as having human characteristics, form, or personality. They are *symbolic* descriptions that help to make God's attributes, powers, and activities real to us. Scripture says to *seek His face*; *His hands are not tied*; *He is not deaf* (ears), etc. But such language doesn't mean God actually has physical ears, hands, and a face like we do.

Using anthropomorphic language to describe God isn't wrong—it's biblical. We just need to be careful how we use and understand it. When the psalmist asks: *"Who may enter into Your presence?"*, he is identifying the relational aspect of God; God is not just a greater, inanimate force or an unknowable higher power—He loves, hates, laughs, thinks, wills, etc.

And in any relationship, there is a dynamic of intimacy that runs along a continuum from very close to extremely distant. Where that relationship falls on that continuum determines appropriate access and behavior. Back to the front door analogy: close friends have easy access to our home; casual acquaintances or strangers do not.

The question: "Who has access to intimacy with Yahweh?" (v.1) is answered in v.2: *"Those who lead blameless lives and do what is right, speaking the truth from sincere hearts."* The word 'lead' (*holek*) refers to a person's lifestyle and conduct. The word *'blameless'* (*tamim*) means complete and sincere. The point is that the person who has intimate access with Yahweh is the one whose heart and activities are in harmony with the moral character of God.

How would you rate your intimacy with God right now? Is there an area of your life that you know is out of alignment with His character? The proper response is to repent and surrender that area to Him, then cooperate with the Spirit to conform you into the image of Jesus.

God, I do want to draw closer to You. By Your Spirit, bring that to pass. Amen

MISTAKE
February 15

"Who may worship in Your sanctuary, Lord? Who may enter Your presence on Your holy hill? Those who lead blameless lives and do what is right, speaking the truth from sincere hearts."

Psalm 15:1-2

There are many people who make the tragic mistake by thinking: "Since I'm saved and all my sins are paid for and forgiven, past, present, and future—I can say and do what I want."

Nope. Not true. Not one tiny bit. If you think that, or even worse, if you live that, you're either not really saved or incredibly deceived.

Salvation comes to a person when they repent (admit their moral depravity and desire to turn away from it) and believe (place their trust in Jesus and His substitutionary death on the cross alone to save them). It is a matter of surrendering control of our lives to Him. While this salvation experience is dynamic (i.e., it is a point in time like walking through a doorway of a house), it continues on as a process (moving throughout the house).

Never in that process do we have the option to tell God, "I think I'll now say what I want to say and do what I want to do." That is the opposite of repentance and surrender. It is an anti-salvation attitude. Put plainly, it is sin. And sin always creates distance between us and God. Distance between us and God isolates us from Him and puts us on a path that will end up in pain and loss.

Do we lose the relationship? No. Fortunately, since we did nothing to earn salvation, there is nothing we can do to lose it. But O my, what we lose is still tragic: we lose intimacy with our Lover and Creator. We lose the beauty of experiencing the *"more and better life than you ever dreamed of"* (what Jesus said in John 10:10).

I love Sue—and miraculously she loves me!! But when my words or actions are inconsistent with our love relationship, this lack of integrity and respect creates emotional distance between us. We're still married, and the relationship is intact, but we certainly aren't close and intimate.

What I've got to do to get back on track with her is to repent; I've got to forsake my selfishness/pride and seek her forgiveness. Then the relationship can begin to get healthy again and our intimacy increases.

Remember, intimacy is determined and revealed by appropriate behavior. There is no better life than a life lived in a close, warm intimate relationship with Jesus. None.

Jesus, I do want the "more and better life than I ever dreamed of" life. Draw me closer. Amen

STAND FIRM
February 16

"Such people will stand firm forever."
Psalm 15:5

By God's grace, I visited China ten times in 20 years. One of the customs of the Chinese is to take your shoes off at the door. It was considered unsanitary and inappropriate to bring the outside stuff into the house on the bottom of the shoes.

In a way, the psalmist is saying the same thing. In v.1 he asks the question: *"Who may worship in Your sanctuary, Lord? Who may enter Your presence on Your holy hill?"* David then answers his own question with two responses in v.2, *"Those whose lives and words are right in the sight of God."* Then he gives some specific examples so that we won't miss the point.

Those who experience a warm, intimate encounter with Him are those who, first, don't gossip (v.3). Gossip is sharing negative information about someone with a person who is not a part of the problem or the solution. People who gossip normally do so out of a deep sense of insecurity. In our warped condition, we somehow feel we elevate our standing by tearing down someone else. At its core, **gossip is a power play**: NEVER helpful and NEVER right. It destroys reputations and harms the person you're gossiping about, sometimes tragically. What most gossipers don't get is that it destroys their own reputation as well. One of the worst titles someone can call you is a gossiper. Speaking evil of someone is harmful to all concerned and definitely something that hinders intimacy with God.

David then turns his focus from words to actions. The one who has intimacy with God has a lifestyle that is honoring to Him. David mentions despising *"flagrant sinners"* (v.4), but this only refers to contrast in lifestyle. We should definitely despise the lifestyle of those who are living dishonorably to the Lord and should purpose to *"lead a life worthy of (our) calling"* (Ephesians 4:1). David covers a few more required lifestyles: being generous and just with people, and keeping our *"promises, even when it hurts"* (v.4)!

Here's what God says about people like that: *"Such people will stand firm forever"* (v.5).

Jesus echoed this psalm in His Sermon on the Mount. After telling us how to live a blessed and meaningful life—one that is pleasing & honoring to God—He finishes with: *"If you hear what I'm saying and live this way, you'll be like a house built on a rock. When the storms of life come, you'll be able to withstand them in blessing and security"* (Matthew 7:24-25). If you don't, well—you won't."

God, by Your Spirit, guard my tongue to only speak positively about people and enable me to walk in a manner worthy of Your calling on my life. Amen

THE GOODNESS OF GOD
February 17

"I said to the Lord, "You are my Master! Every good thing I have comes from you."
Psalm 16:2

Sitting in a coffee shop early this morning, I'm meditating on the truth of those words and reflecting back on the goodness of God in my life. I won't bore you with a protracted history of my life but suffice to say that whatever is good *about* me, whatever good has come *from* me, whatever good has come *to* me—has everything to do with my Master, Jesus!

I didn't say it's been easy. My life has been filled with many tests He's asked me to endure. These past 18 months I've been weathering the harshest storm in my life thus far. Sue's diagnosis of cancer as I was transitioning out of being Lead Pastor at Rush Creek for 25 years, and the awful cancer treatment—five months of chemotherapy, twenty radiation treatments afterward, the body aches, the nausea, the full-body loss of hair, the fatigue, the isolation—has been a major test for us both.

But the truth is that much of the good in my life has actually emerged out of some of the worst circumstances. First, my salvation came out of the pain, suffering, and sacrifice of my Master. Everything else flows out of that. I had to die to self to be able to live in Him. I continue to choose to die. When I don't, I experience the discipline of my Master—and even that has ended up being a good thing. Only He could make it so.

The NASB translates v.2 this way: *"I have no good besides You."* What a realization: I have no good besides Him. In fact, there is no good without Him. Being in Him and Him in me, knowing Him and being known by Him, loving Him, and being loved by Him, learning from Him, and yes, even suffering for Him, is the best there is in this life.

In the worst part of this recent challenge, I was at one of our campuses, worshipping without Sue because she couldn't get out of bed. One of the vocalists began to sing:

All my life You have been faithful. All my life You have been so, so good.
With every breath that I am able, I will sing of the goodness of God.

As I stood there singing, then weeping, my heart overflowed with gratitude at the realization that God has always been faithful, and He has always been good to me. You can too. Focus on His goodness and be overwhelmed with gratitude.

God, I agree: You have been good to me and so faithful. Enable me to see it more clearly. Amen

UPSIDE DOWN
February 18

"Lord, you are my portion and my cup of blessing; You hold my future."
Psalm 16:5

Psalm 16 is overflowing with great verses and wonderful truths. It's one of my favorites and has sustained me through many failures, trials, and heartaches.

In v.5, David reminds us of a value system that is completely upside down and different than the world's. He says that God is our portion. This harkens back to when the Israelites finally did possess the Promised Land, they were to divide it amongst eleven tribes. The twelfth tribe, Levi, was to serve as the priesthood for all of Israel. They never owned any land and were permitted to live in 48 different cities throughout Israel. Deuteronomy 18:2 says, *"Although Levi has no inheritance among his brothers, the Lord is his inheritance, as He promised him."*

God would be their portion, their supply, and their inheritance.

When my parents died, there was no estate to inherit. We're not sure there will be any from Sue's parents. We've tried to be good stewards of what God has provided and there may be some inheritance for our kids once we're gone—though we are trying to spend it at the rate we run out of money the day we die! Our kids are so good. They aren't concerned with having an inheritance; they want us to enjoy life and enjoy life with us as long as possible.

The question is this: who was more satisfied and fulfilled? The tribes who had land or the tribe who had the Lord? The world system values possessions, right? The more you have the more you are; the more you have the more life you have. But is that really true? The most miserable people I've ever known are those who have a lot of money and possessions.

The mature believer realizes the pleasures of what this world has to offer are severely limited and strives to live for the pleasure of the One who created, loves, and redeemed them. It's upside-down relative to the world, but right-side-up relative to ultimate reality.

Which would you choose? Material possessions or the abiding sense of His pleasure. The psalmist reminds us that WE don't hold our future; God does. Choose the One who holds the cup of blessing! If you do, you will be able to say with David: *"The boundary lines have fallen for me in pleasant places; indeed, I have a beautiful inheritance"* (v.6).

God, rid me of my 'this world' materialism and put me right-side-up in what I value and aspire to. Amen

AIN'T NO THANG
February 19

"I know the Lord is always with me. I will not be shaken, for He is right beside me."
Psalm 16:8

I pride myself on proper grammar usage, but sometimes a slang word or phrase just fits better. Such is the phrase, 'Ain't No Thang.' According to the Urban Dictionary, it's a phrase that means, 'No big deal.' I recently watched Kansas City Chief cornerback, Bashaud Breeland (5'11', 185 lbs), try to tackle Tampa Bay Buccaneer tight end Rob Gronkowski (6'6", 270 lbs). It was like a bb bouncing off a tank! I think I might have heard Gronk say as he ran into the endzone, "Aint no thang!"

David is reflecting on the challenges of his life, which were many. He reminds himself that God is his constant companion. This is a foretaste of the incarnation of Jesus (God in the flesh), who is also called Immanuel, which means, *"God is with us"* (Matthew 1:23). This promise that God is with us is THE most important truth to hold on to when times get difficult. He hasn't abandoned us. He doesn't disappear like a fickle friend when you need Him the most. God reassured Jacob (Genesis 28:15), Moses & Israel (Deuteronomy 31:8), Joshua (Joshua 1:9), Isaiah (Isaiah 41:10), and others who came before David, that He would be with them. And David has experienced that for Himself. He doesn't get caught up in temporary emotions; he clings to the promise of God. What a great promise! That no matter what happens, no matter where we find ourselves, Jesus promises: *"I am with you always, even to the end of the age"* (Matthew 28:20).

Not only is God with us, but He is also for us. It's not that He is just near, it is also that He watches over us. Like the little boy running from a bully and finding safety beside his dad, God watches over us with our best interest in mind. Paul said it this way: *"If God be for us, who can be against us?"* (Romans 8:31).

Because God is with us and God is for us, David proclaims: *"I will not be shaken!"* (v.8). He is confident that whatever comes his way, it will not throw him off, it will not defeat him, and "It ain't no thang!" We can be like David, unshaken, undaunted, and unafraid—when we cling to Him and His promise.

God, by faith, I do hold to the promise that You are at my side and that whatever comes against me, ain't no thang. Amen

THE SECRET SAUCE
February 20

"You reveal the path of life to me; in Your presence is abundant joy;
at Your right hand are eternal pleasures"
Psalm 16:11 (CSB)

Plato said, "Pleasure is the greatest incentive to evil." Didn't realize Plato was the first Debbie Downer! Actually, pleasure presents itself to us as something good, attractive, enjoyable, and satisfying. Of course, because of our brokenness, some pleasures are harmful to us, others, and an affront to God—such as adultery, pornography, lying, stealing, etc. But there is a whole slew of pleasures that are good and wholesome—such as snuggling with your honey, playing with your child/grandchild, walking amongst nature, or eating pizza! Some pleasures are fleeting, some are lasting, but then some are eternal. THOSE are the pleasures I want to experience more of, right?

David finishes this amazing psalm with a great summation: "You show me how to live, Your presence brings me joy, and You give me pleasures that are forever." Notice the progression: Path->Presence->Pleasure. This pattern is seen throughout Scripture.

God's path is delineated by His word. If you go back and reread Psalm 1, you'll see that there are two paths, one leads to life and one leads to death. The path to real and genuine life is the path set out in Scripture. That's why it is so critical that we become students of the Bible— that we can know what His path is, how to follow it, and how to get back on it when we lose our way.

God's presence is felt and experienced most satisfyingly when we walk His path. The times in my earlier life when I wandered off His path, wandered away from His will—those times were marked with a feeling of estrangement, not intimacy. This is why we need to keep short accounts with God—humbling ourselves and confessing our sin when it occurs so that our intimacy is maintained. Sensing the close presence of God is EVERYTHING this side of heaven and is the secret sauce that brings bubbly joy.

God's pleasures are handed to us along the way. They are acts of grace, i.e., the favor of God in, through, and around us, in our relationships, marriage, parenting (sometimes!), career— only He can bring lasting pleasure to the routines of life. The great thing is that this handing out, this granting doesn't stop when we quit breathing—as David says, they are pleasures forever! FOREVER! They start right here, right now, and they never quit!!

Follow this hope-filled progression: walk His path, seek His presence, experience His pleasures—it will bring Him pleasure!

God, thank You for Your word. By your grace, enable me to walk your path to experience more and better life than I ever dreamed of. Amen

APPLES

February 21

"Keep me as the apple of Your eye; hide me in the shadow of Your wings."
Psalm 17:8 (NIV)

The first time I remember seeing Sue was at First Baptist Church, Houston, Texas. It was a Sunday night (yes, we had Sunday night church in those days), and the place was packed. I was standing down in front of this 4,000-seat auditorium chatting with friends when I spotted her as soon as she walked in the door: beautiful, shapely, long blonde hair halfway down her back. Mm, Mm, Mm! I still can be in a crowd of hundreds of people—like at church or a mall—but I promise you I can spot Sue in a matter of milliseconds. Why? Because my eye is trained for beauty and this beauty is at the center of my heart.

In this psalm, David is being hard pressed by his enemies. We're not sure if this occurs early in his life when he was being hunted by Saul, or late in his life when he was being chased by Absalom, his son. Whenever it was and whatever it was, he was appealing to Yahweh to protect him.

In v.8 he makes two huge requests in a matter of sixteen words. Both are in keeping with his close relationship with Yahweh.

The first request he makes of God is, *"Keep me as the apple of Your eye."* That's not an expression used often nowadays. The phrase was originally an idiom that referred to the pupil of the eye. It became a figure of speech to communicate that something or someone was cherished above all others. It carries with it the idea of both focus and affection.

When I look at Sue, I still can't believe she's mine—not in a possessive sense, but in a relational sense. We belong to each other—and she sure is high on my scale of focus and affection.

David calls on Yahweh to keep him as the apple of His eye. God doesn't need reminding—David does! In times of danger and trouble, we sometimes feel isolated, alone, and vulnerable. We need to be reminded that in Christ, we are the apple of His eye. It's natural for believers to call out to our Daddy (*Abba*) and be assured that His eye is on us and His affections are for us.

If you are in Christ, Daddy's got His eye on you. You are not alone. His heart pounds with affection for you. And He whispers: "That one is Mine!"

God, You are amazing that You would call me Your own and love me as you do! Thank you!

WINGS
February 22

"Keep me as the apple of Your eye; hide me in the shadow of Your wings."
Psalm 17:8 (NIV)

God has blessed us with ten (10!) grandchildren!! Presently they all live in the Metroplex so we can see them just about as often as we'd like. I can take one of them to the park where there are scores of other children. All the kids on the playground are cute, but I have a special affection for the one I took there. I keep my focus on her because I love her, because she is special to me, and because I want to protect her.

The psalmist (David) is in danger: *"Show me Your unfailing love in wonderful ways. By Your mighty power You rescue those who seek refuge from their enemies"* (v.7). We're not exactly certain of the source of his angst, but whatever and whoever is causing it has prompted him to call out to Yahweh.

In his appeal, he makes two huge requests. The first we looked at yesterday, *"Keep me as the apple of Your eye."* The apple of the eye is a phrase that means someone is the object of your focus and affection.

The first appeal is about affection; the second appeal is about protection: *"Hide me in the shadow of Your wings."* This is not to be taken that God has literal wings. It is another euphemism to describe God in common terms.

Wings are common in our world. The hummingbird's wing is about 1.5 inches and can beat up to 90 times/second! The albatross wing can be as long as 6 feet carrying the bird 600 miles without stopping! What is common amongst all birds is that they protect their hatchlings from danger by covering them with their wings.

God is featured many times in Scripture as The Protector. Jesus referenced this when entering Jerusalem towards the end of His ministry: *"Jerusalem, Jerusalem!! How often I wanted to gather your children together, as a hen gathers her chicks under her wings, but you were not willing!"* (Luke 13:34), *"But the Lord is faithful, and He will strengthen and protect you from the evil one"* 2 Thessalonians 3:3.

What do you need protection from today? Fear? Anxiety? Sin Habit? Attacks from our Adversary? Run to the Great Protector and hide under His massive wings. He cares for you.

God, I do need your protection. Hide me under Your wings!! Amen

NDE

February 23

"I called on the Lord, who is worthy of praise, and he saved me from my enemies."

Psalm 18:3

Have you ever had a Near Death Experience (NDE)? I have—many times! I can count eight times in my life I should have been killed dead as a doornail. Someday I'll tell you about them.

David had a number of NDEs as well. The superscription above this psalm says, *"For the choir director. A Psalm of David, the servant of the Lord. He sang this song to the Lord on the day the Lord rescued him from all his enemies and from Saul."* David wrote this song after an NDE with King Saul, who was incredibly jealous of David. David was loved and respected by the people, Saul was not; David had been tabbed as the new king, Saul was on his way out; David had the Spirit of the Lord on him, Saul had some form of an evil spirit that pushed him into rages. The result was that he tried to murder David multiple times, finally chasing him around the countryside trying to do him in.

We have an enemy who has the same objective for us. The apostle Peter writes: *"Stay alert! Watch out for your great enemy, the devil. He prowls around like a roaring lion, looking for someone to devour"* (1 Peter 5:8). Lions are known for their prowess and their power. They can track the scent of an animal for miles before they close in for the kill. When they have their prey in their clutches—there is no escape.

There is a literal being called Satan. He's called by other titles as well: Adversary, Lucifer, Devil, tempter, god of this age, the accuser, etc. He can only be at one place at one time. But he has a host of demons who do his evil bidding. So whether it is Satan himself (very rare) or a demon(s) he has sent, we are under attack by Satan, our archenemy. He is out to destroy us; to devour us. For those of us in Christ, he can't have our souls, but he can certainly destroy much of what is good in our lives. Jesus said that Satan comes *"to steal and kill and destroy"* (John 10:10). If we let him, he can exert such influence over us that there is little REAL life.

And that, my friends, is the ultimate NDE. Been there; done that. Got the scars. I was 26. I wasn't careful. I stepped into his trap and it took years for me to get out. By God's grace, I did. You can too. Get on His path. Keep calling on Him to deliver you. He will.

God, I need You to rescue me. Deliver me from the clutches of the Adversary. Help!

ATTACKS
February 24

"They attacked me at a moment when I was in distress, but the Lord supported me.
He led me to a place of safety; He rescued me because He delights in me."
Psalm 18:18-19

It was the summer of 1972. "The Godfather" was playing in all the theatres. Bill Withers' "Lean on Me" was at the top of the charts. For me, it was the summer of my discontent.

I was new in my walk with Jesus and frankly, had spent scant time in His word or with Him in prayer. Unfortunately, I was alright with that. The girl I was in love with had broken up with me that Spring, but I was making it. Then I moved to Houston to work for Shell Oil in their downtown offices for the summer. From about the 3rd day there, I found myself battling profound loneliness and depression. I could get through the workday, but by the time I crawled home on the Katy Freeway and walked into my apartment, I could barely make it to the bed before I crumpled in a heap of weeping despair. Weekends were Hades. Thoughts of suicide became all too familiar and the debilitating gloom drowned out any hope of improvement. My enemy was on the attack. When I was my weakest, he came at me with everything he had.

I had acquired a Living Bible; the new paraphrase edition published the previous year by Tyndale. Its green cover and marked pages still sit on my bookshelf. Fortunately, I had decided to take it with me to Houston—it saved my life. I began to pour over its pages, underlining meaningful verses and committing many of them to memory. As the summer dragged on, every evening and most of the weekends I spent devouring God's word. This may sound a bit dramatic, but I felt that if I didn't read the Scripture, I would stop breathing.

David said that in his hour of despair, God led him to a place of safety. I don't know where his was, but I know where mine was: The Bible. To this day I believe it literally saved my life. I learned that lesson almost 50 years ago and it has sustained me through countless more assaults from the enemy: when under attack, head to the word of God. Satan will do anything to distract us from the one weapon that can defeat him. You'll recall that when he attacked Jesus in the wilderness, Jesus responded, *"It is written . . ."* and quoted Scripture. After three attempts, Satan left defeated.

Do whatever you have to do to build the word of God into your life. It might just save it.

God, thank You for inspiring and preserving Your word. I will build my life on it. Amen

LIKE A ROCK
February 25

"God's way is perfect. All the Lord's promises prove true. He is a shield for all who look to Him for protection. For who is God except the Lord? Who but our God is a solid rock?"
Psalm 18:30-31

In Bob Seger's song, "Like a rock", he reflects back 20 years to the time of his youth, how he was strong and unbending then—like a rock. He wishes he could be like that again. Truth is, he never was. Humans foster the illusion that they are indestructible and unassailable.

One of the things I observed about Israel the first time I went, was how plentiful the rocks were there. The houses, the walls, the fences are all made out of rocks. Before you can grow a crop, you have to remove the thousands of rocks from the soil. Rocks are a part of the story of Israel.

In ancient times, when battles were fought hand to hand, rocks were critical when hiding from the enemy to avoid capture or getting to higher ground for a tactical advantage. Because of its arid climate, when the rain falls, it can't seep into the hard, dry ground fast enough, so it creates devastating and deadly flash floods. If you're caught in a rain shower in the desert, you'd better climb up as high as you can on the rocks or be swept away.

Rocks are essentially solid and unchangeable. Wood rots away. Soil and sand wash away. But rocks are strong and reliable.

The psalmists never refer to themselves as rocks; they always point to Yahweh as THE Rock.

God is our protection when the enemy comes after us. We don't have enough strength and knowledge to protect ourselves. That's why the psalmists call Yahweh their Rock. God is solid when everything else crumbles. He is a refuge when the floods of adversity come. He is our constant when no one else and nothing else is.

I know better than to look to people or possessions or power or popularity to sustain me when under attack. Like soil and sand, they disappear quickly when the torrents come. Like wood, they burn away when the heat is turned up. God is my Rock!! Is He yours??

God, I declare that You are my Rock. I trust in You to be my Constant when everything seems to be falling apart and drifting away. I love You. Amen

SUREFOOTED
February 26

"He makes me as surefooted as a deer, enabling me to stand on mountain heights."
Psalm 18:33

I mentioned a couple of days ago about my NDEs (Near Death Experiences). The second one was at Glen Eyrie, a beautiful retreat center in a castle nestled in the mountains just outside Colorado Springs. I was there on spring break with about 200 college kids my sophomore year. One afternoon I got the bright idea of climbing up a sheer outcrop rising 300' from the ground, in penny loafers mind you! More than once my foot started to slip on the 3-4" wide ledge. One time in particular, I slipped and began to feel my weight go backward. I blindly reached up to grab something and, by God's grace, my hand landed on the slightest of a crack to hold on. Whew! But O, when I got to the top—what a view!!

David, reflecting on his relationship with Yahweh, likens it to a wonderful, yet perilous existence. God's path for him included multiple NDEs with King Saul and Absalom.

God calls us higher and closer, but the journey is not always easy and it's certainly not always safe. C.S. Lewis announces this about Jesus through his character, Mr. Beaver, in *The Chronicles of Narnia* series:

> "Aslan is a lion—the lion, the great Lion." Mr. Beaver said. "Ooh!" said Susan, "I'd thought he was a man. Is he—quite safe? I shall feel rather nervous about meeting a lion." "Then he isn't safe?" said Lucy. "Safe?" said Mr. Beaver; "don't you hear what Mrs. Beaver tells you? Who said anything about safe? 'Course he isn't safe. But he's good!"

One of the books I read almost 50 years ago was *"Hinds Feet on High Places"* by Hanna Hurnard. It's an allegory about a young woman named "Much Afraid," who leaves her Fearing family and heads to the high places of the Good Shepherd. The high places were filled with beautiful and exhilarating panoramas, but the slopes were steep, and the paths were narrow and dangerous. Through her journey, Much Afraid faced her fear by placing more and more trust in the Good Shepherd.

David the psalmist and Ms. Hurnard were right: the closer I get to Jesus, the higher and more beautiful the experience, yet the trail can get more and more dangerous: the challenges are bigger, the risks are greater, the falls are harder. But. It. Has. Been. Worth. It! I wouldn't trade anything for the journey I've been on with Him. Deep valleys and high vistas have been a part of His plan all along—He's been with me every step of the way.

God, grant me the faith to follow You closer and higher. Make me surefooted! Amen

FIGHT CLUB
February 27

"You have armed me with strength for the battle;
You have subdued my enemies under my feet."
Psalm 18:39

The 20th-century arms race was certainly alarming. The century began with weapons like rifles, machine guns, mortars, and 31mm canons. Every weapon developed by a country was counter weaponized by its enemy. The century ended with atomic bombs placed on the tips of rockets that could travel thousands of miles and powerful enough to destroy entire metropolitan areas.

In ancient times, weapons were primarily limited to swords, shields, axes, and bows. Having the right weapons and the honed skill to use them, was the difference between life and death.

David saw himself as a warrior for Yahweh. He needed the right weapons and training to carry the day. God was his source for both.

To walk with God closely and live in victory, the Christ-follower MUST be armed and trained. Otherwise, we stand no chance against our Adversary. There is realization and preparation that must take place to win the battles.

First, we must realize that our enemy is ultimately not another person. This is so difficult to remember in this thing called marriage. Irritation, hurt, anger, disappointment with our spouse won't get resolved until we accept the fact that there is something else going on; something unseen. There are dark, demonic forces trying to create wedges and destroy intimacy between you and your spouse. It's true in all relationships: *"For our struggle is not against flesh and blood, but against the rulers, against the authorities, against the cosmic powers of this darkness, against evil, spiritual forces in the heavens"* (Ephesians 6:12).

Second, it takes more than realization—it takes training. The weapons available are listed in Ephesians 6:13-18, including integrity, Christ-likeness, the unshakable peace of Christ, a strong and mature faith, the hope of the gospel, the word of God, and prayer. I will tell you this: the last two weapons are, in my view, the most important. Every other weapon is acquired and developed by knowing and following God's word. And yet, many if not most believers leave this weapon virtually untouched. No wonder they can't overcome adversity, discouragement, tragedy, and emptiness.

There is one more weapon that is often ignored. We'll talk about it tomorrow.

God, forgive me for taking lightly the need to train with the weapons You've given me. Grant me a deep hunger for Your word. Amen

FIGHT CLUB 2

February 28

"You have armed me with strength for the battle.
You have subdued my enemies under my feet."

Psalm 18:39

I love that scene in *Indiana Jones* where Harrison Ford is faced by a guy with a huge, curved sword. The guy goes through about 10 different threatening gyrations with it and everyone in the crowd knows it's the end for Indiana Jones. Then, nonchalantly, Ford pulls out his pistol and casually shoots the guy dead. Swords are no match for pistols.

David was armed with physical weapons but ours are more powerful! Yet few believers know how to use them effectively to defeat temptation, emptiness, shame, anxiety, and sin habits. Yesterday we briefly discussed the weapons mentioned in Ephesians 6:12-17, the most important is knowing and using the word of God. Every other weapon is acquired and developed by knowing and following God's word.

But there is one more incredibly powerful weapon listed in the passage that believers don't employ often enough or effective enough: *"Pray in the Spirit at all times and on every occasion. Stay alert and be persistent in your prayers"* (Ephesians 6:18).

Are you trained to pray effectively? Most believers pray—but from what they tell me, it's not very effective. James 5:16 (CSB) says, *"The prayer of a righteous person is very powerful in its effect."* You don't have to throw up lame prayers and respond impotently to Satan's attacks.

You can LEARN how to pray powerfully. A good book to help is my friend Gary Miller's book: *"Talk Less, Pray More."* Tim Keller's book, *"Prayer"* is good. Phillip Yancey's *"Prayer: Does It Do Any Good"* is a great book. I have a section in my *"Pathways"* book. Effective praying takes intentionality and time to develop.

When I was in Korea back in 1982 visiting the world's largest church, Pastor Paul Cho shared this insight: "Prayer very hard work. Prayer hardest thing I do. Whoever wrote the song, 'Sweet Hour of Prayer', only prayed 10 minutes!"

You and I can pray for anything anytime from anywhere. It is the one remote-controlled weapon we have. Learn to call the firepower of God down on and into the attacks of the enemy and see the difference it will make.

God, like Your disciples asked You: teach me to pray. Amen

GLORY
March 1

"The heavens proclaim the glory of God. The skies display his craftsmanship."
Psalm 19:1

When I was in high school, I took calculus, chemistry, biology, physics, and earth science. College brought more calculus, chemistry, biology, and physics, along with geology and statistics. Some say there is a struggle between science and faith. Not for me. The more I learn about science affirms my faith, not weakens it.

David, the great composer, begins this masterpiece with one of the more memorable openings ever! I can picture him sitting out in the shepherd's fields outside of Bethlehem, late at night staring up into the heavens and being absolutely overwhelmed with its vastness and beauty.

In the mid-1970s, I was in Big Bend National Park way out in West Texas. Standing under the cloudless sky at midnight revealed a canopy of stars I had no idea were viewable with the naked eye. My response was pure worship. What an incredible God who could create all of that. I was in awe of this awesome God. Interestingly, until the early 1920s, most astronomers believed that the Milky Way Galaxy contained all the stars of the Universe! Edwin Hubble demonstrated that there were many more galaxies in the universe. Science informed my faith. Now astronomers estimate as many as two trillion galaxies populate the universe. Science continues to inform and strengthen my faith.

The secularist can look at the same wonders, not just in astronomy, but in anatomy or biology or geology, and conclude no intelligence caused it. That's their prerogative. I contend that their position, like mine, takes faith. I also contend that their position takes more faith because it only explains the how; it does not attempt to explain the why. And without the why, there is even more mystery, not less. God created the universe to display His power and His grandeur. Beyond that, it is the backdrop for a drama, played out on a stage called earth, where His redemptive love is on display.

Astronomers conjecture there is a star born somewhere in the cosmos every second! Amazing!! Each declining star and each new star declares the importance, the power, the awesomeness, the glory of its Creator.

This morning I join them and say GLORY! Google a picture or two of Hubble's pics and say out loud, "GLORY!"

Yahweh, I do join the stars and galaxies and declare You are glorious! Amen

SOUL CARE
March 2

"The decrees of the Lord are trustworthy, making wise the simple.
The commandments of the Lord are right, bringing joy to the heart.
The commands of the Lord are clear, giving insight for living."
Psalm 19:7-8

Every human has a soul. The soul is the non-physical essence of life: our mind, our will, and our emotions—our personhood —the who of what we are. It is imperishable: some souls will spend eternity with God; some souls will be separated from God for eternity. Dallas Willard said, "Our soul is like an inner stream of water, which gives strength, direction, and harmony to every other element of our life."

How's your soul? A few years ago, I started asking myself that question. I ask it to those I am mentoring. You can't really answer the question off the cuff; it takes a good bit of honest reflection. Willard spoke of the "inner stream." There have been times in my past when it was hardly noticeable. In my present life stage, there are times that the stream is just a trickle marked by nagging anxiety, or a feeling of being adrift, or a constant weariness.

Soul care is a BIG topic in today's world, though not everyone is speaking the truth about it.

David does, however. In this psalm, he moves from 'general revelation' to 'specific revelation;' from God's nature on display in creation, to the beauty and centrality of His word. He points us to the mysterious, miraculous, 'mazing nature of God's word: it charges the dead batteries of our soul. The prophet Jeremiah discovered the same thing: *"Your words were found, and I ate them. Your words became a delight to me and the joy of my heart (soul)"* (Jeremiah 15:16; CSB).

God's word makes our soul healthy. How so? David gives us three reasons. First, it makes us wise. Calling someone 'simple' was a nice way of saying they were clueless. Wisdom on the other hand is the ability to correctly size up a situation and know what to do—BEFORE we suffer pain. Second, God's word brings joy to our hearts. For the believer, hearing and reading the Scripture turns on the faucet of anticipated good (joy) because we see the true path to walk in times of difficulty. Third, God's word gives us tremendous insight on how to live right. To live right is to live in the favor and blessing of God.

How's your soul? The one true medicine (or vitamin) for the human soul is the word of God. Get you a big ol' dose of it!

God, my soul needs to be healthier—I will digest Your word! Amen

SELF-EXAMINATION
March 3

"May the words of my mouth and the meditation of my heart
be pleasing to You, O Lord, my Rock and my Redeemer."
Psalm 19:14

A few weeks ago, we celebrated Valentine's Day. Love birds made or bought sweet-sounding cards, went out for a special meal, sat a bit closer, and kissed a little more often than usual. Romanticism is still alive! While these expressions can foster true love, in actuality, genuine love is based on the desire to please the one you love. You can be a hopeless romantic and shower your mate with all kinds of gifts, but if your spouse doesn't sense your deep-down desire to please him or her, those expressions will only go so far. The essence of love is giving, and how that best shows up is in doing and speaking what pleases them.

David began this incredible psalm with one of the great declarations of all time: *"The heavens declare the glory of God."* He finishes it with one of the great prayers of all time: *"May the words of my mouth and the meditation of my heart be pleasing to you, O Lord, my Rock and my Redeemer."* Ultimately the true believer wants to live a life honoring to God; a life where our words, our actions, and even our hidden desires bring Him pleasure.

When we think about God's general revelation (Creation, vv.1-6) and His specific revelation (Scripture, vv.7-11), the only honest response is honest self-examination (vv.12-14). Self-examination is not easy to do. It requires self-awareness, honesty, and humility.

Self-awareness because most of us struggle to know and understand who we are, including our thoughts, motives, and desires. Harvard Business Review estimates that only about 15% of us meet the criteria for being self-aware. Honestly, it's because we are prone to self-deception. We tend to make little of our flaws while making large the flaws of others. This fault mitigation is a major deterrent to clearly understanding ourselves. Humility because once we peer into the dark corners of who we really are, pride wants to excuse it while humility wants to address it.

David wants his words and even his inner desires to be pleasing to God. After all, He is worthy of that, right? As our Rock, He is our protector and stabilizer. As our Redeemer, He is the one who extends mercy to avoid judgment and grace to live abundantly.

This verse is a short but powerful prayer for the believer who wants to please the One they love. Try speaking it every morning to Your Rock and Redeemer.

God, by Your grace, I do want to please You from the inner-most part of my being. Amen

PERSPECTIVE
March 4

"In times of trouble, may the Lord answer your cry.
May the name of the God of Jacob keep you safe from all harm."
Psalm 20:1

I've been in trouble most of my life! I almost didn't graduate high school—it took a special effort of my high school counselor and a signed dispensation from the Tulsa School District Superintendent to get me out. I was on scholastic probation first 3 semesters at college and was almost kicked out for disciplinary reasons. I almost went to jail—twice—all before I was 21!

I could fill up mountains of paper talking about my troubles.

Some troubles were brought by others, but most have been my own doing. Regardless, I've learned who to run to when I'm in trouble. My journal is full of, **"Hear my cry, O God!"**

God has heard my cries. His answers are not always immediate, but they are ultimate. God is not nearly as in a hurry as I am. Because of that, there have been many times that my cries seem to go unanswered, or if they are, they don't even look anywhere close to what I prayed for. I've cried out for healing for dear friends, rescuing of marriages, salvation for precious lost friends. Under the microscope, those cries sometimes seem to fall on deaf ears.

But with the telescope, I get a broader perspective. I do see His grand scheme and have gained the confidence that He does hear. He is in control, and His loving hand is at work through Jesus and His gospel-bearers.

David speaks to those who would be listening to his poem song. He encourages them to call out to Yahweh when they are troubled. Who else is there to go to other than the Creator of all that is and Redeemer of those who believe? He mentions the God of Jacob. Jacob is an interesting character study. Talk about a hot mess!! This guy was a momma's boy, a shrewd deceiver, a liar, and a thief. Most of his troubles were caused by his own hand and mouth. Yet, God mercifully and graciously forgave and blessed Jacob—though the process was very painful at times.

Regardless of the cause of the troubles in your life right now, know that God is at work in them. Calling out to Him gets us in a position to gain His perspective and understand what He's up to, even if only in part. So don't stop calling out—and keep looking for His handiwork.

God, I do call out to You about my troubles. Enable me to see Your answers. Amen

SPARK
March 5

"May He give you what your heart desires and fulfill your whole purpose."
Psalm 20:4

Last night I was watching the Disney/Pixar movie, *"Soul"* with my grandchildren. One of the themes is the idea that each person has an individual 'spark' that drives them to a happy and productive life on earth. We enjoyed it a lot. When I got up this morning, this verse was staring me in the face! David prays that the heart desire of someone fulfills their WHOLE purpose.

Suffice to say Disney/Pixar doesn't have a clue about where the 'spark' comes from that provides purpose in this life. But God's word does. One thing that is clear from Scripture is that by His common grace, God has enabled human beings, redeemed or unredeemed, to find purpose in creativity, development, productivity, etc. This is a part of the Cultural Mandate in Genesis 1 & 2 to exercise dominion over the earth, to subdue it, and develop its latent potential.

Because of two tandem truths, (1) that each human is created in the one image of God, and (2) each human is created with unique individuality, then each person is going to have a unique 'spark.' That spark can be discovered and used for the benefit of the recipient and whomever he/she deems appropriate, or it can be captured and focused on King and Kingdom.

Philosophers call discussions like this 'teleology' from the Greek word *'telos'* meaning *'end.'* Purposes can be proximate, meaning they are relatively near or short term or they can be remote, meaning they have a distant or ultimate purpose.

That's where verses like Romans 8:28 intersect: *"We know that all things work together for the good of those who love God, who are called according to His purpose"* (CSB). A teacher can have the proximate purpose of preparing and instructing a lesson on grammar so that the student understands and utilizes it. Their 'spark' may even have a more remote purpose in that they want the student to be able to experience the success that comes with mastery of a language. But if the teacher is a believer, the final remote purpose is to bring glory to God in his/her teaching.

Life takes on an incredibly fulfilling dimension when the spark God gives us is discovered, developed, and utilized for the One who gave it to us! Are the desires of your heart fulfilling their WHOLE purpose? What is your spark? Are you using it, not just for yourself or those around you, but for the glory and purpose of God?

God, show me not just what my spark is, but how I can use it for its whole purpose: to please You. Amen

CONFIDENCE
March 6

"Some boast in chariots and some in horses, but we boast in the name of the Lord, our God."
Psalm 20:7 (NASB)

I love football. I can't get enough of it. But there is a growing trend, particularly at the pro level, of uncomfortable amounts of bravado. Many make it all about what they can do, how important they are, how indispensable they are. All because they have an overactive pituitary gland. Spare me!

David is the king of Israel. He actually has something to boast about! But that's not his style, and more importantly, it's not his character. He is about to go into a real battle with real danger. Psalm 20 is one of the 'royal' psalms, those that focus on the king as God's anointed or chosen one. It is written in 1st person plural (we) except for v.6 (I) indicating that David is writing this from the viewpoint of his people, prompting them to pray for their king as he heads into battle.

David anticipates an overwhelming victory. He has an experienced, well-equipped army. The most devastating weapon of his day was the horse-drawn chariot that contained the driver and a warrior with bow, sword, and javelin. To a soldier on foot, nothing could be more terrifying. But David's confidence was not in his mighty army. His confidence was in his mighty God.

That's not to say his preparation and training were worthless. His training prepared him to be an effective tool in the hands of Yahweh. Years earlier as he was about to charge at Goliath, he had already honed the skills necessary to fell the giant, though he proclaimed, *"You come against me with a sword, spear, and javelin, but I come against you in the name of the Lord of Armies."* Skill and training are important. But David knew their limitations. Augustine put it this way, "Pray as though everything depended on God; act as though everything depended on you."

What kind of battle are you in? I hope you are prepared for it. I hope you're training for it: memorizing Scriptures that speak to it, praying and fasting diligently, gleaning insight for the battle from other Christ-followers' podcasts, blogs, and books.

But make no mistake: there is NO victory with our effort alone. Confidence in ourselves is near-sighted foolishness. The kingdom of God operates on faith. God responds to faith. He delivers the faithful. Put your confidence in Him. Take no pride in your preparation. Boast in Him. Trust in Him for victory. Speak His name and claim His power for the victory. Stand firm in your faith and see what this mighty God will do!!!

God, by Your grace I will prepare and train, but I declare that You are the source of victory! Amen

LOOK IT UP!

March 7

"My God, my God, why have You forsaken me?"
Psalm 22:1 (NASB)

The Gospels indicate that after His seven (7!) trials that day, the Romans took Jesus outside the city walls to, "The Place of the Skull" (Aramaic for Golgotha). When you go to Israel, your guide will take you to a place where the outcrop of rock actually looks like a skull, right next to a garden, where Jesus likely was executed and then later buried.

David wrote this psalm about 1,000 years before the crucifixion. There is no doubt that David experienced great torment and pain during his life. But the language of this psalm is clearly exaggerated relative to David's life, as many laments are. Whatever is going on in his life, David is feeling excruciating pain and isolation.

Notably, Jesus uttered these same words when He was on the cross. There is little doubt that the Holy Spirit had prompted David to write this psalm, not just to describe his own situation, but as a foretelling, a prophecy of something greater to come.

What follows this well-known opening is a description of great suffering ending in an execution.

It is a remarkably accurate depiction of the crucifixion of Jesus: being mocked (v.13), stretched out on a cross (v.14, 17), being thirsty (v.15), Gentile soldiers surrounding Him (v.16), His hands and feet pierced (v.16), and soldiers casting lots for His clothing (v.18).

When Jesus spoke these words 1,000 years later (Matt. 27:46, Mark 15:34), what was He saying? Many believe that this was the moment of atonement—when the Father placed the sin of humanity on Jesus and turned away from His Son, who was then sin-covered. In response, Jesus uttered these words. But I believe Jesus was also saying something else—"**Look it up!**" The Psalms were not numbered until the 1500s. Until then, the way a psalm was identified was by quoting its opening verse. So as Jesus hung there on a Roman cross, it is reasonable to conclude that He was directing them then, and us now, to check out a perfectly accurate depiction of His crucifixion 1,000 years before it happened—an unmistakable fulfillment of prophecy. He quoted the first line, so as to say, **"Look it up!"**

Read this psalm slowly and with the account in Matthew 27 or Mark 15 as corroborating evidence. Be encouraged in your faith that Jesus fulfills prophecies of old—and worship Him as The Suffering Servant!

Jesus, thank You for Your willingness to suffer for me and atone for my wicked sinfulness! Amen

MY SHEPHERD
March 8

"The Lord is my shepherd."
Psalm 23:1

One of the most well-known phrases, even in today's secular world, is: *"The Lord is my shepherd, I shall not want."* I learned these words at an early age. I didn't know what all the words meant in this great psalm, but there was something profoundly soothing and deeply satisfying about the words: *"The Lord is my shepherd, I shall not want."*

The shepherd would have been a well-known figure in ancient times—a brave, yet gentle soul. Brave because he would have to protect his sheep from wolves, mountain lions, or bands of poachers. Gentle in that he would have to take care of the sheep from the elements, the terrain, and even themselves. In the heat of the summer days, the shepherd would have to get them out of the sun at times to prevent heatstroke. Conversely, he would make sure they huddled close together to keep them from dying of exposure on the cold winter nights. The terrain could get pretty dangerous at times: cracks and crevices that could snag the sheep or break its leg; brambles that their wool could get caught in and not be able to escape. If a sheep wandered off, the shepherd would go searching for it until he found it. Sheep aren't very smart, so they needed someone to take care of and protect them.

In the life of a sheep, the shepherd was THE leading, protecting, and caring figure 24/7. David knew about this relationship because he grew up as a shepherd boy. As he thought about His relationship with Yahweh, he knew God was his shepherd and he was His sheep. So He sang: The *Lord* is my shepherd.

Jesus invoked this imagery and applied it to Himself: *"I am the good shepherd. I know My own sheep, and they know Me…The good shepherd lays down his life for the sheep"* (John 10:14, 11).

The Lord Jesus is the One who guides me, protects me, and cares for me. The Lord is the one who is gentle and kind. The Lord is MY shepherd.

Is He YOUR shepherd? Who do you look to protect you, care for you, and bind your wounds?

If not, why not? He's the good shepherd! No one else can provide the protection and care that Jesus does. If you're a believer, focus on this: He chased you, He chose you, He rescued you, He redeemed you, He sought you, He saved you, He adopted you and He adores you! Focus on Him!!

Lord, You are MY Shepherd! Thank You for loving and caring for me. Amen

CONTENTMENT
March 9

"I shall not want."
Psalm 23:1 (NASB)

My dad grew up during The Great Depression. I remember stories of how his family of eight made do with what they had: shooting squirrels with a .22 rifle to put food on the table, lots of meatless soups flavored with a hog or cow bone, etc. As a result, my dad would not put up with any complaining from my brother or me about what we didn't have. My generation (Boomer), was much more affluent, pampered, and dare I say it, spoiled! Each generation since has moved further on that continuum. This makes the phrase, *"I shall not want"* or *"I lack nothing"* a bit more difficult to understand. After all, we are surrounded by thousands of opportunities to feel lack; to feel we don't have enough or experience enough.

Because of this, I believe the most difficult characteristic for us to experience in today's world is this thing called contentment. Discontent reigns in our lives. Why is that? We live in the wealthiest and strongest nation in the history of the world. We have so much stuff some of us have to rent storage facilities because we don't have enough space for all our stuff. And still, we long for more stuff, more activity, more experiences.

A sheep didn't really have much. In fact, all he had was the clothes on his back—get it? Wool? On his back? Get it? What the sheep did have was a life under the care of the shepherd—and that was enough.

If Jesus is the Good Shepherd (John 10), then is Jesus enough for you? When your marriage is struggling, is Jesus enough for you? When your health fails, is Jesus enough for you? When you lose a loved one, is Jesus enough for you? When you go through financial hardship, is Jesus enough for you? When you have been rejected, disrespected, and cast aside, is Jesus enough for you?

Augustine wrote, "You have made us for Yourself, O Lord, and our hearts are restless until they find their rest in You." We will never be content and experience deep, soul-satisfying peace until we stop expecting the things of this world to satisfy us—and begin to find our wealth and peace in the inheritance God has given us in Himself.

A better translation of this verse is: *"I have what I need."* In Jesus, I have all that I need.

Forgive me, Jesus! Today I proclaim that You are my Shepherd—and in You I have all that I need. I choose to be satisfied in You! Amen

RENEWED
March 10

"He lets me lie down in green pastures;
He leads me beside quiet waters. He renews my life."
Psalm 23:2-3a (CSB)

One of the maladies of our culture is that most of us feel depleted—almost all the time! The causes are too many to list, although the frontrunners must be hyperactivity and the constant pursuit of possessions, power, and experiences. Very few people know how to get refreshed.

David uses a summary statement: *"He renews my life."* This is an indication that precedes it is why he feels renewed. Yesterday we discussed that the Good Shepherd provides what we need. Recognizing that leads to contentment—so elusive in our culture today. In this passage, David notes that Yahweh lets or leads His people to *"lie down in green pastures."* Sheep never stop eating, which is why the shepherd has to keep them moving or they'll gorge themselves to death. So it is significant that the sheep are lying down in green pastures. This indicates that they are content and satisfied. The shepherd has provided what they need. That's the first condition of a renewed life.

It's interesting to know that sheep are fearful, timid creatures. If they sense any danger, they will keep moving. So the fact that David calls on the imagery of sheep lying down in green pastures indicates they are not just fed, but they also feel safe and protected—the second condition of a renewed life.

Lastly, David draws on a little-known fact that sheep won't drink from moving water. The caring shepherd would build up a little dam or a small harbor in a stream before the sheep would venture a sip and get—refreshed. Jesus calls on us to turn aside and drink from Him: *"If you only knew the gift God has for you and Who you are speaking to, you would ask Me, and I would give you living water"* (John 4:10).

Our world is moving so rapidly. Hurry Disease is epidemic. People are constantly depleted. Want to know how to feel renewed each day? Learn to be content in Jesus. Believe that Jesus is good and sovereign so that you feel safe and secure in Him. And drink from Jesus daily—time with Him in His word and in prayer replenishes our courage, our strength, and our faith.

Jesus—thank You for being the Good Shepherd. Renew my soul today. Amen

PATHS
March 11

"He leads me along the right paths for His name's sake."
Psalm 23:3b (CSB)

On June 28, 2014, Archduke Franz-Ferdinand and his wife Sophie were shot to death in Sarajevo, Serbia, plunging the world into its first global conflict. Tragically, the driver of the open car carrying them made a wrong turn, right into the line of fire of a waiting Serbian nationalist. By the end of WW1, over 17 million soldiers were dead.

Life is full of choices. Each choice takes us down a particular path with outcomes that may be harmless—or devastating. David knew that the responsibility of taking care of sheep meant the shepherd needed to lead them on the right paths. The hill country of Judah can be extremely rough terrain. Cracks, crevices, cliffs could mean the loss of one or more of the sheep. Any shepherd worth his wool would make sure that his sheep stayed on the right path.

Sheep wander and the result is never good. I confess to be a wandering sheep at times. It's part of my broken nature. Fortunately, I'm not left to my own knowledge and understanding to find and walk the right path. The Good Shepherd has made a point to guide His sheep along the right paths through two sources.

The first is the word of God: *"All Scripture is inspired by God and is profitable for teaching, for rebuking, for correcting, for training in righteousness"* (2 Timothy 3:16; CSB). Notice the four trail signs. God's word shows us where the right path is and how to walk it (*teaching*). Before we can get on the right path, we have to recognize we're on the wrong path! God's word does that (*rebuking*). God's word shows us how to get from the wrong path to the right path, which is not easy (*correcting*). Finally, God's word becomes a coach to keep us on the right path (*training*).

The second is the Holy Spirit. The Good Shepherd also guides His sheep through the indwelling Spirit. Jesus called Him *"The Counselor."* The Spirit speaks to our hearts and warns us when we begin to wander down the wrong path. The conviction of the Holy Spirit is bitter medicine and serves as a prompting to stop what we're doing and where we're going.

The path The Good Shepherd has laid out for me is full of His blessing and favor. But it's not about me. When I trod the right path, I bring Him honor. People look and say, "What an amazing God he must love and follow!"

Jesus, thank You for Your word and Your Spirit. Enable me to walk the path they lay out. Amen

THE DEEPEST DARKNESS
March 12

"Even when I walk through the darkest valley, I will not be afraid, for you are close beside me."
Psalm 23:4a

On September 26, 2019, Sue and I began the most significant descent into the darkness that we had ever experienced. Sitting in the oncologist's office, we were told that her breast cancer was the most dangerous, radical, aggressive type. The tumor would need to be removed, then she would need five months of the worst kind of chemotherapy and then 20 radiation treatments. We were devastated. I can't say we didn't/haven't battled fear. But we haven't given in to it and it hasn't dominated us. We insist we *"will not be afraid."*

We trust our Shepherd, so we walk the path He has placed us on with confidence that He is with us and '*close beside us.*' That's a game-changer; it's everything! There is no greater truth, no greater promise than God's promise: *"I will be with you."*

Here is a smattering of some of the verses we have been clinging to that affirms God's presence:

"Have I not commanded you? Be strong and courageous! Do not tremble or be dismayed, for the LORD your God is with you wherever you go" (Joshua 1:9).

"I will be with you when you pass through the waters, and when you pass through the rivers, they will not overwhelm you. You will not be scorched when you walk through the fire, and the flame will not burn you. Do not fear, for I am with you" (Isaiah 43:2, 5).

"I will never leave you or forsake you" (Hebrews 13:5).

One translation of David's famous psalm says, *"Even if I go through the deepest darkness"* (GNT). What is the deepest darkness for you? Does it come when you sit down to pay your bills? Does it come when you walk into your home after work? Does it come when you turn off the lights and head to bed? Does it come when you reflect back on the rejections or regrets or raw wounds you have? Maybe it's your marriage or your health or your loneliness.

Whatever valley He has you in, He hasn't abandoned you. He's there with you. He's here with us and our family—and that's enough for us. I pray it is for you. I do know this: **When you are at your <u>darkest</u>, He is there.**

God, by faith I believe You are with me always, even in my deepest darkness. Thank You. Amen

THE POWER STICK
March 13

"Your rod and your staff—they comfort me."
Psalm 23:4b (CSB)

A number of contemporary movies feature some form of power stick. Star Wars has the lightsaber. Harry Potter has his wand. Thor has his Mjolnir. Even if all of those were actually real, the power stick of God would far surpass all of them put together.

David mentions the rod of God. To the Hebrew, this would be pregnant with meaning. At one point when Yahweh spoke to Moses from the burning bush, God told him to throw down his staff on the ground (Exodus 4:3) and it became a snake. It must have been a poisonous one because Moses ran from it! Then God told him to pick it up by the tail, and it became a staff again. When he laid it down, it was the staff of Moses, but when He picked it up, it became known as the rod of God. Later, that power stick became the source of God's power to deliver them from Egypt, across the dry bed of the Red Sea, and through the wilderness for 40 years. The term is always associated with power.

A shepherd normally had a number of accessories he would carry with him at all times: a water pouch for hydration, a knife to cut something, and also a staff which was a long stick with the familiar curl on the end of it. With the staff, the shepherd could redirect the sheep if one was straying away or use it to pull a sheep out of the mud, ditch, or crag. The rod would have been a shorter, heavier, clublike weapon used to defend against predators like the wolf or mountain lion.

These two power sticks were used by the shepherd for the **direction** and **protection** of the sheep. The shepherd-king David was well familiar with both. He counted on the Lord to give him direction in life and correction when heading down the wrong path: *"He leads the humble in doing right, teaching them his way"* (Psalm 25:9). He also counted on the Lord to protect him from his enemies: *"David sang: 'The Lord is my rock, my fortress, and my savior; my God is my rock, in whom I find protection. He is my shield, the power that saves me, and my place of safety. He is my refuge, my savior, the one who saves me from violence"* (2 Samuel 22:2-3).

As David thought about the Lord as his shepherd, he knew he could count on God to guide him in life and protect him from his enemies. That brought him great comfort. And it should us as well.

God, Thank You for being my Guide and my Protector. I take comfort in YOU! Amen

FEAST AND FAMINE
March 14

"You prepare a table before me in the presence of my enemies"
Psalm 23:5a

I love parties! Big gatherings with lots of great food, great drink, great friends, great stories, and tons of laughter—it doesn't get much better than that. Those things don't just happen. Someone takes the time and care to procure and prepare the food, get the house or venue ready, and then pull off the event. All of that is good, but what really makes the evening is not the food, but the company. I've been to gatherings where the food was awesome, but the people there were less than appetizing. Not fun.

Normally we party with folks we like and want to be with, friends and acquaintances that are interesting—and interested in you. There is a genuine give and take of questions, discussion, stories with people who you enjoy. But in this verse, David paints the image of a feast with some unusual guests—his enemies! The picture he's painting is that he's having a great time while his enemies are not. You can almost sense him saying: "In your face, dudes!"

We have enemies. Some are demonic. Satan is called our adversary, our accuser, and the evil one. He is out to *"steal, kill, and destroy"* (John. 10:10). If you're a Christ-follower marked with His blood and sealed by the Holy Spirit, Satan can't have you. Your soul is secure and your salvation is imperishable and irrevocable. But make no mistake about it: Satan can still steal, kill, and destroy much in our lives, including our joy, peace, and hope—if we let him.

Some of our enemies are human. They have stolen, killed, or destroyed much in our lives and brought great pain, suffering, and grief. You may have had a few or a lot of enemies in your life. Me—church work brings a lot of enemies.

Regardless, it seems that God intends to provide a victory banquet for us while our enemies will have to watch! Maybe they're watching now as you have, by God's grace, overcome the suffering they inflicted on you. You're stronger. You're healthier. You're joyful. You're more intimate with God. You have risen above their personal miserableness that they tried to inflict on you, and you are living in abundance.

There will be a victory banquet when this is all over. We'll feast with all the best of everything the Shepherd can provide. Satan and his peeps will have to watch. How excruciating for them to be present and famished while we feast and rejoice!

God, thank You for the grace to overcome the attacks of my enemies. To You be praise! Amen

ESSENTIAL OIL
March 15

"You anoint my head with oil"
Psalm 23:5b

A few years ago, someone gave me a vial of essential oil to help me with something I don't really remember! I had never heard of them, but I found out they were a big deal. The essential oils industry has grown from about $17 billion in 2017 to almost $27 billion. I read an article that said there are five basic essential oils that make life better. Who knew?

But there was one oil not listed in any of my research that is the best of all: the anointing oil applied to the head of a royal or an important guest. In the Bible, oil always represents something good; something God. Oil would be used in a common way as in fuel for lamps. Scented oil would be used in uncommon ways like coronations of royalty. The presence of oil meant God's blessing and provision; the absence of it signified His curse and judgment.

When arriving at a home, the host would honor the guest by having their feet washed and their head anointed with scented oil. It was a sign of great esteem. It would also be soothing and relaxing after a long, hot, arduous journey by foot. They didn't have showers with pressure heads that make you feel like you're standing under a waterfall, so this was the next best thing. David drew on this deep heritage of oil to accentuate the fact that he had been invited into the presence of Yahweh as both a royal (he was king of Israel) and special guest.

In the Old Testament, Both Moses and Isaiah related Yahweh's message to His people that they would someday become a kingdom of priests and a holy nation. That happened in a limited sense, setting up what the New Testament writers realized hundreds of years later: *"You are a chosen people. You are royal priests, a holy nation, God's very own possession"* (1 Peter 2:9.) Christ-followers are the royal priests and make up the nation of God!

God chose YOU! He invited YOU! YOU have been ushered into the very presence of the living God as a royal and a special guest! To be sure, you don't deserve it (me either!), but by His grace and through the blood of Jesus, He has welcomed YOU as His own.

Imagine Him pouring scented oil on His hands, so much it leaks between His fingers, then placing those hands on your head, looking into your eyes, gazing deep into your soul, and saying, Welcome, my friend!" Now THAT is essential oil!

Yahweh, I can't grasp why You invited me into all of this blessing—but thank You! Amen

OVERWHELMED
March 16

"My cup overflows"
Psalm 23:5c

One of my daily routines is to get up and head for the Keurig for a cup of joe. Recently I had an early morning meeting that required me to use a go-cup. Too late I realized that the go-cup was smaller than my regular cup. The coffee first filled, then flowed over the lip of the cup.

David didn't have a Keurig, but he understood the concept of a cup being overwhelmed by something. After discussing God's presence during his 'deepest darkness,' and God's protection from and victory over his enemies, David now uses three short words to form a phrase that expresses the overflowing provision and blessing of God.

Every once in a while, I pause long enough to survey the grace of God in my life; let its abundance overwhelm me. I need to do it more often. Because I'm one of those folks who is always pressing on looking for the next hurdle, next mountain, next opportunity, I find it difficult to be in the moment and enjoy the blessings as He is giving them to me. I'm working on it!

When I do survey the wondrous cross and all the blessings God has poured out on me as a result, I am usually overcome with raw emotion. I am overwhelmed by His benevolent activity in my life. Now is one of those moments.

First and most—I was His enemy and He took me in. He rescued, redeemed, and adopted me. I still can't believe He did it. Beyond that, when I had such a low view of my potential, He gave me favor in a way that has been no less than miraculous. When I've failed, He hasn't given up on me. When surrounded by enemies, He has delivered me from their grasp. When in the depths of despair, He has pulled me out and breathed courage and hope into my soul.

And then there is my family. Just about every time they are over, the eight of us adults sit at the dining table discussing, teasing, laughing, crying, while the ten grandkids are tearing down the house (!), and I pause for a moment to see, to sense, and to know—my cup overflows. Not half full. Not mostly full. Not just to the top. But overflowing; over the top; superfluous.

If you're in Christ, you have a cup as well. It's overflowing. You just have to pause long enough to see things as they really are. When you do, you will be overwhelmed by the overflow.

God, thank You for being so gracious to me. Open my eyes to see more and my heart to appreciate more. Amen

THE DAILY DOUBLE
March 17

"Surely Your goodness and unfailing love will pursue me all the days of my life."
Psalm 23:6a

The 'daily double' was a phrase initially utilized in parimutuel betting. Others have used it, including McDonald's and Jeopardy. It's the idea of doubling the win or the pleasure.

David now turns our thoughts to two of God's awesome attributes. First, His goodness. Psalm 34:8 says, *"Taste and see that the Lord is good."* It's not that God just does good; He IS good. He is the source of all that is good. 'Good' is what is desirable or preferable. He is the ultimate definition of good and the Definer of it. When He does something, it's good because He is good.

This trait gets scrutinized when something happens in our lives that is clearly not good: Sue is diagnosed with cancer, a drunk driver kills your loved one, your husband abandons you, etc. Even the best of us questions God's goodness in those times. We can only sort it out by accepting fact that God didn't do it; He's not responsible for humanity's brokenness. The badness in the world does not negate the goodness of God. It does cause us to seek His goodness in the midst of it. Only God can bring goodness into a bad situation (the cross is His ultimate act of goodness). When Paul writes that God *"makes all things work together for good"* (Rom. 8:28), he is reminding us of that attribute of God.

The 2nd wonder-filled attribute David mentions is God's love. The Hebrew word is *'chesed'*, meaning covenant love. A covenant in the Bible is more than a contract; it's about a relationship between two people who make binding promises to each other. If the promises are broken, so is the relationship. God's love for the believer, demonstrated on the cross (Romans 5:8) is a unilateral covenant—once established through faith in Jesus and His atoning death, it only depends on Him for its continuance! Bottom line: God's love at its core is not an emotional feeling, it is a determined and permanent decision. Don't get caught up in thinking God has to keep proving His love for you. If you do, you'll doubt it with every trial. You'll struggle with feeling loved instead of resting in His love. God's love is unfailing, unfaltering, unconquerable, and unfathomable! Hallelujah!!!

God's goodness and love began when He chased us down and captured us for Himself—and because He is always with us, His goodness pursues us each and every day. David was so convinced of these twin truths that he stated they are certain (*surely*).

God, thank You for Your overwhelming, never-ending goodness and love! Amen

NO WORDS
March 18

"I will live in the house of the Lord forever."
Psalm 23:6b

David comes to the end of THE most well-known song in the 3000 years of its history. The capstone phrase he chooses to finish the song with captures all that has gone before it: *"I will live in the house of the Lord forever."*

This simple statement breaks into three assurances that should bring calm to all who qualify for them. First, David says he will live. Remember Psalm 1 tells of two, and only two paths that humans trod: one leading to life and one leading to death. **Both paths are designed to intensify the farther along them you go.** The life of the true believer, the one who has surrendered control to Christ, is on the path marked with increasing amounts of love, joy, peace, and purpose. It's *"more and better life than you ever dreamed of!"* (John 10:10). When we transition out of this realm, we will be nothing but LIFE--no pain, sorrow, shame, or death!!!

Second, David talks about *"the house of the Lord."* This could refer to the temple in Jerusalem, or its predecessor, the portable tabernacle. Regardless, it was considered by the ancient Jew to be the place where God would descend, meeting with the priest who represented Israel. It was considered the dwelling place of God on earth. Because only priests could enter the inner sanctum to meet with Yahweh, the notion that David could dwell in the presence of God was revolutionary. Jesus expanded on this (John 14:2-3) the night He was betrayed:

> *In My Father's house are many dwelling places; if it were not so, I would have told you; for I go to prepare a place for you. If I go and prepare a place for you, I will come again and receive you to Myself, that where I am, there you may be also.*

The true believer will ascend to a real place in the presence of the Creator and Redeemer of all that is—the Lover of our souls whose passionate love drove Him to the cross and now awaits us with open arms!

The final assurance is that this delectable, astonishing, transcendent, beyond this world existence is not temporary; not 90 years, 90 million years, but forever. The Good Shepherd not only guides, provides, calms, protects, and conquers, He welcomes us into an existence that never grows boring, tired, empty, hurtful or limited. In fact, there are **no words** that can fully describe what awaits those of us who are in Christ!!

Jesus, I can't grasp what awaits me, but I am so grateful You have personally prepared it for me!

SOVEREIGNTY
March 19

"The earth is the Lord's, and everything in it.
The world and all its people belong to Him."
Psalm 24:1

There is not a more fundamental truth in Scripture than this: *"In the beginning, God created the heavens and the earth"* (Genesis 1:1). *"Heavens and earth"* is a *merism*: a linguistic and rhetorical term where two contrasting words or phrases express the totality or completeness of something. We might use the merism, "high and low" to say that we've looked all over for our lost phone.

Our psalmist, David, is harkening back to the first words of Scripture and reminding himself and his readers that God created the earth, the people on it, and therefore He is sovereign overall.

The creator of anything determines its purpose and has supreme authority over it.

We run into trouble when we forget that all we have is Yahweh's. It's easy to adopt the false notion that my possessions, house, car, job, plans, investments, calendar, marriage, family—my life—is mine. How foolish! No doubt I am His steward of those things He has entrusted to me. As a steward He expects me to handle them properly, **as He would**. But ultimately, I own nothing, I have nothing, I am nothing apart from Him. I need to be reminded of this: everything belongs to God. He is the Supreme Ruler, Power, and Authority over all that is.

That goes for my cancer-prone wife, Sue. What I mean is, she belongs to the Lord. He has placed her in my life as an incredible gift these 40 years, but He is the Determiner of her days and future, not me.

That means I have to hold on to her loosely. Cherish her, yes. Care for her, yes. Protect her, yes. Love her, yes. But she is not mine. He can and will do with her as He pleases. He is sovereign over her, her body, her life, her everything. I must trust that God is sovereign—but also that He is good and loving.

If I can't, terror creeps into my heart—indicating that I'm holding on too tightly. When I pray, "God, Sue is in Your hands. I trust You with her," there is a large measure of peace in my soul. God is in control—I'm not. I have to be at peace with that. Today I am.

God, today I confess that You, not me, are sovereign over my life. I surrender to You. Grant me peace. Amen

THE RECEPTION

"Who may climb the mountain of the Lord? Who may stand in his holy place?"
Psalm 24:3

I'm one of those who is fascinated by the history and customs of the British Royals. Queen Elizabeth, presently 94 years old, has reigned 68 years and seems to be loved by her millions of subjects, though very few have actually had a personal audience with her. For the fortunate few, there are protocols in place that must be followed for the queen to receive the guest.

David asks the question: "Who can climb, ascend, go up to where the Lord is?" After all, Yahweh is much more lofty and superior than any earthly royal. To be received into His presence, certain protocols are required. They are comprehensive and cover the totality of a person spiritually, physically, and socially.

First is the requirement of desires and conduct that are in alignment with the character of God: *"Only those whose hands and hearts are pure"* (v.4). This speaks to both our actions (*hands*) and motivations (*heart*). Is our lifestyle one that is pleasing to God; one that resists being involved in immoral activity? And how is our heart? Do we seem right on the outside, but inside we are far from it? And why do we do what we do? Are we doing it to advance ourselves or to serve the Lord and others?

Second, are we looking to the things of this world to give us what only Yahweh can: *"Only those…who do not worship idols and never tell lies"* (v.4). Money and possessions are the most obvious and sinister gods. Jesus talked more about them than He did faith and prayer together!! But there are other idols we sleep with including family, popularity, or entertainment. Spiritual adultery will hinder us from experiencing the fullness of being in God's presence.

David's encouragement for an ethical life does not mean that our works make us righteous—such a life flows out of a right relationship with Yahweh. He says plainly, *"They will receive the Lord's blessing and have a right relationship with God their savior."* At the core of the right relationship with God is that it is received; that HE is the Savior, we're not.

Don't think for a moment that we can act and desire what we want—and gain a reception with the King of Kings. He looks to bless and support those who seek Him and worship Him in spirit and in truth. (v.6)

God, by Your Spirit, purify my motives and my actions that I may be fully received and enjoy Your presence. Amen

THE TRILOGY
March 21

"Open up, ancient gates! Open up, ancient doors, and let the King of glory enter!"
Psalm 24:7

Now we come to what many believe is the last episode of a trilogy found in three successive psalms. When you step back and look at Psalms 22, 23, and 24, you can find a connection between them and Jesus, the Messiah.

Psalm 22 can be viewed as our Lord's excruciating death, beginning with: *"My God, My God, why have You forsaken me?"* The verses following this cry are an amazingly accurate depiction of His crucifixion 1000 years before it actually occurred: Jesus being mocked (vv.7-8), bones out of joint (v.14), pierced hands and feet (v.16), casting dice for His garments (v.18), etc.

Psalm 23 can be seen as our Messiah's time in the tomb. It is a picture of serenity even in the presence of death: *"the shadow of death"* (v. 4), Jesus at rest, having completed the task of atonement (v.2), they prepared a feast and victory party played out in front of His enemies when He walks out of the tomb (v.5), etc.

Psalm 24 is a glorious psalm signifying the victory and ascent of a king: *"Open up, ancient gates! Open up, ancient doors, and let the King of glory enter. Who is the King of glory? The Lord, strong and mighty; the Lord, invincible in battle"* (vv.7-8). When kings returned victorious from battle, the citizens would crowd the road leading to the city, look over the ramparts, or wait inside the gate—all to cheer and praise the conquering king.

As you read this short psalm, you'll see the connection between it and the resurrection/ascension of our Lord Jesus. He walked out of the tomb demonstrating that He was conqueror over sin and death. Forty days later He ascended to the right hand of the Father where He now reigns in victory!! If anyone had a pure heart (v.4) and was in a right relationship with the Father (v.5), and therefore could ascend the holy hill and stand in the holy place (v.3), it would be JESUS!

Jesus, thank You for Your willingness to suffer the shame of the cross, allow Yourself to be buried in death, and then walk out of the tomb proving Your power over sin and death! I worship You in Your exalted and ascended position at the right hand of the Father! Amen!!!

THE TROUBLES
March 22

"Turn to me and have mercy, for I am alone and in deep distress.
My problems go from bad to worse. Oh, save me from them all!"
Psalm 25:16-17

If you know anything about British history, you know that the relationship between England and Ireland has been thorny at best. In 1922, except for six northern counties, Ireland became an independent and sovereign nation. Those six northern counties became known as Northern Ireland and remain under British rule. For 30 years, from the early 1960s to the 1990s, civil unrest filled its streets with bombs, arson, assassinations, and a brutal form of street justice. This period is called The Troubles because there was constant trouble without any solution in view.

We don't know what was going on in David's life and what he was dealing with at the time of this writing. That is to say, David was always in so much trouble we can't pinpoint which crisis prompted this psalm!

To get the full impact of his despair, you must read the entire psalm. It breaks down nicely into what is called a chiastic pattern:

> A. Trusting, hoping, and praying (vv.1-5)
>   B. Prayer and forgiveness (vv.6-7)
>   C. Guidance for sinners (vv.8-10)
>   B. Prayer and forgiveness (v.11)
>   C. Guidance for God-fearers (vv.12-14)
> A. Trusting, hoping, and praying (vv.15-21)

David is pleading with God for guidance, forgiveness, protection, and a way through or out of a dire circumstance, i.e., The Troubles.

I'm familiar with the territory. Even in my 70th year, I am still so prone to do stupid, foolish stuff. My insensitivity to the Spirit, my lack of wisdom to see the outcome of my actions/words, my penchant for letting my flesh influence my decisions—keeps me embroiled in The Troubles, necessitating a constant call to God: *"Do not let me be disgraced"* (v.2); *"Show me the right path* (v.4); *"For the honor of Your name, O Lord, forgive my many, many sins"* (v.11); *"Protect me! Rescue my life from my enemies"* (v.20).

David says over and over again: "I put my trust in You. I put my hope in You." Life can be so overwhelming. Our brokenness and the brokenness of this world continue to wreak havoc on us and those we love. Like David, cry out: *"Remember me in light of Your unfailing love"* (v.7).

He does remember. He will deliver. Put your trust in Him. Put your hope in Him. Echo David's plea: *"O Lord, I give my life to You. I trust in you, my God!"* (vv.1-2). *Amen!!*

AFRAID
March 23

"The Lord is my light and my salvation— so why should I be afraid?
The Lord is my fortress, protecting me from danger, so why should I tremble?"
Psalm 27:1

I went skydiving for my 60th birthday. Many questioned my sanity. Admittedly, I had to deal with a good bit of anxiety at first. The "what ifs" were eating me up. But I reasoned that though there was some risk, it was not enough to keep me from doing it. I chose trust, trusting the company who would take me up to 12,000' and throw me out of a perfectly good airplane—but trusting more that God was sovereign and the worst thing that could happen is I'd be with Jesus in about 45 seconds! From the moment I jumped, it was—AWESOME!!

My fears have not only been about antics like parachuting: Sue's cancer, the prospect of getting old and all its associated challenges, financial viability without a steady income, the health and safety of my children and grandchildren. In all cases, I ask myself a simple question: "Why am I afraid?"

The answer is not always flattering. Even the best of Christ-followers deal with fear. The reason we do is—wait for it—we don't really trust God completely. Puritan John Flavel wrote, "The spring and cause of fear is unbelief." That's why we must keep growing in and affirming our faith. Fear is a natural human response to warn of possible danger. It can be healthy or unhealthy; reasonable or unreasonable. Once the heart is anxious, we should ask: "Do I have reason to be afraid?"

Here's the deal: fear is a signal to trust God. It can actually build faith just as resistance builds muscle. The believer who exercises the mind of Christ reasons that: 1. Fear is a warning system that is not always reliable; 2. Fear is a signal to trust in an always reliable God; 3. Fear is an impetus to pray and claim His promises; 4. Fear should not dominate my heart and mind. Ultimately fear becomes a decision: Will I respond according to my fear or my faith?

That's what David is doing here. He affirms that God's light will give us hope and direction; that only He can rescue us from our sin, brokenness, and fear; that He is a fortress who will protect us—and any adversity that reaches us fits into His loving, sovereign plan for us. When we look to ourselves or others for hope, rescue, or protection—fear will creep in and cripple. Instead, look to Him and confess:

Yahweh, I affirm my trust in my loving and sovereign God. I release my attempt to control my life and those I love. Amen

ONE THING
March 24

"One thing I have asked from the Lord, that I shall seek: That I may dwell in the house of the Lord all the days of my life, To behold the beauty of the Lord And to meditate in His temple."
Psalm 27:4 (NASB)

In the movie, *City Slickers*, Curly, played by Jack Palance, is giving sage advice to Billy Crystal's character, Mitch. Curly asks, "Do you know what the secret of life is?" "No", Mitch responds. Curly holds up one finger and says, "One thing. Just one thing. You stick to that and everything else don't mean (beans)." Mitch says, "That's great, but what's the one thing?" Curly responds: "That's for you to find out."

Well, David answers that question for Curly, Mitch, for me, for you—for all humanity. The one thing that rises above all other things in life, the one thing that is the secret to an exciting, fulfilling, love-filled life is this: Seeking the Lord and His presence each and every day. That's it! If you do that in good times and bad times, in plenty and in poverty, when it's easy and when it's hard, you'll experience the blessing of God and truly flourish in life.

The problem for us is that our culture excels at multiplying options. We love our options, don't we? The more options we have, the better we feel about ourselves. Starbucks boasts 80,000 drink options. At Pizza Hut you can design your own pizza in one of 1,000 options. Consumerism has driven people to choose a church based on options that best suit their personal preferences of time, style, dB level, dress, and even coffee.

We struggle with focus. Singularity is a grind. We can't seem to prioritize what is most important. The result is that we have become a dissatisfied people. Options are not the key.

David discovered the key: "This ONE thing," he says, *"above all else I will seek."* Seeking the Lord, His person, His presence, His pleasure, His purpose—that's the secret to an amazing life.

What is your '*one thing*'? To be a great doctor, mom, athlete, entrepreneur, or salesperson? To be liked, respected, or wealthy? If it is ANYTHING other than to seek the Lord and desire to spend time with Him and please Him—it will ultimately leave you wanting.

It's not complicated. God said, *"You will seek Me and find Me, when you seek Me with all your heart"* (Jeremiah 29:13). Focus on Him. Make Him your "*One Thing*"!

God, I do want you as my One Thing; what and who I seek after with a whole heart. Amen

FACE OR HAND?
March 25

"When You said, 'Seek My face,' my heart said to You, 'Your face, O Lord, I shall seek.'"
Psalm 27:8 (NASB)

Early on in my relationship with Sue, I sought her for mostly selfish reasons: she was beautiful, funny, smart, godly—and for some reason she liked me! But upon analysis, those reasons were fairly self-centered; they were largely about me and how she made me feel. But as my love has matured, it has also purified. I am compelled to seek her pleasure, her presence, her delight— for her sake, not mine. I love to be and act in a way that brings a smile to her face.

But the selfish person that I am, I still find myself seeking her hand; that is, seeking her for what she can do for me: fix dinner, run errands, be my trophy wife at parties, etc. To be sure, she loves me and wants to please me, so she is more than willing. But nobody wants to be sought only for what they do. Truth is, the more I love her, the less I seek her hand and the more I seek her face. When you seek someone's face, you seek their pleasure. When you seek their hand, you seek what they can do for you.

We're made to seek, to pursue, to acquire, to achieve. But our brokenness compels us to seek after stuff 'n things with greater passion than we do God. That's when our lives begin to go down the wrong path, the opposite of a flourishing life.

God commands us to seek His face. This concept is prominent all the way through the Bible. That simply means we pursue our relationship with Him out of a desire to love and please Him more. The true believer has an innate desire to please God. But much of the time our motives are suspect. We find ourselves seeking Him for what He can do for us.

I have to admit it's easy for me to slip into an attitude of seeking God because of what He can do for me: heal Sue of cancer, protect my family, inflate my 401k, get a new owner for the Cowboys, etc.

Why do you seek God? Take a moment and write down a few reasons, good and not so good.

Remember: When we seek God's hand, we seek what He can do for us. When we seek His face, we seek His pleasure, not ours.

Seek His face, and you'll get His hand!!

God, by Your grace, I will seek Your face and Your pleasure. Amen

WAIT FOR IT—

March 26

"I would have despaired unless I had believed that I would see
the goodness of the Lord in the land of the living. Wait for the Lord.
Be strong and let your heart take courage; yes, wait for the Lord!"
Psalm 27:13-14 (NASB)

This wonderful psalm finishes with a flourish of faith. David acknowledges that this great trial is pressing him to the point of despair. Despair always indicates a lack of hope.

Maybe you're at that point in your life right now. You're experiencing despair about something or about someone: your marriage, your job situation, your finances, your health or that of a loved one. The possibilities are endless.

Despair is all about expectations and control: we have expectations of outcomes and timing, and we want to control those. When those expectations are not met, we begin to lose a measure of hope that can eventually turn into despair.

Expectations are not bad. Parents should expect their children to act in a godly manner and should actively guide them that way. I can expect that Sue will remain cancer-free, but there's not much we can do beyond chemo and radiation to bring that about. We also have expectations of timing. We want relief from our suffering, answers to our prayers, and solutions to our problems as soon as possible. Who doesn't? But let's face it—ultimately, we can't control very many outcomes.

The antidote for despair is waiting on God. Waiting on God is a critical teaching in the Bible. One of my favorite memorized verses is Isaiah 40:31, *"But they who wait for the LORD shall renew their strength; they shall mount up with wings like eagles; they shall run and not be weary; they shall walk and not faint."* Waiting on the Lord is not a passive thing. It means to seek the Lord and trust in Him. Those are very active responses to trials and troubles. Simply put, waiting on God means to transfer expectations and control to Him: "God, I call out to You about this. I want to cooperate with **YOU**, not control **IT**. I place this in Your hands." That brings uncommon peace and rest to our souls. Not easy, but necessary.

We use the phrase "Wait for It—" to signal that something good is about to happen and if we rush it, we'll miss or spoil it.

God has something good in store for you—wait for it!

God, draw me to Yourself and enable me to trust and transfer my expectations to You. Amen

GIVE UP
March 27

"I pray to you, O Lord, my rock. Do not turn a deaf ear to me.
For if You are silent, I might as well give up and die."
Psalm 28:1 (NASB)

I've never been in any protracted physical danger—though those who ride with me would disagree! I have been in protracted dangers of a different sort. My mind goes back to the summer/fall of 1972 when I was deeply depressed with thoughts of suicide, the years of 1977-79 when I had absolutely lost my way and was acting in ways I now cannot imagine, 1984 when my job was coming to an end and I wasn't sure how I would provide for my family, 1994-95 when I was within a gnat's wing of getting fired at Rush Creek after being there less than a year, and then there was 1999-2000 when one-third of the church just up and left. I'm just warming up, but you get the point.

A study of David's life reveals that he was constantly in great physical danger from Saul, the Philistines, and even his own son, Absalom. His psalms are filled with pleas for God's protection and intervention. This particular psalm begins with jarring honesty: "God, if I don't hear from You, I might as well give up."

Trials and problems should always prompt us to turn to The Great Problem Solver. David calls to Him as his *"rock"*; a metaphor signifying strength and power. That's a good reminder for us: we can load Him down with our burdens—He can take it!

But David also confesses that if God doesn't respond to his plea, he might as well *"give up and die."* There are those problems and trials that are so urgent, so critical, if we don't hear from God, we don't know how we're going to make it.

Early on in our fight with Sue's cancer, there were times we felt like David. I pride myself at being a darn good problem solver. Those who know me would affirm that. But there are some problems that only Yahweh can solve.

Make your plea—and then listen for His answer. My experience indicates His answer always starts with His word. Search it for your solution. Pour it into your heart. And listen for the Spirit to speak.

If you do, you won't give up. You will find the way to press on. You will see His provision and sense His presence. You will.

God, hear my cry. Show me Your way. Grant me the grace to endure. Amen

BUST OUT!

March 28

"Praise the Lord! For He has heard my cry for mercy. The Lord is my strength and shield.
I trust Him with all my heart. He helps me, and my heart is filled with joy.
I burst out in songs of thanksgiving."

Psalm 28:6-7

Sometimes when I get caught up in my problems and trials, all I do is call out to God for deliverance. Of course, God wants us to come to Him with our concerns, but when I get focused on the problem, on the trial, I lose focus on the God who can do something about it.

In this psalm (like so many he wrote), David was in physical danger. When you read the psalm, you see that he is calling out for mercy and help from Yahweh. But right in the middle of his plea, he busts out in praise and thanksgiving! He praises God for hearing his prayer. He praises God for being his strength and protection. The interesting thing is that there is no tangible reason for him to do this! He's still under attack and in danger!! In fact, in v.9 he moves from praise back to plea.

God invites us to plea, and David takes Yahweh up on His offer. But David's faith moved him to bust out in a higher form of prayer—praise. Praise focuses totally on God. It gets our eyes off of ourselves and our problems and catches us up in the glory, splendor, and sufficiency of God.

Every time of prayer needs to include a time of praise. Here is a great exercise to build into your daily prayer time: identify a few attributes of God (His sovereignty, omnipotence, holiness, etc.) and begin to brag on Him about them. We do that with our kids—why not do it with our Creator?

There is something elating when we bust out in praise, even when our hearts are burdened.

Forty-plus years ago there was a powerful song by a group called the Imperials that got me through a dark, dark patch in my life. One refrain went like this:

Praise the Lord, He will work through those who praise Him,
Praise the Lord, for our God inhabits praise.
Praise the Lord, for the chains that seem to bind you,
Serve only to remind you, that they drop powerless behind you,
When you praise Him.

God, in the midst of my pain, I choose to praise You. You are worthy of my worship no matter the circumstance. Amen

THE STORM
March 29

"The voice of the Lord is powerful; the voice of the Lord is majestic"
Psalm 29:4

Spending most of my life in Oklahoma and Texas, I've experienced countless thunderstorms. I am fascinated by them: the lightning that cracks the sky wide open, the thunderclaps that can almost knock you out of bed, the winds that bend and shake trees like rag dolls. Few natural phenomena are as powerful as a storm.

They can also be frightening. Many a child has run into their parent's bedroom in hopes of escaping the terror and hearing the assuring words, "Don't be afraid. You're with me now. You'll be ok."

Take a moment and read the 11 verses of this psalm. When reading Scripture, it's always good to underline or highlight words or phrases that are repeated. Seven times in vv.3-9 David employs the phrase, *"The voice of the Lord."*

The God of the Bible is a God who speaks.

Throughout Scripture we find Him speaking from a burning bush, booming from a clear sky, and whispering quietly outside a cave. He spoke through prophets, donkeys, angels, and dreams.

In this psalm, David hears God speak in a storm: gale-force winds, bolts of lightning, and jarring thunder. At the end, he affirms that God is sovereign over the storms—a huge realization in the midst of the storm.

Are you in a storm right now? They come in all different forms: life-threatening diseases, job losses, financial ruin, marriage struggles, abandonment—you fill in the blank.

God still speaks in the storms.

The writer of Hebrews reminds us: *"Long ago God spoke to our early fathers in many different ways. But in these last days He has spoken to us through His Son"* (Hebrews 1:1-2). When a storm is raging in your life, find shelter in Jesus. Spend time in His word and listen for His voice. If you do, you'll discover what David proclaimed at the end of this psalm: *"The Lord gives His people strength. The Lord blesses them with peace"* (v. 11).

God, I needed to be reminded that You are sovereign over the storms and that You speak in the midst of them. I'm listening. Amen

ANGER AND FAVOR
March 30

"For His anger lasts only a moment, but His favor lasts a lifetime!"
Psalm 30:5a

I loved my dad. Raised in the Great Depression, WW2 Marine who fought on Iwo Jima, he could be tough. When I needed discipline, he didn't hesitate to apply his belt to my seat of learning! He loved me too much not to. I would wail for a while, but afterward, I was at peace and so was he. He didn't harbor anger; he dealt with my variant behavior and was done with it.

Some folks have a hard time reconciling the love of God with the anger of God. But we can't avoid the fact that both Old and New Testaments reveal that God experiences anger, Paul put it this way, *"Notice how God is both kind and severe"* (Romans 11:22).

God disciplines His children: *"For the Lord disciplines the one He loves"* (Hebrews 12:6).

Discipline is not the same as punishment. Jesus took the punishment for our sin on the cross. Too many believers get this way wrong. Because they're going through a trial, they'll say, "God is punishing me." Nope. Not true. Not by a long shot.

But He does discipline. He loves us too much not to. In my experience, He utilizes two switches: His Spirit and trials. When the believer ignores God's will, the Holy Spirit will become grieved in us (Ephesians 4:30). That is a sickening feeling that doesn't really go away. You can try to ignore it, stuff it, even drown it, but He's in you and He's not going away. The balm for this malady is confession and repentance: *"God, I confess I sinned. I will turn away from it. By Your grace, may it be so."* Done. Over with. Move on.

But if we harden our hearts, God will step back and let adversity discipline us. That is NOT to say ALL adversity is God's discipline. Much of our adversity is not necessarily our fault, it is the result of living in a broken world. But when trials do come, we must examine our hearts to see if there is any unconfessed sin, then respond with brokenness and realignment to His will.

Sometimes the consequences of our rebellion are alleviated quickly; others play out for a long time. Regardless, what we must keep straight in our minds is that God doesn't harbor anger against us. He is for us, not against us (Romans 8:31). God will use trials, deserved or undeserved, to purify us and make us more like Jesus. Believer, know this deep, deep in your soul: *"His favor lasts a lifetime!"* Actually—it lasts for an eternity!!

God, I accept the loving discipline of Your hand. Teach me Your ways. Amen

EMOTIONS
March 31

"Weeping may last through the night, but joy comes with the morning."
Psalm 30:5b

Emotions make terrible taskmasters. To be sure, God experiences emotions and, made in His image, we are outfitted with an array of emotions ourselves. But we place too much value on them at our peril. One of the most critical perspectives a person can have is to know that feelings are transient and such poor indicators of reality. It's not easy. Depending on the circumstance, our feelings can get us to believe that it's always going to be this way and we are always going to feel this way.

Maturity realizes that such is not the case. Emotions in the spiritually healthy person are tethered to the truth of Scripture. Romans 12:2 reminds us: *"Don't copy the behavior and customs of this world, but let God transform you into a new person by changing the way you think. Then you will learn to know God's will for you, which is good and pleasing and perfect."* Notice that the Holy Spirit led the Apostle Paul to write that transformation and the flourishing that is good and pleasing, doesn't come with how you feel, but how you think. Reading, memorizing, and meditating on the Bible keep our emotions on a short leash and in healthy condition.

I can tell you from experience that linking my thoughts and actions to Scripture has saved my bacon many, many times. There were periods in my marriage I felt it was never going to get better. But it did. How tragic would that have been if I had acted on those feelings? There were times in my ministry where I felt I just couldn't do it anymore; couldn't deal with the disappointment and pain. But I did. When my dad died suddenly at age 57, I had never, and still have never felt such acute pain. It took quite a while to process my grief. But I did. Tens of thousands of times I have felt something was not going to change and therefore I couldn't endure it. But I did.

The psalmist reminds the believer that God is in the restoration business. He restores what has been taken from us. This broken world can devastate, but God can and will restore. Sorrow and despair may come, but joy and peace can overcome in the heart that trusts in Yahweh. He loves to give us new mornings: *"The faithful love of the Lord never ends! His mercies never cease. Great is His faithfulness; His mercies begin afresh each morning"* (Lamentations 3:22-23).

God, I purpose to not allow my emotions to rule me but renew my mind by being a better student of Your word. Amen

TIMING

April 1

"Weeping may last through the night, but joy comes with the morning."
Psalm 30:5b

Recently I was visiting with a couple who is going through a terrible ordeal. Their pain and grief was and is significant. Both of them are incredibly strong believers and possess great faith, but **great faith does not inoculate us from great sorrow.**

David touches on a very important sequence here that his son, Solomon, articulated years later: *"There is a time and a season for everything . . . a time for weeping and a time for laughing"* (Ecclesiastes. 3:1, 4).

How do you handle grief? Grief is a God-given response to the loss of something or someone dear: grief at the loss of a job, the loss of innocence, the loss of a loved one. It may surprise you that God grieves. When Jesus' good friend, Lazarus, died, Jesus stood outside his tomb watching others grieve, and the Scripture says: *"When Jesus saw her (Mary, Lazarus' sister) crying, and the Jews who had come with her crying, He was deeply moved in His spirit and troubled. 'Where have you put him?' He asked. 'Lord,' they told Him, 'come and see.' Jesus wept"* (John 11:33-35; CSB). The phrase *"deeply moved"* means an intense, strong, visceral feeling, and the word *"troubled"* means acute emotional distress. His grief prompted the shortest verse in the Bible, *"Jesus wept."* He didn't just shed a tear or two. He wept hard.

Don't be afraid to grieve. Grief, not the circumstance, is good. Grieving is absolutely necessary so that you can move on to joy. There is a timing to this whole grief and joy thing. If you rush through the grief, you'll mitigate the joy that is to follow. If you spend too long in grief, you'll have a hard time getting to the joy.

As their eyes welled up with tears, I told this couple that it was certainly a time for weeping. But I also assured them that there would be a time of rejoicing in the future as they saw God's loving, sovereign hand at work through all of this.

Weeping may last through the night, but rest assured that there is a sunrise of joy out there for you.

God, by faith I believe what You promise will come true for me. Amen

SHELTER
April 2

"O Lord, I have come to You for protection; don't let me be disgraced.
Save me, for You do what is right. Turn Your ear to listen to me; rescue me quickly.
Be my rock of protection, a fortress where I will be safe. You are my rock and my fortress.
For the honor of Your name, lead me out of this danger."
Psalm 31:1-3

In 2002, I was trying to figure out how to get some quality time with my two sons before they headed off in different directions. Ben was going back to college and Brad would start two-a-days for football in a couple of weeks. I decided that we needed to go wildlife viewing in Glacier National Park in Montana. I had just read the book, "Wild at Heart" by John Eldredge. In the book, he exhorted men to be comfortable and confident in their manhood. I gave my boys the book, told them to read it and we'd discuss it on the trip. It was such a rich time. Besides talking about our God-ordained manhood, we drove and hiked from daybreak to dawn seeing fox, moose, antelope, elk, and black bear. What we wanted to see more than anything was a grizzly bear. We did eventually, but that story for another time...

One afternoon we were up on a mountainside above the tree line when we got caught out in a violent hailstorm. There was nowhere to shelter except under a few rocks jutting out of the mountainside. Ben and Brad crawled under one and I found another. We were safe. I still have that picture of them huddled together peering out over the valley.

Do you feel in danger? Threatened? There is really only one place you can seek shelter and be safe: not **A** rock, **THE** Rock!

David calls on God to, not just hear him, but shelter him from danger. Ultimately, only God can protect us. We can disinfect everything and everyone in our house, tighten our seatbelts until we hurt, try to bubble wrap our kids—but at the end of the day, we must trust a loving, sovereign God.

David also reminds us that it's not about us—it's about The Rock: *"For the honor of Your name"* (v.3). How will I act in danger? What/who will I turn to and trust in? Will those around see fear or faith in me? Will they be drawn to the Rock because of me?

Danger has a way of revealing the true answers.

For His name's sake, for His honor, for His reputation, I turn to and trust in Him.

Like a Rock, He is my shelter!!

God, You are my Rock, my Shelter, my protection. I trust in You!!

CONTROL
April 3

"My times are in Your hands."
Psalm 31:15 (NASB)

Have you ever been white water rafting? Rapids are divided into five navigable categories: Class One is like ripples in a bathtub. Class Three are much faster rapids with waves 4-5 feet high. Class Five rapids are. . . AWESOME! Big waves, big vertical drops, big currents, big rocks to avoid—people die doing these! I've done Class Fours and Fives a bunch of times. They put you in a raft with 4-10 people and a guide at the back using a slightly larger paddle to try to keep the raft going in the right direction. When the guide says paddle, you paddle like crazy. When he/she says stop, you stop. Essentially, you have very little control. If you didn't have the guide, you would die. Literally.

Life can be like that. There are those times when it seems everything going on around us is chaotic, random, unpredictable—even dangerous. Fear is the natural result. As an example, I've noticed that parenting continues to evolve toward bubble-wrapping children! It's not because parents feel they are in control; it is because they feel helpless to protect. It's a common malady for all of us. Life can feel so totally out of control.

Truth is, we never were much in control anyway! We like to think we can protect ourselves and our loved ones, that we can control circumstances, that we can determine our future—but it's an illusion.

When David was up against it, when his own skill, knowledge, and determination met their limitations, he had the wisdom to utter one of my favorite prayers: *"My times are in Your hands."*

Let go of what you can't control anyway. It only leads to fear and frustration if you don't. The one thing you can control is your choice. Choose to transfer your faith from yourself to the One who holds your future in His hands. It doesn't relieve you from responsibility. But it does relieve you from fear.

A song back in the '70s put it this way: "Put your hand in the hands of the One who stilled the waters; put your hand in the hands of Him who calmed the sea."

Pretty good advice cause—He's got the whole world in His hands!

God, by Your grace, I commit to placing my family and all I hold dear in Your hands. Amen

UPSIDE DOWN
April 4

"Oh, what joy for those whose disobedience is forgiven, whose sin is put out of sight!
Yes, what joy for those whose record the Lord has cleared of guilt!"
Psalm 32:1-2

In the 16th century, Felix Platter proposed that the pupil of the eye functions as an optic and the retina as a receptor. This was proved correct by Rene Descartes a century later. You may not know this but the image that appears on your retina located at the back of your eye—is actually upside down! God made our brain so that it automatically flips the image right-side-up!

Such is the nature of grace. Grace is an upside-down thing. We all fall short of God's standard of moral perfection (Romans 3:23). Because of our sin and rebellion against this holy and righteous God, we deserve His judgment. Not for just a moment, or a season, but for eternity.

But where sin abounds, grace superabounds (Romans 5:20)! It makes no sense!! I deserve God's judgment, but through Christ, He gives me favor!!! That's upside down.

When I pause long enough to take a sober look at my inner self and my actions that flow out of it, I am genuinely repulsed. I see greed, selfishness, pride, deceit, lust, prejudice—and that's just for starters! I know what I deserve from a righteous and holy God, and I shudder to think of one minute of His wrath, let alone an eternity of it.

Yet, through and because of Jesus' debt-satisfying death, I am no longer a candidate for His gallows, but for His grace. That's upside down! That God would, not just be willing to, but want to forgive me and wipe clean my guilt is—beyond my ability to fully grasp.

What happens when the believer catches glimpses of this? Notice what David said: the heart is flooded with grief that we rebelled, gratitude for His grace, and joy that He has set us free from the penalty of all this!

I'm still baffled. All I know is that I need more of Him and more of His grace for this upside-down life of being a Jesus-follower.

Jesus, thank You so much for taking my sin on Yourself so that I might be an object of Your love, not Your wrath. Amen

MY HIDING PLACE
April 5

"For You are my hiding place; You protect me from trouble.
You surround me with songs of deliverance."
Psalm 32:7

In 1980, Michael Ledner wrote the song, *"You Are My Hiding Place"* based on this verse. As a Christian musician, he spent much time in the Psalms—the songbook of the Hebrews.

Michael's life was far from idyllic. His marriage was falling apart and eventually ended in divorce. He would sit alone in his one-room apartment on his bed with his guitar reading the Psalms to gain comfort. It was there he was inspired to write the song. A year later he traveled to Israel to visit friends. Israel was embroiled in conflict with terrorists in Lebanon who would launch rockets or raid settlements into northern Israel, so he stayed in the south of Israel. When he played the song for his friends there, they insisted he play and sing it over the phone to their friends in the north who were sheltering from the rockets. He began singing the words over the phone as he heard the explosions going off in the background:

> *You are my hiding place. You always fill my heart with songs of deliverance.*
> *Whenever I am afraid, I will trust in You.*

Could be your life is falling apart—bombs going off all around you. As I write this, I am so burdened by people in my own life who are experiencing the damage of living in a broken world: infidelity, life-threatening disease, newborns struggling to live, grieving spouses, profound loneliness, chronic depression, families at war with each other, financial catastrophes, chemical dependency—I could go on, but it is so overwhelming.

Maybe you are overwhelmed this morning. King David and Michael Ledner have a word for us: we can find shelter and comfort in Yahweh. HE is our Hiding Place. Hiding in a Person is totally different than hiding in a place. Places can change or deteriorate over time. Yahweh is unchanging. Places can be overrun by powerful forces. Yahweh is unconquerable and all-powerful. Places can be remote and difficult to get to. Yahweh is in the heart of the believer and accessible by just a whisper.

And get this—when we shelter in Him, we hear Him SINGING! He surrounds us with songs of deliverance assuring us that, by His grace and power, we will get through and overcome!!

Run to Him, hide in Him, and listen . . .

Yahweh, I confess that YOU are my Hiding Place. Enable me to hear You singing. Amen

BREATHE
April 6

"The Lord merely spoke, and the heavens were created.
He breathed the word, and all the stars were born."

Psalm 33:6

Hold your breath for a moment—long enough to feel a bit uncomfortable. Go ahead. The ability to breathe is a part of the life-giving element called the *"nephesh."* Nephesh can be translated as *soul* or *breath*. We see it first in Genesis 2:7, *"Then the Lord God formed the man from the dust of the ground. He breathed the **breath** of life into the man's nostrils, and the man became a living person."* Until God breathed into the formed, but unalive Adam, he would have no life.

The psalmist grabs the concept of God breathing something into existence when he writes in v.6, *"He (Yahweh) breathed the word, and all the stars were born."*

One of the realities we must keep central in our perspective always is that God is sovereign and supreme over all that is. Why is that so? Because He created all that is. He did so just by speaking and breathing everything that is into existence. As Creator, He decides what each creation's purpose is and what part He wants it to play in His plan.

Yahweh's 1st recorded words were *"Let there be light"* (Genesis 1:3). Actually, in the original Hebrew text, there is the singular proclamation: *"Light!"* God took a breath and declared, "LIGHT", and guess what? There was light!! The God of the Bible is so powerful that He merely had to speak the universe into existence. The rest of the Bible demonstrates how God didn't just create and then step away, but that He has stayed personally involved in the goings-on of His creation.

This is absolutely critical for us to remember when life becomes difficult. Circumstances are NOT out of His control. Chaos is NOT the guiding principle of reality. God is.

The psalmist reminds us that Yahweh is still in control. When we accept and count on that to be true, three life-giving realities emerge: 1) He is our hope, so hope can never run out (v.20); 2) He is our joy, so our joy can never be depleted (v.21); 3) His love surrounds us, so we can never wander beyond it (v.22).

Breathe. Breathe in His word and breathe in the life He wants for you.

God, I bow before you as my Creator and Sovereign. Enable me to breathe in the life You have for me. Amen

TASTE BUDS
April 7

"O taste and see that the Lord is good!"
Psalm 34:8

We all have our favorite foods: pizza, pasta, burgers, brats, steak, seafood—makes me hungry just thinking about it! We literally crave the food we want to eat: stomach grumbles and saliva glands tune-up. Get the prayer over with and LEMME EAT! Our taste buds come alive, and if you're like me, you probably eat too much when your favorite dish is before you!

The psalmist reminds us that we can taste of the Lord. What he means is that God is to be experienced like a good meal; that our spiritual taste buds can be so delighted in Him; that we can and should crave Him.

The problem is that if we're not careful, we love other foods more than Him: affirmation, belonging, sex, money, hobbies, travel—the world offers unlimited entrees! Worse, the Deceiver makes his bill of fare look more scrumptious than what the Lord offers. But I can tell you from experience, eating from Satan's menu brings heartburn in horrific ways.

Because of Sue's cancer, I learned that one of the side-effects of chemotherapy is that the taste buds are adversely affected. The patient can still eat, but it is just not satisfying. Spiritual cancer ruins our tastebuds, yet we keep eating more and more of the world's smorgasbord and finding it less and less satisfying.

So how do we train our spiritual tastebuds? 1 Peter 2:2-3 (ESV) expands on this: *"Like newborn infants, long for (crave) the pure milk of the word, that by it you may grow up into salvation-if indeed you have tasted that the Lord is good."* One of the miraculous dynamics of God's word is the more time you spend in it, the hungrier you get for it! Time in the Scripture greatly increases our appetite for God.

Set aside time each morning to spend time in God's word. Read the Psalms—I try to read five psalms a day. Or read a chapter out of the Gospels each day, or go to YouVersion and follow one of their reading plans, or whatever—just be intentional about intaking the Word of the Living God! You'll begin to experience God's power and presence like never before.

And when we do experience Him, taste of Him—He's good. He's real good. In fact, He's better than any other meal this world offers! Taste and see just how good the Lord can be.

God, by Your grace, I commit to a daily reading of Your word. Grant me a greater hunger. Amen

LONG AND PROSPEROUS
April 8

"Does anyone want to live a life that is long and prosperous?
Then keep your tongue from speaking evil and your lips from telling lies!
Turn away from evil and do good. Search for peace, and work to maintain it."
Psalm 34:12-13

We humans scurry around the planet frantically looking for something that eludes most of us: a genuinely full and satisfying life. David gives us a great key to open the door to the extraordinary life we seek: watch your mouth (your speech), watch your feet (your walk), and watch your hands (work for peace in your relationships).

Words matter and we need to be careful how we use them. Ephesians 4:15 says, *"Instead, we will speak the truth in love, growing in every way more and more like Christ, who is the head of His body, the church."* Speak the truth in love. Get that right and a whole lot of life is right. It's not as easy as you might think. Jesus said in Matthew 12:34, *"For the mouth speaks from the overflow of the heart."* Whatever is in our hearts makes it to our lips. Yikes!

I have a terrible flaw in my heart that makes its way to my lips all the time: pride. I tend to fashion my words in a way that portrays me better than I really am and my position stronger than it is. This shows up in so many ways, but maybe most deplorably when I argue with Sue. When we get into a tiff, I tend to insist my perspective is the right one, so I'll fashion my words in a way that paints my position on the matter more right than I should. And that's wrong. Then pride really kicks in and I become entrenched in my position and struggle to let go of it.

Can I get a witness??

The only way out of the deadlock is for me to speak the truth in love. Truth is, I can't be certain my position is true on just about anything. My perspective is always biased toward me. I love Sue more than my opinion or perspective on anything, so I must decide to turn from my evil pride (repent), speak truth to her in love, and seek peace.

But it's not just about my words, my actions have to back it up. So I look for ways to affirm my love: touch her, hug her, clean up the kitchen...

The better I get at this, by God's grace, the more full my life is.

God, by Your Spirit, kill the pride in me that leads to a less than full life and prompt me to speak the truth in love. Amen

PRICELESS
April 9

"How priceless is Your unfailing love, O God! People take refuge in the shadow of Your wings. They feast on the abundance of Your house; You give them drink from Your river of delights. For with You is the fountain of life; in Your light we see light."

Psalm 36:7-9

There used to be a Master Card commercial that showed a young boy and his father attending a baseball game. The narrator: "Two tickets--$28. Two hotdogs, two popcorns, two sodas--$18. A real conversation with your 11-year-old son—priceless."

David reminds us there is one blessing above everything else to be valued: God's unfailing love—It's priceless!! You'll recall that the Hebrew word for *"unfailing love"* is *chesed*, or *covenant love*. God loves the whole world (John 3:16), but there is a unique love for those of us who have entered into this covenant with God through the blood of His Son, Jesus.

Notice three benefits and blessings of those who walk in God's unfailing love. First is security—we can *"take refuge in the shadow of Your wings."* Imagine the expansive wings of an eagle protecting her little eaglets from predators and the elements. When trouble comes, we can hide in Him and sense His love and protection. Knowing that I can take refuge in Jesus when trials come—priceless!

The second blessing is abundance. The psalmist uses the imagery of feasting and drinking. Jesus often used such imagery to describe the abundant life (*"More and better life than you ever dreamed of."* John 10:10) and Kingdom living (*"The Kingdom of Heaven . . . is like a banquet."* Matthew 22:2). Abundant joy. Abundant peace. Abundant love. Abundant best. Interestingly, David identifies *"Your river of delights"* as the source of our abundance. The Hebrew word for '*delights*' is *eden*. We know Eden as the incredible garden where God placed Adam and Eve; where they and all creation were in harmony with God. It's also the place where disobedience and rebellion destroyed that harmony and left all of creation in need of redemption. By using this phrase, David touches on the human need for restoration; to be redeemed and restored to our original, pre-fall condition. That's what sanctification is all about: the restoration of the image of God in the life of the believer. To experience this Holy Spirit restoration and experience God's abundant best in this life—priceless!

Third, direction. When we walk in God's light (obedience to His word), we obtain light and direction in the chaos of life: *"In Your light we see light."* To see His path and walk in it with confidence—priceless!

God, Your faithful love is PRICELESS! Thank You! Amen

WITHERING HEIGHTS
April 10

"Don't worry about the wicked or envy those who do wrong.
For like grass, they soon fade away. Like spring flowers, they soon wither."
Psalm 37:1-2

Is it just me or do you also notice that many non-believers (people who willfully disavow Jesus or people who say they know Jesus but don't really act it and therefore don't really believe) seem to gain prosperity and power while we who do believe don't get more and better? People like Bill Gates, George Soros, Jeff Bezos who have everything this world can offer, but don't give homage to the One who provided it. I would think we should get some of what they have. Don't you? We're children of God, co-heirs with Jesus, destined to rule and reign for eternity—so why don't we get preferential treatment??

Listening to some preachers and believers, they agree. They insist if you're not wealthy and healthy, you're either not a believer, have sin in your life, or don't have enough faith. Rubbish!

The Bible warns us not to determine the favor of God based on the trappings of this world.

David's song here affirms that. We must get this straight: there will be an accounting at the end of the age. The REAL value system will be revealed. I promise you that we will see how worthless money and power really are.

Every Spring, Sue plants some flowers that are seasonal. They bloom and are beautiful—until it gets hot. When the 100+ degree days come, they wilt and die.

Like spring flowers, the heat of God's judgment and reckoning will burn away all earthly and temporal benefits—and those who count on them—so that only what and who HE values will remain. Those outside of Christ who have risen to the heights of power, influence, and prosperity will wither away when Jesus shows up.

So, I don't need to waste a second wondering why others (the unbeliever) have what I don't. They don't have what I have! Somebody's going to end up empty-handed and eternally impoverished. Not gonna be me! How about you?

God, enable me to see and hold on to this perspective. Thank You for my salvation—the greatest possession of all. Amen

THE HEART'S DESIRE
April 11

"Take delight in the Lord, and He will give you your heart's desires."
Psalm 37:4

I love that scene in "The Christmas Story" where Ralphie is in the department store to see Santa. When Santa asks what he wants for Christmas, he freezes. The impatient Santa puts him on the slide to get rid of him, but suddenly Ralphie remembers and shouts, "I want an official Red Rider carbine-action 200 shot range-model air rifle!" Santa responds, "You'll shoot your eye out, kid"—and then shoves him down the slide.

If we're not careful, we'll see God as The Great Santa Clause, sitting around at the North Pole of Heaven waiting for us to ask what we want so that He'll fill our lives with whatever we desire.

God is not Santa Clause.

Look again at the verse. What a great promise—and how greatly misunderstood! The key to grasping the power of this promise is in the first phrase. It is the seminal, first condition necessary for the second phrase to come true: delighting yourself in the Lord. The second condition—receiving the desires of your heart—is a result of the first condition—delighting in Him.

What does it mean to delight in the Lord? BIG topic! To delight in something is to take or experience great pleasure. So basically, to delight in God is to find great pleasure in who He is.

Who is God? What attributes does He possess that reveal His personhood? You could make a pretty long list: holy (totally set apart & different), sovereign (supreme in power & authority), just (upholding what is right), omniscient (all-knowing), omnipotent (all-powerful), eternal (no beginning or end), love (the fountain of mercy and grace), and so on.

As I've mentioned before, early on in my marriage I delighted in what Sue did for me. So when she didn't do what I wanted, my delight diminished. My love was pretty shallow. As we mark our 40th anniversary this year, I can honestly say that I delight more in who she is, so that what she does isn't nearly as important. Get this: the result of delighting in who she is brings delight in me for what she wants, not what I want. Her wants become my wants; her desires become my desires.

Delight yourself in who God is and your heart will align with His. This first condition leads to the second condition: He will give you the desires of your heart. And those gifts are the best!

O God, I desire to delight in You for who You are, not what You do. May it be so!

YOU KNOW THIS

April 12

"The wicked borrow and never repay, but the godly are generous givers."
Psalm 37:21

All the way through this psalm, David has been contrasting the character, desires, speech, and actions of the godly with the ungodly, the righteous with the unrighteous, the true believer, and the fake believer. In this verse, he points out the difference when it comes to money.

You know this. What we do with our money is the key indicator of our relationship with Jesus. You know this. Jesus talked more about money and possessions than He did faith and prayer!

You know this.

Jesus was always doing and saying unordinary things. One day He decided to sit down opposite the offering box in the temple area and just watch as the people put their offerings in. You can find the story in Mark 12:41f and Luke 21:1f. A widow (there was no social security so unmarried women, particularly older widows were amongst the poorest) walked up and put a couple of pennies in the box. Jesus whooped and hollered about it because it was all she had to live on: *"Everyone else gives out of their abundance, but she gave out of her poverty!"*

One of the great lies Satan perpetrates is that generosity increases with more income. We buy into that lie when we say to ourselves: "I have debts and diapers and doctors' bills—when I get clear of all this financial responsibility, I'll be more generous." Truth is, survey after survey affirms that the more money we earn, the less percentage of it we give! It is never easy to be generous, particularly in hard times. Fear sets in and we worry if we'll have enough.

But godly folk overcome their fears with faith. They love when it's hard, they serve when it's hard, and they give when it's hard. Generosity is born out of a sense of gratitude. Hard times should make us more, not less, grateful for what Jesus has provided for us in this world—and in the one to come.

You know this.

So be more generous. Begin with God's chosen instrument to carry His good news—His church. The church you attend needs your generosity now more than ever. And here's the thing: you'll be more joyful and content the more generous you are!!

Jesus, I know all this. Thank You for generously pouring Yourself out for me. I will take my generosity up to the next level. Amen

3-D
April 13

"The Lord directs the steps of the godly. He delights in every detail of their lives.
When they fall, they will not be hurled headlong, for the Lord holds them by the hand."
Psalm 37:23-24

When my children were learning to walk, it was always so fun to watch them learn how. It's been a treat again with my ten (10!) grandchildren. After watching these thirteen grow up through the years, I know there are different ways of learning to walk. One pulled up on something and then ventured out. One rocked back and forth on hands and knees until they figure out how to stand from there. One got their right foot going but not their left, so they just went in circles!! So fun!

But one experience was common: they stumbled and fell. At that point, the loving parent would come alongside, bend down, and grab the child's hand to steady them as they learned to walk.

What a wonderful 3-D picture of our Lord as we learn to walk!

First, He DIRECTS our steps. We are not left alone to figure life out on our own: *"Trust in the Lord with all your heart; do not depend on your own understanding. Seek His will in all you do, and He will show you which path to take"* (Proverbs 3:5-6). He has given us direction in His word, and through His indwelling Spirit, He guides us along the way. We have only to read and listen to find His direction for our lives.

Second, He DELIGHTS in us and *"every detail"* of our lives. We who believe the Scripture know He is an incredibly personal God who cares about us and cares for us. There is nothing going on in your life that He is not interested in. Jesus was talking about this one day when He said, *"The very hairs on your head are all numbered"* (Luke 12:7). Of course, that number is changing constantly as we get older—but you get the point! As a believer, you are the apple of His eye. He loves watching you learn to walk.

Third, He DELIVERS us through, not from, danger. There is no guarantee of deliverance from, just deliverance through. Hard times will come. We will stumble. Pain and scars will be a part of our story. But all along the way He will be walking beside us, holding our hand, and keeping us from headlong destruction.

What a loving, caring, wise, and powerful Heavenly Father!

Heavenly Father, thank You for being so attentive to me as I stumble and grow. I love You! Amen

THE LAND
April 14

"Put your hope in the Lord. Travel steadily along his path.
He will honor you by giving you the land."
Psalm 37:34

In my 20's when I was working in Houston, I would drive in to the rural areas for business. I used to dream about buying a tract of land and building a big house on it. I now live in a house not so grandiose as I imagined, on a lot where the backyard grass can be cut with scissors!

Land. It is something we can literally possess. Ownership and control of land has been the source of pride, security, and even conflict since the beginning.

David could have been referring to the struggle to win back and maintain the land God had promised to the Hebrews from the days of Abraham. He could have also been speaking to those who had lost their land to the unscrupulous. Regardless, David is saying there is a way to obtain what has been promised but taken away.

God has promised land to every believer. Not terra ferma, but something far more valuable. In the Old Testament, everything revolved around the Promised Land, aka, Israel. Moses led the Hebrews out of slavery in Egypt toward it; Joshua got them into it. The Promised Land in the Old Testament is a symbol of the Abundant Life in the New Testament. Not the promised land but the promised life! The life that is *"more and better than you ever could have imagined!"* (John 10:10).

How sad it is to know that most Christ-followers are not possessing that land; that life. Instead of experiencing great joy, peace, freedom, and all that makes life good, they constantly struggle with defeat, guilt, fear, shame, frustration, emptiness—all that makes God's promise seem so elusive.

I was there for a season. It's been a long time since, but I remember it well. My pride, sin, and self-sufficiency were killing me. It. Was. Awful.

But I kept repenting. I kept hoping and believing He would get me through. I kept trying to walk His path, even though I stumbled terribly. I kept in His word and kept on my knees calling out for His mercy and the life I longed for. By His grace He brought me into the land and life He promised, and it is good—so, so good, I can't even express it!

Hope in the Lord. Repent and travel His path, not yours. Stay at it. He will bring you into the land.

Jesus, I want that 'more and better life' You talked about. By Your grace, bring it to pass. Amen.

CALLOUSES
April 15

"O Lord, don't rebuke me in Your anger or discipline me in Your rage!"
Psalm 38:1

I've never been very good with my hands. All of that talent bypassed me and went from my dad to my brother. Every time I try to fix something, it gets worse. I do remember my high school and college days when I worked construction jobs, digging ditches, pushing heavy wheelbarrows around, carrying heavy bags. It felt good to be able to do something worthwhile with my hands. They got rough and calloused.

There is an eternity of difference between calloused hands and a calloused heart.

This psalm is a song of guilt and sorrow. David has become entangled in some unknown (to us) sin and God has disciplined him in a way that has brought a significant level of pain and struggle. He calls out to God to remember him with compassion. As you read through the psalm, underline the phrases David uses to describe the seriousness of God's discipline: arrows striking deep in his heart and blows crushing him (v.2), his health broken (v.3), overcome with guilt and grief (vv.4-6), and debilitating soul-fatigue (vv.7-8).

One of the most important features of the Spirit-filled life is passed over and ignored far too often: the discipline and correction of the Lord.

I get it. As a pastor, I'm always wanting to speak words of encouragement and hope. But if the believer doesn't understand and respond to God's discipline, we CANNOT experience the fullness He has for us.

We don't have to experience God's discipline. There is a better way. Callouses build up on our hands because of repeated friction. The resistance creates the hardness. When we sin, the Spirit sends a signal that we've violated God's moral standard. If we get the hint and repent, all is well and good. But if we ignore Him, resist Him, a callous begins to form on our hearts. If our resistance continues, we become insensitive to the Spirit and, in many cases, may not even be aware we're sinning. At that point, a loving Father will then orchestrate circumstances to get our attention. David got the point and in vv.18-22. He confessed his sin and called on God to deliver him from his painful circumstances.

Is your heart soft and sensitive to the rebuke of the Spirit? Or have you let it get calloused and hard? Ask God to soften your heart and make it sensitive to His promptings. Then call on God for help and deliverance. This is the path to a victorious and flourishing life.

God, show me where my heart has grown callous to You. Hear my cry. Amen

VAPOR

April 16

"Lord, remind me how brief my time on earth will be. Remind me that my days are numbered—how fleeting my life is. You have made my life no longer than the width of my hand. My entire lifetime is just a moment to You; at best, each of us is but a breath."

Psalm 39:4-5

There is nothing like danger to remind us how fragile life is.

Subconsciously we believe our bodies are indestructible and are going to last forever. That perspective shows up in a number of ways. For a risk-taker like me, it means you do any number of stupid things foolishly believing you won't get hurt or worse: rowing a canoe off a 15' waterfall just to see what it's like, or snow skiing at twice the speed of your skill level or chasing after grizzlies without a gun.

For others, it's over-eating or over-drinking or over-whatever and thinking that it's not that bad and your body can handle it. And some folks foolishly believe that their body is strong enough to avoid any serious diseases, so they cast caution to the wind. But when danger shows up, it tends to sober us about the frailty of our bodies.

David writes this psalm apparently while still in the danger of Psalm 38. He calls on God to remind him that in the scheme of things, life is brief and can be shattered easily. He needed to reorient his life and put his hope in Yahweh.

On a cold morning when you breathe, a vapor appears for just a moment—and then it's gone. Life is just a vapor: here one moment and gone the next. Are you investing your minutes in things that last for eternity—people, the word, the Gospel, the Kingdom? It's time to re-evaluate; reset priorities; re-focus on what is truly valuable and important.

Hurry—you don't have much time left.

God, show me what I'm wasting my life on and enable me to invest in what truly matters. Amen

VANITY
April 17

"We are merely moving shadows, and all our busy rushing ends in nothing. We heap up wealth, not knowing who will spend it. And so, Lord, where do I put my hope? My only hope is in You."
Psalm 39:6-7

In contemporary culture, the word vanity has come to refer to someone who has too much pride in their appearance or abilities. Vanities are pieces of furniture specifically designed to help us look better.

But historically the word refers to wasted effort, ambition, or achievement. David's son, Solomon, wrote an entire book (Ecclesiastes) about vain pursuits. This was a guy who built gardens, seaports, palaces, walled cities, a standing army, and the Jerusalem temple. He had more notoriety, money, and women than he knew what to do with. His assessment: it was empty. It was vain. Even with all that, he was left with profound hopelessness and emptiness.

His dad, David, hit upon the same conclusion: *"We are merely moving shadows, and all our busy rushing ends in nothing"* (v.6).

This is a fact: the more we put our hope and meaning in the 'things' of this world—family, jobs, sports, financial security, relationships, health—the less genuine, enduring hope we have. Why? Because those are all temporary and fleeting; they are not designed by God to be the ultimate source of hope.

By the way, when God puts those 'things' in your life and you honor them as such, they can bring a great deal of joy, pleasure, contentment, and a filling satisfaction. But the wise person knows that the pursuits of this world are nothing unless God is at the center of them and the reason for them.

David's point is that ultimately there is only one source of hope that can never be diminished or removed: Yahweh. I can hope that Sue never experiences cancer again, but I can't be certain. I can hope the beauty of the marriages of my three/six children will last a lifetime, but I can't be certain. I can hope that my ten grandchildren will embrace Christ, walking with and counting for Him all the days of their lives, but I can't be certain.

What I can be certain of is that Yahweh is faithful and true; that He is good and loving; that God's judgment for my sins has been paid for and covered by the blood of Jesus and I will spend eternity with Him in a place that is beyond description. He is unmovable, unshakable, and unlosable. Put your hope in Him!

God, to whom or what shall I look for hope? I confess: my hope is in You. Amen

THE PITS
April 18

"I waited patiently for the Lord to help me, and He turned to me and heard my cry.
He lifted me out of the pit of despair, out of the mud and the mire.
He set my feet on solid ground and steadied me as I walked along.
He has given me a new song to sing, a hymn of praise to our God."
Psalm 40:1-3

I recently learned the 'rest of the story' about the time one of our church buildings burned to the ground back in 2005. The initial firemen who went up to the 2nd floor to find the source of the fire, found themselves engulfed by smoke. In such cases, the firemen usually retrace the hose they carried with them back to safety. Without going into detail, by the time they escaped, their oxygen was almost depleted. Seconds made the difference between life and death.

Despair is that way. It feels as if someone is standing on your air hose, and you are dangerously close to suffocating and dying; seasons in life of protracted discouragement that lead to profound despair.

Discouragement can occur fairly often: didn't get the job I wanted; a relationship didn't work out; I under-performed on a test or a project; I'm struggling to control my weight. These discouragements come and go in the normal routines of life.

Despair is different by degree and duration: it is a situation that continues to be unresolved despite our best efforts. It drains our hope down to alarming levels. We find ourselves in an emotional quagmire, a deep, dark hole that seems impossible to escape from.

I found these verses in the summer of 1972. The pit was deep, deep, deep. It was debilitating. It lasted for months and months. When you're struggling to stay alive, each second feels like an eternity. I still don't know how I was able to function in my job.

But I do know how I eventually got out: I kept reciting these words and kept calling out to God and hoping beyond hope that He would pull me out—and He pulled me out. Deliverance was months away, but I kept claiming, kept hoping, kept reciting, and kept calling out to the Rescuer.

Since then, I've been singing a song of praise (v.3). And when I've found myself in the pits, I have followed the same pattern, sung the same song—and He has delivered me again and again.

He will for you as well. Keep singing.

God, I call out to You. Lift me out of this pit of despair. Make me more like Jesus in the process.
Amen

DOXOLOGY
April 19

"Praise the Lord, the God of Israel, who lives from everlasting to everlasting. Amen and amen!"
Psalm 41:13

We don't do it much anymore, but when I was a kid growing up in church, we would sing the doxology almost every Sunday:

Praise God from whom all blessings flow;
Praise Him, all creatures here below;
Praise Him above, ye heavenly host:
Praise Father, Son, and Holy Ghost.

The word *doxa* is Greek and means *'glory and splendor'*. The suffix *ology* from the Greek word *logos* meaning *'word or speak.'* A doxology is a short hymn or song of praise.

In this psalm, David is once again besieged by his enemies; even his best friend has turned against him. He calls out for God to rescue him from his adversaries, a common theme in the Book of Psalms. But at the very end, he strikes a different note and breaks into a doxology: *"Praise the Lord, the God of Israel, who lives from everlasting to everlasting. Amen and amen!"*

Sometimes we get caught up in our pleading and forget our praising! The result is that our focus is wrong: we get preoccupied with the difficulty rather than the Deliverer.

The best way to respond to adversity is to break out in praise and worship of our amazing God!! Begin to meditate on His nature and character. If need be, google the attributes of God.

Then begin to praise Him for each one. David selects two: God is a covenant God, and He is an eternal God.

God chose Israel to be His people and established a unilateral covenant with them; that is, He alone bore the responsibility to maintain the arrangement. For those of us who are in Christ, He alone upholds the permanency of the relationship. Jesus said, *"No one can snatch you out of My hand"* (John 10:28). He is faithful when we are not. That my friend, is praiseworthy!!

Yahweh is also eternal. Everything else comes and goes, rises and falls. But only God is the One *"who is, and was, and is to come"* (Revelation 1:8). He's been around, and will be around, for you. David ends his doxology with two amens. Amen means *'so be it'* or *'that's right'* or *'uh-huh!'* God's faithfulness in times of adversity is worth at least a double amen! Shout it!!

God, I do and I will worship and sing to You. You are worthy of my total songs of praise. Amen

STAY THIRSTY, MY FRIEND
April 20

*"As the deer longs for streams of water, so I long for you, O God.
I thirst for God, the living God. When can I go and stand before Him?"*
Psalm 42:1-2

Years ago, friends of mine let me use their lake house on Possum Kingdom Lake for study breaks. Early in the morning, white-tail deer would make their way down to the lake. On the way, they would feed on the corn from a spreader my friend had set up. I loved sitting out on the porch watching them move quietly, ears twitching and noses in the air making sure all was safe.

Deer are beautiful creatures, aren't they? So nimble, so timid, yet strong and fast. They need as much as 5 quarts of water a day to function properly. Humans need just 2 quarts. That means deer are looking for or hanging out around water much of the day, particularly in warm weather. If they don't find water, they're in trouble.

The psalmist draws a parallel between the deer and our souls. There is much confusion about the human soul. The Hebrew word is *nephesh*. It refers to the life principle that makes us alive; a being. In Genesis 2:7 God breathes life (*nephesh*) into Adam. We don't have a soul; we ARE a soul.

Our soul has appetites and needs that require attention: we need love, we need relationship, we need purpose. Our greatest need is for the One who breathed life into us.

But in our brokenness, we try to satisfy the need with everything but Him: success, wealth, approval, activity, pleasure, comfort, etc. These don't really satisfy our down deep soul thirst.

The psalmist has recognized just that. Only time with Yahweh will quench the thirst. Not one little sip on Sunday, but a daily and continuous lapping from His stream—the only water that really refreshes.

One day Jesus was chatting up a woman who had tried to satisfy her soul thirst with everything but. His words to her speak to us: *"Anyone who drinks this water will soon become thirsty again. But those who drink the water I give will never be thirsty again. It becomes a fresh, bubbling spring within them, giving them eternal life"* (John 4:13–14).

Are you thirsty for God? Searching for His refreshment throughout the day? If not, pray for it. This is a request God is just waiting to answer! Begin each day in His word. You'll get thirsty.

Stay thirsty, my friend!

God, make me thirsty for YOU and Your word. Hear my cry. Amen

SMILE!

"O my soul, why be so gloomy and discouraged? Trust in God! I shall again praise Him for His wondrous help; He will make me smile again, for He is my God!"
Psalm 43:5 (LB)

Have you ever heard the adage: "It takes more muscles to frown than to smile"? Turns out that the science is confusing on this. One researcher found it takes 43 muscles to frown and only 17 to smile. Another found it took 12 to frown and 11 to smile. Bound up in this notion is the definition of a smile and a frown. I found at least eight different findings by researchers, leading me to conclude that the adage is probably not true.

What is true is how difficult it is to smile when life has become painful and discouraging.

There is no superscription at the beginning of this psalm and some scholars believe that Psalm 42 and Psalm 43 were, at one point, the same psalm. Regardless, in both psalms, the psalmist is crying out to God about how oppressed he is, how painful his life is, how distant he feels from God. He sheds tears, feels heartbroken, and is grief-stricken. He continues to mention how discouraged he is.

There is nothing like adversity to get us in touch with our real needs: job loss, sickness, loss of loved ones, family turmoil, or constant anxiety. The psalmist is in trouble and is well aware of his need. It makes him thirsty for God because he knows that only God can help him.

He commences to self-talk to get his mind off of his feelings and on to the truth.

There was a popular song that had the phrase, "I know what I was feeling, but what was I thinking?" The songwriter was lamenting how his feelings were overriding his reason and the result was not good. Our feelings are such poor indicators of the truth. Pay too much attention to them and you'll get in real trouble.

Look beyond the circumstance, look beyond your emotions, and focus on the truth. Put your hope in Jesus: He will get you through. Put your trust in Jesus: He has been and will be faithful. Praise Jesus: He is worthy of your worship because He created you and redeemed you.

Follow the psalmist's lead: have a little talk with yourself. Remind yourself of how great your God is. Praise Him for His faithfulness and goodness in your life. He will make you smile again for HE is your God!

O God, get my eyes off my problems and on to You. You are my God—make me smile again. Amen

CREDIT

April 22

"Only by Your power can we push back our enemies;
only in Your name can we trample our foes."

Psalm 44:5

When Sue was diagnosed with an aggressive form of breast cancer, we were devastated. Sue's internal constitution has always been easily disrupted. We could be watching television and out of nowhere, she would say, "I think I'm going to throw up!" So that Thursday morning when the doctor told us she would have to go through chemotherapy and radiation, we imagined six straight months of toilet-hugging misery. And then, of course, there were the 'what ifs' that began to flood our minds and bring fear into our hearts. It took a few days, but we regrouped and faced the enemy head-on.

Prayer was our first weapon. We called out to God for strength, for courage, and of course, for healing. We asked for a special demonstration of His grace that would heal her without going through the chemotherapy and the radiation therapy. But once the lumpectomy was done, it was clear that those two treatments were unavoidable. It was now our prayer that His common grace, working through doctors and medicine, would be the instrument of His healing.

What is obvious from reading the latter part of the psalm is that Israel is in serious trouble. They are being assailed by an enemy and it appears that Yahweh is asleep at the switch—*"Wake up, O Lord! Why do you sleep? Get up! Why do you look the other way? Why do you ignore our suffering and oppression?"* (vv.23-24).

I have to admit that in those early days of Sue's diagnosis, similar thoughts and feelings crept into my heart and mind. We were up against an enemy that we felt absolutely powerless against.

The first half of the psalm is a reflection on Israel's history; how God had defeated their enemies as they moved in and possessed the Promised Land—and gives credit where credit is due: *"They did not conquer the land with their swords; it was not their own strong arm that gave them victory"* (v.3). And then he states the obvious: *"Only by Your power can we push back our enemies; only in Your name can we trample our foes"* (v.5).

What enemy are you up against? Do you feel like God is not attentive to your plight? Give credit to Him for times past when He has strengthened you, and by faith, wait for the strength and courage to endure and triumph.

God, hear my cry! I can't do this on my own. Grant me victory over this foe. Amen

ENTITLEMENT
April 23

"We collapse in the dust, lying face down in the dirt."
Psalm 44:5

One of the growing cancers in our American culture is the idea of entitlement: the attitude that we are entitled to a growing list of things; that it's our right to have something or be treated a certain way. Recall that powerful phrase offered in the Declaration of Independence: "We hold these truths to be self-evident, that all men are created equal, that they are endowed by their Creator with certain unalienable Rights, that among these are Life, Liberty and the pursuit of Happiness." The framers of the Constitution identified those rights in the Bill of Rights, among them religious freedom and freedom of speech. Sadly, according to some, those unalienable rights include free college education, free sex changes, and even free cell phones! Entitlement is a cancer.

If we're not careful, this cancer creeps into our relationship with God. When adversity enters our lives, we are likely to make the claim, "Wait a minute God! I don't deserve this. I've loved You, served You, testified to Your power, I've been faithful to You. What's the deal?"

Psalm 44 has two parts to it: in the first, the psalmist is bragging about how God defeated Israel's enemies when they moved into the Promised Land (vv.1-8); in the second, the psalmist is complaining that God has abandoned them (vv.9-26). Apparently, Israel was going through a series of military defeats and the enemy was wreaking havoc on them. The psalmist is beside himself pleading for God to intervene. His main point: we don't deserve this ordeal.

When I begin to complain about God's treatment of me, such protests reveal a sense of entitlement; that I have a right to be treated a certain way. Essentially, I'm telling God He's making a big mistake here and He needs to wake up and do what I think is right.

God doesn't owe us anything good. What we deserve is His judgment! It's only by His grace that we experience or have anything positive in our lives. That being true, gratitude should always be our baseline: *"Be thankful in all circumstances, for this is God's will for you who belong to Christ Jesus"* (1 Thessalonians 5:18).

It's ok to call for God to hear and answer: *"Rise up! Help us! Ransom us because of your unfailing love"* (v.6). But don't appeal based on what you think you deserve; appeal based on His love and mercy. If done well, it will be well with your soul no matter how He responds.

O God, hear my prayer. I don't deserve Your grace and mercy, but I'm counting on it! Amen

JIT
April 24

"God is our refuge and strength, a very present help in trouble."
Psalm 46:1 (NASB)

You probably recognize the title, JIT. It stands for Just In Time. JIT is an inventory management strategy that reduces the cost of storing products that are to be sold. Before JIT, companies would order goods from the manufacturer and store them in a warehouse until sold. Buying the land, building the warehouse, staffing the warehouse, etc. added a considerable amount to the cost of the product. With the advent of JIT, companies have reduced their need for warehousing considerably by moving the product straight from the manufacturer to the customer, Just In Time for its usage.

I love this opening verse to Psalm 46. It reminds me that we don't have to wait for the delivery of God's help in times of trouble. Whenever there is a need, God delivers in the moment, JIT. The key is looking to Yahweh for the help we need.

In times of trial, humans always look to something or someone for help. The humanist will look to himself and dig a little deeper, try a little harder, and dive into the self-help section of B&N.

The materialist will look to acquisition, go shopping, and count on the dopamine rush to relieve the fear and stress. The alcoholic will look to the bottle, drink a little more, and hope that it will give him the courage to get through. The love addict will look to her relationships and depend on friendships, romance, or sex to get her through.

The psalmist has an infinitely better idea: look to the One who is more powerful, more wise, and more loving than anyone or anything in creation. God is always near; always ready to help the believer. We don't have to wait for Him to show up or His power to kick in—He's with us and in us right now.

He will help. His help may not be what we desire, but it's always what we need. Always. Look to Him for comfort, for courage, for strength, for peace, for hope. He's ready. Always.

And whatever you may need tomorrow, or next month, or next year—He'll be there with you and for you with the help you need—Just In Time!

Yahweh, thank You for being the Ever-Present God. I love You and trust You! Amen

BE STILL

April 25

"Be still, and know that I am God!
I will be honored by every nation. I will be honored throughout the world."

Psalm 46:10

In an emergency, very few people can keep their heads on straight. Most people run around like chickens with their heads cut off (chickens actually do that!) My eldest son is a fireman. The remarkable thing about first responders is that they run toward danger while everyone else runs away from it. When he arrives at a fire, he dons his gear, including an oxygen tank and a helmet outfitted with communication equipment. The comms are there so that the fireman on the outside can give him direction and warn him of danger he can't see or know.

Psalm 46 is about the psalmist's confidence in the power of God, particularly in times of trouble and chaos. You must read this whole psalm! There are so many incredible verses about God's power: *"So we will not fear when earthquakes come and the mountains crumble into the sea."* (v.2), *The nations are in chaos, and their kingdoms crumble! God's voice thunders, and the earth melts! The Lord of Heaven's Armies is here among us; the God of Israel is our fortress"* (vv.6-7).

Up to this point, the song has been in the 3rd person, but now God speaks up for Himself: "STOP! BE STILL!" It's like He's clapping His hands trying to get their attention. His message is short and sweet: "Remember who I am! Remember what I'm about! I am The Almighty God. I brought everything that is into existence just by the power of My voice! No power can begin to match Mine. Nations bow to MY will. The whole earth is full of MY glory. Before you do anything else, get that straight."

Keeping that straight is our problem. In times of adversity, too often our first move is to get busy to protect or provide or solve or scurry. That is a recipe for disaster, anxiety, and fear.

Our first move should and must always be to stop, acknowledge, and be in awe of Yahweh. Being in awe prompts worship, and worship prepares us for the battle like nothing else.

There is much to be done after that, yes. But nothing to be done before that.

Are you anxious and fearful? Under attack? Scurrying around trying to fix the problem? Stop. Breathe. Get your comms on and listen, be still, and sense the power of our God. Remember that He is Yahweh, maker of heaven and earth. And worship Him.

Yahweh, teach me to be still—and know that You are God! Amen

RECLAIMING
April 26

"For the choir director: A psalm of the descendants of Korah."
The superscription to Psalm 47

The gospel changes people. A guy in my past was pretty rough: high school dropout, motorcycle gang, tattoos before they were in vogue, spicy language—big body and big personality. But when he met Jesus, his life was radically changed. He would read the Bible I gave him and ask all kinds of questions. Once he said, "I was reading in 1st Philothinos the other day…". Of course, there is no 1st Philothinos, but that didn't matter. He was hungry for God and His word and the Spirit was transforming him inside out.

You'll notice that this and the last few psalms (12 overall) were attributed to the sons of Korah. *Sons* can, and does here, mean descendants. Korah was an infamous character who, 100s of years prior, led a revolt against Moses (and therefore God) while Israel was in the wilderness (Numbers 16). The end result is that the earth opened up and swallowed him! Yikes!! Be mindful of that when grumbling against church leaders!

Tracing Korah's descendants is an interesting study. By the time of David, three of Korah's descendants, all brothers, had risen to the high position of being keepers of the entrance to the Tabernacle and choir leaders to the congregation of God. One, Asaph, became even more prominent in writing and leading the songs of Israel. Can you imagine that? The descendants of a wicked, rebellious scoundrel, who sowed seeds of discontent amongst the congregation and got swallowed up by the earth---actually ascended to one of the highest positions possible!

Here's my point: regardless of the darkness of your family's history or even your own past, your future is as bright as the promises of God. Our God is a kind and compassionate God, abounding in loving kindness. No matter how messed up your past is, God is ready to reclaim your future! *"Do not remember the past events, pay no attention to things of old. Look, I am about to do something new; even now it is coming. Do you not see it? Indeed, I will make a way in the wilderness, rivers in the desert"* (Isaiah 43:18-19; CSV).

You do not have to be chained or held back by what has happened in your past. There are consequences of errant choices, yes. But we can learn from them and count on God to use them in our lives. And we can live in the present with hope for a bright, incredible future because of His amazing grace through Jesus! God is still in the reclamation business!

Jesus, I am so grateful that You saved me. Keep the reclamation job going! Amen

THE HAPPY CLAPPIES
April 27

"Come, everyone! Clap your hands! Shout to God with joyful praise!
For the Lord Most High is awesome. He is the great King of all the earth."
Psalm 47:1-2

I love corporate worship! Singing amongst the congregation of God gets me pumped. Sometimes I am overcome with God's goodness and grace, and I weep. Sometimes I'm overwhelmed with His presence and bow in reverent awe. Sometimes my body sways with the music—worship is supposed to be a 'full body experience'! Sometimes the words deserve some clapping because they are so powerful. I call it the happy clappies. Yesterday we sang *"Great Are You Lord"* by All Sons and Daughters. There's a place where the music builds and we sing:

> *All the earth will shout Your praise, our hearts will cry,*
> *these bones will sing—Great are You, Lord!*

I couldn't help but clap loudly at that magnificent truth! That's biblical. Clapping and applause is a form of worship seen throughout the Bible. Even the trees clap in praise to God (Isaiah 55:12)! The Hebrew word for clap is *taqa*, appearing 65 times in Scripture. It means to '*clatter, clap or strike*'. We're instructed to clap our hands for God and lift our voices in praise to Him.

Nothing irritates more than to be in a worship service and watch as folks who **SAY** they love God stand like mute statues, hands at their sides instead of exuberantly making joyful praise to God. Occasionally I'll ask why that is the case. Their response: "That's just not who I am."

Well, let me say this—it ain't about them! It's about the God who loves them so much He crawled up on an old rugged cross to save them. It's about the gratitude and praise that **WILL** flow out of a redeemed heart into our bodies and onto our lips. It's about joining the saints who have gone before us, who have joined the choirs of angels around the throne singing, *"Holy, Holy, Holy is the Lord God Almighty—who was and is and is to come!"* (Revelation 4:8).

We will shout and cheer on our favorite team, right? We will clap for a wonderful performer, right? But we won't clap and shout for the One who created us and redeemed us and welcomed us into His family? Rubbish!!

He is the Lord Most High! He is the great King of all the earth. He's certainly worthy of more than slightly moving lips and limp arms. Get over yourself and get the happy clappies! You'll settle into it and be glad.

God, You are worth my unrestrained praise and worship. I love You. Amen

ENTHRONED
April 28

"For God is the King over all the earth. Praise Him with a psalm.
God reigns above the nations, sitting on His holy throne."
Psalm 47:7-8

Henry VIII, who ruled England from 1509-1547, was a brilliant and ruthless king. Like all monarchs, his highest priority was to keep his power and stay on his throne. Many a king before and after him was deposed, then either deported or executed. His second priority was to extend his rule by producing a son who would be the future king. In that quest, he married six times, doing all he could to maintain his throne and legacy.

Psalm 47 is what is called an 'enthronement' psalm. The throne was the place of power. These kinds of psalms focus on the fact that Yahweh is the ultimate, sovereign ruler over all the earth, enthroned over all creation. A common theme in the Psalms is how Yahweh defeated Pharaoh and Egypt to free the Hebrew slaves. The psalmists also often reference God's provision in the wilderness those 40 years, and most importantly, His defeat of the nations who were in the Promised Land so that Israel could possess it. This psalmist wanted to make clear who was on the throne and wielding power through all of that.

That was then, over 3,500 years ago. But as in most Scripture, there is not only the past at play, but also the present and future as well.

Let's talk about the present. There are many powerful nations in our world. Some, like the U.S., Russia, and China are superpowers. Collectively, they possess enough nuclear power to kill nearly every human on earth. Their financial, technological, and industrial power dominate the global economy. All of this and more causes heightened anxiety in much of the world. Believers need to remind ourselves that no nation, the U.S. included, is more powerful than God. In fact, all the nations together are impotent in the face of the sovereign God, Yahweh.

And at the end of the age, all nations and rulers will kneel before Him to be held accountable for how they used or abused the power that He gave them. That includes Putin, Xi, Trump, and Biden. Every knee will bow, and every tongue will confess that Jesus is King, Ruler, and Sovereign (Philippians 2:6-11).

Believers can take heart and be encouraged and comforted by this truth during trying times. Circumstances are not random and chaotic. Yahweh is still on His throne. He's still in control. Rest in that knowledge. *"God is the King over all the earth!"*

God, I praise You for Your power and authority. As Your subject, I submit to and trust You. Amen

PRIDE
April 29

"They trust in their wealth and boast of great riches."
Psalm 49:6

I don't consider myself wealthy, but in comparison to most of the rest of the world, I guess I am. The net worth (the totality of money & house, & other possessions) for the average adult worldwide is about $7,000. In the U.S. it's about $70,000.

There is a certain pride that creeps into the soul of someone with money. Subtly, and sometimes imperceptibly, those who are wealthy perceive themselves, not just better off, but better. Sadly, as I examine my own heart this day, I confess that I have the disease that plagues the wealthy.

I do have compassion for the poor. I launched a whole ministry at my church, built a million-dollar building to house it, and recruited thousands of people to fund it and serve in it. Sue & I drive down a street in our town known for day workers who are hoping to get hired for a few hours, giving away food, blankets, and gift cards. I give money to the down-and-outs on the corners. Maybe you do as well.

But I am ashamed of the thoughts that sometimes come to me from the deep, dark recesses of my soul: "Why didn't you buy a less expensive car, so you'd have food?" "Why didn't you study in school so you'd have a better job?" "I'll bet you have a nice tv at home." "Why in the world don't you save some money rather than live paycheck to paycheck and find yourself in this predicament?"

That is nothing but deplorable, wicked pride speaking. Truth is, I didn't choose what country I was born in, choose my parents, choose my I.Q., choose the schools I went to, choose my personality, or choose much of anything else that delivered my wealth to me. Yet I've placed myself in a superior position. I survey my wealth with the attitude: "Look what I, I have done."

There's really nowhere to hide here. Only to confess. Only to repent. Only to call on the Spirit in me to keep transforming me to be more like Jesus.

Join me.

O God, I am a prideful person. Forgive me and change me from the inside out. Enable me to be aware of this pride when it creeps in and realize all I have is from You. Amen

BANKRUPTCY
April 30

"Yet they cannot redeem themselves from death by paying a ransom to God.
Redemption does not come so easily, for no one can ever pay enough."
Psalm 49:7-8

The man I worked for in the oil business was a multi-millionaire and because of his money, thought he was better than most and good enough to please God and get into heaven.

Psalm 49 is a polemic against the false pride and security that wealth brings. You may not think of yourself as wealthy, but compared to most, you likely are. There is something about money that causes false expectations: that it insulates us from trial or tragedy and lifts us above the fray and frailty of more common folk. To some extent that is true. The wealthy have access to excellent healthcare and often are on a 1st name basis with their doctors, while many poor are left to use hospital emergency rooms for their healthcare needs, attended to by whoever is on duty at the time. The poor are more susceptible to a full range of diseases than the wealthy. The average lifespan difference between wealthy and poor in America is about 15 years. However, the psalmist points out that your money can't insulate you from tragedy and it can't protect you from heartache.

Money also creates the expectation of immortality. The really wealthy even have businesses and estates that they think will carry their names into the future (vv.11-12). Your wealth means nothing to death. It will come to you, and when it does, you won't be able to bargain with God, no matter how wealthy you are. Why? Because in God's economy, rightness is the currency, and we have none of it; we are totally bankrupt. We have nothing of value to offer that would compel God to accept us. The great prophet Isaiah put it like this: *"All our righteousness is like filthy menstrual rags"* (64:6) to God. The apostle Paul affirmed that assessment: *"There is no one righteous, not even one"* (Philippians 3:10).

We can't buy our redemption because Jesus already purchased it: *"For Christ also died for sins once for all, the just for the unjust, so that He might bring us to God"* (1 Peter 3:18). To receive this rightness, right standing with God, we must first admit we are morally bankrupt. Pride rejects that notion, but humility is the only way forward. Then we must believe that Jesus alone provides the only righteousness God accepts. He alone can provide redemption, secured by His death, burial, and resurrection. If you have never confessed your bankruptcy, now is the time. There is no promise of tomorrow. Place your faith in Him alone and become truly—wealthy!

Jesus, if I never have, I do now confess my moral bankruptcy, and by faith, claim the redemption You purchased for me on the cross. Thank You!! Amen

ME TOO!

May 1

*"For the choir director: A psalm of David, regarding the time Nathan the prophet
came to him after David had committed adultery with Bathsheba."*
The superscription to Psalm 51

Few psalms are as well-known and loved as the 51st. The reason? Anyone who reads it identifies with David in some way. As we read his blunt confession, there is something in us that cries out: 'Me too!'

A little background is helpful. By this point, David has transitioned from shepherd to king. His heart for God has become distracted, possibly even calloused. This is dangerous territory for anyone, particularly one of God's leaders. A one-sentence history is in the superscription above. You can read the full account in 2 Samuel 11 & 12. It's high drama! In summary, from his palace David notices a beautiful woman bathing one day—men are definitely stimulated by visuals (hence pornography), and he wants her. As king, he rules over all subjects and commands her to come to him (notice the illegitimate use of power). They sleep together and Bathsheba gets pregnant. Because she is married, the problem is compounded.

David tries elaborate schemes to cover it up, but that NEVER works. Eventually, he has her husband, Uriah, killed. No one knows about it except his henchman, Joab. Whew—problem solved, right? Not right. **Private sin never stays private**. Jesus warned, *"Whatever you have said in the dark will be heard in the light, and what you have whispered behind closed doors will be shouted from the housetops for all to hear!"* (Luke 12:3).

Sin always has consequences. First and foremost, God sees and God knows. He is a just God and He never turns a blind eye. So God sends His prophet, Nathan, to David to confront him with his sin.

Psalm 51 is the result. David is guilty of lust, adultery, lying, coveting, and even murder. Awful, right? How could someone who knew and loved God do something like that? But here's the Me Too moment: I'm not any better than David. Same with you. If you doubt that, here's what Jesus said: *"I say, if you are even angry with someone, you are subject to judgment! I say, anyone who even looks at a woman with lust has already committed adultery with her in his heart"* (Matthew 5: 22, 28).

Psalm 51 is a roadmap for sinners: it shows us the way to move from guilty to forgiven, from fear to peace, and from chains to freedom.

God, help me to see the smugness I have about my own sin. Speak to my heart. Amen

THUMBS UP!

May 2

"Have mercy on me, O God, because of Your unfailing love.
Because of Your great compassion, blot out the stain of my sins."

Psalm 51:1

In Ancient Rome, gladiators would fight in the Coliseum, usually to the death. Once it became apparent one of the fighters was defeated and helpless, the victor would look to the crowd, and eventually to an official, as to whether to grant mercy or finish him off. If they thought the defeated gladiator fought valiantly, sometimes they'd hold their thumbs up, and mercy was granted. Thumbs down and—well, you know.

Upon being confronted with his sin, David's first step was and is always the best step: he began pleading for God's mercy. God is a just God, and as such, demands justice for violating His moral standard. God calls this violation sin. But fortunately, He is also a merciful God, so He is ready to withhold His judgment when rightly called upon. Gaining mercy instead of judgment for his sin is certainly David's intention.

Unlike the gladiator scenario, God's mercy is not based on how well we perform or on any other merit, it is based on God's *chesed*: the Hebrew word for *covenant love, lovingkindness, unfailing love*. If the person calling for mercy is in a covenant relationship with God through faith in Jesus, then they are extended mercy when it is honestly appealed for. I have called and pled for God's mercy many times—and He has granted it, not because I deserve it, but because, of my faith and trust in Jesus alone. My faith makes me His child (John 1:12) As you know, loving parents love to extend mercy.

Notice that David asks for mercy, not because He deserves it, but because God is loving and merciful: *"Have mercy on me, O God, because of your unfailing love."* We don't deserve mercy. We appeal for mercy without any justification for it.

When we sin, our first/best response always is to confess it as sin. Don't ignore it, justify it, deflect it, make an excuse, blame someone else— deal with it properly and own up to it. Once you have humbled yourself and confessed your sin, then you're in a position to appeal for God's mercy.

"The sacrifice you desire is a broken spirit. You will not reject a broken and repentant heart, O God" (v.17). Fortunately, the honest appeal for mercy always brings a thumbs up!

God, I pledge to deal with my sin properly—confess it honestly and humbly. I'm so grateful You pledge to grant mercy when I do. Amen

FILTHY

May 3

"Blot out the stain of my sins. Wash me clean from my guilt.
Purify me from my sin."
Psalm 51:1b-2

Our kids had a penchant for getting filthy dirty when they played in the yard, climbed trees, and played in the drainage ditches. When they'd come in, it was nearly impossible to get all the dirt off. The dirt would even be in the itty-bitty lines in their necks—it looked like a dirt necklace!

Notice the three verbs David uses in quick succession: blot, clean, & purify. David knows that sin is a wretched thing in God's eyes. He knows that it has made him filthy. He wants it to be washed away. He wants to be—clean. He restates this desperate desire in v.7, *"Purify me from my sins, and I will be clean; wash me, and I will be whiter than snow."*

There is something about being immoral that leaves a human feeling dirty. It's universal. Not just big immoral lapses like David's—we lapse morally many, many times a day.

Let's say you only lapsed morally 3 times a day; i.e., only 3 times a day you said something unkind, did something selfish or thought something you know was wrong. Three times a day—you'd be a saint! Multiply that by 365 days. Then multiply that number by your age. That would be over 76,000 sins for me! And that's only 3 moral lapses a day. Honestly, there are times when I feel like I've lapsed 76,000 in one day! Maybe now you get the magnitude of our sinfulness, our filthiness. We are unclean and we know it.

We may try to medicate it away with pills or drink. We may try to ignore it by engaging in distractions: shopping, recreation, travel, entertainment. We may try to rationalize it by deciding it's not that bad. But none of that will bring the cleansing that all humans long for. Our own efforts to be clean just cover up the dirt.

When I was a kid, I would come in after an evening of playing outside, dirty from head to toe. Mom would tell me to go take a bath, put on my pajamas, and get in bed. I must confess to you that many times I did two out of the three!

You may look clean on the outside, but do you know how to get clean on the inside? It begins with what we talked about yesterday: confession. Here's the Christian's bar of soap: *"If we confess our sins, He is faithful and just to forgive us our sins, and to cleanse us from all unrighteousness"* (1 John 1:9).

God, thank You for providing a way for me to get CLEAN!! Thank You, Jesus!! Amen

INSIDE OUT

May 4

"Create in me a clean heart, O God. Renew a loyal spirit within me."
Psalm 51:10

When I was a kid, every summer my dad put my brother and me in the yard to pick weeds. I hated it; I loathed it. To get my assigned patch done quickly, I would grab the top of the weed and pull, usually leaving the root. Soon it was back. To do it properly I needed to use a "special tool" that would get at the root. Getting the root out was the key to getting rid of the weed.

Here's the thing about sinful activity: it won't change until there is a heart change; until it's rooted out of the heart. We can get all religious and go about this completely backward by trying to change exterior issues without addressing the critical, inner issues: "I'm not going to overeat anymore; not going to over-drink anymore; not going to see her anymore; not going to—whatever anymore." That's going after the behavior without going after the cause.

David understood this. In the midst of his contrition, he called out for God to change him from the inside out. He recognized it took something he didn't have and couldn't do. His first word here is what? *"Create."* He knows that only God can perform the necessary miracle of creation.

The believer must realize that overcoming sin habits is an inside-out process; the root of the sin habit must be removed. The 'special tool' I mentioned earlier is the word of God in conjunction with the Spirit of God. Memorizing and meditating on God's word has a mysterious and wonderful transforming effect: *"Do not be conformed to this age, but be transformed by the renewing of your mind, so that you may discern what is the good, pleasing, and perfect will of God"* (Romans 12:1-2). Renewing the mind means changing how we see, perceive, and think.

The indwelling Spirit provides the power to overcome: *"The Spirit of Him who raised Jesus from the dead lives in you"* (Romans 8:11). The same Spirit who had the power to raise Jesus from the dead is resident in YOU!

Get into the word and get the word into you. Ask the Spirit to take control of your life in every way; to change your desires and make you more like Jesus. As the inside of you changes, so will the outside. Real, lasting change happens from the inside out.

God, thank You for Your word and Your Spirit. As I invest and surrender, change me from the inside out. Amen

RESTORATION
May 5

"Restore to me the joy of Your salvation."
Psalm 51:12

I have done a good deal of counseling in my ministry. So many that I have tried to help struggle with various levels of anxiety or depression. I share what has been true in my own life, and what is revealed in Scripture: much of our inner struggle comes from unconfessed sin. All sin, large or small, is abhorrent to Yahweh. Without Jesus, humans will suffer His eternal and just wrath for the tiniest little moral flaw. Each sin carries with it a weight that burdens us. We may try to ignore it away, drink it away, cover it with comforts or experiences, but it's still there. There is only one way to get the burden lifted.

Fortunately, God has provided what is necessary for us to dump the gloom that settles over us. Psalm 51 is a roadmap for sinners: it shows us the way to move from guilty to forgiven, from fear to peace, from chains to freedom, from gloom to joy.

David has committed adultery, deceit, and murder. Once confronted with His sin, he knows the only way out of his guilt is not to go make excuses or empty promises. God is looking for much, much more. And frankly, so is David. David doesn't just want to alleviate his feelings of guilt, he wants to sense the joy that comes with knowing he has pleased his Creator.

It's a characteristic of love that you want to please the ones you love. The more you love them, the more you want to please them. It may mean sacrifice or hardship for you, but the payoff is the joy you feel when you see you've pleased them.

When we confess our sin, we see it for what it is and what it costs. That results in brokenness. Brokenness softens our hearts so that we want to turn away from that sin (repentance) and live differently. We call on Him to change us from the inside out so that we will live in a way that pleases Him. And THAT, my friend, is where true and lasting joy is found. It is meant to be continuous and overflowing. Jesus put it this way: *"Your joy will overflow! No one can rob you of that joy!"* (John 15:11; 16:22).

But you can't get there without beginning at the right place: confession. Start that path; begin the honest conversation and discover the unspeakable joy that awaits you.

Jesus, thank You for being the sacrifice the covers my sin. By Your Spirit, enable me to see and confess my sin that I might fully enter into Your joy. Amen

CLEAN!

May 6

"You do not desire a sacrifice, or I would offer one. You do not want a burnt offering.
The sacrifice You desire is a broken spirit.
You will not reject a broken and repentant heart, O God."
Psalm 51:16-17

There is an eternity of difference between the soul and the body. One is physical, the other is the element of life itself. Every human body has a soul until it dies. The body ceases to exist eventually, but soul continues.

There's another difference: the body can get clean by taking a shower or bath with a generous lathering of soap. The soul can't be cleansed that way. When we feel grimy on the inside, it takes a special something to feel clean again.

We come to the end of this remarkable admission of David about his awful and deplorable actions with Bathsheba and her husband, Uriah. He's needing a soul-cleansing and he knows how to get it.

David makes a very unusual statement for a Hebrew well versed in the sacrificial law. The Mosaic Law stipulated that there should be five different kinds of sacrifices practiced regularly, some daily. Without getting into the gory detail, there were occasions where the blood was so deep in the tabernacle and later the Temple, that it came up to the knees of the priests making the sacrifices. That's a lot of blood; a lot of sacrifices.

Fundamental to the practice of sacrifice is the concept of atonement where the person confesses: 'I know I'm guilty, I deserve death, but I offer this animal to die in my place.' Tragically, some ancient cultures even sacrificed humans to appeal to their god to obtain soul cleansing.

Created in the image of the morally perfect God, all humans instinctively know we aren't morally perfect, despite our desire to be so. We sense that some form of atonement must be made. The Hebrew sacrificial law provided the process. This is why it is so unusual for David to make this statement: "*You do not desire a sacrifice, or I would offer one*" (v.16). The sacrifice was to be an outward expression of an inward realization: "I am guilty, and I am broken about it." This is what God is after when we sin—brokenness and repentance.

Jesus made the ultimate and final sacrifice on the cross so that animal sacrifices are no longer necessary!! But God is still after brokenness and repentance.

You want to get rid of the moral dirt on your soul? Accept the reality that your sins, large and small, required Jesus to pay for them with His blood—and let it break you. Then claim the cleansing that only He provides. Nothing else will make us clean.

Jesus, thank You for being the Lamb of God who took away the penalty and awfulness of my sin. By faith, I accept the cleansing that You provided on the cross. Amen

FOOL'S GOLD
May 7

"Only fools say in their hearts, 'There is no God.'"
Psalm 53:1

There are places around the U.S. that (for a fee) let you look for, pan for gold. During the 20th century, there was a fair amount of interest in trying to find gold (Au). Usually what they found was not Au, but FeS2, Pyrite—Fool's Gold. Why that name? Thinking they've found something valuable, they discover (after taking it to an expert) their time and money were foolishly wasted.

This verse (Psalm 53:1) is identical to Psalm 14:1. It is an indictment by God Himself, now explicitly made twice in the Psalms. In our Psalm 14 devotional, we examined the prospect of the practical atheist; i.e., the person who claims to be a Christ-follower but whose daily life is lived without much regard for Him—the practical atheist.

But there is another kind of atheist: the one whose pride is so pervasive they cannot see the overwhelming evidence for Yahweh. God calls them fools. It doesn't mean they're not smart. In fact, many are brilliant. It just means that they fail to apply their intelligence properly from God's perspective.

There is more than enough data in nature, humanity, and the cosmos to make a logical case for Yahweh. So much so, it takes more faith to believe in a godless universe than one with God. As Timothy Keller says, "You cannot doubt Belief A, except from a position of faith in Belief B." In other words, to resist faith in Yahweh, you must have faith in something/someone else.

In my interaction with 100s of atheists/agnostics through the years, only a handful have possessed the intellectual honesty to examine the evidence on both sides with equal vigor. When they do, their previously held notions are rocked. Sadly, very few atheists have the integrity to actually examine the data. They will give lots of reasons. But from my experience, there is one underlying reason for their atheism: they reject Yahweh's moral absolute authority over their lives; they want to be God, not Him.

To be sure, every human struggles with this malady—we all think we know better than God! It's called sin. It began when our 1st parents decided they knew best and disobeyed God, thrusting all creation into this awful brokenness. The wise seek the cure that can only come from Yahweh. The fool seeks his own solution. Underneath it all is their insistence that they are God; that they are the sole determiner of what is best for them.

Sad—and foolish. Do you know an atheist? Stop right now and pray God will open their eyes to the truth. *Amen*

THREATS AND FEAR

May 8

"Come with great power, O God, and rescue me! Defend me with Your might.
Listen to my prayer, O God. Pay attention to my plea."

Psalm 54:1-2

One of the scariest scenes in any movie is in Jurassic Park 1. Two children are in the commercial kitchen while a velociraptor is trying to eat them. They kept trying to find places to hide from it, and more than once I thought they were done for.

David is feeling threatened and scared. Someone has told King Saul where he is hiding. This is happening between the time David was chosen by God to be king and when he actually was installed as king. During the interim, King Saul was hunting him down and trying to kill him. No wonder he felt threatened and afraid!!

David did what we should do when we feel threatened and afraid: he appealed to Yahweh for help.

Notice the verbs David spits out in quick succession: come, rescue, defend, listen, pay attention. Do you get the idea that David felt a sense of urgency? Notice too why David appeals to God: He is powerful; He is mighty; He is God! As it turns out, God did deliver David from the hands of Saul—He had a greater purpose in mind for David.

Are you feeling threatened and afraid? There is really only one place to go, and that is to Jesus. Remember He said, *"Come to me, all of you who are weary and carry heavy burdens, and I will give you rest"* (Matthew 11:28). Rest is the idea of relief from the strain; a soul-peace in the midst of the fray.

Call out to Him. Keep calling out to Him. Ask Him to show you the purpose of the threat. What is He working to accomplish in you and through you? Trust Him to deliver you from the fear: *"Cast all your cares and burdens on Him because He cares for you"* (1Peter 5:7).

Feeling threatened and afraid is an ordinary human response. Responding with prayer and faith is extra-ordinary.

He is powerful. He is mighty. He is God!

God, when I feel threatened and afraid, I will call out to You. I pray You will show me Your purpose in the threat and that I will count on You to deliver me from fear. Amen

IN THE CAVE

May 9

"But when I am afraid, I will put my trust in You. I praise God for what He has promised. I trust in God, so why should I be afraid? What can mere mortals do to me?"

Psalm 56: 3-4

The background on this psalm is very, very intriguing. David has just been warned by his best friend, Jonathan, that King Saul intends to kill him. He runs away to the Philistines, Israel's archenemy. He realizes his mistake and acts insane in order to avoid imprisonment or worse. He then finds a cave to hide in isolation (1 Samuel 20-22). He was alone and being hunted by multiple enemies.

There is something about trial and adversity that causes a sense of isolation, of loneliness. Others may attempt to encourage, but still, there is the lingering sense that we are alone to deal with our problems.

And there is some truth in that. There's an old song that puts it this way: "You gotta walk that lonesome valley, You gotta walk it by yourself, Nobody here can walk it for you, You gotta walk it by yourself."

The fear caused by adversity hides away in a cave deep in the recesses of our souls. We can keep busy, entertain ourselves, and surround ourselves with people, but when the head hits the pillow and the lights are turned out, we are left to face the fear on our own.

It is in that aloneness that we come face-to-face with our faith. We will reach out to God or we won't. If we don't reach out, there is no way to escape the aloneness. But if we do, we affirm God's help as David does in this psalm: *"When I'm afraid, I will put my trust in God; I will not fear what threatens my life; I will choose to worship Him because He is faithful."*

In this particular season of my life (the past 20 months), I've found myself in the cave at times: a major life transition, Sue's cancer, a pervasive pandemic, political and social unrest, and more—have caused a great deal of unrest in my soul.

But what I've experienced, once again in my life, is that when I affirm my faith in Yahweh—God joins me in the cave!

God, when I am in the cave, please come join me! I can make it without others but can't make it without You beside me. Thank you! Amen

HE KNOWS
May 10

"You keep track of all my sorrows. You have collected all my tears in Your bottle.
You have recorded each one in Your book."
Psalm 56:8

Recently I was reading a biography of Thomas Edison, the great 19th-century inventor. On matters of faith, he said he assumed there is some fantastical force that is responsible for the universe consistent with Genesis 1, but wholly rejected any concept of a <u>personal</u> God.

Mr. Edison did not read his Bible.

From the first few pages until the last, Yahweh is depicted as a God who is intimately acquainted with and interested in the affairs and details of our lives.

After Yahweh speaks creation into existence, He seemingly gets down on His hands and knees in the terra ferma to form and fashion man with his hands, then bends over him to breathe life into his lungs (Genesis 2:7). Later He sends His Son to become one of us; to enter into our humanity to identify with us and redeem us (the Gospels). Jesus let us know that the very hairs on our heads (if there are any!) are known by God. Jesus was tender with children, fed the hungry, healed the sick, delivered the demonized, and wept with the bereaved.

In this psalm, we are informed that God logs our sorrows and captures our tears in a flask. Whether David's description is literal or figurative makes no difference. The point is that The Great I AM sees what's going on in your life right now—and He cares.

Don't buy into Edison's view of God. Don't give in to Satan's whisper that He doesn't care. Don't lose heart in the midst of your hardship. God knows. God cares. God listens. He still comforts. Your pain is very personal to Him. Call out to Him as David did. I love how David ended this psalm: *"So now I can walk in Your presence, O God, in Your life-giving light"* (v.13).

And know this: at the end of the age God will do away with our tears. There won't be any need for the book of sorrows or the tear jar: *"He will wipe every tear from their eyes, and there will be no more death or sorrow or crying or pain. All these things are gone forever"* (Revelation 21:4).

Hallelujah!

God, I love You! Thank You for being so caring about the details of my life; for caring about and entering into my trials and suffering. Draw me closer to You. Amen

WINGS

May 11

"Have mercy on me, O God, have mercy! I look to you for protection.
I will hide beneath the shadow of Your wings until the danger passes by."
Psalm 57:1-2

The wings of birds are amazing creations. They enable a bird to fly at great speeds and, depending on the bird, great distances.

A hummingbird's wings flap about 80 times per second—only slightly faster than the frequency that our daughter spit up when she was a baby! On the other end of the spectrum, the wingspan of an albatross is 12 feet and takes as much as 2 seconds to flap its wings!

Whether large or small, the wings of most adult birds provide a safe covering for their chicks. Before the fledglings can fly, they are extremely vulnerable to other birds or animals of prey, so the adult will cover their chicks until the danger passes. I've seen videos of parent birds fighting off other birds trying to steal eggs or take young chicks. Fascinating.

When young David was hiding from King Saul, he felt extremely vulnerable. He imagined himself as a young fledgling, unable to fly away from the danger, so he called on Yahweh to cover him with His wings.

We can do the same. Sometimes life comes at us like a predator attacking our marriage, our children, our health, or our livelihood. We feel threatened and vulnerable.

When that occurs, we can call out to God and ask Him to hide us under His wings; to protect us until the danger has passed. We'd like to bubble wrap ourselves and those we love for protection against harm. But truth is, we can only muster up so much protection. That means this call needs to be made often and passionately.

Call out to The One who loves you; who describes Himself over and over again as Protector. Rest under the cover of His wings.

And feel His heart pound for you.

God, I need Your protection. My loved ones need Your protection. Cover us with Your wings and enable us to feel Your heart pound for us with great love. Amen

FROM AND THROUGH
May 12

"Be exalted, O God, above the highest heavens! May Your glory shine over all the earth."
Psalm 57:9 & 11

In the midst of great peril, David does a remarkable thing: he breaks into a chorus of praise! Twice in this short psalm, he repeats this refrain: *'Be exalted, O God! May Your glory shine!'*

No doubt David, in this psalm, is counting on God to give him victory over his assailants. But underlying his petition is his recognition that God is to be exalted, not him.

When life comes at us; when we are being threatened and attacked in some way, it is so easy to make the situation about us: "I can't believe this is happening to me; this is going to ruin me; what did I do to deserve this?"

But there is something greater at play here: the glory and fame of God. We would love, every time we were attacked, for God to vanquish our foe and us to escape unscathed. The charlatan preachers out there hold this up as the perfect picture of God's will: that we can avoid hardship, we can avoid disease, we can avoid financial trouble—if we really have faith.

It's a lie.

Through the ages, Godly people have suffered greatly. There are those times in the believer's life where God's path for us leads us through suffering. It's in the enduring, trusting, and persevering through, that God gains glory.

Delivering us through and delivering us from. When God delivers us from, we should praise Him. And we do gladly, right? But when He delivers us through, the praise is a higher form. Why? Because we get no immediate physical benefit for ourselves. If we praise Him in trial and tragedy, it is only because of our faith and trust that He will eventually work it out for His glory and ultimately for our good.

So whether life is good for you now, or incredibly difficult—pray that God will be exalted in the highest way. *"So that the proof of your faith, being more precious than gold which is perishable, even though tested by fire, may be found to result in praise and glory and honor at the revelation of Jesus Christ"* (1 Peter 1:7). Regardless of whether God delivers you from or through, let praise be on your lips. He is worthy!

God, I ask that you deliver me FROM this trial. But if it's not Your will, then I pray that You will grant me the faith and courage necessary as You get me THROUGH this adversity. Amen

BUT AS FOR ME

May 13

"But as for me, I will sing about Your power.
Each morning I will sing with joy about Your unfailing love.
For You have been my refuge, a place of safety when I am in distress.
O my Strength, to you I sing praises, for You, O God, are my refuge,
the God who shows me unfailing love."

Psalm 59:16-17

Through my many years of life and ministry, I've been around all kinds of people with all kinds of perspectives about God. Some are angry at Him. Something has happened in their past—the loss of a loved one, an unanswered prayer, a failed marriage—and they blame God.

Some are disappointed in Him for similar reasons. They feel as if He let them down and they are hurt and disillusioned. Some are disinterested in Him. They go throughout their day with hardly a thought about Him—unless of course, they experience some trouble in their lives. When it comes, their disinterest dissipates, and they decide to come knocking at His door.

And then there are people like David. I count myself in that group. When I get up, my thoughts run to Him. He puts a song in my heart. I read His word and see His unfailing love on its pages and worked out in my life. He has been and is my Refuge and my Strength.

It wasn't always like this for me. I would have been counted in all those groups at various times—the angry, the disappointed, the disinterested.

But through the years I've fallen more and more in love with Him. He is the center of my life—He IS my life! It's hard to put into words, but Paul gets close: *"For from Him and through Him and to Him are all things"* (Romans 11:36 ESV); *"But whatever things were gain to me, those things I have counted as loss for the sake of Christ. More than that, I count all things to be loss in view of the surpassing value of knowing Christ Jesus my Lord, for whom I have suffered the loss of all things, and count them but rubbish so that I may gain Christ"* (Philippians 3:7-8; NASB).

Others may ignore Him or resist Him or curse Him, **But As For Me**, each morning I will sing with joy of His power to transform, His protection from the Enemy, His strength to get me through, and His incredible, unfailing love.

How about you?

Lord, draw me to Yourself. I will spend more time with You in prayer and in Your word. Fan the flame of my heart for You. I love You. Amen

THE BANNER
May 14

"But you have raised a banner for those who fear you—
a rallying point in the face of attack."
Psalm 60:4

Maybe it's difficult for the 21st-century citizen to understand the importance and strategic necessity of a banner during a battle in ancient times. But surely, you've seen more than one movie where a young soldier carrying the flag is cut down and someone else drops their weapon, picks up the flag, and carries it onward. A flag is a type of banner. It encourages the soldiers to fight on; a rallying point in the face of attack.

David was a warrior king. He and his nation faced opposition from all sides. They were constantly engaged in war. When the battle was hot and victory hung in the balance, they looked to the banner of Israel to remember why they were fighting—and it encouraged them to press on.

In so many ways, we are in a battle. We fight the effects of our brokenness and the brokenness of others every day. We fight off the selfishness that threatens our marriages, fight off the self-gratifying appeals of a materialistic society, we fight for our children's and grandchildren's hearts and minds in the midst of an insane, godless culture. In short, we daily fight the Enemy who opposes God, the word of God, the people of God, and the things of God.

Are you tired of fighting? Feeling defeated? Look to the Banner! Lift Him up in your heart and mind. He was lifted up on a cross for you. He conquered sin and death so that you could walk in victory. He loves you with an everlasting love. Look to Jesus and rally yourself to His cause and for His glory.

Fight the good fight. Be encouraged, pilgrim: *"You have already won the victory, because the Spirit who lives in you is greater than the spirit who lives in the world"* (1 John 4:4).

God, I feel the struggle. I look to You to give me strength and courage to fight the good fight! Amen

VALIANT
May 15

"Through God we shall do valiantly,
and it is He who will tread down our adversaries."
Psalm 60:12 (NASB)

I've always been intrigued by the word *valiant*. It's not a commonly used word. It means 'possessing or showing courage or determination.' Synonyms more commonly used are brave, courageous, and mighty.

But there is something about *valiant* that catches the eye: dauntless, fearless, lion-hearted. In the Old Testament Hebrew, the word is *raggi* and is applied to those who are courageous, particularly soldiers of war.

God, the real author of these psalms, contends that through Him, we can be valiant; we can face our foes with undaunted courage. David was fighting Edomites; we fight a foe far more evil and powerful.

Satan and his minions are the 2nd most powerful force in the universe. 1 Peter 5:8 warns us: *"Be sober [well balanced and self-disciplined], be alert and cautious at all times. That enemy of yours, the devil, prowls around like a roaring lion [fiercely hungry], seeking someone to devour"* (Amplified Bible).

We sense that, don't we? There are times we hear him roaring. There are other times we can almost hear him breathing next to us. He makes deceitful appeals to our fallen sin nature and together they team up against us hoping to entice us to think, speak, and act opposite of our calling in Christ.

He attacks. He deceives. He destroys. We would have no hope of resisting him—apart from Jesus. But in Christ, we can experience victory! *"But thank God! He gives us victory over sin and death through our Lord Jesus Christ"* (1 Corinthians 15:57). *"If God is for us, who can be against us?"* (Romans 8:31). *"And this is the victory that has overcome the world-our faith"*

(1 John 5:4).

He will *'tread down our adversaries.'* Believe that. Stay close to Jesus. Don't lose heart. Be lion-hearted in times of adversity and temptation. The Lion of Judah is with you!!

Jesus, I praise You as the Lion of Judah. Thank you for being beside me through this. If You are for me, who could possibly be against me! Thank you! Amen

A LOVE TAP
May 16

"Let all that I am wait quietly before God, for my hope is in Him.
He alone is my rock and my salvation, my fortress where I will not be shaken."
Psalm 62:4-5

If you are a student of the Psalms, you'll recognize certain words and themes reiterated over and over again. These two verses contain a nice summary of them: hope, rock, fortress, and rescue.

This is why I love the Psalms so much: nearly every one of them is written by someone in trouble. They are afraid, they are angry, they are discouraged, they're feeling hurt, betrayed, sad, or lonely.

The psalmists realized that what they needed was something unearthly, something uncommon to get them through. They needed a love tap from Yahweh.

Once again David finds himself in a tight spot. He faces a situation that calls for an unearthly, uncommon response. He knows that he needs to reaffirm his faith in the God who has come to his rescue many times before.

Jesus said, *"Here on earth you will have many trials and sorrows. But take heart, because I have overcome the world"* (John 16:33).

When we find ourselves in a tight spot, there is only one first step to take: reaffirm our faith in the One who has gotten us through so many times before. Reread these verses and put yourself in them and emphasize Him: "God, **You** are **my** Rock—strong & mighty. **You** are **my** fortress—I can hide in and be secure in **You**. **You** are **my** salvation—only **You** can rescue me."

Twice David says, *"I will wait quietly before God"* (vv. 1 & 5). That's the key: in times of trouble, get time with God. Reaffirm His power—He's overcome the world, for crying out loud! Reaffirm His faithfulness—He has been there for you all along the way.

The result is a love tap from Yahweh that will get you through.

Lord, You are my Rock. You are my fortress. I need a love tap from You! Amen

HEARING PROBLEMS
May 17

"God has spoken plainly, and I have heard it many times: Power, O God, belongs to You; unfailing love, O Lord, is Yours. Surely You repay all people according to what they have done."
Psalm 62:11-12

If you've ever had children or been around them much, you know that they have a hearing problem: you must keep telling them the same things over and over again! When we ask them why they didn't do what we asked, what's their response? "I forgot." There is a difference between audibly hearing and hearing with a mind to obey.

We can't be too critical of them—we have the same issue. God has to keep telling us the same things over and over again, doesn't He? Here David attests to the fact that God has told Him many times two important truths.

First, that He is omnipotent; all-powerful. We forget that. That's the reason we feel afraid, or discouraged, or confused, or hopeless. We forget that all power belongs to Him. Jesus informed Pontius Pilate, the Roman governor officiating His trial, of just that truth: *"Jesus answered, 'You would have no power over Me at all unless it were given to you from above'"* (John 19:11). We forget and think that earthly powers are supreme.

The second truth is that His love is faithful, constant, and unmerited. We can hardly grasp that since ours is so fickle and self-centered. The result is that we feel unloved by Him when troubles come our way; we interpret His love based on circumstances. We forget that *"God proves his own love for us in that while we were still sinners, Christ died for us"* (Romans 5:8; CSB). The cross is the ultimate indication and proof of God's love, not events or situations. He reminds us over and again that adversity is an opportunity for us to strengthen our faith.

Will you believe God loves you even when tragedy or abuse strikes? Will you believe God is omnipotent when life feels out of control? God says again: "Just because this is happening to you doesn't mean I'm not powerful—this person will pay for their abuse. It doesn't mean I don't love you—the cross ought to be proof enough. Trust Me—I know what I'm doing!"

He has said that to me over and over again—because I have a hearing problem!

God, I affirm again that you are the All-Powerful God and that Your love for me is supreme. I again choose to trust You with the circumstances of my life. I trust You. Amen

MINE!

May 18

"O God, you are my God."
Psalm 63:1

Psalm 63 is one of the most loved psalms of all time. It is said that the early Christians held it in such high regard that they were compelled to sing it every day. There is far too much to unpack in a single sitting. Its beauty and depth require us to move through it slowly.

The superscription indicates David wrote this in one of his wilderness experiences. He had so many, it's difficult to pinpoint which one! That resonates with me: I've been in the wilderness so many times I can't keep track of them!! If I had written them down, there would be trailer loads of journals chronicling them all.

David begins this song with the greatest of all affirmations: *"God, you are MY God!"* In Hebrew, the common word for a god is *'el'*. Ancient cultures featured a large number of gods, mostly fertility gods. Pagans would count on those gods to grant them offspring, good crops, and plenty of livestock. These gods were local; i.e., they were different depending on where you lived. As you moved through different regions, you'd encounter different *els*. There were lots of *'els'*.

El is the front part of one of the names of the God of the Bible, *Elohim*, translated 'The God' or 'The Living God.' From Abraham on it's clear that the Hebrews knew their *El* was different: universal, not local; not just powerful, but all-powerful.

David is staking a claim of possession on this God: "Elohim, You are MY El" He's defining relationship, not ownership. David knows that his relationship with Elohim places him in a superior position relative to his enemies and their *els*.

As believers, we can make that same claim. We certainly have enemies that assail us. Our increasingly secular society is assaulting almost every belief and value we hold as Bible-believing Christ-followers. Beyond that, the brokenness of this world and the people of it and in our lives is overwhelming at times.

We need to affirm again and again that Elohim is our El—and if He is for us, really, who can be against us?

God, You are MY God! I am so grateful that You have chosen and adopted me as Your child. I love You!! Amen

FIRST THINGS FIRST
May 19

"O God, you are my God; I earnestly search for You."
Psalm 63:1

Growing up, I heard my dad say often: "Put first things first." I didn't actually heed that advice until in my 20s. Occasionally I still fight to live by that principle.

In this great psalm, David is on a quest. He is searching for something that satisfies and fills him like nothing else. That something is Someone.

He begins with the greatest affirmation to ever be made: *"O God, you are MY God!"* David is staking a claim of possession on this God. He's defining relationship, not ownership. He wants to be with, spend time with, and enjoy the presence of his God.

The Hebrew word for *'earnestly'* can also mean *'early.'* Both are in view here. When you are desperate for something, you wake up with it on your mind.

When Sue and I lay in bed at night praying (and spooning), I finish our prayer time with this request: "Wake us up with thoughts of You." We want our last thoughts and first thoughts to be about the Lover of our souls.

For decades, the first thing I do—after I get my cup of joe—is to seek God. When the kids were small, I'd have to get up mighty early, sometimes as early as 4:30 am. But I knew, and I know, that the first of my day needs to be spent seeking God: "What first lays hold of the heart in the morning is likely to occupy the place all the day" (Clarke).

Some call this a 'Quiet Time.' Some call it 'Devotional Time.' Older generations would call this 'The Morning Watch.' Doesn't make a bit of difference what you call it—only that you prioritize it and make it the first and best part of your day.

Seeking God early is the best decision I make—each and every day.

Join me.

If you want some help to know how, my *Pathways* book has helped thousands of people establish this in their lives. You can get it on my website: www.nextlevelleadership.org

O God, You are MY God! I will seek You earnestly and early. You are worth whatever effort I must make to establish time with You as my top priority. I love You! Amen

DESPERATION
May 20

"O God, you are my God; I earnestly search for You. My soul thirsts for You;
my whole body longs for You in this parched and weary land where there is no water."
Psalm 63:1

Once, when I was snorkeling off the coast of Jamaica, I wanted to dive down to get a shell on the ocean bottom about 40' deep. I took a big breath and headed down. By the time I got there and picked out the shell I wanted, I was out of air. I started swimming for the surface in a panic. The last 10 seconds were excruciating—I was desperate for air and would have died without it!

Can you recall a time you were desperate for something? At the age of 33, God called me to preach and pastor. My heart burned with a passion for it. It dominated my thoughts and desires. I'd wake up and go to sleep longing for it—desperate to pastor and preach.

David crafted this song in a way that revealed his desperation for God. He begins with the greatest affirmation to ever be made: "God, you are MY God!" He's defining relationship, not ownership. And this relationship was so intimate that it created a sense of desperation in him.

It's time to take an accounting. Think about the desires of your heart. What do you spend most of your time wanting and trying to fulfill? Make a list right now of the top 5. Hopefully knowing and loving and spending time with Jesus is on the list. Here's mine:

1. Jesus
2. Sue
3. Family
4. Kingdom Impact
5. Relationships

Frankly, it's hard to limit it to five!! To be honest, there are times I allow any one of those

(or a few others) to climb to the top of the list; climb on the throne of my heart. I am a broken man in desperate need of transformation.

My prayer for myself, and for you, is that we would be desperate for God; that His Spirit would fan the flame of our hearts for Him above all other affections; that we would, and we will, be desperate for Him.

God, I find myself being desperate for so much of what this world has to offer. Forgive me! And remake me to look and be more like Jesus. Amen

GLIMPSES
May 21

"I have seen You in Your sanctuary
and gazed upon Your power and glory."
Psalm 63:2

If you have a chance to go to Israel, you'll see just to the east and south of Jerusalem is what is called the Judean wilderness. I used to think it was like the wilderness in Alaska or Montana. Not so; not even close. It is an arid area much like parts of New Mexico, Nevada, or Arizona. We call it desert. Water is available only by digging wells or finding spring-fed streams.

David is in the Judean desert—not exactly a garden spot. He's apparently being hounded by his adversaries. Not much water. Not much food. No internet. No Starbucks. Nothing really positive going on in his life circumstantially. Needless to say, he's in a tough spot.

But his spirit is buoyed because of one thing: in times past he has seen, caught glimpses of the power and glory of God.

He had seen God's power and glory when he took on Goliath: a young boy going against Hulk Hogan with a beanie flip. He certainly had gotten glimpses when God gave victory over his enemies in various battles. We all love it when we see God show up in difficult circumstances, don't we?

But here David is speaking of the times he has seen God's glory and power, not in circumstances, but in worship.

There is something that is singularly stunning about special moments in God's presence. There are those times when we're gathered with other believers, lifting voices of praise to Him, not for what He has done (interceding in our difficulties), but for who He is: sovereign, omniscient (all-knowing), all-wise, holy, righteous, merciful, gracious, patient, etc.

Or maybe times when we're by ourselves, seeking Him in the Morning Watch, reading His word, thinking on His love and goodness and greatness—and we are overcome by His presence.

These worship experiences sustain us in the wilderness. These glimpses of glory are as life-giving as anything this side of heaven. Gain them. Experience them. Cherish them.

And remember them.

God, enable me to see Your power and glory right now; just a glimpse! I worship You for who You are and I trust You will draw close to me. Amen

BETTER THAN LIFE
May 22

"Your unfailing love is better than life itself; how I praise You!"
Psalm 63:3

"It's to die for!" My aunt Mary Jeanne's fried chicken was beyond amazing. The best part about it was the cracklins'—pieces of the fried dough that remained in the skillet after the chicken was removed. Combine those with some cream gravy and her fried chicken—O my! It was to die for!!

That idiom (It was to die for!!), usually meant in jest, reveals the notion that some things are incredibly valuable. David uses the phrase *"better than life itself"* to say that nothing is more valuable than God, even his very life.

We make that valuation daily. People will die in attempts to gain money. They'll exchange their lives in pursuit of success. They'll die seeking thrills. They'll die trying to protect those they love.

David holds the love of God in such high regard that he counts it more valuable, more precious than his own life. Genuine believers agree with him. This reality holds many applications, though we only have time for a few.

If we believe God's love is better than life, we will seek Him early and often, sitting at His feet in order to experience that great love. The rest of our life only finds meaning, our other loves are only deepened, when we seek Him, the Lover of our soul.

If we believe God's love is better than life, our trials and even tragedies don't debilitate us because they don't become the ultimate reality in our lives—God's love is the ultimate reality. His love, not trial, not tragedy, overwhelms us instead.

If we believe God's love is better than life, we face death with a completely different outlook. Death becomes a kind of filter to us: as we pass through it, all the pain, all the suffering, all the failure, all the abandonment, all the injustice is left behind. Once we pass through, His love for us is then seen and sensed perfectly.

God's faithful love IS better than life.

God, thank you for Your great, unfailing love. It is better than anything this life has to offer. Amen

GOOD POSTURE

May 23

"I will praise You as long as I live, lifting up my hands to You in prayer.
You satisfy me more than the richest feast. I will praise You with songs of joy."

Psalm 63:4-5

I've always admired people with good posture: back straight, shoulders back, head not leaning forward but in alignment with the upright spine. I have none of that! I've never had good posture and now I'm paying for it.

In vv.1-3, David has already said a mouthful about The One True God and his relationship with Him. He now transitions to a posture of praise.

A posture of praise is something internal. It begins with the recognition of the greatness of God. When I think about Yahweh, His magnificence, His power, His creativity, His holiness, His justness, His omniscience, His sovereignty, His grace and mercy—my soul is prompted to break out in praise for The Glorious One. He is so worthy of every bit of praise I give Him—and more.

A posture of praise is not just internal, but external as well. Like all things spiritual, what is real on the inside usually makes its way to the outside.

When I was younger in my faith, I saw people lifting their hands in praise and worship and it made me feel—uneasy. They were a distraction to me. I didn't get it. I bought into the idea that what is intensely personal should be intensely private.

My confession is this: I believe they had a better understanding of and a more intimate relationship with The Great I AM than I did. Their inside posture was better than mine. That showed up, not just in something like hand-raising, but how they lived.

Thankfully, my posture has gotten better. I have no hesitation to raise my hands in praise now—prompted by my growing understanding and awareness of my great and awesome God. More importantly, my overall spiritual posture is much better and shows up in how I live. I'm light-years from having it all worked out, but I take heart in that my posture is improving!

God, enable me to gain a better posture spiritually; one that is quick to praise You and steadfast to live for You. Amen

FITFUL SLEEP
May 24

*"You satisfy me more than the richest feast. I will praise You with songs of joy.
I lie awake thinking of You, meditating on You through the night."*

Psalm 63:5-6

I am so envious of people who sleep well—drop off to sleep quickly and stay asleep through the night. I'm married to one. After our prayer time, we'll be in bed engaged in a little pillow talk. She'll ask me a question and by the time I say my 10-word response, my answer is met with either stone silence or a slight nasal sound! That's all it takes for her to drop off into la la land.

Sometimes I can feel her body go limp while I'm praying!

I've never been a good sleeper. For most of my life I have stayed awake long after my head hit the pillow. And if I wake up, I often struggle to go back to sleep. That's bad news for an aging man! Events, experiences, conversations (real and imagined) take over my brain and keep sleep at bay.

David apparently had the same problem. After all, he writes this while being hunted by folks who want to kill him! During his fitfulness, he spent his time contemplating the goodness and provision of God.

That's a good word for me. When life is stressful and I have so many challenges and opportunities that I can't turn my brain off, it's good to make my 'awake in the middle of the night' time more profitable. Keeping a notepad by the bed to write something down so I can release it helps. But I've learned that praying and reviewing Bible verses is even more helpful. I'll pray for my family, events, and people that come to mind. I begin to count my blessings, and I sense the fullness He has infused into me through His Spirit. Pretty quickly my soul is quieted, my brain relaxes, and I drop off to sleep.

Wish I had learned that a long time ago!

God, remind me to meditate on you when I wake up in the middle of the night. You are worthy of that! And I pray that the sleep You do give me is sufficient for the day. Amen

STUCK ON YOU

May 25

"Because You are my helper, I sing for joy in the shadow of your wings.
I cling to You; Your strong right hand holds me securely."

Psalm 63:7-8

In the 2003 movie, *Stuck on You*, Matt Damon and Greg Kinnear play two conjoined twins who have turned their circumstance into becoming the fastest cooks in town. It's a funny movie.

David employs language in these verses that highlights his closeness to Yahweh. *"In the shadow of Your wings"* denotes the presence and protection of God. The image that comes to mind is that of a defenseless fledgling hiding close to or under the protective wing of its parent. *"I cling to You"* reinforces that idea. David has chosen to stay glued to Yahweh. It's like he's saying to God, "I'm sticking close to You like white on rice! I'm talking close!" And with good reason: David is in need of God's protection.

David looks to God's right hand to hold on to him. Of course, such language is what is called *anthropomorphic language*: assigning human attributes to God. *Right hand* is a figure of speech, a metaphor, to help us understand a particular characteristic of God. The use of the phrase, *right hand,* always signifies mercy, honor, and power in the Bible. David is counting on the strength and power of God to hold on to him in this crisis of his. When a child is afraid, sticking close to a parent is the natural thing to do. David is sticking close to God, counting on His strength and mercy to protect him. That brought joy, not fear, to his heart.

We live in a time where there is too much insecurity and too little joy. People cling to various things: jobs, money, possessions, relationships—not necessarily bad, but certainly fragile and uncertain. Down deep we know that what we cling to is fleeting and temporary, and it fosters insecurity. It's like leaning against a rickety fence instead of a brick wall. So when that rickety fence is threatened, falls down, or is taken away, we're in trouble. Security comes from leaning against the immovable, indestructible God. So that when the torrents threaten to sweep you away, His right hand will hold on to you.

Stick close to Him—because of His great love, He's stuck on you!

God, I look to You, lean on You, depend on You for protection and strength. Draw me nearer, O Lord, to Your precious, bleeding side. Amen

PAYDAY

"But those plotting to destroy me will come to ruin. They will go down into the depths of the earth. They will die by the sword and become the food of jackals. But the king will rejoice in God. All who swear to tell the truth will praise him, while liars will be silenced."

Psalm 63:9-11

David has been focused on God and it has set his heart to singing. But now he turns his attention to his problems: his close relationship with God did not take away his troubles—he's being hunted by his enemies. **Intimacy with God does not insulate us from adversity.**

David is calling on God to destroy his enemies. He uses *imprecatory* language: *'may my enemies come to ruin, be thrown in the abyss, die by the sword, and be eaten by jackals.'* Doesn't sound very, um, Christian, does it? After all, Jesus told us to love our enemies.

But David touches on something that needs to be discussed more these days: the justice of God. The same Bible that says God is love, says God is just. There will be an accounting for injustice at the end of the age.

It's tragic that our country is still struggling with racism and injustice. Few things infuriate me more. God is just and holds humanity accountable for injustice. Believers who insist on moral and ethical behavior in areas of abortion and LGBTQ+ issues should also insist on it in matters of justice.

Those who suffer injustice should insist that matters be resolved justly in this world. However, as long as sin persists in the human heart, solutions will surely remain unsatisfactory.

There are other victims of injustice besides racism. Believers are being attacked and belittled in our own country because of our trust in Jesus. The perpetrators do their best to remove His values from the public square and wantonly treat Christ-followers with disdain and contempt.

In all cases, those who commit injustice will come before The Great Judge, at the end, face to face. There will be no argument. There will be no escape. It will be much worse for them than to be eaten by jackals.

There will be a payday, someday. So take heart and look to heaven for the grace to endure.

God, You said You hate injustice. Make me more like You. And when I am treated unjustly, may I not look for vengeance, but for the grace to endure. Amen

GLAD WRAP

May 27

"The righteous man will be glad in the Lord and will take refuge in Him."
Psalm 64:10 (NASB)

The word *glad* means pleased, delighted, and grateful. David uses it often. Here he indicates what brings him pleasure: the Yahweh Himself. I love that phrase, *"glad in the Lord"*! It makes me—glad!! A smile comes into my heart and makes its way to my face.

To be glad is to experience the positive emotions of rejoicing, delighting, taking pleasure in something. What makes you glad? I hope there is a ton in your life that makes you glad: your marriage, your children, your grandchildren, travel, hobbies, etc.

But there are times when there is very little in our lives that makes us glad. Circumstances seem overwhelmingly sad, not glad: sickness, loss of a loved one, job troubles, financial stress, a dying marriage, a wayward child, etc.

David reminds us that if nothing else makes us glad, we can be glad in the LORD. This is not some pie in the sky, head in the sand perspective. He has been and is in real trouble. Harassed. Threatened. Betrayed. Bludgeoned by gossip. Yet he declares that he is glad in the Lord.

Why? First, we have to recognize that David says it is the righteous who are glad in the LORD.

That word *righteous* primarily means *'right standing or right relationship.'* To be in right standing is to be someone who has satisfied the requirements God makes to be in a right relationship with Him. Faith is that requirement. *"The just, the righteous shall live by faith"* (Habakkuk 2:4, Romans 1:17). David's faith was looking forward to the cross; our faith is looking back at the cross.

All that to say: we who are in Christ can rejoice in the fact that we in a right relationship with God—we are SAVED! We will never suffer His judgment and wrath. No matter what happens to us in this life, good or bad, it does not even begin to compare to the eternal inheritance we stand to gain in the life to come!!

When that realization comes into full focus, joy can begin to take root in our hearts regardless of circumstances. We can be wrapped in glad, if in nothing else, in the LORD. That's good enough for me.

God, enable me to see more clearly the great value of the salvation You have given me and to be glad in You, no matter what else is going on in my life. Amen.

CHOSEN
May 28

"What joy for those You choose to bring near, those who live in Your holy courts.
What festivities await us inside Your holy Temple."

Psalm 65:4

In 1978 I was chosen out of a large group of applicants to participate in an exchange program through Rotary International. Five of us were selected to go to England and represent the Houston area chapters. Each of us was chosen because of our profession: one guy was a hospital administrator, one was in agribusiness, one was a professor, one an attorney, and I represented the oil industry. We were outfitted in new clothes and treated like celebrities. When we got to England, we were wined and dined like royalty for five weeks!

I'm sure you've wanted something, worked for something, but had to wait to see if you would be selected for it. The less chance you had, the sweeter the exhilaration when you discovered you were chosen.

In this psalm, David is shaking his head at the reality that God chose him to be king of Israel: punk kid, runt of the family, lowly shepherd, poet, and musician. Why in the world would Yahweh choose him to lead His people at such a critical time? Against all odds, Yahweh chose David.

I have yet to fully understand why God would choose me. Like David, I'm still shaking my head. It doesn't make sense! Someone else might be chosen because of their piety, position, wealth, or celebrity. I didn't and still don't have much of that. There was no good reason for God to choose me. In fact, God had every reason to bring His judgment and wrath on me because of my moral and spiritual bankruptcy.

Yet. God. Chose. Me!

I love what Paul says in Ephesians 1:4, *"Even before He made the world, God loved us and chose us in Christ to be holy and without fault in His eyes."* David said, *"What festivities await us inside Your holy Temple."* Before God created anything, I was on His heart—and He was storing up great things for me.

I do believe that one must choose God, but that's a no-brainer. Only a fool would not. But that God would choose me—I'm still shaking my head!

God, thank you for choosing me. I know I don't deserve anything but Your judgment, but I am forever grateful for Your unmerited favor in my life. Amen

BRAGGIN'

May 29

"Come and listen, all you who fear God, and I will tell you what He did for me."
Psalm 66:16

Every (good) parent loves to brag on their children. I could fill page after page of reasons why my kids are awesome. But I've got a friend who takes bragging on children to an art form. I've known him a quarter of a century and he never ceases to amaze me at how he finds new ways to brag on them. If you didn't know better, you'd think these kids (now adults) were so good, any one of them could fill the spot if there was ever a vacancy in the Trinity!

David is bragging on God. He does that a lot in his writing. The reason of course is because God is worth braggin' on! He begins this psalm by exhorting God's creation: *"Shout joyful praises to God, all the earth! Sing about the glory of His name! Tell the world how glorious He is. Say to God, 'How awesome are Your deeds!'"* (vv.1-2). He then points to the most well-known demonstration of God's power in Israel's history as proof: the crossing of the Red Sea.

Israel's deliverance out of Egyptian slavery and the crossing of the Red Sea is THE seminal event in the Old Testament. It correlates with the salvation experience of the New Testament. Just as Yahweh delivered the Hebrews out of slavery to Egypt, He delivers sinners out of slavery to sin. Just as God's judgment was averted by splashing the blood of a spotless lamb on the doorposts, so it is averted by splashing the blood of the Lamb of God on the heart.

Each true believer has a story of God's deliverance from sin. We call it our salvation story, our testimony. It's not to be kept a secret; it is to be told again and again to all who will listen. It's our opportunity to brag on God for His mighty work in our lives. It's powerful and no one can dispute it. Tell the people He has placed in your lives. Like David, say: *"Come and listen . . . and I will tell you what He did for me"* (v.16).

God, thank You for saving me! By the power of Your Spirit, embolden me to tell others what a great God You are and what You have done for me. Amen

LISTENING
May 30

"If I had not confessed the sin in my heart, the Lord would not have listened."
Psalm 66:18

In one of my favorite movies, *The Princess Bride*, Miracle Max (Billy Crystal) is being hounded by his wife for misstating what young Wesley said ('to blave' instead of 'true love'). As she chases him around the room, he keeps saying, "I'm not listening!" One of the best scenes—ever!

David understands the importance of 'getting the ear' of God: he must be honest with Him in every way, particularly about sin.

When we think, say, or do something wrong, it's a part of our human nature to try to hide it. We got that trait from our first parents. After they disobeyed and ate the forbidden fruit, they went into 'hide and seek' mode. What a crazy notion: that we can hide from God! The Bible is clear: He knows everything at all times. There is nothing He is unaware of.

And yet, we try to hide our sin from Him. We ignore it, trying to convince ourselves it's no big deal. We justify it, thinking that it is the normal human reaction. We deflect it, blaming someone else. Or we mistakenly believe that as Christ-followers, that our sin doesn't impact our relationship with God.

Well, it does. For the true believer, sin doesn't change the status of our relationship with God, but it does impact our intimacy with Him. It's similar to marriage. If I say something unkind or treat Sue with impatience, it doesn't change our status: we're still married. But it does impact our intimacy—we will not enjoy any real closeness until I've confessed to her and sought her forgiveness. I can try to talk to her about other matters, but she isn't really listening to me because there is something between us. She hears, but she isn't listening!

To be clear, as a believer in Jesus, all my sin—past, present, and future—was nailed to the cross and paid for in total by the shed blood of Jesus (Colossians 2:14 et al). Amen! Confession doesn't get more forgiveness from God; that has already been granted for all of eternity. Hallelujah!! My confession is because I realize I have acted in a way that is not consistent with our relationship and I regret it. Confession removes the hindrance to our intimacy and clears the channels so that God is not just hearing me, but listening!

God, make me more sensitive to the sin in my life. By Your grace, change me to be more cooperative with Your Spirit and more like Your Son. Amen

THE BLESSING
May 31

"May God be gracious to us and bless us and make His face to shine upon us."
Psalm 67:1 (ESV)

If this verse sounds familiar, it seems David fashioned it after Aaron's blessing on God's people en route to the Promised Land. You'll recall that God made Aaron, Moses' older brother, the first high priest of Israel. He instructed Aaron to bless His people a certain way:

> *Thus you shall bless the people of Israel: you shall say to them,*
> *The Lord bless you and keep you;*
> *the Lord make His face to shine upon you and be gracious to you;*
> *the Lord lift up His countenance upon you and give you peace."*

Numbers 6:23-26 (ESV)

Notice that *the LORD* (*Yahweh*) is mentioned three times. Once would have sufficed, but God wanted His people to get the point that He and He alone was responsible for all of life's goodness: "Listen, My people—when things go well with you, remember I'm the reason. When you enjoy wealth and health, remember I'm the reason. **Don't get caught up in the blessing and forget the <u>Blessor</u>!"**

I love the phrase found in both passages: *"make His face to shine upon us."* This is something familiar to just about every parent. I've got a zillion examples, but let me share just a few: when Ben finished basic training, when Brit had our first grandchild, when Brad was inducted into West Point. If you could have seen my face those moments, it was shining as bright as the sun!

However, as gleaming as my face was, it would not begin to compare to God's face as He looks upon His children who are cooperating with His Spirit and being transformed into His image.

Have you repented of your sinful nature and placed your trust in Jesus alone to save you? Then you are a child of God (John 1:12)! Are you growing in your faith walk, learning how to live daily by and through His Spirit in you? Then His face is beaming as He looks upon you.

Pray for His grace in your life. Seek His pleasure and approval in all you do.

Know that you are blessed and highly favored. And look to heaven to see God's shining face.

God, thank You for loving me and blessing me with so much. I don't deserve it; I don't deserve You. But I desire Your blessing today and to see Your smile. Amen

THE REASON

"May Your ways be known throughout the earth, Your saving power among people everywhere.
May the nations praise You, O God. Yes, may all the nations praise You."

Psalm 67:2-3

Yesterday we looked at v.1 and David's call for God to bless His people; for His face to shine in favor on His people. Everyone wants God's blessing, right? We want His favor in every part of our lives. But let's place this in context: the rest of the psalm is about the nations. That's why this psalm is called by many, The Missionary Psalm.

Why does God bless us? Is it just for our own benefit? Or does He have a higher reason for it?

The blessings of God have both an immediate and a higher purpose. The immediate is that our Heavenly Father wants to bless us and favor us with good things (Matthew 7:11).

But His blessings are not to be hoarded. He blesses us so that we might bless others. Generosity is the trademark of a truly grateful heart. What percentage of your blessing do you hoard? I've known so-called believers who keep close to 100% for themselves. Others take great pride in giving 10% away when they could do more. Such attitudes and actions reflect a lack of understanding of the higher purpose of God's blessings.

The greatest reason, the highest purpose for God's blessing is to make His glory and His gospel known to the nations. God is all about gaining glory for Himself. If this were the supreme objective of a human being, we would say he/she is arrogant to think so highly of self and so worthy of praise. But in God's case, He IS high; He IS perfect; He IS everything. He IS worthy of all praise.

And He wants to be worshipped by ALL peoples. He wants His good news to be offered to people of every tribe, every tongue, and every ethnic group.

Use your blessings to advance the glory of His name. Give at least 10% to your church. Give more to special mission offerings. Give more to worthy ministries that carry the name of Jesus around the world. Go on mission trips. Pray about planting your life somewhere else in His world to start a church. Then you will discover the joy of the ultimate reason for His blessings in your life.

God, forgive me for not being more generous with Your blessings. By Your Spirit, I will give more away and invest more in kingdom work. Amen

RUN!

June 2

"Rise up, O God, and scatter Your enemies.
Let those who hate God run for their lives."
Psalm 68:1

"Run for your lives!" This is a phrase that has been used so many times in music, literature, and cinema. A wild beast or a scary alien or an overwhelming force is on the attack. There's no use staying and fighting—to do so would mean certain death: "Run for your lives!"

David begins this psalm by loosely quoting Moses as the Hebrews were in the wilderness: *"And whenever the Ark set out, Moses would shout, 'Arise, O Lord, and let Your enemies be scattered! Let them flee before You!'"* (Numbers 10:35). In doing so, David announces to his people that just as Yahweh defeated the Hebrew enemies in the wilderness, so He will do the same for them.

What is an enemy to a child of God? Any force that opposes God, the word of God, the people of God, or the things of God. That takes in quite a bit, doesn't it? Let's focus on two.

The first is our fleshly desires. Satan and his demons roam the earth seeking to devour us (1 Peter 5:8). One of their strategies is to whisper and appeal to our fleshly nature. Although our sin has been forgiven through Jesus, our sin nature is still resident in us—and will be until we are delivered from this fallen body. Satan tempts us to give in to those desires rather than the desires of and for God. We find ourselves fighting off lust, greed, selfishness, anger, complacency, and a myriad of other fleshly desires.

The second enemy we fight is fear: fear of sickness, fear of death, fear of failure, fear of rejection, fear of . . . This in spite of the fact that the most often repeated phrase in the Bible is, *"Don't be afraid!"* God doesn't want us to be afraid. Circumstances may become testy or tragic, enemies may be coming at us from every angle, but we are not the ones who should be afraid—THEY should be afraid!

Do what Moses did. Do what David did. Do what the saints have done for millennia—call on Yahweh to scatter His enemies—and watch them run!!

Yahweh, I call on you to scatter these enemies that are attempting to defeat me by stealing my joy and peace. I stand firm in my faith that You are more powerful than any enemy that comes against me. Amen

SQUIRRELS
June 3

"Blessed be the Lord, who daily bears our burden."
Psalm 68:19 (NASB)

My study has a window that opens to our front yard where there are trees and lots of squirrels. Squirrels are fun to watch. They run up tree trunks, across limbs, down the trunks, and across the lawn as if they don't have a burden or care in the world. I told Sue one day, "I sometimes wish I was a squirrel." She said, "You'd be squashed in the street."

Generally speaking, the younger a person is, the fewer burdens; the older, the more burdens we have. Burdens, weights, come in various forms and from various sources.

One source is responsibility. When I was single, I only had me to take care of. Then I tricked Sue into marrying me and I had more responsibility. Then she tricked me into having kids and the responsibility increased. Add to that a mortgage, bills, college for kids, church leadership, aging parents, an ill spouse —that's a lot of responsibility. The weight of it all makes me long for the squirrel life!

Another source of burden is the consequences of our past sins: sexual immorality, failed marriages, overindulgence of food, drink, possessions, experiences, debt, etc. When we confess, to be sure, God forgives. But the consequences of our choices sometimes stay with us the rest of our lives.

Everyone has burdens. The question is: what do I do with my burdens? Do I carry them alone? If so, I will be so weighted down that life will become dreary and overwhelming. I'll miss out on the joy and peace God has for me.

The answer is to give those burdens to the Burden-Bearer. Jesus said, *"Take my yoke upon you. Let Me teach you, because I am humble and gentle at heart, and you will find rest for your souls. For My yoke is easy to bear, and the burden I give you is light"* (Matthew 11:29-30).

Notice Jesus didn't say we'd have no burdens, like squirrels. He said that our burdens would be light. Why? Because when we choose to follow Him and ask Him into our burdens, He shoulders up under the weight of it all, so that we carry only the light load. Joy and peace follow.

Lord Jesus, I confess You are the Burden-Bearer. I want to follow You in all things. I call out to You to lighten the load. Thank you! Amen

DROWNING
June 4

"Save me, O God, for the floodwaters are up to my neck.
Deeper and deeper I sink into the mire; I can't find a foothold.
I am in deep water, and the floods overwhelm me."
Psalm 69:1-2

Growing up, the creeks in my neighborhood were concreted for flood control purposes. During the spring downpours, they would fill up quickly, moving the water swiftly downstream. The water was fascinating to watch as it rumbled under the bridges and on to its destination. Pieces of wood and debris on top of the choppy water were at the mercy of the water's power, traveling 15-20 mph.

Home from college one spring break, my brother and I were standing on a bridge after a huge rain. I got the bright idea to jump the 15 feet into the raging water. Immediately I knew it was a mistake. I swam to the concrete side trying to get out, but the speedy current just scraped me across the course concrete, tearing the skin from my hands and chest. At that moment, I thought I was going to die. I cried out to God to save me.

A quarter-mile later, the creek turned, the concrete ended, the banks widened, and the current slowed a bit. I headed for the dirt bank multiple times, tried to grab hold, but the mud would give way and downstream I went again. I knew that about a half-mile up ahead, the creek went into underground drainage pipes. Time was running out. Finally, I found a place to hold on and pull my upper body up out of the water until I could find the strength to get out completely.

Because the dirt in the desert of Israel is so hard and the land so parched, any rain at all creates flash flood conditions. David knew that and compared his present circumstance to that of getting caught up in a flood.

There have been many floods in my life. Not in creeks, but in great trials: a season of deep depression, another of high anxiety, many professional missteps and disasters, and periods of my family, marriage, and financial life that kept tugging me under. Each time, like David, I called on Yahweh: *"Save me, O God!"* And He did. Like that day in the creek, I don't know how He has done it—but He has—and He does. He will for you.

O God, when I am overwhelmed and being tugged under by the raging waters of life, I will call on You to save me and get me through. Amen

IMPACT
June 5

"O God, you know how foolish I am; my sins cannot be hidden from You.
Don't let those who trust in You be ashamed because of me,
O Sovereign Lord of Heaven's Armies.
Don't let me cause them to be humiliated, O God of Israel."
Psalm 69:5-6

I love how honest David and the other writers are in these psalms. Here David is pleading with God: "Don't let my foolish and sinful actions negatively impact others."

Believing parents certainly should ask this of God. What a weighty responsibility He gives us with each child. Having parented three, I have a pretty good sense of the duty incurred. Sue and I prayed for each of them to grow up with hearts drawn toward God. We prayed Luke 2:52 (and many other verses) for our children: *"Jesus grew in wisdom and in stature and in favor with God and all the people."* We wanted them to grow up to follow Jesus and His path in every way.

But we (mostly me) were far from the perfect example. My inner brokenness spilled out all the time into my family. It was quite messy! If you haven't discovered this yet, it's important to know: **what comes out of you when life shakes you is what's in you.** What was in me, and still is to some degree, was a lot of impatience, selfishness, and sinful foolishness. It's a miracle my kids didn't turn out hellions! To this day, I continue to pray, as David did, that my family not be ashamed and humiliated because of my brokenness.

But this doesn't just apply to parenting; any caring believer would make the same request. I want my lifestyle, my social media posts, my demeanor towards my neighbors and workmates, to influence others toward, not from, Christ.

It's one thing to desire this; another to live it. The Spirit-filled life is the key. The Spirit is the power in us to transform and enable us to live the way Jesus commands—and we desire. God commands us (Ephesians 5:18) to be filled with the Spirit. Simply put, that means to surrender control to Him; to be dominated by Him. This must occur multiple times daily as we breathe out/confess our sin/self-control—and breathe in His forgiveness and His control.

Holy Spirit, I confess I've been controlling my life instead of You. Forgive me and fill me. Dominate my life in every way today. Amen

ON WHAT BASIS?

June 6

"Answer me, O Lord, for Your lovingkindness is good;
According to the greatness of Your compassion, turn to me."
Psalm 69:16 (NASB)

David is drowning. Life's circumstances are pulling him under. This is a man that seems to move from one crisis to another. Identify?

Years ago, when I began turning to the Psalms to breathe life and peace into my soul, I noticed that one of the recurring themes was the one stated in this verse: the petitioner calls on God to help and rescue, not based on any personal merit, but solely on the basis of God's love and mercy.

Twice in this short verse, David does just that: *"Answer me . . . for Your lovingkindness is good; According to the greatness of Your compassion, turn to me."*

If we're not careful, we think that God owes us something. After all, we're His children trying to live for and serve Him, right? So why can't we expect, even demand that He do our bidding?

Well, God does not owe us anything.

Before I was saved, all I deserved from God was His judgment and wrath. Once I repented and placed my faith in Jesus alone, that deserved judgment was removed and I was made in right standing with God. Hallelujah! God did that, not because I deserved it, but out of His love and grace, He responded to my faith and saved me. He didn't have to, but man, am I glad He did!

It's really not different on this side of salvation. I still don't deserve His love. I can't come and ask that He do something based on my merit. I can only appeal to Him in the name of Jesus. (John 14:14) Not my name, not my authority, not my merit. Only pride and arrogance compel me to think that I deserve His unconditional love.

I've needed His answers to my prayers for over 50 years. I've needed His rescuing more times than I can count. He has answered and He has delivered. But I never once deserved it.

When you think about it, praying and asking God to respond based on His love and compassion leads to assurance and peace. Who He is and what He has is far better than anything I've got!

God, I do come to You in the name of Jesus. I'm appealing to Your love and compassion: help me. Amen

BALANCE
June 7

"Let all who seek You rejoice and be glad in You;
And let those who love Your salvation say continually, 'Let God be magnified.'
But I am afflicted and needy; Hasten to me, O God!
You are my help and my deliverer. O Lord, do not delay."
Psalm 70:4-5 (NASB)

These two verses seem polar opposites, don't they? Verse 4 is extolling the greatness and goodness of God. Verse 5 is in stark contrast, focusing on the pain and need of the psalmist. It's like David is saying, "God, I know You're great and wonderful. But I need help, and I need it NOW!"

This is important to remember when approaching God. I have a tendency to run into His presence and start rattling off my requests: "Hey God. Good to see You. I need this and that and such and such . . . see you later." After all these years, I still find myself sometimes entering into the presence of the Holy God, hurried and impatient, spitting out my requests and demands as if I've got better things to do and need to get on to them. Ugh!

On the other hand, I notice in our daily prayer time together, that Sue never starts out with requesting. She always begins with praise. This is a wise move. It's the right move.

There needs to be balance in our prayer time. If we are too rushed to praise God for who He is, it reveals a skewed value system. Do we seek God for who He is or for what He can do for us? Both are ok as long as we keep first things first and strive for balance.

I love how the Spirit prompted David to phrase verse 4 *"Let all who seek You rejoice and be glad in You."* I want my motives toward God to be purified; that is, to want Him, not just for what He can do for me, but for who He is. I want to be glad in Him. If there is imbalance to be made, let me be unbalanced toward praise.

God, I confess that sometimes I come to You selfishly. You deserve my unmitigated praise. Purify my motives for coming to You so that I seek You, most of all, because of who You are, not because of what you can do for me. Amen

160

A GUIDE

"But I will hope continually and will praise You yet more and more. My mouth will tell of Your righteous acts, of Your deeds of salvation all the day, for their number is past my knowledge."
Psalm 71:14-15 (ESV)

We don't know exactly who wrote this psalm. From the text we can conclude he was an older man who was, once again, anticipating God's help in times of trouble. God had been faithful to deliver him through his many years and once again he is placing his hope in Yahweh in a difficult situation.

Wisdom is not limited to the aged, but those of us 'up in years' should have considerable amounts of it, garnered through the many years of trials, failures, and experiences. If you don't have someone much older than you speaking into your life, you're missing a great blessing. He or she has probably seen and/or been through just about every challenge you have or will experience. Like a grey, grizzled guide, they have been down the path that you're presently on and can offer invaluable insight into your journey. They can't walk the path for you, but they can walk the path with you, offering perspective, prayer, and encouragement.

In these verses, the elderly man is confirming his faith and hope in Yahweh. As we grow older, we find that, in their brokenness, people will disappoint us; we discover that all the stuff we thought made life purposeful and meaningful—really doesn't! As a matter of fact, the suicide rate of my generation (Baby Boomers) is rising at an alarming rate. Some have labeled us the "Suicide Generation." Why? We are the most affluent and successful generation of any before us or after us. I conjecture it is because we have put our hope in the stuff of this world, and it has left us empty and hopeless.

This wise old man, whoever he is, has learned to put his hope in God. He has learned that no thing and no person can satisfy him deep in his soul. As he looks back over his life, he has experienced so many times when God worked in his life, he can't even count them! Do yourself a favor: find someone with grey hair (or no hair) and foster a relationship with them. You won't regret it.

God, grant someone who can be a grey, grizzled guide for me—I need them speaking into my life. Amen

INVEST

June 9

"O God, you have taught me from my earliest childhood, and I constantly tell others about the wonderful things You do. Now that I am old and gray, do not abandon me, O God. Let me proclaim Your power to this new generation, your mighty miracles to all who come after me."

Psalm 71:17-18

For decades, my life verse was Jeremiah 29:11, *"For I know the plans that I have for you,' declares the Lord, 'plans for welfare and not for calamity to give you a future and a hope"* (NASB). Looking forward in my life, I found great comfort in knowing that God had a wonderful future for me. This gave me great assurance as I moved through life's challenges.

At age 60, the Lord brought Psalm 71 to me. I began to see that His future for me was to leverage my past on behalf of younger men and women who have so much of their future ahead of them. It's not that I wasn't doing that already, but sensing a God-ordained shift in my soul, I memorized these as my new life verses. Now my life centers around investing in the next generation of leaders to help them discover and live out God's great plans for them.

Each of us has the opportunity to invest in the next generations. Parents have the great privilege to invest in their children in ways that help them discover and live out God's great adventure for them. Here's a clue: the adventure is not about helping them become a great athlete or student or entrepreneur. These are ordinary aspirations. God has something far more extra-ordinary in store for them.

In 2008 I became a grandparent. I had no idea. The sheer joy of being a grandparent surpasses almost all experiences of my life. We love investing in them. Sue FaceTime's all 10 of them regularly, reading Bible stories and creating ways for them to interact with these great Bible truths. I'm working through Keller's *The Reason For God* with my 11-year-old by Zoom! We recognize each child's particularity and pray daily for each of them to discover God's unique great adventure.

Don't waste your position and your experience. Invest in the next generations, for your sake, for their sake, for God's sake.

God, help me to see who You want me to invest in and enable me to help them discover Your wonderful future for them. Amen

MYSTERY
June 10

"You who have shown me many troubles and distresses will revive me again,
and will bring me up again from the depths of the earth."
Psalm 71:20 (NASB)

Here we are back at the subject of suffering. This elderly man does not question God as to why he suffers; he only asserts that God is in control of it. The difficult word here for us to grasp is '*shown*'. The Hebrew word (*ra'ah*) means "*to see, understand, reveal, examine, inspect, show.*"

As much as it troubles us to think about it, God is actively involved in the introduction of suffering into our lives. Because suffering seems so anti-loving, we struggle to grasp the reality that God is somehow involved in it—except to deliver us from it.

We've just stepped into a space that is filled with mystery.

In the book of Job, Satan comes to God raising the prospect of bringing suffering to Job. God's response is insightful for us. Yahweh says to Satan, *"You can touch Job here, and here, but you cannot touch him here"* (Job 1:12). There's so much of this I can't grasp, but what I do grasp is that even Satan is the maidservant of God. God is not the cause of pain and suffering, but the controller of it. If we believe in a sovereign God, we must accept the truth of this mystery.

But that's not the only truth in this mystery. Another truth is that God is a loving and merciful God. He acts, in every way, toward His children with love as His motivation. If He '*shows*' us pain, it is for our good.

Thomas Watson, the 17th century Puritan put it this way: "Troubles befall us for our profit. Afflictions teach us. The school of the cross is a school of light. It shows us more of our own hearts. Sharp afflictions are to be the soul as a soaking rain to the house. You don't know there is a leak until it rains." In other words, suffering reveals the need to draw closer to God. And that's a good thing! Joseph said it better in Genesis 50:20 when he said to his dastardly brothers, *"You meant evil against me, but God meant it for good."*

God, I trust that You are in loving control of all that goes on in my life. Enable me to see Your great love and purpose in it all. Amen

MORE MYSTERY

"You who have shown me many troubles and distresses will revive me again, and will bring me up again from the depths of the earth."
Psalm 71:20 (NASB)

Yesterday we tackled the foggy subject of suffering. The elderly psalmist does not question God as to why he suffers, only asserts that He controls it. We struggle to grasp how a loving God can be actively involved in our suffering—except to deliver us from it. But if we believe in a sovereign God, then we must accept His control in all things.

It's a mystery, to be sure. But there are some lights in this fog that give us bearings. Two lights I mentioned yesterday: 1) that Satan is the handmaiden of God; that God is not the cause of suffering, but the controller of it; 2) that God introduces suffering out of His love for us; it draws us closer to Him and in that, He works all things together for our good.

There are at least two more lights in this fog. One is that God does everything for His own glory. You might ask, "How does my suffering bring glory to God?" Because if we trust God only when our lives are good and easy, that doesn't take much of what God treasures greatly—faith (see 1 Peter 1:7). But when we bear up in suffering and **trust** that He is in loving control, it prompts us to ultimately fall to our knees and worship Him as the sovereign God that He is. He's worthy of praise even when our circumstances are awful.

Another light in this fog is the fact that God will grant us the strength to get through our trials: *"You will revive me again, and will bring me up again from the depths of the earth."* I can testify from experience, that God's promises that He will be with us in the fires and the floods are real and true (Isaiah 43:2). Each time I have come out on the other side stronger and better for it.

And one day, pilgrim, our journey will be finished. Ultimately our Father will deliver us from all suffering. Then we'll be in His presence, fully and completely, where there is no pain, there is no suffering, there is no grief, and there is no death.

God, there is so much here I don't understand. But I do trust in You and Your love for me. I can say by faith: You have brought this into my life for Your glory and for my good. Amen

THE END GAME
June 12

"Praise His glorious name forever! Let the whole earth be filled with His glory.
Amen and amen!"
Psalm 72:19

The psalmist finishes this psalm with a doxology (word or song of praise) that extols the glory of God. The glory of God is the end game of all that God is and does.

In the Old Testament, *glory* carries the ideas of brightness, weightiness, and majesty. In the New Testament, it speaks of fame, honor, and beauty. The glory of God, then, is all that is beautiful and famous about God.

God is all about His glory. As Creator of all that is, He's due that! Fortunately for us, that's not the only thing He is about (i.e., love and mercy). But we can know that above all things and behind all things is His intent to be glorified.

The heavens declare His glory (Psalm 19:1)! The whole earth is full of His glory (Isaiah 6:3)! He became flesh and dwelt among us so that we could see His glory (John 1:14)! Jesus died on a cross and was resurrected on the 3rd day for His glory (Philippians 2:5-11)! He meets all our needs according to the riches of His glory (Philippians 4:19-20)! What we suffer now pales in comparison to His glory that will be revealed to us (Romans 8:18)!

Back to the psalm. It says God's name is glorious. In many cultures, certainly the ancient Hebrew culture, the person and their name were synonymous. Their names were to signify their character, heritage, or future. If you insulted their name, it was like a curse. If you said something good about their name, it was a blessing to them.

Whenever you see *LORD* in all caps, it signals God's personal name, Yahweh, which translates to "I AM." The One who is I AM, is the One who is, and was, and is to come—all at the same time!! Eternal and ever-present.

To praise His name is to praise Him. We must glorify Him with our lips and with our lives: *"So whether you eat or drink, or whatever you do, do it all for the glory of God"* (1 Corinthians 10:31).

To that, we join the psalmist and say, Amen, which means, "So be it!" Or, "True that!"

God, I join heaven and earth in praising Your glorious name. By Your Spirit in me, enable and empower me to praise You with my life. Amen

BUT THEN

June 13

"When I tried to understand all this, it seemed hopeless until I entered God's sanctuary.
Then I understood their destiny."
Psalm 73:16-17

Our psalmist, Asaph, is wrestling with one of the great questions this life has to offer: why is it that the godless seem to live a prosperous and easy life, while the godly always seem to suffer adversity and scratch out a meager existence?

Like Asaph, I find myself envying people that have stature and money. Bill Gates doesn't appear to know God, let alone love Him. Same with Warren Buffett and Jeff Bezos. Why do they get all the money? If God gave me that kind of wealth, I sure would do something better with it than they are. Why doesn't God put people like Franklin Graham or Beth Moore or Marty Collier in the great halls of power in Washington, Moscow, and London? God raises up one and puts down another (Psalm 75:7), so why not raise up people like that to run countries?

Like all sin, envy doesn't grasp the whole picture. There are many wealthy individuals who love and serve God and many godly leaders in the halls of power. Still, I can't figure out what God is up to. It's frustrating.

And it's personal. I remember 40 years ago when my dad suddenly died at age 58, I was devastated. One evening a few weeks later, Sue and I were watching the news and some wicked soul was flaunting his power and wealth. It was obvious that it was all about him, to the detriment of his family and friends. In a moment of rage, I kicked my TV tray, spreading Sue's nicely made meal all over the den. I yelled, "Why would God let that guy live and let my dad die!!"

When Asaph contemplated all this, he scratched his head. I do too.

But then—Asaph went into the presence of God and it changed everything for him. He got the true picture of what is and what will be. I can tell you that I've learned this lesson a zillion times. When life doesn't make sense, when I find myself doubting God's plan or love, I only need to come into His presence and worship Him. It changes me. Worship reorients the heart of the worshiper to trust this sovereign, loving God we serve.

God, when I begin to doubt what You're up to, remind me of the But Then. Draw me to Yourself to worship You—and leave running the universe to You. Amen

THE REAL THING
June 14

"Whom have I in heaven but You? I desire You more than anything on earth.
My health may fail, and my spirit may grow weak,
but God remains the strength of my heart; He is mine forever."
Psalm 73:25-26

What a great couple of verses! What an extraordinary perspective!! After complaining about how the wicked seem to prosper while the righteous get the scraps, the psalmist heads to the sanctuary to meet with Yahweh—and everything changes. There is something about worshiping God that resets our hearts and gives us a healthier orientation. In his time with God, God shows Asaph the destiny of all who are indifferent to Him, particularly the wealthy and powerful in this world.

The worshiper sees his own contrasted future, one that is much more preferable than those he envied: *"Yet I still belong to You; You hold my right hand. You guide me with your counsel, leading me to a glorious destiny"* (vv.23-24).

We get so caught up in the trappings and pursuits of this world, don't we? The glitter and glitz catch our eyes and capture our hearts. We find ourselves chasing after stuff that only lasts a few decades at best—and miss the real thing that truly enriches our hearts and lasts for eternity.

Coca-Cola use to run an ad campaign with this chorus, "It's the real thing." The inference was that Coke stood above and apart from all other soft drinks.

Asaph sees clearly now that Yahweh is the Real Thing. He understands that there is nothing else, no one else that even begins to approach the true value of an intimate relationship with God. For true believers, God is our destiny. Heaven is a place, yes; but it is so much more. If God is our destiny in heaven, why not enjoy and love Him more on earth?

On earth we're still broken, to be sure. Our health will fail us. Our faith will get tested and fatigued. But at the end of the day, God is—and will be—the strength of our hearts! We are His, and He is ours. It will be this way forever and ever and ever and ever and . . .

He's the Real Thing.

God, enable me to see the futility of chasing worldly pursuits as if they bring lasting value to my life. Draw me closer so that I fall more in love with You. Strengthen my heart, MY God. Amen

THE JUDGE
June 15

"But God is the Judge; He puts down one and exalts another."
Psalm 75:7

Psalm 75 is a song written in anticipation of victory. It is set to a well-known tune at the time, "Do Not Destroy." Both the words and the tune declare that God will not destroy the righteous, but the wicked will surely perish.

The proud and haughty are warned not to get too caught up in their own self-worth. If they have wealth and power, it was granted to them by Yahweh. God grants power and wealth to whom He desires and then holds the grantee responsible for how the grants are utilized. Arrogance will be met with stiff reprisal; if not in this world, certainly in the one to come.

Asaph, the author, was the great writer and singer of David and Solomon's time. His family (Korah) had faced disgrace and judgment in the days of Moses (see April 26th, Psalm 47) But here he has been elevated to a position of influence and respect. His infamous ancestor had met the judgment of God, but he personally had been exalted by God.

God puts down one and raises up another. It's the decision of a sovereign God. He's the judge, not us. He has His own criteria based on His own plan. He will judge; He will decide who will be exalted for whatever reason and time He determines. The same goes for those He decides to put down.

This has been true throughout history. Charles Spurgeon wrote, "Empires rise and fall at His bidding. A dungeon here, and there a throne, His will assigns. Assyria yields to Babylon, and Babylon, to the Medes. Kings are but puppets in His hand; they serve His purpose when they rise and when they fall."

Every good thing we have comes from God (James 1:17). Every position, every promotion, every possession you have ever received came from the Father of lights. Be overly generous daily with your gratitude to Him for what He has given you, great or small. Utilize what He has granted in a way that brings pleasure to Him and advances His kingdom.

And remember, He exalts one—and puts down another. He's the Judge who decides. Trust Him!

God, I am so grateful for the good things You have brought into my life. Since they are from You, they are more than adequate. Thank you. Amen

HORNS

June 16

"I will cut off all the horns of the wicked, but the horns of the righteous will be lifted up."
Psalm 75:10 (CSB)

The horns of oxen or rams were signs of power and strength. In fact, in an agrarian culture, the ox was the most powerful animal, pulling loads many times their weight. When you go to Jerusalem, you can walk underneath the Temple Mount and see some of the largest blocks in the world, a few weighing 80 tons—all pulled by oxen!

Asaph has been highlighting the power of God in this psalm, warning the proud to stop being haughty and to cease opposing God and His people. Here at the end of the psalm, God speaks up for Himself, as it shifts to first-person: *"I will cut off all the horns of the wicked."* This is personal to God. As sovereign of the universe, He is offended and angered by those who will not submit to His authority. The enemies of Israel, God's chosen people, had better stop harassing and opposing Israel because to oppose His people was to oppose Him—and God would not tolerate it.

The Bible has this unique characteristic that when it speaks, it usually has an 'already-now-not yet' dimension to it. It was true then, there is truth in it now, and it will be fully true in the future.

God has declared that He personally will step in and cut off the horns, render powerless, the nations and peoples who oppose Him. There will be a final accounting at the end of the age. After all, He is The Judge (v.7).

This speaks to every believer who has been abused, who has been abandoned, who has been persecuted, who has suffered prejudice and injustice for the sole reason that they didn't have the power to resist their oppressor. And this speaks to all believers who look at the world system that opposes God, the word of God, the people of God, and the things of God—and wonder if justice will ever reign.

The story is not finished, so don't lose heart. The day is coming when the god of this world (Satan) and all who do his bidding will meet their end. Their horns will be cut off. And the horns of the righteous, those who bear the righteousness of Jesus, will be lifted up (see Revelation).

Count on it!

God, when I feel powerless against the forces of this world, I will look by faith to Your final act of justice. Amen

STRONG-ARMED
June 17

*"When I was in deep trouble, I searched for the Lord.
All night long I prayed, with hands lifted toward heaven, but my soul was not comforted."*
Psalm 77:2

The psalmist is put out with God. He feels as if Yahweh has been indifferent to his plight; that his suffering is being ignored. His hands were lifted in prayer all night long, but he is not comforted. He finally confesses, *"I am too depressed to pray"* (v.4).

This experience is not unusual among believers, is it? There are times when the 'dark night of the soul' leaves us wondering why God is letting this happen; wondering if it will ever be different; wondering if God really loves us.

This despair is common territory to someone who suffers a great loss of some kind: a loved one, a marriage, a career, our health, an injustice. Whatever the cause, we are left to deal with our emotions. Emotions are real and they can be raw. They can be a wonderful companion or a cruel taskmaster. When tethered to fact and faith, they are a great blessing. When allowed to run independently, they are a terrible curse.

Asaph finally gets insight, *"But then I recall all You have done, O Lord; I remember Your wonderful deeds of long ago"* (v.11). At this point, he begins to recount a few facts, particularly the crossing of the Red Sea. Here and in other parts of Scripture, this unbelievable miracle is recalled over and over again to strengthen the faith of Israel.

When I find myself in a situation like Asaph, fearful and doubtful about things, I have learned to look backward. I go back into my prayer journal and look at all the times God answered my prayers. My memory is engaged in recalling times in my life where He came through for me in hopeless times. When my present and future seem overwhelming, I look back to see how faithful God has been in the past. I look back—and then I look up.

The psalmist finishes with this, *"O God, Your ways are holy. Is there any god as mighty as You? You are the God of great wonders! You demonstrate Your awesome power among the nations. By Your strong arm, you redeemed Your people"* (vv.13-15).

I've been strong-armed by God many times!

Lord, I look back in my past and see how faithful You have been. Thank You. I will look up and see how awesome and strong You are—and not be afraid. Amen

PASS IT ON

June 18

"That the generation to come might know, even the children yet to be born, that they may arise and tell them to their children, that they should put their confidence in God and not forget the works of God, but keep His commandments."
Psalm 78:6-7(NASB)

I remember my dad telling stories about growing up in the Great Depression. I remember stories of him fighting on Iwo Jima in WW2. I remember stories of how God led him to my mom. I've told them to my kids. There is a mysterious quality about stories that connect us to people and events in ways nothing else can.

Psalm 78 is a *maskil*. The root word is *sakal* which means to have or give insight; to teach. The writer is giving a heads up that this is a teaching psalm. He emphasizes this in v.1, *"O my people, listen to my instructions. Open your ears to what I am saying."*

What is it that the Holy Spirit laid on Asaph's heart that must be taught? When you read the entire psalm, you see that it is largely a recounting of God's faithfulness to deliver the Hebrews out of Egypt and provide for them in the wilderness even in their disobedience. Other times of God's intervention are included in the psalm.

These stories of God's power and provision were to be passed on from generation to generation. But sadly, the parents and leaders often failed in their duty.

If you are a Christ-follower, you have a story of God's deliverance and provision. It's called your testimony, your account of God's gracious and miraculous rescue from sin and its penalty.

As a parent, grandparent, leader, and influencer in your community of faith, this is a story that must be repeated from generation to generation. Do your children know your story? Do your grandchildren? Pass it on!

But you certainly do have more stories, right? Stories of when you saw God's hand at work in your life. Stories of His provision. Stories of His protection. Stories that highlight the glory and majesty of what Jesus has done and is doing in your life.

Pass them on!

God, You have delivered me so many times. You have provided for me in so many ways. I want to be a good steward of those stories and pass them on to the next generation. Amen.

THE SHEPHERD

June 19

"So he shepherded them according to the integrity of his heart,
and guided them with his skillful hands."
Psalm 78:72 (NASB)

The 'he' in this verse is David. This fairly lengthy psalm recalls the rebellious history of the stiff-necked Hebrews despite God's mighty works on their behalf. From the time God delivered them out of Egypt, 40 years in the wilderness, even when He took them into the Promised Land—they struggled to stay obedient. As an example, read vv.52 56.

You would think that after all God had done for them, they would be so thankful and willing to follow His commandments that instructed them how to live under His blessing, right? I mean, who in their right mind would not want to live under God's blessings?

We can't be too critical. We WANT to be obedient; we want to live under God's blessings, but we wander, we drift away, we struggle to keep God first in our hearts and lives—not ideally, but really. After all He has done for us, like the Israelites, we still rebel; we still sin.

Perhaps you've heard the story about the little boy who was afraid of the thunderstorm in the middle of the night. He cried out, "Daddy, I'm afraid!" His dad assured him, "You're ok, buddy. God is in there with you." A big thunderclap hit again: "Daddy, I'm really afraid now." The dad said, "That's ok little buddy, God is in there with you. You'll be alright." After the next loud thunderclap, the boy said, "Daddy, I know God is in here with me—but I need someone with skin!"

God raised up David for His people; someone with skin who would shepherd His sheep: a man of integrity; a man who cared for God's people with skill.

Every sheep needs a shepherd with integrity and skill. If you're not committed to a local body of believers, you need to find one and get plugged in. The worship style is important, yes. The ministries for your teens and children are important, yes. But nothing is more important than being under a shepherd who loves The Good Shepherd; someone with skin who leads with integrity and compassion. That's my pastor! I pray you have one as well.

God, thank you for my pastor. Enable him and empower him to lead us with integrity and skill. And when he gets discouraged, I promise to encourage and pray for him. Amen

SHEARING THE SHEEP
June 20

"Then we Your people, the sheep of Your pasture, will thank You forever and ever,
praising Your greatness from generation to generation."
Psalm 79:13

Psalm 79 was apparently written after Nebuchadnezzar and the Babylonians laid siege and eventually destroyed Jerusalem and its Temple in 586-87 B.C. As you read through this short psalm, you get a summary of the awful destruction of the city. Jeremiah, the great prophet and eyewitness to the calamity, recorded part of the scene in Jeremiah 52:12-24.

God had warned His people for centuries that they had wandered away and allowed other gods to take root in their hearts, violating the first commandment: *"You must have no other gods but Me"* (Exodus 20:3). They drifted into syncretism, i.e., the merging together of belief systems. They worshiped Yahweh, yes, but they also worshiped other cultural gods such as Baal, Asherah, and Moloch. The One True God did not and will not stand for this. He cajoled, then warned, then eventually brought a terrible punishment on them. He sheared His sheep.

Maybe He has sheared you. You fashion yourself as a true believer, but you've allowed yourself to worship other cultural gods like financial security, entertainment, sex, alcohol, or the powerful 21st Century god, comfort. They get your affections, your time, and your money. They lead you to walk out of marriages, miss out on family time, throw your money at them, and eventually leave you empty and used.

God will not play 2nd fiddle to anyone or anything. His Spirit will warn us by convicting our hearts. If we ignore Him, harden our hearts toward Him, He will eventually begin to shear us. I know from experience that His discipline can be utterly devastating. I also know that He disciplines those He loves (Hebrews 12:5-11) and His intent in doing so is to rid us of the wickedness in our hearts and purify our love for Him.

Feel sheared right now? Repent. Turn away from your gods. Make conscious decisions to serve and love Him first and foremost. He will grant grace and mercy and begin to restore what has been devastated. He loves His sheep.

God, I do turn from my idolatry of those gods. By your grace, refine my love and devotion for You. As Your sheep, I will praise Your name to those in my life and tell them of Your rescue. Amen.

FROWN OR SMILE?

June 21

"Turn us again to Yourself, O God. Make Your face shine down upon us.
Only then will we be saved."

Psalm 80:3, 7, 19

Any good parent understands the great value of discipline for character development in a child. It's not as much about punishment as it is love: "I love you too much to let you do this."

The context of this psalm seems to be a time when the Northern Kingdom (Israel split into two kingdoms in about 930 B.C.) was being attacked by the Assyrians about 721 B.C. God had raised up the Assyrians to discipline His people for their worship of other gods.

Some believers struggle to accept the fact that God disciplines His people. They wonder how God would bring pain to those He loves. Yet all through Scripture Yahweh is portrayed as a God who loves His people too much to let them get away with what they're doing.

Sometimes His discipline is extremely painful. Hebrews 12:6 says, *"For the Lord disciplines those He loves, and He punishes each one he accepts as His child."* That word *punishes* means to punish severely, even whipping. Ouch!

The psalmist makes essentially the same plea three times in this psalm, verses 3, 7, & 19, to indicate that he is dead serious about his request. He's asking God to take three actions. First, that God would turn back toward His people. We know this as a metaphor describing disfavor; that God is not happy with them. The psalmist is wanting God to turn back around and show favor once again. The second request is similar: that God would smile at them again. Because of their behavior, God is portrayed with a frowning face in v.16. Children want to please their parents; we prefer smiles over frowns. The third request is the result of the first two: that God would rescue them. They needed relief that only He could give.

Do you need relief? Need God's rescue? Then align yourself with His will. Is there any sin that you are holding on to? Let it go. Surrender all to Him. Seek His pleasure instead of your own. Then the transforming power of His Spirit in you will begin the rescuing, restorative process that only He can deliver. That will turn His frown into a smile.

God, I do want to align myself with Your will. I surrender all I am, all I have to You. I want to sense your favor; your smile. May it be so.

OPEN WIDE
June 22

"Open your mouth wide, and I will fill it with good things."
Psalm 81:10

When my eldest child was just a baby, we'd put him in a highchair, strap the bib around his neck, and shovel pureed vegetables down his throat. My mental picture of him forever will be of both his arms flapping like a bird, eyes bright with anticipation, mouth wide open waiting for each spoonful. As loving parents, we wanted to give him what tasted good, what was good for him, and in amounts that were good for him. It's what parents do!

Our Heavenly Father wants to do the same. This psalm depicts Him wanting to give the children of Israel the good stuff of life. That's why He relieved their heavy burdens (v.6), rescued them from Egypt (v.10), and provided for them in the wilderness (v.7).

But Israel didn't want God, only the good stuff He could provide: *"But no, My people wouldn't listen. Israel did not want Me around"* (v.11). They thought they knew better how to live (v.12) and walked their path instead of His (v.13). Instead of opening their mouths wide for the good stuff God wanted to give them, eventually they shut them tight and looked for food elsewhere.

Do you get the fact that God wants to feed and fill you with the best? Jesus said a mouthful when He said, *"I came so you can have an amazing life here and in heaven; more and better life than you ever dreamed of!"* (John 10:10; RDB). More and better life than you ever dreamed of—who wouldn't want that?

To get that, we need to want Him, to love Him, and to please Him. Otherwise, we just use Him for our own selfish desires; to only want Him around when we want something. No one wants to be treated that way; certainly not The Great I AM.

Fall in love with Jesus. When you love someone, you want to please them, right? Fall in love with Jesus. He promises to give us more and better than we could ever imagine.

The more I fall in love with Him, the clearer I hear Him say, "Open wide!"

God, thank You for loving me so much that You sent Your Son to declare it and demonstrate it. By Your grace, enable me to draw closer to You and experience the good stuff You have for me. Amen

THE WEAK

June 23

"Rescue the poor and helpless; deliver them from the grasp of evil people."
Psalm 82:4

The psalmist is calling out for God to rescue those who are weak and oppressed. He is calling on those in authority to stop rendering decisions in favor of the powerful and to champion the cause of the poor, the needy, the fatherless, the weak.

This theme is particularly highlighted in the writings of the prophets. Over and over again God reveals His heart and compassion for those who are weak and vulnerable. Isaiah heard this from Yahweh:

> *Free those who are wrongly imprisoned; lighten the burden of those who work for you. Let the oppressed go free, and remove the chains that bind people. Share your food with the hungry, and give shelter to the homeless. Give clothes to those who need them, and do not hide from relatives who need your help.* Isaiah 58:6-7

God's heart for the weak is not just revealed by the prophets, but all through the Scripture. In the Books of the Law, He prescribes that widows and immigrants be provided for (Deuteronomy 10:9-10). In the gospels we see Jesus moving through crowds of the weak, displaced, and hurting, responding with divine compassion (Matthew 9:36). The epistles (letters) point to the compassion of Jesus and encourage us to follow His example (2 Corinthians 1:3-4). And James, the half-brother of Jesus, warns what is in store for us if we don't share our wealth and influence with those less fortunate than us (James 5:1-6).

If God has been generous enough with me to save me, to rescue me, to forgive me, and adopt me, shouldn't I be generous with others? If He has blessed me with a job, and a house, and food, should I not be willing to share those blessings with others?

This shouldn't be driven by guilt—only gratitude and joy for what Jesus has done for you. We were weak and He came alongside us to help, to strengthen, and to provide. Let's be like Him.

God, thank You for the eternal blessing of salvation and the temporal blessings of food and shelter. Remake my heart to be more like Your generous heart. Amen

HATE

June 24

"O God, do not be silent! Do not be deaf. Do not be quiet, O God. Don't You hear the uproar of Your enemies? Don't You see that Your arrogant enemies are rising up? They devise crafty schemes against Your people; they conspire against Your precious ones."

Psalm 83:1-3

The context of this psalm is probably found in 2 Chronicles 20 when the enemies of Israel gathered to overthrow King Jehoshaphat and capture Jerusalem. Regardless, the topic of this psalm is one of the overarching themes of the Bible: God has enemies, and by association, so do we.

If you're a true believer, you live in a world that hates you. Jesus said, *"If the world hates you, remember that it hated Me first. The world would love you as one of its own if you belonged to it, but you are no longer part of the world. I chose you to come out of the world, so it hates you"* (John 15:18-19).

The Psalmist mentions *crafty schemes*. That is the same language used in Ephesians 6:11, *"Put on the full armor of God so that you can stand against the schemes of the devil"* (CSB).

It follows that Satan has a whole system of schemes to oppose God, the word of God, the people of God, and the things of God. This world system promotes values and perspectives opposite of God's as revealed in Scripture. As Bible believers, we find ourselves in constant conflict with the world system.

When we hold to the biblical view on life and oppose abortion, the world hates us. When we hold to the biblical view of marriage and oppose same-sex marriage, the world hates us. When we hold to the biblical view that salvation is imparted only by grace through faith in Jesus alone, the world hates us.

King Jehoshaphat called the people to pray, and Israel was victorious. Prayer is what leads God's people to victory—and faith that ultimately, we will be on the winning side, even though it feels like we're losing right now. Jesus said it right, *"I have told you all this so that you may have peace in Me. Here on earth you will have many trials and sorrows. But take heart, because I have overcome the world"* (John 16:33).

Get used to the hate.

God, I pray that my worldview lines up with Yours, and that if people despise me, it is because I love and follow You. Grant me the grace to do it. Amen

PRESENCE
June 25

"How lovely is Your dwelling place, O Lord of Heaven's Armies.
I long, yes, I faint with longing to enter the courts of the Lord.
With my whole being, body and soul, I will shout joyfully to the living God."
Psalm 84:1-2

Psalm 84 is one of my favorite psalms. It is a pilgrimage psalm describing the blessedness of the one who journeyed to the temple to pray.

The temple, of course, was in Jerusalem. To the Jew, it was the place where heaven met earth; where God met man. It was the centerpiece of worship for all Jews regardless of where they lived. Some of the journeys to the temple were long, strenuous, and even dangerous. But time in the presence of the Yahweh during one of the feasts, like Passover, was worth it. Those who lived close would go to the temple regularly, some even daily. Worshipers would enter the outer courts of the temple singing and lifting up their voices in praise. There was nothing quiet about it!

The temple, and its portable predecessor, the tabernacle, housed the Ark of the Covenant and symbolized the presence of God. Indeed, there were instances where God's presence showed up in incredible, observable ways. (1 Kings 8:10-11; Isaiah 6) But no single dwelling houses the infinite God: *"This is what the Lord says: 'Heaven is My throne, and the earth is My footstool.*

Could you build Me a temple as good as that? Could you build Me such a resting place?'" (Isaiah 66:1).

Genuine worship has never been about the place; it's always been about the presence. The psalmist was excited to come into the presence of the Lord. All true believers are drawn to the presence of the Living God to worship Him.

Notice the language: *"with my whole being, body and soul."* If I've said it once, I've said it a thousand times: worship is a full-body experience! It starts deep in the soul and makes its way to the body. I often wonder about those who stand placidly in corporate worship—what's going on inside of them, or, what's NOT going on inside of them?

Regardless, to come into the presence of the Creator of the Universe and the Lover of our Souls is something that we should long for. If it isn't, ask the Lord why.

O God, show me what is keeping me from desiring more of Your presence. Fan the flame of my heart for You. Amen

ANGEL ARMIES
June 26

"How lovely is Your dwelling place, O Lord of Heaven's Armies."
Psalm 84:1

Angels are referred to at least 273 times in 34 books of the Bible. Yet they are never really discussed. Their appearance in Scripture is always incidental to some other topic or event. When they are mentioned, they inform us more about who God is and what He is up to.

Most people are fascinated by the idea of angels. There certainly have been many books, movies, and TV shows with angels as central characters. This has led to a lot of misconceptions about angels.

A few basic facts. Angels are beings created by God to serve Him. They are immaterial, though at times visible. They are more wise and powerful than us, yet because they are not created in God's image, they are not as valuable as humans. Somewhere in history some of them rebelled against God and became 'fallen angels' or demons as we call them. They oppose God and His work. Those that remain obedient to Yahweh serve different and various purposes.

The psalmist mentions heaven's armies. Some translations use the term *hosts*. The Hebrew word is *tsaba* and carries the idea of warfare. So, these are angels serving God in spiritual warfare—and there are a bunch of them! But hear this: just because we can't always see them, doesn't mean they're not there. They are fighting for God and for those of us in Christ.

In 2 Kings 6:8-16, Elisha the prophet was surrounded by the army of Aram with orders to kill him. His servant began to panic. Elisha said, *"Don't be afraid! Those who are with us are greater than those against us."* Then he prayed for the servant to see with spiritual eyes. The result was that the servant saw they were surrounded by angels and *'chariots of fire'* (Great movie!).

Listen. If you are in Christ by faith, then Christ is in you. The Living God resides in you, not some building, and *"greater is He who is in you than he who is in the world"* (1 John 4:4). When you feel surrounded, overwhelmed, discouraged, panicky—open your eyes of faith and see that the LORD of hosts has deployed His angel armies to surround you!

God, I choose to believe that You are fighting for me. By your grace, I will trust in You, not my circumstances and not my feelings. Amen

VALUED
June 27

"Even the sparrow finds a home, and the swallow builds her nest and raises her young at a place near Your altar, O Lord of Heaven's Armies, my King and my God!"
Psalm 84:3

Sparrows are the most common bird on the planet. Some ornithologists spend lots of money and travel to remote parts of the world to view rare birds such as the New Caledonian Owlet-Nightjar in, you guessed it, New Caledonia, or the Great Indian Bustard in, yeah, India. But nobody really travels anywhere to see one of the gazillion sparrows in the world.

There's a universal economic principle: the more of something there is, the less value is assessed to it. When I was a kid, I collected rare coins. The market value was far more than face value. I had books and books of rare coins—until my brother raided them without me discovering it and bought popsicles from the ice cream truck one entire summer!

The psalmist purposely speaks of the sparrow finding a home in the temple, the "dwelling place of God." His point: the most common of all animals is valued and welcome in the presence of God Almighty.

Jesus often mentioned sparrows: *"What is the price of five sparrows—two copper coins? Yet God does not forget a single one of them. And the very hairs on your head are all numbered. So don't be afraid; you are more valuable to God than a whole flock of sparrows"* (Luke 12:6-7). I love that phrase, *"Yet God does not forget a single one of them."*

So, if God never loses track of a sparrow, how much more does He keep up with you? If the sparrow is so valued by God, how much more are you? If the sparrow is welcome to find a home in the presence of God, how much more are you?

Our world places value on people for all the wrong reasons: wealth, power, beauty, fame. I don't have much of that, thus very little worldly value. But God valuing me? Get out!!

God values us, not because of who we are, but because of who He is: *"For God so loved the world, that He gave His one and only Son, that whoever believes in Him will not perish (become valueless) but have eternal life (in His presence)"* (John 3:16; RDB). You are invaluable to Him!

God, thank You for loving me and giving Your son to die for me. What amazing value You place on me! Thank You! Amen

REST

June 28

*"Even the sparrow finds a home, and the swallow builds her nest and raises her young
at a place near Your altar, O Lord of Heaven's Armies, my King and my God!"*
Psalm 84:3

Swallows are another interesting bird. They never seem to touch the ground; always flitting around, always hunting small insects, and even can feed their fledglings mid-flight!

It's interesting to me that the psalmist mentioned these two birds in v.3. Yesterday we saw that the sparrow symbolizes commonness; that even the most lowly and insignificant of us are welcome in the presence of the Lord. The swallow represents restlessness; that even the most ill at ease or unsettled of us can find rest and peace in the presence of the Lord.

We are certainly a people who struggle with finding rest and peace. Our hyperactivity is creating a nation of folks so over-committed and in constant motion that the level of anxiety amongst all ages has been rising at alarming rates for years. Some studies indicate that 40% of Americans suffer notable levels of anxiety. My sense is that it is more—and rising.

There are many causes for our anxiety and inner restlessness, but the most common is stress. Work stresses us out and so do our finances, relationships, and constant busyness—and that leads to anxiety. There are many good responses for anxiety, but for now, let's tackle the first and most important one: learning to come into God's presence to discuss it, surrender it, and leave it with Him.

Jesus said, *"Come to me, all of you who are weary and carry heavy burdens, and I will give you rest"* (Matthew 11:28). There you go! You want to begin to gain victory over your anxiety and find rest? Come to Him with whatever is causing you anxiety. Surrender it, and your will concerning it, to Him. And then leave it with Him. Our anxiety occurs if any of those three steps break down. We want to handle it ourselves. Wrong move. We don't want to trust God with it. Wrong move. We keep taking it back after we've laid it before Him. Wrong move.

The rest you seek begins in the presence of God: discuss it, surrender it, and leave it with Him.

Nothing else really works.

God, I do come to You with these anxiety-producing issues. I want your will, not mine. I do leave them with You. Bring me peace. Amen

THE MIDDLEMAN
June 29

"What joy for those who can live in your house, always singing your praises."
Psalm 84:4

It wasn't only birds that lived in the temple, but also the ministering priests. The priests lived in various Levitical cities in Israel and took turns serving in the temple located in Jerusalem. When it was their turn, the temple was equipped with rooms for the priests to stay in.

The priests interceded before the Lord on behalf of the nation of Israel and offered sacrifices on behalf of the people. If you were a Jew, you could not make your own sacrifice, you had to come to the temple with your sacrifice (or purchase it there) and let the priests do it for you and intercede for you so that your sin would be atoned for. All official interactions between God and man were done through the priest. The priest was the middleman.

On this, the New Testament is abundantly clear in two matters. First, there is no more need for sacrifices to atone for sin. Jesus made that ultimate sacrifice on the cross: *"It was the precious blood of Christ, the sinless, spotless Lamb of God. God chose Him as your ransom"* (1 Peter 1:19-20). There is absolutely no need to make sacrifice or penance. There is no other way to be united to God: *"For Christ also suffered for sins once for all, the righteous for the unrighteous, that He might bring you to God"* (1 Peter 3:18). Hallelujah!

The second matter is this: the middleman has been cut out and made obsolete! This issue, Priesthood of the Believer, was a big part of the Reformation. We don't need priests; we ARE priests! Jesus is our great High Priest (Hebrews 4:14). If we are united to Him through faith, we share in this priesthood: *"You are living stones that God is building into His spiritual temple. What's more, you are His holy priests. Through the mediation of Jesus Christ, you offer spiritual sacrifices that please God."* (1 Peter 2:4-5)

As priests, we have direct access to God. We don't have to go through any human being. We live in His house and can go straight into His presence to pray and praise and worship. Amazing!

Jesus, thank You for clearing out the separation between me and the Father and opening the way for me to live in Your house with constant and eternal access to You. Amen

THE SPOTTER
June 30

"What joy for those whose strength comes from the Lord."
Psalm 84:5

If you've ever lifted weights or done any kind of resistance training, you know this dynamic: you begin doing your reps and feel pretty strong, but pretty soon the muscle you're working out gets worn out. No matter how strong you are, your strength gets sapped.

When I go to the gym, I'll see guys over on the bench press. One guy will be lying on his back pushing up huge amounts of weight while the other guy is 'spotting' him. Because the muscle runs out of strength after a certain number of reps, at the end, the lifter sometimes can't get the weights back on the rack. If he didn't have a spotter, the bar would drop down on his neck!

Life can wear us down. It saps our strength. The dad who works 60+ hours a week to provide for his family and stays involved in their lives in the evenings and weekends knows that. The stay-at-home mother who wrestles with preschoolers all day knows that. The working mom who pushes hard all day and then pushes hard at home more knows that. The single mom— one of the strongest creatures on earth—REALLY knows that!

The husband who keeps loving even when his wife is acting unlovable knows that. The person who is the caregiver of a loved one with chronic medical issues knows that. The one who struggles with anxiety or depression knows that.

At some point, our strength fails us. There is no shame in that. Even Jesus (God in the flesh) had strength limitations: He was worn out at the well and stressed out in the garden.

When our strength fails, we need a spotter: someone who can make up for our weakness. Fortunately for those of us who are believers, we have THE Spotter! When David had no strength left, he *"found strength in the Lord"* (1 Samuel 30:6). Paul encouraged the Ephesian believers who were in the midst of great spiritual warfare to *"Be strong in the Lord and in His mighty power"* (Ephesians 6:10).

The muscle fatigue in weightlifting actually builds muscle and strength. In the Christ-life, increased strength comes as we learn to rely on The Spotter sooner and better.

God, I confess I do feel weak and worn out. I call on You to strengthen me for the task You have set before me. Amen

THE PURPLE ROOM
July 1

"What joy for those whose strength comes from the Lord,
who have set their minds on a pilgrimage to Jerusalem."
Psalm 84:5

The psalmist begins verses 4 and 5 with the same phrase, *"What joy for those..."* Some translations read, *"How blessed are those..."* In v.4, the joyful, blessed ones are those who live in the temple. In v.5, the joyful, blessed ones are those who are on a pilgrimage to the temple. Many Jews who traveled to Jerusalem to be a part of one of the feasts, such as Passover or Pentecost, had far distances to go. The journey was strenuous and tiring. The psalmist is saying there is blessedness in the temple, but there is also blessedness in the journey.

There is certainly something incredibly wonderful about worshiping the Lord, whether alone in our time with Him or with the congregation of God. We can kind of leave our stress and worry there and be lifted up in His presence. So good. So wonderful. But there is something indispensable about the journeys of life that get us there.

I remember a story a friend told me decades ago. She went to a women's health club in Houston to help her with her weight. They ushered her into a purple room that was decorated beautifully. Pictures of slender and smiling women hung on the walls. They gave her some tea and a cookie. They talked to her about all the nice classes they could offer her to improve her health. She was thrilled and couldn't wait to sign the contract and pay the first year's fee.

A few days later she went to her first class. In five minutes, she was exhausted and soaking wet. All she could think about was the purple room. She wanted to be back in the purple room. Everything felt good in the purple room. It was thrilling to be in the purple room. But, she realized, to be like the ladies on the purple room walls, she had to go through the journey to get there.

There is something about the difficulties of life that make the worship experience better. Don't discount them. Count them as a blessing.

God, thank you for the journey You've set me on. Don't let me miss the blessing of it. Amen

REFRESHMENT
July 2

"What joy for those whose strength comes from the Lord,
who have set their minds on a pilgrimage to Jerusalem. When they walk through the
Valley of Weeping, it will become a place of refreshing springs.
The autumn rains will clothe it with blessings. They will continue to grow stronger,
and each of them will appear before God in Jerusalem."
Psalm 84:5-7

On the way to join in on one of the Jewish feasts in Jerusalem, pilgrims (travelers) would undoubtedly encounter various hardships. After all, there was no Holiday Inn, no McDonalds, and no drink stations at non-existent rest stops. Some apparently would pass through a place called the Valley of Baca. The word *Baca* carries with it the idea of tears and weeping, or of dryness and drought.

Walking with Christ is not for the weak or woozy. We are not insulated from trial or tragedy. The Bible is full of examples of God-blessed individuals who suffered greatly from Abraham and Sarah (who struggled with infertility for decades), to Joseph (who was hated by his family, sold into slavery, and thrown into jail). Fast forward to Mary and Joseph (who had to flee the country), to our Jesus (who was dissed His entire ministry, tortured within an inch of death, and finally hung naked on a cross at a crossroad). His disciples did not fare much better.

And there are times of dryness in our relationship with Jesus. A relationship is not transactional, that is, one cause always results in an expected result. A relationship is fluid; it experiences ebbs and flows. There are times I feel very close to Jesus and other times that He seems so distant.

In our journey toward heaven, we will experience want and weeping; suffering and shortage. All of this is for our good. Thomas Watson, a 17th century Puritan put it this way:

> Troubles befall us for our profit. They show us more of our own hearts.
> Sharp afflictions are to the soul as a soaking rain to the house.
> You don't know where the leaks are until it rains.

Sometimes our hardships are our doing; sometimes not. Regardless, along the way God promises periods of refreshment. Each time we push through times of dryness or heartache, our faith strengthens, and we are drawn closer to Him: *"They will continue to grow stronger, and each of them will appear before God"* (v.7).

God, I need refreshment today! Hear my cry. Amen

SELAH

July 3

"O Lord God of Heaven's Armies, hear my prayer. Listen, O God of Jacob. Selah"
Psalm 64:8

Here, midway through the psalm, the sons of Korah hit the pause button. That's what *selah* means: to pause or to emphasize by pausing. You know when you're telling a story or making a statement and you want the importance of something you said to sink in, you pause. Selah.

Looking at v.8, we see at least four reasons for the pause. First, as we've examined, the previous verses are talking about how blessed people are who enjoy the presence of God and who are blessed in the journey to come into His presence. Second, the phrase, *O Lord God of Heaven's Armies* is repeated. This is acknowledging the fact that there are myriads of angels circulating around creation doing the bidding of Yahweh and fighting for His beloved. We take heart in knowing that there are more forces for us than against us. Third, there is the call for God to listen. That's what prayer is, a dialogue with God. We can come to Him with our problems and burdens—and He listens! He's not deaf. He's not disengaged. He is deeply interested in what troubles us.

Finally, there is the phrase, *O God of Jacob*. If you've studied Jacob's life, you might really wonder about this. Jacob was a scoundrel; a trickster. He conspired with his mom, deceived his brother, broke his dad's heart, and wrestled mightily with the idea of surrendering to God.

You see this phrase all through the Old Testament. Why God of Jacob? There's no God of Moses, no God of David, no God of Elijah. You get the point. Why God of Jacob?

Because Jacob was no role model. Jacob didn't deserve blessing; in fact, just the opposite. He was one broken, self-absorbed dude. Yet God chose to bless him. That's the idea of grace, right? Unmerited, undeserved favor.

I can identify with Jacob: flawed moral character, deceiving, manipulating, ill-tempered, impatient—I'm a hot mess! But God CHOSE me! He RESCUED me from certain doom! He ADOPTED me into His family! He has INDWELT me with His presence! He has BLESSED me in ways I cannot fully grasp or estimate! He has RESERVED a place in heaven for me! O God of Russ!

Selah!!

God, thank You for Your gift of salvation. I don't deserve it—but oh how grateful I am for it! Amen

THE KING

July 4

"O God, look with favor upon the king, our shield! Show favor to the one You have anointed."
Psalm 84:9

Psalm 84 is about the joy that comes for those who seek the presence of God. The temple is where the ancient Jew made his way to worship God. There was joy in the journey and joy to finally be in the place where (in their view) God resided.

Because the temple was a physical, earthly place, it was subject to certain physical, earthly realities. The psalmist prays that the king of Israel, the one with physical, earthly power, would enjoy the favor of God so that the temple would be protected from harm from other nations.

As it turns out, because the temple was a physical, earthly place, the kings could not always protect it. Solomon built the first temple in about 950 B.C. It was magnificent. Unfortunately, because Israel turned its back on Yahweh, He raised up Nebuchadnezzar and the Babylonians who tore down the temple in 586 B.C. It was partially rebuilt by Ezra and his friends in about 535-515 B.C. Herod the Great (the Herod who tried to kill baby Jesus) greatly expanded the temple in 20 B.C. Jesus worshipped in it and predicted its total destruction, which occurred in 70 A.D. by the Romans. The only building on that site now is the Muslim structure known as the Dome of the Rock. Point: kings couldn't/can't protect it.

In actuality, God has never been restricted to a place. We don't need a place to worship Yahweh. We can seek His presence no matter where we are or what's going on. There is a King who can protect—His name is Jesus! He is the Messiah, the anointed One. He doesn't protect a place; this King protects His people. He is the shield and guarantor of our salvation; the lover and protector of our souls. No force can take or destroy what He protects: *"I give them eternal life, and they will never perish. No one can snatch them away from Me"* (John 10:28).

If you are in Christ and Christ is in you, then your redemption, your relationship with God, your access to God, and your place in heaven are secured, not by your effort or strength, but by your King Jesus!

Jesus, thank you for spilt blood on the cross that sealed this deal; that is stronger than anything that will come against me. Amen

LOVE LANGUAGE

July 5

"A single day in Your courts is better than a thousand anywhere else! I would rather be a gatekeeper in the house of my God than live the good life in the homes of the wicked"

Psalm 84:10

The psalmist places such high value on being in the presence of God that he makes some grandiose statements: "A day with You is better than a thousand anywhere else; just let me hold the door for You—it's all I need!"

Sounds pretty radical, right? But such is the language of love. We would expect young lovers to make statements similar to these: "In vain I have struggled. It will not do. My feelings will not be repressed. You must allow me to tell you how ardently I admire and love you" (Jane Austin). "You are my heart, my life, my one and only thought" (Sir Arthur Conan Doyle).

Words like these have been expressed between lovers since the beginning. I might have uttered a few myself. The reason is that when love is involved, everything else pales in comparison. Passion of the heart shoves other realities to the back of a closet so that nothing else really matters. But honestly, while I may have said stuff like that when I was younger, I didn't really know what I was talking about. Young love is usually stupid love! But now after 40+ years of marriage with this wonderful woman God has given me, my love has matured. Words can't quite fully express the depth of my love for Sue. Yet, reminiscent of the Bee Gees, words are all I have.

The psalmist is saying about his Lover that he would rather be with Him than be with anyone else or be anywhere else. I am familiar with this. There are times I am so caught up with the Lover of my soul in reading my Bible or in worship that time seems to fly. I want more of THAT! I want more of HIM!

My love for Jesus has matured, but unfortunately, I still have a long way to go. I get distracted. I become too hurried. I give my affections elsewhere. Sad, but true. My desire is to be more like the psalmist and to be like that all the time. One day…

God, forgive me for letting life limit my time and passion for You. I do love You. Fan the flame. Amen

THE SUN
July 6

"For the Lord God is our sun and our shield. He gives us grace and glory. The Lord will withhold no good thing from those who do what is right."

Psalm 84:11

I love this verse for a whole lot of reasons. There are many times in the Bible where God is referred to as a shield, but this is the only place where God is explicitly called the sun. Biblical writers undoubtedly resisted the comparison because of the dominance of solar deity worship.

To the ancients, the sun represented power, life, warmth, and light. It was probably the most dominant feature and force in their lives. We know now that it is literally the center of our physical existence.

I love that the sun comes up every day. Regardless of what happened the day before, each day is brand new; a new beginning. I need that. Some days are really hard. Some days are really dark. Some days are really painful. I'm glad to know that I get a new start each morning. In the midst of a time of great pain and suffering, Jeremiah wrote, *"Your mercies are new every morning; great is Your faithfulness"* (Lamentations 3:23). Today is a new day to live in and by God's mercy and grace.

I love that the sun shines on my face. When the moon shines on me, I can't feel it. But the sun warms my face, and it feels like—it's shining just on me. It feels so personal. Proverbs 7:2 says that I am the apple of God's eye. That means that He gazes at and watches me closely. Zechariah 2:8 says that whoever harms me, harms God's most precious possession. I feel the warmth of His love.

I love that the sun gives light to my day. Until 200 years ago, humanity had no way to see at night without a torch or candle. Daybreak gave them limitless illumination. When I don't know what to do or which way to go, God and His word enable me to see more clearly where I am and the path in front of me: *"Your word is a lamp to guide my feet and a light for my path"* (Psalm 119:105).

The Son is my sun!

God, I praise You for being my sun. And even when I go through seasons where dark clouds seem to blot You out, I know You're there for me—and that is comforting. Amen

GIFTS
July 7

"For the Lord God is our sun and our shield. He gives us grace and glory."
Psalm 84:11

God's love language is gifts. Maybe you've read *The Five Love Languages* by Gary Chapman. From his counseling practices, Chapman came to believe that each person has one or more love languages to express or receive love. Gifts is one of them.

God expresses His love by giving gifts (Romans 5:8). The psalmist says that God gives us grace and glory. Grace has to do with favor; glory has to do with honor. Grace always comes first, then the glory.

We talk a lot about grace: the unmerited favor of God. We are saved by God's grace and we are transformed by His grace (Ephesians 2:8-10; 2 Corinthians 9:8).

But the psalmist points to the end result of grace: glory. The Hebrew word is *kabod* (*kawbode*) and carries the idea of heaviness, importance, honor. The end game of all God does is His glory. To glorify God is to magnify His fame and greatness. Sanctification (being reshaped from our old, broken condition into the image of Jesus) brings God glory. The more I look like, sound like, act like Jesus, the more I draw attention to His transforming power. God saves us for His glory, and He changes us for His glory.

But there is something else here, and the psalmist touches on it. Believers actually share in God's glory! Jesus said in John 17:22, *"I have given them the glory You gave me, so they may be one as We are one."* Paul builds on that, writing, *"And since we are His children, we are His heirs. In fact, together with Christ we are heirs of God's glory"* (Romans 8:17).

God gives glory and honor to us now and later. The now part means that He honors us with His favor. He honors us with His salvation. He honors us with adoption. He honors us with His name. He even honors us with suffering.

But the greater glory for us is yet to be revealed. Ultimately the righteous will be held up before all the unrighteous, all the skeptics, all the ridiculers—and affirmed that we got it right (Revelation 20:11-15)! What an honor! What a gift that will be!

God, thank You for saving me and bestowing honor on me. I don't deserve it, but I am so grateful! Amen

THE CURRENT
July 8

"The Lord will withhold no good thing from those who do what is right."
Psalm 84:11

The current in a river is the movement of the water moving downstream. If you've ever been canoeing on a river, you know it's important to find where the current is the strongest so that you can make the best progress. If you don't, you'll drift toward the bank where it's slow or you get in a whirlpool that is hard to get out of. You're still in the river, but you're not making much progress.

Reread Psalm 84. It speaks of amazing intimacy with our Creator and Redeemer: the rest, peace, and joy we have in Him; how loved and valuable we are to Him; the gifts that He pours out on us; the protection He gives us. Who would not want all of that you can get?

But there is a catch. In order to experience all the blessings of this psalm, we must find where the current of God's blessings is strongest. The current is strongest when we live our lives consistent with God's will and desires.

The CSB translates this verse, *"He does not withhold the good from those who live with integrity";* the ESV, *"No good thing does he withhold from those who walk uprightly."* It's clear that God is interested not just in behavior, but motives as well. Both must be aligned with His will and His desires for us to experience His abundant life.

Does the good parent reward the child who pays no attention to boundaries, willfully disobeys, acts in ways that bring dishonor to the family name? No wise and loving parent would do that. God is the wisest and most loving parent ever. He's not going to reward bad motives and bad behavior.

God wants to give good things to His children (Matthew 7:9-11). He possesses a strong current of love in His heart for you. So get yourself into the mainstream of it. God's Spirit in you will get you there as you seek His desire and will. Pour into His word. Pray for transformation. Walk daily with Him in integrity. And enjoy the current of His love.

God, I do want to experience more of You and more of Your blessings. By Your grace, draw me to You and Your word—and align my will and desires with Yours. Amen

ETA

July 9

"O Lord of Heaven's Armies, what joy for those who trust in You."
Psalm 84:12

I love to travel. I actually keep a toiletry pouch and a travel bag stocked with the basics ready for my next trip. I'm always planning my next trip. One of the necessities of travel is figuring out the itinerary: when do we leave, what flight or route do we take, and when will we get there. The Estimated Time of Arrival (ETA) on any leg of the journey is a critical component of planning.

Psalm 84 is a pilgrimage psalm describing the blessedness of the one who journeyed to the temple to pray. It breaks nicely into three sections: longing (vv.1-4), traveling (vv.5-8), and resting (vv.9-12). For the psalmist and his contemporary readers, there was the longing to get to the temple, the journey to experience what was desired, and the satisfaction and tension release once they arrived at the destination.

For us, the parallels are obvious. First, there must be the longing to be in the presence of The Most High God. We don't have to travel to Jerusalem to worship, but there must be a desire, a passion to draw aside each morning to worship Him and continue throughout our day. Jesus told us, *"If anyone is thirsty, let him come to Me and drink"* (John 7:37; CSB). Pray for a thirst and a longing for God.

Second, there is the journey as we learn to live out what we desire. Along the way, there are setbacks, failures, disappointments, and hardships. We don't like them at the time, but once we've cleared them, they become for us another of a large collection of experiences where God's grace enabled us to move through and overcome (Romans 8:28).

Third, there is the rest that comes when we learn to trust Yahweh with the details of our lives. The psalmist says, *"O Lord of Heaven's Armies, what joy for those who trust in You"* (v.12).

There is a peace and a rest that attends those who commit their ways to the Lord (Proverbs 16:3). We fear (lack of rest) because we don't trust. That's crazy since He's the LORD of Heaven's Armies!!

I haven't arrived yet, but my trip has been awesome, and my ETA is certainly closer.

God, draw me to Yourself and enable me to focus more on You. I trust You on this journey. Enable me to rest in You. Amen

HELP!
July 10

"Now restore us again, O God of our salvation. Put aside Your anger against us once more. Will You be angry with us always? Will You prolong Your wrath to all generations? Won't You revive us again, so Your people can rejoice in You?"
Psalm 85:4-6

In times past, Israel had experienced the blessing of God on their land (v.1), but when the psalmist wrote this, it only seemed like a distant memory. He pleads with Yahweh to restore and revive them again.

Our country needs the same. After 60 years of civil rights legislation and hundreds of supreme court cases, racism seems as divisive today as in the Jim Crow days. We've spent over 25 trillion dollars of government money (plus trillions of private money) trying to eradicate poverty, yet the poverty rate is about the same as it was when the Johnson administration declared "The War on Poverty" in 1965. The legal killing of pre-born babies is still the law of the land, with 50 million abortions reported to the CDC since 1973. Our history of slavery, the greed of robber barons, past and present, and the genocide of Native Americans during our western expansion are just a few of our national sins. If God is a just God, He's exacting a measure of it right now.

We're the most powerful country ever. The richest, too. Our forefathers established the American Experiment in 1776 and since then we've been the envy of the world. But we're decaying from the inside out. Money won't fix it. We've proved that. Legislation won't either.

In our recent struggle with a pandemic, the national aspiration was to get back to normal. Normal is not good right now. We need something abnormal; something supernatural.

In verses 1-2, the psalmist remembers a previous time when the nation suffered. Apparently, there was a national response of contrition and repentance that brought a heavenly response. He calls on heaven to respond again. That's what we need to do now.

The challenge is this: forgiveness and blessing are always predicated on contrition and repentance. I don't sense a national mood to repent. The question is: will Christ-followers spend more energy and time influencing heaven than Washington? Washington does not hold the answer; heaven does. Jesus had no interest in trying to help Caesar get it right; His eye was on the church and His appeal was to heaven.

God help us. Amen

ALL EARS

"I listen carefully to what God the Lord is saying, for He speaks peace to His faithful people."
Psalm 85:8

When someone asks you if you're interested in some important information, you might respond with the phrase: "I'm all ears." It's an idiom that expresses a keen interest in hearing something correctly; something important.

The psalmist has been praying for God to bring restoration to His people. He wants to hear from heaven about his circumstance. So he says, *"I will listen."* The ESV says, *"Let me hear"*, indicating a heightened awareness of the need to hear correctly. The NLT adds the word *carefully* to emphasize that we need to be all ears when we ask God to speak to us.

I often hear people say, "The Lord told me…" or "The Lord said to me…". Many times what follows out of their mouth cannot be from the Lord. How do I know? Because it's contrary to the already revealed will of God. The Scripture is our ultimate basis for faith and behavior. God is not going to tell you something that is different from what He has already told us in Scripture. You can't believe how many times a couple has told me that God told them it was ok to divorce their spouses and get married to each other, or others justify their gay lifestyle because God said it was ok.

Culture is not our final authority, neither the latest pop philosophy. We are not the final authority; God and His word are. If you want to know God's will for your life, dig into His word. The answer is there. But you have to be all ears. **You have to be willing to study and discover—but then you have to be willing to listen and obey**.

Notice the psalmist says that God *"speaks peace to His faithful people."* Digging into God's Word and discovering His will in the circumstances of life brings peace. It just does. His word directs us how to respond to being treated unfairly, how to handle money, how to treat difficult people, how to deal with grief and loss, how to deal with fear and anxiety—whatever ails you.

Go to the Lord through prayer and His word—and go saying, "I'm all ears, Lord."

God, I need to hear from You. I will search Your word and listen for Your voice through it. Amen

STRANGE BEDFELLOWS
July 12

"Unfailing love and truth have met together. Righteousness and peace have kissed!"
Psalm 85:10

Strange bedfellows is an idiom that refers to a peculiar alliance or combination. Examples abound, but maybe the most well-known is: "Politics makes for strange bedfellows." The psalmist combines two seemingly opposite concepts that leave us scratching our heads—and he does it twice!

In the first, he combines love and truth. Truth is precise. It is unambiguous. It is unbending. It isn't swayed by emotion or prejudice. 2 + 2 = 4 whether you like it or not. Our planet is a sphere even if you think it's flat. The Dallas Cowboys won't win another Super Bowl under its present ownership. That's the fact, Jack!

God is all truth and no lie (Titus 1:2). His moral character is spotless and pristine. Ours, however, is anything but. The truth about us is that we are hopelessly flawed; that in our brokenness, we reject God and His will. As a result of our wickedness and rebellion, we deserve His condemnation (Romans 3:23, 6:23, 8:7).

Oddly, the psalmist joins truth with love. The great Hebrew word for 'unfailing love' is *chesed* which is covenant love; loyal love. Scripture affirms that *"love covers a multitude of sins"* (1 Peter 4:8). One of the wonderful characteristics of this kind of love is that it looks beyond our fault and sees our need. In Christ, the truth of my depravity is swallowed up by the vastness of God's love!!

The second strange combination is righteousness and peace. You would think that righteousness and peace would be in opposition to each other—and normally they would be. My unrighteousness positions me for the wrath of God. We don't talk much about the wrath of God, but folks, if God's love is beyond anything we can imagine, so is His wrath. I wouldn't want to experience one millisecond of it. Outside of Christ, that's what I deserve—for eternity!

But in Christ, I don't get what I deserve—I get something indescribably better! I don't experience His wrath; I experience His peace; His *shalom*. Shalom carries the idea of harmony, wholeness, completeness, welfare, and tranquility. I want all of that I can get—and I can get all of that in Jesus.

In Jesus, love and truth, peace and righteousness have met. Inconceivable!

Jesus, thank You for demonstrating Your love on the cross and reconciling me to the Father! Amen

MAKING A WAY

July 13

"Righteousness will go before Him and will make His footsteps into a way."
Psalm 85:13

When I was a teen, I sometimes went hunting with my dad to a place in the Cookson Hills of Oklahoma. In getting to a good hunting spot, we had to trudge through some very dense underbrush. He would take his machete and whack the underbrush creating a path for me to follow him.

At the end of this great psalm, the author paints a picture of Yahweh going before us and making a way for us. It's interesting that he says God's righteousness goes before Him; His own motivation to act is His righteousness. The righteousness of God is one of the more prominent attributes of God in Scripture. It carries with it the idea of being straight, being just, always acting and doing what is right. He is not deterred or influenced by outside forces. God always acts exactly and consistently with His character and desires regardless of anything else.

We, on the other hand, are definitely influenced, deterred, discouraged, and even defeated by outside forces. Circumstances rise up and create a heavy underbrush that at times seems impossible to get through. We can't seem to find the way. We desire to move through, get beyond, overcome, but we can't always act in the right way to get the job done. We need help.

There were more than a few times as a pastor that circumstances covered me up and just about swallowed me. As the shepherd of God's flock, I knew that if I didn't find the right path forward, the consequences for me and for those who were following me would be disastrous. But God made a way.

When Sue was diagnosed with triple-negative breast cancer, the most aggressive, radical form, suddenly we were surrounded with fear, anxiety, confusion, uncertainty—even some anger. We didn't know how we were going to get through it. But God made a way.

I won't bore you with the details of my countless jungle experiences, but I have learned that sticking close to my Father and following Him has always been the best decision to make, and the only way to move forward. Whatever is going on in your life, follow Yahweh. He will make a way.

God, I know the only way forward is to follow You. That's my intent. By Your Spirit, enable me. Amen

BEND DOWN

July 14

"Bend down, O Lord, and hear my prayer; answer me, for I need Your help."
Psalm 86:1

Through the years, we've had friends who had swimming pools. I personally think it's better to know people who have pools than to have a pool myself. I recall one time when we were at some friends' house that had a pool. A small child, maybe 3-4 years old, was playing on the steps leading down into the pool, lost his balance, and went in over his head. Dad, who was near, stepped down into the water, bent over, and pulled the child to safety. He got his pants wet and killed his phone, but the child was saved.

What a great picture of the Christ-life. It began with us being in such peril and danger because of our sin, that God bent down from heaven. He stepped into our world, our skin, to rescue us. We call it the incarnation. Chili con carne is chili with meat, right? Incarnation means God with meat; God in the flesh.

The incarnation was an act of condescension. He stepped out of His lofty, perfect, holy, pristine, glorious abode and stepped into this cesspool we call earth. He didn't have to. But out of His love and for His glory, He bent down—as low as low could be. He became one of us to live the perfect life so that He could die the perfect death for us. It cost him more than some wet pants and an iPhone. It cost Him His life. He paid for our sin with His precious blood and ransomed us from the domain of death and hell.

There was an old hymn we used to sing that captures this reality:

> *I was sinking deep in sin, far from the peaceful shore;*
> *Very deeply stained within, sinking to rise no more.*
> *But the Master of the sea, heard my despairing cry;*
> *From the waters lifted me, now safe am I.*
> *Love lifted me. Love lifted me.*
> *When nothing else could help, love lifted me!*
> *Love lifted me. Love lifted me.*
> *When nothing else could help, love lifted me!*

Jesus, thank you for loving me so much that You bent down and snatched me from certain damnation. I give You praise and thanksgiving! Amen.

BEND DOWN AGAIN
July 15

"Bend down, O Lord, and hear my prayer; answer me, for I need Your help."
Psalm 86:1

God has blessed Sue and me with ten grandchildren. Russell (yes, named after me!!), is 2 years old. When he sees me, he runs to me with his arms open wanting me to pick him up. Nothing better!

I notice that if he falls and hurts himself, or if he feels one of his sisters has been a little rough with him, he'll run to his mom or dad: arms lifted up, panic or pain in his eyes, looking for a little love and rescue.

The 86th Psalm begins with the superscription, A Prayer of David. The Hebrew word, *tephillah,* means *prayer.* It is used other times in the Psalms, but Psalm 86 is known simply as The Prayer of David. Of this psalm and David, Spurgeon wrote: "The man of sincerity, of ardor, of trials, of faults, and of great heart, pleads, sobs, and trusts through all the verses of this psalm."

David knows who to run to when he's in trouble. It's notable that David uses the title, *Adonai,* seven times when referring to God. Adonai means *master* and it emphasizes God's power and authority. David runs to the One who is mightier than any of his enemies. You can imagine David running to this great God with his arms out and calling out for Him to bend down and give him a little love and rescue.

Are you in need of a little love and rescue? Maybe it's not just a little you need. What is causing your panic or pain? As I write I have a dear friend I've known 40 years who is in the OR getting a 7" mass taken out of his chest. He's running full speed to God with his arms wide open. I've got another friend whose wife has quit trying in the marriage and is stepping out on him. He's running. I've got another friend whose bout with cancer was thought to be over, but now she is battling it once again. She's running. I've got other friends whose adult children are unbelievers, and it is breaking their hearts. They're running.

Run to Him. He's Adonai.

Adonai, I do run to You with this pain and panic. Bend down and envelop me with Your love and mercy. Hear my cry. Amen

CONNECTION

"Protect me, for I am devoted to You.
Save me, for I serve You and trust You. You are my God."

Psalm 86:2

In v.1, David called for God to bow down and listen to his plea for help. His reason: he is a needy man.

In v.2 David adds a second reason God should bend down: their relationship. 'Help me God—I'm one of Yours!'

Notice that David uses faith language throughout this verse. The only way to be connected to God, to be in a relationship with Him, is by faith. We cannot earn our way or buy our way into this connection. A connection with God only comes by faith. Jesus said, *"I am the only way, the only truth, the only life. No one comes to the Father except by believing in Me"* (John 14:6). It's always been through faith alone in the Messiah (pre & post appearance) that creates the connection between God and us. If you've never made the decision to stop trusting in yourself and start trusting ONLY in Jesus to save you and introduce you to the Father—stop right now and place your faith and trust in Him ALONE. The eternal connection will begin at that moment.

David says, "I am devoted to You." The word here for devotion is *chaciyd* (*kaw-seed*) and carries the idea of piety and holiness as a result of a full-of-faith life. David says, "I am faithful to You. I serve You. I trust in You. You are my God. HELP!"

A note of caution. David is giving God reasons why He should bend down and listen; why He should step in and help. But he isn't demanding, and he isn't pouting. He isn't saying, "After all I've done for You . . ." God doesn't owe us anything. The Christ-life comes to us by grace, and it continues by grace. Our faithfulness to Him is not for His benefit; it's for ours.

But we can still run to Him. In fact, He tells us to! His promise is that He will take us into His arms and comfort us. It's not a response of insulation, but one of intimacy. Our connection to Him must be enough. It is.

Father, I am grateful to be connected to You through faith in Jesus. Gather me up. Hear my cry. You are enough. Amen

SO
July 17

"O Lord, you are so good, so ready to forgive,
so full of unfailing love for all who ask for Your help."
Psalm 86:5

In this Prayer of David, he has called for God to bend down and listen to his plea for help. His reason: he is a needy man (v.1). Another reason David believes God will bend down is their relationship: they are connected (v.2).

Here's a third reason he's asking God to bend down: he knows the amazing character of God (vv.3-5). He believes it is God's nature to listen and answer.

In v.3 David asks for mercy. The root word means to show favor; to have compassion. Someone said that "compassion is your pain in my heart." Jesus showed compassion when He saw people suffering and wandering in spiritual darkness (Matthew 9:36). Compassion doesn't just sense the pain and suffering; it enters into it as He did. David calls on God to have compassion on him and relieve the pain.

Then David asks for joy, *"Gladden the soul of Your servant, for to You, O Lord, do I lift up my soul"* (v.4; ESV). In times of trouble and trial, the soul grows dark; heavy. The imagery is David holding up his weighted soul and asking God to touch it, to lighten it, to brighten it.

Read v.5 at the top of the page again. Notice the three so's: God is **so good, so ready to forgive, so full of unfailing love**. That's a mouthful right there! That little word *so* is such a powerful word. In this context, it means "to such a great extent." It acts as a superlative. God is not just good, He is SO good. He's not just forgiving, He is SO ready to forgive. He's not just loving, He is SO loving.

I don't know about you, but when I read these verses and contemplate their meaning, my soul is lightened and brightened! He is SO good. The goodness of God is indicative of His desire to be generous with His blessings toward us. He is SO quick to forgive. He does not hold grudges. Once we repent, His forgiveness swallows up our sin and He remembers it no more (Hebrews 8:12). He is SO full of unfailing, steadfast, unbending, undefeatable love.

God, I praise You for being so, so, so amazing! I love You!! Amen

INCOMPARABLE

July 18

"No pagan god is like you, O Lord. None can do what You do!"
Psalm 86:8

Some things in life are so different, there is nothing really to compare them to. Standing on the rim of the Grand Canyon, it's obvious there is nothing else like it. Sitting at my dinner table with my wife and my six adult children, listening to them talk, laugh, tell stories, discuss hard issues—I realize there is nothing else like it. As good as these experiences are, they don't compare to experiencing intimacy with the One True God.

There are lots of gods in this world. The ancients tended to worship the sun, the moon, the stars, and a myriad of fertility gods. Americans worship possessing, experiencing, thrilling, purchasing, passion seeking, hyperactivity, our children, alcohol, sex, and the ultimate 21st-century American god, comfort. We'll do *anything* to avoid the anti-god, discomfort.

We worship these gods because we believe they will meet a certain need; they fill a place in our soul that feels empty. But like all false gods, they're packed with promise but in the end, only deliver pain.

David says it right: "There is no god like You, God! None of those other gods can do what You do!!" This is one of those seven times David uses the title *Adonai* in this psalm when he addresses God. It means *master* and carries the ideas of power and authority. He is alluding to the fact that the other gods do not have power; they do not have authority. They can't deliver what they promise.

I'm reminded of the First Commandment God gave His people: "*You must not have any other god but Me*" (Exodus 20:3). He knew that in our brokenness, we have a tendency to look to other gods to satisfy us. Because He is insulted to share His glory with another god, and because He loves us too much to let us chase something that will only lead to pain and suffering, He commands us to worship and live only for Him.

He is incomparable. There is no god like our God. He is sovereign, all-knowing, all-wise, kind, compassionate, and full of unfailing love. Only He can deliver us, help us, bind up our wounds and heal us. Only He can forgive us and lift us up. Only He has provided a way to thrive in this life and the life to come. That's MY God!!

God, You are MY God. There is none like You. I love You and worship You. Amen

UNITED WE STAND
July 19

*"Teach me your way, O Lord, that I may walk
in Your truth; unite my heart to fear Your name."*
Psalm 86:11 (ESV)

When Sue and I have a disagreement, my tendency is to expect her to see my position, to hear my heart, to move my direction. But because she's normally right, I'm learning to see her position, hear her heart, and move her direction. I have found that in all relationships, making the first move toward the other's perspective is the wise thing to do.

If you read this psalm in one sitting, you'll notice there is a subtle shift between v.7 and v.8. In the first 7 verses David is calling on God to move his direction: "Bend down, hear me, protect me, save me, be merciful to me, give me joy." David's focus is on David.

But at v.8 that changes: "No god is like You, You're amazing, the nations will bow to You, only You are God, I praise You." David's focus has shifted to God.

The wise person recognizes that if there is a distance between us and God, it's up to us to move first: *"Come close to God, and God will come close to you"* (James 4:8).

David says, "I'm moving Your direction. I want you to teach me the real truth about life. I want to find Your way of how to see and how to live. Unite my heart with Your heart."

You probably know the phrase: "United we stand; divided we fall." It's based on the teachings of Jesus (Mark 3:25), but the specific phrase was popularized by Founding Father, John Dickinson, when he wrote, "The Liberty Song."

We must unite our hearts and minds with God's truth; with God's heart. That's the key to being able to withstand the assaults this world throws at us. As long as we cling to our version of the truth, our version of what's right, our perspective on our marriage, our parenting, our finances, our country—there's not much chance of avoiding falls great and small. Buy into the perspectives of this world, and I assure you, there's no chance of standing.

Get in the word of God. Read it and study it. That's where you discover real truth on the issues of life. That's how you unite your heart and mind with God's.

God, I'll get into Your Word. Unite my heart and mind with You. Amen.

THESE WORDS

July 20

"But You, O Lord, are a God of compassion and mercy,
slow to get angry and filled with unfailing love and faithfulness."

Psalm 86:15

These words speak to us from ancient past until this very moment. They will speak deeply in our souls until the very end.

These words are found throughout Scripture. They were first uttered by God Himself to Moses on Mt. Sinai, revealing His very nature: *"Yahweh! The Lord! The God of compassion and mercy! I am slow to anger and filled with unfailing love and faithfulness"* (Exodus 34:6). This was AFTER the Hebrews had worshipped the golden calf! Slow to anger, yes!

These words also show up in two other of David's psalms, 103:8 and 145:8. Instead of God proclaiming His own nature, David has come to recognize these personal characteristics of his God. As many times as David was in danger, discouraged, threatened—he knew this personally.

These words show up in the Minor Prophets. God sent Jonah to share about God's love, but Jonah resisted because the Ninevites were THE most hated people in the eyes of Israel. They had raided, ransacked, raped, and enslaved Jews for over a century. After Jonah got disgorged, he did go preach to his enemies, and they repented. Jonah got so mad, he said, *"I knew this would happen! That's why I ran away. I knew that You are a merciful and compassionate God, slow to get angry and filled with unfailing love. Just go ahead and kill me now!"* (4:2-3). Talk about a pity party!

The prophet Joel was warning Judah that their idolatry was inviting God's discipline. Joel pled with them to repent: *"Return to the Lord your God, for He is merciful and compassionate,*

slow to get angry and filled with unfailing love" (2:13). Sadly, they didn't listen to Joel or God. So the holiness and justness (equal characteristics of this God) emerged: Jerusalem and its prized Temple were destroyed.

Finally, there is Nehemiah who was with the returned exiles in Jerusalem reminding them, that from the days of Moses, Yahweh was a *"God of forgiveness, gracious and merciful, slow to become angry, and rich in unfailing love"* (9:17).

These words speak to us from ancient past until this very moment.

God, from ancient past to this very moment, these words speak to me. Thank You for highlighting them in Scripture and in my life. Amen

THESE WORDS AGAIN

July 21

"But You, O Lord, are a God of compassion and mercy,
slow to get angry and filled with unfailing love and faithfulness."
Psalm 86:15

These words speak to us from ancient past until this very moment. They will speak deeply in our souls until the very end.

Because David does not mention a specific situation within the psalm, we are left to wonder what prompted his writing. No doubt it could have been a time when King Saul was trying to kill him. Or later in life when his ongoing battle with the Philistines had become critically dangerous.

But there is one circumstance that stands out as the most painful danger in David's life. Many scholars believe this was written when his son Absalom rebelled, ran him out of town, and tried to hunt down and kill him.

There's not enough room here to tell the whole sordid story. Read about it in 2 Samuel 13-19. It speaks to integrity and accountability in marriage and parenting. Can you imagine being hated and hunted by your own child? I can't.

But many of you can. I have a number of friends whose children have grown to adulthood and somewhere along the way, come to disrespect, distance, or even forcefully and callously disconnect. No parent is perfect, but few would deserve this. I can imagine only a few things in this life more painful. As a parent, you work to provide, sacrifice, and protect with your very life this creature God gave to you. And then to have them turn their backs? Many times, grandchildren are kept from seeing their grandparents as the ultimate form of torture. Awful. Not only does this violate the 5th Commandment, but it is also one of the most un-Jesus-like actions anyone could do. If you're the adult child reading this, God holds you responsible to fix the situation.

Regardless, we have to find a way to get through times like this. In the midst of his pain and fear, David reminded himself and us that there is Someone who cares; Someone who is kind and compassionate; Someone who is not rejecting us; Someone who is filled with unfailing love.

David's situation with Absalom ended tragically. But this kind and compassionate God got him through it. And He will you as well.

God, when I feel threatened or rejected, turn my eyes on You and set my heart at peace. Amen

THESE WORDS AGAIN AND AGAIN
July 22

"But You, O Lord, are a God of compassion and mercy,
slow to get angry and filled with unfailing love and faithfulness."
Psalm 86:15

These words speak to us from ancient past until this very moment. They will speak deeply in our souls until the very end.

These words have a history and a context. But ultimately, they reveal the nature and character of God. This would not be a complete list of His attributes, but it certainly is a wonderful list!

Yahweh is full of compassion. The Hebrew word used here is only employed when referring to God's compassion. His compassion is unique. Compassion carries the idea of, not just willing, but being able to enter into the suffering of someone else and to do something about it. No one knows your suffering like God and no one can enter into it and touch it like He can. I remember watching Louis Armstrong sing the spiritual that started with, "Nobody knows the trouble I've seen; nobody knows but Jesus." Yup.

Yahweh is full of mercy. Mercy is what causes someone in a higher position to show favor and help someone in a lower position. The Hebrew word here is also employed only when referring to God. God, who is in the highest of highest positions, has an infinite distance to reach down to help and show favor to us—His depraved, fallen, broken likenesses. We can't bridge it, but through Jesus, He did.

Yahweh is slow to anger; He is patient. I know that how I act many times could invoke God's wrath because He hates sin. But as a child of God (John 1:12), His infinite love for me swallows up His anger. Think about that: God's love swallows up His righteous anger toward my sin! As a loving parent, He still disciplines me but does so with patience and affection.

Yahweh is filled with unfailing love. *Chesed* is God's covenant, faithful love. Once directed toward the believer, it does not depend on us to maintain it. God's love does not vary based on emotion or circumstance. Grasp that, and your life changes dramatically!

Yahweh is faithful. He is faithful to Himself, faithful to the truth, faithful to His promises, faithful to His children, faithful to the end.

That is our God!

Lord, I praise You for who You are. What an amazing God!! Amen

A SIGN

"Send me a sign of Your favor. Then those who hate me will be put to shame,
for You, O Lord, help and comfort me."
Psalm 86:17

This psalm began with David calling for God to bend down and listen. He ends the psalm by calling for God to send a sign of favor. The first is a plea for reception; the second a plea for action.

There is something about being heard that brings peace to the soul. When my heart is troubled, it gives me peace to know that the Lord God Almighty, maker of heaven and earth, is listening.

But there are those times I look for God to act; to do something about my situation. And if He's not going to change the circumstance, to at least let me know that I'm going to get through it. That's what David is doing: calling on God to give him a sign for good; a sign of favor; an indication that he's going to get through this difficult time.

Maybe you're at a time in your life when you need a sign from God that you're going to get through this. I can assure you, you will. But you have to back up and get a biblical view of what it means to get through. Sometimes getting through has little to do with the change in circumstance. Sara prayed her husband would stay and fight for their marriage, but when he walked out, God got her through. Mike prayed that God would heal his wife's cancer, but when she died, God got him through. When the Clarks prayed for their business to survive, and it didn't, God got them through.

What was the sign that got these and others through? They found a promise in God's word that sustained them and got them through: *"When you go through deep waters, I'll be with you. When you walk through the fire, it won't consume you"* (Isaiah 43:2). It doesn't say there'll be no high water or fire—just that God will be there and get us through. There are hundreds more promises to cling to.

The ultimate sign of God's favor is the cross. Be mindful of His pain, His suffering for you, to demonstrate His great love for you. That'll get you through. Promise.

Jesus, thank You for Your great love for me; because You got through, I will too—by Your grace. Amen

JOY
July 24

"Singers and dancers alike will say, 'My whole source of joy is in You.'"
Psalm 87:7 (CSB)

If you've never been to Jerusalem, you have missed being in the greatest city on earth. I've been to most of the great world cities: New York, Paris, London, Moscow, Rome, Beijing, and Hong Kong to name a few. But nothing compares to Jerusalem.

It's not that big: fewer than 1 million people—half the size of Arlington, TX. Yet its influence in world culture, religions, and politics is incredibly leveraged. Judaism, Islam, and Christianity count it as their city. The world keeps its eye on this city.

For Christ-followers, it holds special significance for many reasons. It was the place where Abraham offered Isaac as an offering to the Lord, though God gave a last-minute reprieve. It was where the Hebrews established their capital and built the Temple. Most importantly, it was the place where Jesus offered Himself up as an offering—no last-minute reprieve this time. After three days in a borrowed tomb, He stepped out into a Jerusalem sunrise—always a stunning sight.

David most likely sat on the throne of Jerusalem at the time of this writing. The psalm celebrates the fact that Jerusalem was the center of the universe: the nations were coming to it for favor and recognition.

But Jerusalem is not about the past as much as it is about the future. The Apostle John, in his Revelation of Jesus Christ, writes about the New Jerusalem (Revelation 20-21). It will be a place that bustles with activity, where there is no darkness, pain, or suffering; a place with beauty beyond description. It will be the residence of those whose name is written in the Book of Life (Revelation 3:5) and who are clothed in righteousness through the blood of Jesus (Revelation 5:9). Most importantly, it will be the place where God and blood-bought believers exist in perfect harmony together.

The psalmist mentions those who play and dance in celebration of their Jerusalem. But folks, they could not imagine the singing and dancing that will occur in the New Jerusalem. Knowing this fills my heart with joy. In fact, all the rivers and streams of joy begin in the heart of God and flow into the hearts of those who believe and anticipate the Great Reunion with Him in the New Jerusalem.

God, I look to You for joy. Stream it into my heart. Amen.

THE DARK NIGHT
July 25

"You have taken away my companions and loved ones. Darkness is my closest friend."
Psalm 88:18

The Dark Night of the Soul. Some of the greatest believers have suffered through it. "This is no ordinary fit of depression, but it is a depression that is linked to a crisis of faith, a crisis that comes when one senses the absence of God or gives rise to a feeling of abandonment by Him" (Sproul).

Welcome to what some call, "The saddest Psalm." In the other psalms, there is real pain and suffering, but after crying out for mercy, the psalmist gains some sense that God hears and will respond. In the end, he finds hope.

Not this psalm. There is nothing but darkness and despair all the way through. Knowing that, you might think that you'll skip this one. After all, who needs more discouragement in their life?

But God included it in Scripture for a reason. Truth is, many if not most believers go through a serious testing of faith at least once in their lives. For some of us, it's constant.

It happens when we feel our suffering or the suffering of a loved one goes unnoticed and our prayers go unheard. At some point, we feel as if God is not listening or He doesn't care. Sometimes faith becomes so weak, the sufferer begins to even doubt the reality of God.

The Bible never tries to hide or cover up the weaknesses of its characters. In this case, the psalmist has been in spiritual depression for some time without any prospect of progress. He cries out to God day and night. He lives in darkness constantly. He wonders how his death by depression can bring God glory. This is not a passing pang but a prolonged agony. His faith is waning.

What does the psalmist do? What do we do if and when this malady overtakes us? Hold on. Get in the Word. And pray. Only God can get you through this. Most importantly, pray for stronger faith, as did the grieving father in Mark 9:24, *"I believe; help my unbelief!"*

There is hope in knowing that this won't last forever; that our suffering will be totally removed and replaced by infinite joy one day. Night will turn to morning; darkness into light. Promise.

God, when I feel distant and dark, draw close to me and shine Your light into my soul. Amen

EMPTY PROMISES?

July 26

"I will sing of the Lord's unfailing love forever! Young and old will hear of Your faithfulness. Praise the Lord forever! Amen and amen!"

Psalm 89:1 & 52

When you read those two verses, you might think this is an uplifting, lofty, heavenly psalm of praise. It does contain those elements but sandwiched in between are some hard realities and truths that describe the 'on the ground' difficulties we deal with on a regular basis.

Psalm 89 contains all the elements found in the Book of Psalms: praise, prayer, promises, power, despair, doubt, disappointment, destruction, deliverance, goodness, evil, and so on. It's long (52 verses), but worth the read. The psalmist addresses the age-old question: What do we do when great promises become great disappointments; when the goodness of God seems obscured by the evil of this world?

We're not sure of the historical context. Some scholars conjecture it was written during the time of David's grandson, Rehoboam, when Egypt invaded Judah, or as a result of the Babylonian conquest of Jerusalem. Regardless, it's a time when it seems as if God's promises and goodness seem to be nowhere in sight.

It breaks nicely into three movements:

1. God's promises based on His character (vv.1-14). Here the psalmist praises God for His unfailing love, His faithfulness, His righteousness, and His power and glory on display in creation and throughout history. What a great God!
2. God's promises bestowed on His chosen one (vv.15-37). The psalmist recalls God's covenant with David and the promises made to him and to his descendants; how David's dynasty will reign forever. What a great promise!
3. God's promises blackened by crisis (vv.38-51). Despite all of this, the circumstances are bleak, the love of God is in question, and the promises seem broken. Here the psalmist pleads for God to awaken His love and remember His promises. What a great disappointment.

There's too much in this psalm to cover in just a few daily devotions. But if you're someone who grapples with why a great and good God would allow such pain and suffering in your life and in your world, then stay tuned.

God, I know You to be good and faithful. Open my eyes to see You and Your purposes more clearly. Amen

WHY DOES GOD PROMISE?
July 27

"I will sing of the Lord's unfailing love forever! Young and old will hear of Your faithfulness.
Your unfailing love will last forever. Your faithfulness is as enduring as the heavens."

Psalm 89:1-2

Do you ever find yourself in the midst of a struggle thinking: "God, why is this happening to me? You promised me the abundant life; a life filled with Your favor and goodness!" After all, as believers, God has *"given us such great and precious promises"* (2 Peter 1:4), right?

You'll recall yesterday's flyover of this psalm: God's promises based on His character, God's promises bestowed on His chosen one, and God's promises blackened by crisis.

Let's talk about the nature of God and these promises. Why does God promise us anything? He doesn't owe us anything. He's not obligated to guarantee anything. What compels Him to promise in the first place?

There are over 1,000 commands in the Bible and over 5,000 promises. The difference between a command and a promise is this: in a command, God tells us how we should act; in a promise, He tells us how He will act. In Genesis 1 & 2, God gave commands: be fruitful, multiply, subdue the earth, don't eat that fruit, etc. But beginning with Genesis 3, God begins to make promises. Why? After Adam and Eve rebelled, all of creation, especially humanity, became tragically broken. God needed to intercede; God chose to act in a merciful way that provided in the midst of the brokenness.

That's the nature of God's promises: to help us in our brokenness. The nature of God's promises is based on the very nature of God. The first section of this psalm touches on some of the nature of God: His faithfulness, might, sovereignty, righteousness, and justice.

But it seems that God's unfailing love and mercy is the primary attribute that prompts Yahweh to step into our brokenness and make promises. It is His nature to help.

This is critically important to remember when adversity strikes. God is not aloof; He is not disinterested in our suffering. It's not in His nature to be so. It's impossible for Him to look the other way, or worse, act unlovingly toward His children.

Don't add to your suffering by doubting God's love for you. Focus on other reasons for the calamity. There is the path to peace.

God, I again affirm and am grateful for Your unfailing love for me. Amen

ARE GOD'S PROMISES RELIABLE?
July 28

"Young and old will hear of Your faithfulness.
Your unfailing love will last forever. Your faithfulness is as enduring as the heavens."
Psalm 89:1-2

One morning in children's Sunday School, the teacher was using the squirrel as an object lesson about the importance of being prepared: "What lives in trees and jumps from limb to limb?" No one raised their hand. "What has a bushy tail and flips it all the time?" No one raised their hand. "What hides nuts in the ground?" Finally, one little boy slowly raised his hand and said, "Well, I know the answer must be Jesus—but it sounds like a squirrel to me."

If we're not careful, we look at a question like, "Are God's Promises Reliable?" and respond with a non-thinking, Sunday School answer: "Sure, God's promises are reliable." The problem is, when trouble strikes, when storms begin to decimate our lives, our shallow understanding of God's nature and the nature of His promises leave us bewildered and defenseless.

If you answered the question, "Yes they are reliable," then why are they reliable? The psalmist gives us the reason right off the top: God's promises are reliable because God is reliable; He is faithful. Three times in the first two verses the psalmist points to the faithfulness of God.

Faithfulness is the characteristic that insists on doing what has been promised. To be faithful in marriage is to be and act how you pledged in your wedding vow. To break a vow, to violate a pledge means that you lied—not necessarily at the time you made it, but at the time you broke it.

It's not in God's nature to lie. In fact, He is truthful to the core. This is asserted all the way through the Bible (Numbers 23:19, Proverbs 12:22, John 1:14; 14:6; 16:13, etc.). Because it's impossible for God to lie, when He speaks, when He makes a promise, it is true and it will happen. God is faithful and His promises are true and reliable.

If God is not faithful, He is a lying, cheating, awful being.

But the Bible insists, and I bear witness, that God is absolutely and eternally faithful to who He is and what He says. As Paul says, *"If we are unfaithful, He remains faithful, for He cannot deny who He is"* (2 Timothy 2:13).

God, I believe in You, and because I do, I trust that You are faithful. Amen

WHEN A PROMISE ISN'T
July 29

"Your unfailing love will last forever."
Psalm 89:2

The psalmist speaks of God's enduring, unfailing love; one of the foundational promises God makes to His people throughout the Bible. In the Old Testament, God repeats it: *"I have loved you, My people, with an everlasting love. With unfailing love I have drawn you to Myself"* (Jeremiah 31:3; see also Deuteronomy 10:15, Isaiah 43:4, 63:9, Hosea 11:1). This was God's promise to Abraham's descendants, but those promises are transferred to us: *"For all of God's promises have been fulfilled in Christ with a resounding "Yes!"* (2 Corinthians 1:20).

The New Testament affirms God's love for His people: *"See how very much our Father loves us, for He calls us His children, and that is what we are!"* (1 John 3:1; see also John 3:16, 15:9, Romans 8:35-39).

In most of these Scriptures, the promise of God's love was made in the midst of great hardship and difficulty. The O.T. prophets were speaking when Israel/Judah were being besieged by their enemies and eventually pillaged and exiled. The N.T. writers were speaking in the midst of great persecution.

The point here is that God's love is not circumstantial. It is not dependent on circumstances and it is not affirmed by circumstances. God's love for His people is not dependent on anything other than His own nature to love us unconditionally. Even when we don't act lovingly toward Him, He still loves us— *"nothing shall separate us from the love of God"* (Romans 8:39).

But it is also equally true that God's love is not proved by circumstances. There is a strain of heresy out there claiming that if God really loves you and you really have faith, you'll be healthy and wealthy. Not true. Tell that to Jeremiah in prison or the martyred Apostles or Jesus on the cross.

If we're not careful, we buy into that strain from a different angle: we believe God's love means we won't suffer, and we question His love when we do. We've wrestled with this dilemma in other writings, but suffice to say God's love is ultimately proved, not by our comfort, but by the discomfort of Jesus on the cross (Romans 5:8).

When we talk about God being faithful to His promises, make sure you get the promise straight.

God, thank You for Your promise of unconditional love. Enable me to believe it when circumstances say otherwise. Amen

PROMISED TO WHOM?

July 30

"The Lord said, 'I have made a covenant with David, My chosen servant.
I have sworn this oath to him: "I will establish your descendants as kings forever;
they will sit on your throne from now until eternity."'"
Psalm 89:3-4

When Sue and I stood in the chapel of First Baptist, Houston on Saturday evening, April 11, 1981, I made a promise to her. Honestly, I was too scared at the moment to remember what I promised! It's still all a blur. But I do know that while there were lots of people in attendance, I only made the promise to her and God.

There are some promises in the Bible God made to everyone (John 3:16), but most of His promises were to a people or a person. Remember, this psalm is about God's promises based on His character, bestowed on His Chosen One, and blackened by crisis.

When you read vv.15-37, you see what God promised David AND his descendants: *"I will make him my firstborn son, the mightiest king on earth. I will love him and be kind to him forever; my covenant with him will never end. I will preserve an heir for him; his throne will be as endless as the days of heaven"* (vv.27-29).

This promise was only partially fulfilled in David's lifetime, but ultimately fulfilled in guess who? Jesus!

> *You will conceive and give birth to a son, and you will name Him Jesus. He will be very great and will be called the Son of the Most High. The Lord God will give Him the throne of his ancestor David. And He will reign over Israel forever; His Kingdom will never end!* Luke 1:31-33

God's promises to David of joy, strength, power, and victory—and being the object of God's unending faithful love—were ultimately and perfectly fulfilled in Jesus.

But guess what? For those of us who are in Christ, those promises extend to us as well! In Christ, I am God's son. In Christ, I have an abundance of real life. In Christ, greater is He that is in me. In Christ, nothing can separate me from God's enduring love. In Christ, I will live forever. In Christ, I am an heir. In Christ, I will reign with Him.

All of this and more is only partially in view now. But one day we shall see it all so clearly.

Until then, Lord, give me faith to believe what I can't see clearly now. Amen.

WHEN GOD'S PROMISES HAVE GONE DARK
July 31

"But now you have rejected him. You have renounced your covenant.
You have broken down the walls of protection. You have made his sword useless.
And refused to help him in battle."
Psalm 89: 38-40, 42

Has this ever happened to you? You get a call and the person on the other end chit chats about whatever, and then says, "The real reason I'm calling you is…" The psalmist began his call to God by touting the reliability of His promises based on His character, particularly His faithful, enduring love. He then recalled how the promises were made to His servant, David, his descendants, and people. We know now that these promises were fulfilled in the ultimate descendant, Jesus, and by extension, to all believers.

But beginning with v.38, the psalmist gets down to the real reason he's calling out to God: he feels that God has reneged on His promises.

There have been times in my life when it seemed God's promises seemed untrue; when awful circumstances caused me to doubt God's faithfulness and love.

The reason was that I lost perspective. I was too focused on myself. Too preoccupied with MY plans and too disinterested in HIS plans. I didn't see the big picture. God made those promises to David in about 1000 B.C., but they weren't fulfilled for a millennium. Even then, there is still another fulfillment that won't occur until the end of time. When God's promises seem to have gone dark, I need to shine the light of Scripture into my soul and gain God's perspective on my situation. It has always made the difference.

One more thing: don't forget that this earth is not our home. Shine the light of these verses into your soul: *"Dear friends, I warn you as temporary residents and foreigners"* (1 Peter 2:11); *"Their god is their appetite, they brag about shameful things, and they think only about this life here on earth. But we are citizens of heaven"* (Philippians 3:19-20); *"For this world is not our permanent home; we are looking forward to a home yet to come"* (Hebrews 13:14).

God, keep reminding me that this world is not my home; that Your promises are still true whether I feel them or not; that I'm just passing through and someday all will be made right in Your presence. Amen.

SINGING
August 1

"I will sing of the Lord's unfailing love forever! Young and old will hear of Your faithfulness. Your unfailing love will last forever. Your faithfulness is as enduring as the heavens."
Psalm 89:1-2

If you know Sue and me, you know that we see things so differently. I see black, she sees blue. I think up, she thinks down. Occasionally our difference in perspective prompts frustration or hurt feelings. Regardless of that temporary angst, I still love her deeply. Eventually the reasons I love her crowd out anything else.

That dynamic is likely to occur in any relationship, particularly our relationship with God. Because God's perspective can be so different than ours, there are those times when we are hurt, frustrated, or even angry. But for genuine believers, it doesn't change the fact that we love God deeply. Eventually, the reasons we love and worship Him crowd out everything else.

Before we leave Psalm 89, let's circle back and gaze at the opening verses. Read them again. Regardless of his frustration with God, the psalmist's bedrock conviction was that God was faithful and that His unfailing love would last forever and ever. Amen.

I love Yahweh! I can't fully grasp who He is. I don't understand all that He's up to. I get frustrated, hurt, even afraid based on the circumstances He has sovereignly introduced into my life. But O my, do I love Him.

When everything else in my life seems to be shouting otherwise, I come back to this bedrock conviction: God possesses unfailing, enduring love for me in Christ Jesus. He created the universe as a backdrop and the earth as a stage for this great drama. He knelt down in the dirt, forming me and fashioning me in His image. He took on human flesh for the purpose of rescuing me from my slam-dunk guilt and punishment. He adopted me and brought me into His family and *"He has given me the Holy Spirit to fill my heart with His love"* (Romans 5:5). In this fallen, broken, chaotic world, He is working all things out according to His will, for His glory and for my good. Eventually, He will do away with all this mess and I'll be with Him in perfect harmony.

Why wouldn't I love Him? And because I love Him so much, I just have to SING!

God, I do love You. I confess that. I believe that. Bless You! Amen

NO BEGINNING
August 2

"Lord, through all the generations You have been our home! Before the mountains were born, before You gave birth to the earth and the world, from beginning to end, You are God."

Psalm 90:1-2

Everything about you had a beginning: your conception, your first step, your first grade, your first car, your first date, your first child, and so on. As believers, we might be able to comprehend the idea that eventually we will live forever; it's not fully graspable, but we get the idea of no ending. What is absolutely impossible to grasp is the other end of the continuum: no beginning. Every effect in our life had a cause. So how can there be a reality that had no cause; that had no beginning?

Yet, that is exactly how the Bible portrays Yahweh: Genesis 1:1, *"In the beginning, God;"* John 1:1, *"In the beginning was the Word;"* Revelation 1:8, *"'I am the Alpha and the Omega—the beginning and the end,' says the Lord God. 'I am the one who is, who always was, and who is still to come—the Almighty One.'"* He not only has no end, but He had no beginning. He always will be and always has been (brain explosion!).

God created all things, including time. Time is a creation. We experience life on a space-time continuum: day 1 is first, day 2 is second, Thursday, then Friday, last year, this year, and so on. Life unfolds one day at a time. But God is outside of time; there is no 'one day at a time' with Him. "God views the whole span of history as vividly as He would if it were a brief event that had just happened. But He also views a brief event as if it were going on forever...all events—past, present, future—with equal vividness" (Grudem). This is why the psalmist says in v.4: *"For You, a thousand years are as a passing day, as brief as a few night hours."*

I love the statement, "**When understanding ends, let worship begin**." We can't understand it, but we can worship Him for it: *"For everything comes from Him and exists by His power and is intended for His glory. All glory to Him forever! Amen"* (Romans 11:36).

The Great I AM—worship Him!

God, there is so much about you I cannot grasp; You are transcendent. Because You are literally AWE-SOME, I praise, worship, and surrender to You. Amen!

NO NEED
August 3

"Before the mountains were born,
before You gave birth to the earth and the world, from beginning to end, You are God."
Psalm 90:2

It seems that my whole life has been driven by need. When I was a baby, I cried because I needed food (or a diaper change). As I got older, I needed friends, a bike, a car, an education, a job, money, a house, a wife—I'm a needy guy.

But God is not. He doesn't need a thing. Never has; never will. Scripture says, *"He is the God who made the world and everything in it. Since He is Lord of heaven and earth, He doesn't live in man-made temples, and human hands can't serve His needs—for He has no needs"* (Acts 17:24-25); *"And who has ever given to God, that He should be repaid?"* (Romans 11:35).

When we think about God and His eternality, as we did yesterday, we have to also think about His *aseity*, the fact that He is absolutely self-sufficient in every way. God has never needed more joy—He possesses it in infinite supply; always has and always will. He doesn't need more patience or power or food or fellowship or love. Whoever He is and whatever He possesses, He is and possesses all in infinite, never-ending quantities. It's a part of His eternal nature.

The psalmist reminds us of Yahweh's eternal nature and that He existed before He created. He is not dependent on creation; creation is dependent upon Him. He is not bound by time like us; He is outside of time. In other words, He doesn't wear a watch or own a calendar.

You would think that since God is eternal and without need, there would be no creation. But at some point, He decided to begin stuff. When I say, "at some point", that's when time began. His creation included humans, whom He gave volition (will; Genesis 1 & 2), which eventually brought the Fall (and His curse; Genesis 3). Fortunately, because He is love, in an incredible act of mercy, He initiated a process to redeem His creation through Jesus the Messiah.

We are utterly dependent upon God for everything. He has unilaterally acted mercifully on our behalf. He doesn't need us, but wants us. He wants you—all of you.

God, You don't need me, but I need You. Here's my heart. I love You.

BREVITY
August 4

"Teach us to realize the brevity of life, so that we may grow in wisdom."
Psalm 90:12

Have you heard of the 'holiday paradox?' It's a theory about why time seems to move faster the older you get. When we are younger, everything is new, new experiences, new observations, new skills, etc. Our brains log and retain those kinds of stimuli more than repetitive or mundane experiences. As we grow older, the brain doesn't pause to log and retain as much, thereby creating the sense that time moves faster. There are other theories. All I know is that the older you get, the faster it seems that life and time is passing. You get to my age and time is passing faster than an Amazon delivery truck!

In vv.1-4 we examined the eternality of God. He never had a beginning and He will never have an ending. He always will be and always has been. When God created, one of His creations was time. He lives outside of time; He is timeless.

Not so with us. We have a limited time here on earth. Verse 10 says we may get 70 or 80 years. The author of this psalm, Moses, lived 120 years. I don't want to live that long. I do want to live long enough to dance at a couple of my grandkids' weddings. If I do, it will undoubtedly be embarrassing to my family!

Moses' prayer was that, not only do we need to learn how brief life is, but because it is brief, we need to make the most of it. One translation says, *"Teach us to number our days carefully"* (CSB). That's the idea of being purposeful about how we invest whatever days God gives us. You realize, don't you, that God gives you every breath you breathe? It's not like He breathed life into you and checked out. He is literally the air that we breathe. When it suits Him, you'll stop breathing.

The reason to live purposely is not to increase our productivity or our fame or fortune. For the believer, the purpose for living purposely is to please our Maker with how we live: *"That we may present to You a heart of wisdom"* (NASB).

When you get up every morning, is your one purpose to live wisely for the Lord? To live in a way that leverages all God has given you to please Him and bring Him glory? Make the most of your moments for your Maker. Life is too precious not to.

God, today I will live wisely for Your sake. Amen

DISCOURAGEMENT
August 5

"But even the best years are filled with pain and trouble; soon they disappear, and we fly away."
Psalm 90:10

The superscription attributes this psalm to Moses, making it the oldest of all the 150 psalms.

Moses experienced a lot of heartache in his life. After being run out of Egypt for murdering a guy, he spent 40 years in the backwoods of the Sinai. In a flash, he goes from being a well-groomed, privileged member of Pharaoh's household, to a fugitive living in one of the most desolate places in the world. Talk about a financial and career catastrophe! He left behind all his friends and family—and for 40 years he lived in relative isolation and obscurity.

Then God speaks to him from a burning bush. God doesn't say, "Ok, you're suffering is over. Head to Cabo or Playa and enjoy your days." No, He tells Moses to go back to Egypt! In those days of dueling with Pharaoh, he must have lived in constant fear knowing that at any moment Pharaoh's men could burst through the door and cart him away for execution.

After the death angel passed over and their subsequent release, Mo leads the Hebrews back into the Sinai for what should have been a 2–3 week trip. But because the stiff-necked Hebrews rebelled against God, Moses not only didn't get to go into the promised land but had to lead these rabble-rousers around in the desert for 40 years! They were a constant pain in his patooey. Finally, they made him so mad he threw a temper tantrum at the Lord, which did not end well for him.

Somewhere in the midst of all of this, Moses pens this psalm. His anger, pain, and discouragement are raw and obvious. These are words of someone who is in the midst of prolonged suffering.

Three thoughts. First, the Bible does not try to hide the suffering and failures of those on its pages. Second, the Bible refuses to spin a narrative that those who walk in faith and obedience have an easy life. 21st Century American believers need to understand that for most of the history of God's people, the way of faith, has been a way of pain and adversity. Third, Moses is one of the most revered figures in all of history. Not a bad reward.

God, I purpose to walk with You by faith, regardless of the outcome. You are my reward. Amen

RAINY MORNINGS
August 6

"O satisfy us in the morning with Your lovingkindness,
that we may sing for joy and be glad all our days."
Psalm 90:14 (NASB)

As I write, it's 6 a.m., raining and dark. There are flashes of lightning illuminating our street and thunderclaps rattling the dishes in the cabinets.

I love the rain—unless I'm camping out in a tent! For some people, rain in the mornings is a downer. They'll use terms like dreary, bleak, even depressing.

But I don't really feel that way when it rains. I see it as a part of God's overall plan. If we had sunshine all the time, we'd end up a desert. Whether it's sunshiny or rainy, I'm just glad it's morning.

What a great metaphor to help us grapple with difficulties and trials. The 90th Psalm is a psalm that reveals the pain and frustration of Moses as he's trying to lead 3 million people through the wilderness. He's complained about the brevity and meaningless of life. He's accused God of treating him unfairly and without mercy. He's moaned under the weight of hardship and struggle.

But a couple of times in the psalm he puts in a gleam of hope (v.14). In doing so, he's acknowledging that a touch from God is all that he really needs to endure and move forward. As each day begins, a touch is all he needs to get him through the day.

When it's dark and rainy in our lives, we need to hold to this perspective: God allows adversity to achieve His great and mysterious purposes (which we've discussed in previous devotions).

The point here is that rain and sunshine are a part of His plan. It actually makes the pain and fear worse if we resist that reality. ***If we reject it, we're rejecting Him.*** Accepting the dark and rain sets us up to seek the touch of God in a way we will really be able to sense it. And when we sense the touch of God, when He speaks to our souls about His enduring love, we are able to sing about it. Not just one morning, but each morning while He gives us breath.

Even if it's dark and rainy.

God, thank You for the sunshine and the rain in my life. Enable me to see both as a part of Your plan. Help me to sense Your unfailing love regardless. Amen

SANDCASTLES
August 7

*"Let the favor of the Lord our God be on us; establish for us the work of our hands—
establish the work of our hands!"*
Psalm 90:17 (CSB)

Recently my family made a trip to the beaches of the Gulf. We rented a beach house and spent a week playing in the surf and sand. My three sons decided they would build a mammoth sandcastle. They spent just about all day working on it using various-sized buckets and molds, building moats, parapets, and spires to give it the look of one of those medieval castles. It was fun watching these 30-somethings working in the sand like schoolboys. After hours of labor, they posed for pictures by their day-long effort. That evening, as we looked out at the ocean from our beach house, there was the castle—a testimony to their sweat and effort.

The next morning, you guessed it, the tide had come higher on the shoreline than expected and washed it all away. You could hardly tell where the castle had been, so powerful was the force of the water.

No one wants to work hard and then see their efforts be for nothing. This must have been Moses' thinking as he penned the last words of this psalm. He had worked overtime trying to take care of three million people and moving them through the desert. He had complained about life's brevity and futility. At the end he blurts out: "God, don't let all this be for nothing!"

Truth is, everything we do will be examined and assessed for its Kingdom value. Everything. The primary test is this: *"So whether you eat or drink, or whatever you do, do it all for the glory of God"* (1 Corinthians 10:31). It doesn't matter if you are washing cars, doing laundry, seeing patients, or teaching kids—everything is assessed for Kingdom value. If not done for the glory of God and with the desire to build His kingdom, it will end up like the sandcastle.

Nothing is more tragic than the specter of a wasted life.

Sue quotes a phrase from a plaque her grandma had on a wall:

> Only one life 'twill soon be past.
> Only what's done for Christ will last
> C.T. Studd

God, for Your glory and by Your grace and Spirit, establish the work of my hands; purify my motives so that all I do will last. Amen

THE MOST EXCELLENT PSALM
August 8

"He who dwells in the shelter of the Most High will abide in the shadow of the Almighty."
Psalm 91:1 (NASB)

Few psalms are as well-known and loved as this one: "This psalm is one of the greatest possessions of the saints" (G. Campbell Morgan); "In the whole collection there is not a more cheering psalm" (Charles Spurgeon).

We don't know who wrote this psalm. Some scholars conjecture it was Moses, responding to his own dark 90th Psalm with a psalm of light. Others think it was David because of some terms used so commonly in David's other psalms.

Do yourself a favor and read the whole psalm right now. It'll take you about 60 seconds.

This psalm is every bit as beautiful and comforting as the 23rd Psalm.

Older saints will remember the person and story of Corrie ten Boom. Her Christian family sheltered Jews in their home in Haarlem, Netherlands during WW2. Her family was eventually discovered and sent to the concentration camps.

On the night before they were discovered and captured, Corrie's father asked her brother to read Psalm 91. It was the last time she saw her father who died 10 days later. During her time in three different death camps, she kept remembering the 91st Psalm and found comfort in its words. Even though she and her sister, Betsy, were treated cruelly, slept on lice-infested mattresses, nearly froze and starved to death, they persevered by holding on to this psalm. Eventually, only Corrie survived the death camps. She was released "accidentally" on New Year's Eve, 1944 due to a clerical error. She found out later that the women in her cell block were all executed one week after her discharge. She wrote about her experiences in the best seller, *"The Hiding Place."* It is a MUST read.

Life is dangerous. It's risky. Some dangers hide in wait. Some seem random. Some are launched by hostile forces. Others are imagined, but still invoke incredible fear. Psalm 91 is here for us to find comfort in the fact that God is our protection. Storms may rail against us, people may turn against us, but those who abide in The Most High can know that He is for us and watching over us.

God, thank You for inspiring and preserving this psalm for me. Enable me to discover and live out these amazing truths. Amen

BAM!
August 9

"He who dwells in the shelter of the Most High will abide in the shadow of the Almighty.
I will say to the Lord, 'My refuge and my fortress, My God, in whom I trust!'"
Psalm 91:1-2 (NASB)

Years ago, I went to a concert—a little-known fact is that I enjoy classical music. The varied concertgoers drifted in gripping their playbills, chatting, and laughing as they found their seats. As the lights began to dim, the conductor walked out, bowed to polite applause, raised his baton, and suddenly tympany and trumpets shattered the silence as the orchestra feverishly worked through the sonata. It was powerful.

In like manner, the psalmist bangs out an incredible beginning to this great song. The words and concepts in these first two verses are rarely matched in any two verses of the entire Bible.

In these two verses, four wonderful titles or names of God are highlighted. The first is *Elyon*, translated *Most High*. It expresses the incomparable majesty of God. Incomparable because there is no other god that can even begin to rise to His level. The ancient world worshipped many different gods; mostly fertility gods who they hoped would bless them with flocks, herds, and children. They all paled in comparison to this preeminent, Most High God.

The second is *Shaddai*, translated *Almighty*. It carries with it the idea of mountains—the highest, most intimidating presence of the ancient world. Rarely did anyone try to climb a mountain. They went around the mountains; the mountain didn't move or bow to the will of the travelers, they had to submit to its awesome presence.

The third is *YAHWEH*, or the *LORD*. It translates roughly to "*I AM*." This is God's personal name. It was considered so holy and revered that great care was given whenever it was written so as not to defile it by miswriting it; some wouldn't even speak it. The holy and eternal nature of God are captured in His personal name.

The fourth is *Elohim*, translated *God*: "In the beginning, Elohim created..." It carries the idea of judging or determining. It speaks to the sovereignty of this God who creates and determines what is and isn't; what is right and what isn't.

The psalmist brings all of this understanding of God to bear in these first two verses. To what end? More tomorrow!

YAHWEH, I bow before You. Your name is holy because You are holy. I worship You. Amen

SECURE
August 10

"He who dwells in the shelter of the Most High will abide in the shadow of the Almighty.
I will say to the Lord, 'My refuge and my fortress, My God, in whom I trust!'"
Psalm 91:1-2 (NASB)

We live in an age dominated by the need to feel secure. We spend trillions on national security, billions protecting digital information, and over $50 million annually trying to secure our homes. But the security we worry about and pursue most—is financial security.

This psalm is all about security. Notice the four images the psalmist employs. The first is a shelter. It carries the idea of a hiding place. For the ancients, it could be a cave or just a little niche in a rock formation. Believers are found hiding in Christ!

The second image of security is a shadow. To be in the shadow of something or someone means to be close. The psalmist is saying there is security in sticking close to the Almighty One. Bullies run away when the picked-on child runs to his dad. Ain't nobody bigger or badder than our Heavenly Father!

The third secure image is a refuge. This would be more substantive than a niche or a shadow. It would be some kind of structure that would protect from danger. God had the Hebrews set up cities of refuge for those who were accused of murder. They could run to that shelter to avoid the avenging family members and to have their side of the story heard. In Jesus, we find refuge from the penalty of our sin!

The last of the images of security is a fortress. Usually, it referred to a mountain fortress; a reinforced structure located strategically on a high place that could repel the assaults of an enemy. When Satan comes against us, we are safe in our unassailable Jesus!

Combining the four security images with the four names/titles of God (yesterday), creates an incredible panorama of God's protection! Those of us in Christ are protected (shelter, shadow, refuge, & fortress) by the Most High God, the Almighty God, the God who is and was and is to come, the God who created and is the Determiner of what is and ultimately will be!!

So be at peace. Trust in Him. Rest in Him. He's got you.

God, I place my need for security before You. Only You can provide it. Amen

THE MOST HIGH GOD
August 11

"In the shelter of the Most High"
Psalm 91:1

Occasionally as a pastor, one of my members would give me a couple of passes to a sporting event. Usually, the pass got me into areas where only a few people were permitted. I loved walking through security checks like a VIP. I was benefiting from someone else's good name.

Right at the beginning of this psalm, four titles or names of God are highlighted. One of them, *Elyon*, translates *Most High*. It expresses the incomparable majesty and loftiness of God. Fallen humanity worships all kinds of gods, but there is one true, preeminent God who rises far above all of them.

Corrie Ten Boom, who survived the Nazi death camps, told the story of a young Englishman who was held prisoner in a German prison camp for a long period of time. One day he read Psalm 91 and fell to his knees in prayer: "Father, I see all these men dying around me. Will I also die here? I am still young and very much want to work for Your kingdom here on earth." He sensed God say, "Rely on what you have just read and go home."

Trusting God, the young Englishman got up and walked into the corridor toward the gate. A guard called out, "Prisoner, where are you going?" "I am under the protection of The Most High," he replied. The guard came to attention and let him pass, because Adolf Hitler was known as The Most High.

The man came to the gate where a group of guards stood. They commanded him to stop and asked where he was going. "I am under the protection of The Most High," the Englishman replied. All the guards stood at attention as the prisoner walked out the gate. The English officer made his way through the German countryside and eventually reached England where he told how he had made his escape. He was the only one to come out of that prison alive.

The Most High God is more powerful and mighty than any force that can come against us. There is no reason for us to cower in the face of hardship, disease, or attack. If Elyon is for us, who can be against us?

Most High God, I bow before You and pledge to live in the power and privilege of Your good name. Amen

THE TRAPPER
August 12

"He Himself will rescue you from the bird trap"
Psalm 91:3 (CSB)

When I was a kid, my friend and I would place small pieces of bread just outside and under a box propped up by a stick tied to a string snaked through the screen window of his bedroom. The bird would start with the pieces outside the box but eventually get under the box. We'd yank the string and trap the bird, which we would eventually let go.

The psalmist uses this metaphor to highlight the fact that we live in an evil world filled with evil people who intend to do us harm. But there is one enemy above all others—Satan. He uses the same technique that my friend and I used 60 years ago.

First, he has a plan. He is very proactive. The Bible talks about his schemes: *"Put on the full armor of God so that you can stand against the schemes of the devil"* (Ephesians 6:11; CSB). Paul warned us not to be naïve about the devil: *"so that Satan will not outsmart us. For we are familiar with his evil schemes"* (2 Corinthians 2:11).

Here's the thing about Satan's schemes: he has handcrafted one just for you. The scheme that would work on me might not work on you. He knows your weaknesses better than you do. He's been working his plan carefully. He is very smart and he is very patient. He may tempt you to do one little thing today knowing that there's a good chance it will lead you to do something worse in five years and something catastrophic in ten years.

Second, he has a full array of tactics and bait to lure you in—much more sophisticated than little pieces of bread. He'll use your desire to be loved to snare you into sexual immorality. He'll use your desire for meaning to snare you into workaholism. He'll use your desire to accumulate to snare you into consumerism. He has as many baits as there are secret sins in the whole of humanity.

There is one stark difference between two boys having fun, and Satan: *"Be sober-minded, be alert. Your adversary the devil is prowling around like a roaring lion, looking for anyone he can devour."* Satan is out to destroy you, plain and simple.

God, open my eyes to see the areas of my life where Satan is luring me. Rescue me! Amen

THE PLAGUE
August 13

"He Himself will rescue you from . . . the destructive plague."
Psalm 91:3 (CSB)

In the Spring of 2020, a unique and deadly virus practically shut down the entire world. By the end of that summer, over 5.5 million people had contracted the disease and almost 175,000 died from it in the U.S. alone, according to the CDC. Almost every day, Christians were posting prayer needs on social media for loved ones who had fallen ill to the plague.

What are we to make from the confluence of COVID 19 and Psalm 91:3?

To properly interpret Scripture, we must distinguish between general principles, conditional promises, and absolute promises. For instance, Proverbs 22:6 says, *"Train up a child in the way he should go, then when he is old he will not depart from it"* (NASB). Many mistakenly hold this as an absolute promise instead of what it is, a general principle (Proverbs are pithy wisdom sayings that are meant to guide us in the right path, not guarantee results). When their child goes astray, they suffer great guilt because they conclude they were terrible parents—or that God's promises must not be reliable. In fact, neither is correct. Someone can be a great parent (not perfect), but still watch as a child wanders from the faith.

Back to COVID. The psalmist is extolling the protection we have in Yahweh. Does that mean we are absolutely and always protected from harm, from plagues? Nope. The psalmist is not identifying an absolute promise, but a general principle: God's tendency is to physically protect and defend those who trust in Him. I have seen it, experienced it, and believe it. I pray for physical protection for my family multiple times a day and generally God has granted it. But I do have heart disease and Sue's body was wracked by cancer and we both may yet die of COVID. None of this negates the reality that God watches over His beloved. He has a broader perspective than just our few short years on earth.

With a nation and a world reacting with sheer terror, I choose to not fear. I'm not naïve; I just profoundly believe that Yahweh is watching over me and my family—and if He removes His hand of protection, He has good reason. He's God, I'm not.

God, I ask that You watch over and protect me and my loved ones. I trust You no matter what. Amen

PLAGUE AND PROTECTION
August 14

"He will cover you with His feathers; you will take refuge under His wings.
His faithfulness will be a protective shield."

Psalm 91:4

Yesterday we talked about God's physical protection for believers; that it is His tendency to protect us from harm. Still, there is no guarantee in Scripture that we will avoid disease, no matter how much faith we may employ.

However, we should not shy away from praying to and trusting Him for physical protection. Over and over in the Bible, particularly in the Psalms, we see this imagery of God's people taking refuge in, hiding in, being protected by God. The Bible is clear: God responds to the faithful prayers of the saints. I pray daily that God will protect me and my family from maladies, malice, and mishaps. He has covered us with His wings, and we do feel safe.

A story is told by theologian James Boice to illustrate God's penchant for protection:

> Lord Craven, a Christian, was a nobleman who was living in London when the plague ravaged the city in the fifteenth century. To escape the spreading pestilence, Craven determined to leave the city for his country home, as many of his social standing did. He ordered his coach and baggage made ready. But as he was walking down one of the halls of his home about to enter his carriage, he overheard one of his servants say to another, "I suppose by my lord's quitting London to avoid the plague, that his God lives in the country and not in town." It was a straightforward and apparently innocent remark. But it struck Lord Craven so deeply that he canceled his journey, saying, "My God lives everywhere and can preserve me in town as well as in the country. I will stay where I am." So he stayed in London. He helped the plague victims, and he did not catch the disease himself.

I will continue to pray for God's protection for me and mine. I can wholeheartedly testify that God has treated us well; that by His grace, we are blessed, and that He has been and will be faithful. There is such incredible peace in that knowledge.

God, in faith, I do call out for Your protection. In faith, I will leave the results to You. Amen

THOUSANDS FALL
August 15

"Though a thousand fall at your side and ten thousand at your right hand, the pestilence will not reach you. Because you have made the Lord—my refuge, the Most High—your dwelling place, no harm will come to you; no plague will come near your tent."
Psalm 91:7, 9-10 (CSB)

Your firstborn child—for most parents there is a unique bond with that first one. You love all of them equally, but that first one: first pregnancy, first nursery, first delivery, first feeding—few feelings are as strong as with that first child.

We almost suffered tragedy with our firstborn right from the beginning. The first 45 seconds outside the womb, Ben's life was in doubt. By God's grace, he finally began to breathe—and so did we! That bond was now even more powerful. The year was 1982.

Fast forward to Thanksgiving, 2002. Ben's brilliant mind had been mothballed his first year of college. I warned him as he headed off for his sophomore year, to buckle down and get with it. Unfortunately, his midterm grades were abysmal once again. Sue and I agreed something drastic had to be done. So when he was home for Thanksgiving, I sat Ben down at the kitchen table and Sue headed back to the bedroom to cry.

I recounted our previous discussions and then paused to take a deep breath. Gathering my courage, I said, "Ben, we love you too much to let you keep going down this path. We're not going to help you anymore with your schooling. You'll have to find another way to continue your education."

He left. I wept. It. Was. Awful.

Ben ended up enlisting that following Spring in the Air National Guard to pay for his tuition. He went through basic training. His grades were on the upswing. All was good. And then—the U.S. declared war on Iraq. We found out that summer that Ben was going to be shipped out to the war theatre. In a few months, my firstborn was going to be in harm's way in a real way and I kept thinking no way.

Almost a year to the day after our talk in the kitchen my firstborn was at a small, captured air force base in Iraq, surrounded by hostiles who were doing all they could to kill him.

Now Psalm 91 came front and center in our lives. And with good reason. Events were going to unfold that stretched our faith as never before.

More tomorrow…

THE PRAYER
August 16

"Though a thousand fall at your side and ten thousand at your right hand, the pestilence will not reach you. Because you have made the Lord—my refuge, the Most High—your dwelling place, no harm will come to you; no plague will come near your tent."

Psalm 91:7, 9-10 (CSB)

(Continued from yesterday)

When Ben was in high school, he was involved in show choir and concert choir. His senior year they sang, *The Prayer*, popularized by Celine Dion and Andrea Bocelli. From that time on, I linked that song and Ben together in my heart.

When he was in the Middle East, I played that song often. The refrain that always got me choked up was: *"Lead us to a place, guide us with Your grace, to a place where we'll be safe."*

I just now got all choked up again listening to it.

That's essentially what the psalmist was saying in Psalm 91. I had read the psalm many, many times and had memorized the first two verses. But with Ben in Iraq, it became a central part of our devotional life and prayer time. We fought off the fear that would naturally arise with the hope found in these verses.

But it wasn't easy. My dad had fought on Iwo Jima in WW2, and most of his battalion did not come home. A lot of my friends who fought in Nam did not come home. As I studied the psalm, I had to reckon with v.11: *"For he will command His angels concerning you to guard you in all your ways."* I knew Satan used this verse to tempt Jesus in the wilderness: "Go ahead and jump off—God won't let harm come to You" (Luke 4:10). Jesus certainly was supernaturally protected from harm many times (Herod's infanticide, the precipice of Nazareth, etc.), but it was in God's plan to remove that protection for the greater purpose of the cross. So, while I prayed and counted on God's protection for Ben, I knew God might have a grander plan. That realization kept fear crouching at the door every waking moment.

But we kept praying Psalm 91, that God would hide Ben in His shadow and under His wing; that though a thousand may fall around him, no harm would come to him.

"Lead him to a place, guide him with Your grace, to a place where he'll be safe."

More tomorrow…

THE TENT
August 17

"Though a thousand fall at your side and ten thousand at your right hand, the pestilence will not reach you. Because you have made the Lord—my refuge, the Most High—your dwelling place, no harm will come to you; no plague will come near your tent."
Psalm 91:7, 9-10 (CSB)

(Continued from yesterday)

One week after Ben got to Iraq, Saddam Hussein was found in an underground hideaway. Troops had been looking for him night and day for eight months. We mused that since they found Hussein only a week after he got there, they should have sent Ben sooner!

After his tour was over, Ben came home on the C-130 aircraft they had operated in Iraq. When he stepped off that plane onto the tarmac at the Fort Worth Naval Air Station, I can't begin to explain the relief and exhilaration we felt.

But soon he was back over in the Middle East, this time in Afghanistan. Twice! At night, the Taliban would set up positions in the mountains around Bagram AFB and lob mortars into the base. Our forces would copter up, kill them or chase them off, but there was always damage, injuries, and sometimes death. Once again Sue and I were staying close to Psalm 91.

For some reason, the third and last deployment was the most fearful for me. Many times, I would be sitting in my Quiet Time chair at 5:30 am, quiet, still—and get this strange and powerful sensation that Ben had just been killed. This was particularly painful since, as you may recall, the only reason he was there was because I had cut him off financially and he joined the guard to pay for his college. I kept praying, "don't let any harm come near his tent."

One night Ben was sleeping in his little wooden 8 person barracks when a mortar came right over his 'tent,' barely missing it. The explosion was so powerful it knocked him out of his cot. He got up and started to run for the relative safety of a stack of sandbags 100 yards away. As he was running, another shell came right over his head and landed 20-30 yards ahead of him. The majority of the explosion was away from him; had it been coming at him, it would have killed him.

A plea for protection. An implicit trust. A brush with death. A sovereign God. An act of mercy.

Hallelujah!

GOD'S PENCHANT
August 18

"Because he has his heart set on Me, I will deliver him; I will protect him because he knows My name. When he calls out to Me, I will answer him; I will be with him in trouble. I will rescue him and give him honor. I will satisfy him with a long life and show him My salvation."

Psalm 91: 14-16 (CSB)

This great psalm ends with a flurry of eight promises. They create a sweeping summary of God's penchant for protecting His people. I use the word penchant because, as we discussed earlier, not everything that is stated emphatically in Scripture is to be taken or applied with equal weight. Proverbs 16:7 says, *"When people's lives please the Lord, even their enemies are at peace with them."* This is a general principle, not a promise. Jesus even had people in His life who would not be at peace with Him. God promised Solomon in 1 Kings 3 that He would give Solomon wisdom, honor, and riches—which He did. But God also promised him He would give him long, full days IF he obeyed His statutes and commandments.

The eight promises in these verses are conditional, not absolute, promises. They have three boundaries or conditions. The first condition is that we must possess a clinging love for God: *"Because he has his heart set on Me."* The Hebrew word used carries the idea of being pressed and bound together like a saddle on a horse. These promises are experienced when we cling to God and set our hearts to follow Him. This love is not some sentimental emotion, it is the deep desire to please God. We want to please the ones we love, right? Pleasing God is the test of our love for Him.

The second condition is intimate knowledge: *"because he knows My name."* The word, *yadah*, carries the idea of, not just head knowledge, but a close, experiential knowledge. Spending time with God and His word daily is the key to experiencing these promises.

The third condition is prayer: *"When he calls out to Me."* If we call, God will respond. He promises unconditionally to answer us, but His answer is conditional based on His sovereignty. His answer may not be our answer, but it's always the right answer!

God, I desire to cling to You, to know You more intimately, and call on You in faith. May I experience the fullness of Your promises.

PROMISES FOR PROTECTION
August 19

"Because he has his heart set on Me, I will deliver him; I will protect him because he knows My name. When he calls out to Me, I will answer him; I will be with him in trouble. I will rescue him and give him honor. I will satisfy him with a long life and show him My salvation."
Psalm 91: 14-16 (CSB)

This great psalm ends with a flurry of eight conditional promises. Check out yesterday's devotion for those conditions.

The first is for intervening action: *"I will deliver him."* God has stepped in and rescued me from various danger and trouble a zillion times. Usually, it has been because of my own sin or stupidity, but fortunately, He is a compassionate God! Second is the promise of security and protection: *"I will protect him."* I know that if God did not protect me, I'd be dead or worse: a total reprobate in the hopeless clutches of sin.

Third is the promise of answered prayer. My daily journal of God's answered prayers encourages me to continue to pray and trust in His unconditional promise: *"Call to Me, and I'll answer you and show you great and mighty things you've never seen before"* (Jeremiah 33:3).

Fourth is the promise of His presence: *"I will be with him in trouble."* He doesn't promise to keep us from troubles, but to know that He is with us in this trial, is EVERYTHING.

Fifth is the promise of deliverance: *"I will rescue him."* This is similar to the first promise with a slight distinction. The word used carries the idea of not just rescuing but fighting for. God fights for us, and He will have the victory! Sixth is the promise of vindication: *"and give him honor."* The world makes fun of us for our faith and convictions, but one day the truth will be revealed, and we will be vindicated.

Seventh is the promise of a full, rewarding life: *"I will satisfy him with a long life."* Who doesn't want that? Yet long is a relative term. I just want to experience the fullness of God no matter how long my life is.

Eighth is the promise of salvation: *"show him My salvation."* This is the capstone of the other seven promises—that we would end up delivered from sin and made whole in God's presence.

God, thank You for these promises! I want to experience all of them. Amen

THAT'S GOOD!
August 20

"It is good to give thanks to the Lord, to sing praises to the Most High. It is good to proclaim Your unfailing love in the morning, Your faithfulness in the evening."

Psalm 92:1-2

If you've ever backed a trailer up to a dock or down a ramp, you know there's an exclamation you're waiting on from the person spotting you at the back: "That's good!" It means that you've put the trailer where it needs to be; you've got it right.

"It is good" is used twice in these verses and carries the idea that it is fitting and appropriate; just right. Each of them is followed by a couplet that explains what is good.

First, it is good and fitting to give thanks to Yahweh and to sing praises to the Most High. We give thanks to God for what He has done for us: *"You thrill me, Lord, with all You have done for me! I sing for joy because of what You have done. O Lord, what great works You do! And how deep are Your thoughts"* (vv.4-5).

Too many times we are like the nine lepers who forgot to thank Jesus for their healing! Or worse, when times are tough, we think, "What have You done for me lately?" Scripture reminds us to be thankful *"in all things"* (1 Thessalonians 5:18). Take a moment and write down 10 reasons to be thankful to God. Because the psalmist uses God's personal name (*LORD=YAHWEH*), he reminds us this is a very personal thing to Him.

We're also prompted to praise God; to celebrate Him for who He is. Google the attributes of God and take a moment to praise God for just five of them. Don't just say, "I praise You for Your _____. Formulate a few sentences that describe the attribute: "I praise You because You are the Most High God; there is no other god like You; You are higher, You are greater, You are more majestic than anything or anyone else. I worship You." Thanksgiving is offered because of what He did for ME. Praise is offered for who HE is; His virtue, not His activity.

God, I thank You for all You have done for me and I praise You because You are the One True God. I worship and surrender to You. Amen

STILL GOOD!

August 21

"It is good to give thanks to the Lord, to sing praises to the Most High. It is good to proclaim Your unfailing love in the morning, Your faithfulness in the evening."

Psalm 92:1-2

My eldest has just finished building some shelves in his house—measuring, cutting, placing the pieces so that everything fits just right. That's the idea behind the phrase, *"It is good"* used twice here: it carries the idea that it is fitting and appropriate; just right. Each of the two *"It is good"* phrases are followed by a couplet that explains what is good.

Yesterday we examined the first couplet: it is good and fitting to give thanks to God for what He's done and praise Him for who He is.

The second couplet reminds us that it's also good and fitting to proclaim God's unfailing love and to reflect on His faithfulness. His unfailing love, *chesed,* is covenant love. God has bound Himself by a covenant that He made with those in Christ to love us no matter what. This is a unilateral covenant, meaning that once established, it's up to Him to keep it; to keep bound to us; to stay in the covenant. That's good to know, right? If the relationship was based on my love and my performance, it wouldn't last a New York minute! I am so fickle with my affections and inconsistent with my devotion. But not God: *"Nothing shall separate us from the love of God that is in Christ Jesus!"* (Romans 8:39). Because His love is enduring, unlimited, and unending, it's only fitting for me to proclaim it to those around me.

The psalmist says, *"It is good to proclaim . . . Your faithfulness"* (v.2). Because of who He is, God is absolutely and totally reliable to keep His promises to us. His faithfulness is one of the more fascinating attributes of our God. It's partly based on His immutability: He never changes. He doesn't get smarter, wiser, more powerful, or more loving. Because He never changes, He is not capricious about anything; He is constant in every way. It's also based on His omnipotence: if He says it, it will happen. If He pledges it, He will do it.

It is good, right, and fitting to sing about all of this from the time we wake up until the time we go to sleep. What a great God!

Lord, You are great! Blessed be the name of my God!! Amen

HATE SPEECH

"How magnificent are Your works, Lord, how profound Your thoughts! A stupid person does not know, a fool does not understand this: though the wicked sprout like grass and all evildoers flourish, they will be eternally destroyed."

Psalm 92:5-7

Hate speech is defined by the Cambridge Dictionary as "public speech that expresses hate or encourages violence towards a person or group based on something such as race, religion, sex, or sexual orientation." I wonder if the psalmist (and other biblical writers) would be guilty of spewing hate, according to the definition.

He calls people stupid and foolish. He seems to proudly proclaim that some people are actually wicked. Wicked is a strong word: morally wrong; evil. He tops his rant off by claiming that some people are so despoiled, that they will be eternally destroyed. Sounds pretty hateful to me. With the leftist attempts in our nation to squelch free speech, I don't doubt that there will be a time soon when pastors will end up in jail for proclaiming the gospel (salvation for the justified, damnation for everyone else) and teaching biblical morals (marriage is only to be a union between a male and a female, etc.). Of course, the biblical writers (and pastors) are only quoting God. So let's see them throw Him in jail!

The psalmist makes the point that this is all a result of the fact that humans can't grasp the transcendence of God. Even though created in His image, we are so damaged and broken that we can't see or discern reality without His help. So we try to create a god in our image, made up of our distorted perceptions of reality—and that is the definition of stupidity and foolishness.

Here's what God says about Himself, *"My thoughts are nothing like your thoughts,' says the Lord. 'And My ways are far beyond anything you could imagine. For just as the heavens are higher than the earth, so My ways are higher than your ways and My thoughts higher than your thoughts"* (Isaiah 55:8-9).

The prophet and the psalmist both agree: God has His own perspective and His own agenda. If we seek Him and gain His perspective, He will lift us up. To ignore His or insist on another perspective is to be lowered down—deep down. Hate speech? Nah, hopeful warning.

God, enable me to see and live life from Your perspective so I won't live foolishly. Amen

GOT SAP?

"The righteous man will flourish like the palm tree; he will grow like a cedar in Lebanon.
Planted in the house of the Lord, they will flourish in the courts of our God.
They will still yield fruit in old age; they shall be full of sap and very green,
to declare that the Lord is upright; He is my rock, and there is no unrighteousness in Him."
Psalm 92:12-15 (NASB)

The Bible is full of imagery about the transient nature of life: *"Lord, remind me how brief my time on earth will be— how fleeting my life is"* (Psalm 39:4); *"Your life is like the morning fog— it's here a little while, then it's gone"* (James 4:14).

But Scripture takes a different slant when it talks about people who are outside of the faith. Not only is their life brief, but it is also of little value: *"They are like worthless chaff, scattered by the wind"* (Psalm 1:4); *"Just as the weeds are sorted out and burned in the fire, so it will be at the end of the world . . . the angels will throw them into the fiery furnace"* (Matthew 13:40, 42).

Weeds. Chaff. Good people doing good things outside of Christ have no lasting value in God's economy. He may utilize them in this life for His purposes (common grace), but when all is said and done—nothing lasting.

Not so with the person who is in a right relationship with Yahweh through faith. The psalmist likens that person to a palm tree and a cedar tree. Palm trees can flourish in dry climates because they can send roots deep to find water. The cedars of Lebanon are legendary: strong, giant, durable evergreens. The psalmist pictures these planted in the temple courts, in the presence of God, bearing fruit in old age.

In contrast to those who are outside of Christ, the righteous have something to show for their lives, even in old age! Tree sap functions to transport vital mineral nutrients and sugars so that it can live and bear fruit. I love this! In my latter years, I want to drive my roots deeper into Jesus, continuing to bear fruit, making an impact for Him, and proclaiming, *"The Lord is upright; He is my rock, and there is no unrighteousness in Him!"*

God, make my days count for You! May it be so.

YOUR MAJESTY!

August 24

"The Lord reigns! He is robed in majesty;
the Lord is robed, enveloped in strength."

Psalm 93:1 (CSB)

The U.S. has never had a monarch. In part, that's what the revolution of 1776 was about. In fact, one of the battle cries of the colonies was, "No king but King Jesus!" It is fascinating to watch the British as they fawn over their royals. On special occasions, QE sits on her throne wrapped in a jewel-covered robe. It sets her apart; it speaks of dignity, majesty, and power.

The 93rd Psalm is an "enthronement" psalm focusing on the kingship of God. The psalmist begins this brief psalm with an abrupt declaration; a shout: "The LORD reigns!"

The LORD reigns! The Hebrew word for *reigns* is *malak*. If used as a noun, it means king. If used as a verb, it means to reign or rule. Twice in v.1 God is pictured as king, robed and enveloped in majesty and power. Clothing is normally viewed as an extension of the person; it gives insight into character and intent. The Bible makes no qualms about it: God sees Himself as the Supreme Ruler. That's who He is; that's what He's about—and He's dressed for success!

As King, no one has higher authority or power. As King, He commands respect and loyalty. As King, He demands obedience and submission. Jesus said in Luke 6:46, *"Why do you call me Lord, Lord, and not do what I say?"*

This is difficult to swallow. We're bent in a way that causes us to resist absolute surrender to anyone. Recently I've been visiting with a young man who has so many questions about God. He keeps saying that he can't embrace Jesus because he can't grasp the mysteries of the universe. I told him Jesus does not ask us to understand everything; He commands us to follow Him. I know (he doesn't yet) that the young man's objections are not intellectual, but volitional. He does not want to surrender his will to Jesus; he does not want to bow and pay homage to the King.

Genuine believers know this to be true: life in Christ is a life of dying to self; of total surrender; of making His will, our will; His commands, our joy.

Is Jesus King in your heart?

Lord, I bow before You right now. I want Your will, not mine; Your desires, not mine. Rule my life. Amen

NO JUSTICE, NO PEACE

August 25

"O Lord, the God of vengeance, O God of vengeance, let Your glorious justice shine forth!
Arise, O Judge of the earth. Give the proud what they deserve."
Psalm 94:1-2

Psalm 94 is about justice. We place our faith in a sovereign God, but we find ourselves in situations where we are treated unjustly by those who have a measure of power over us. Persecuted believers all over the world are crying out for God to act on behalf of His oppressed people. We need to join those prayers.

The Scripture is clear that God will take vengeance on the enemies of His people. From the Pentateuch, *"Vengeance is mine; I will repay,"* to Revelation, *"With justice He judges and makes war,"* God insists He will bring justice to this unjust world. Trust Him—He will.

But how are we to respond in the face of injustice? Well, it depends. If you and I are the ones being treated unjustly, then God commands us to not respond with vengeance: *"If someone slaps you on the right cheek, offer the other cheek also"* (Matthew 5:39), *"Dear friends, never take revenge. Leave that to the righteous anger of God"* (Romans 12:19).

The common phrase "No justice, no peace" may be within the right of free speech as an American but is outside a biblical perspective if 'no peace' means violence.

If you're not someone who is suffering injustice, then you must be active in interceding for those who are suffering injustice. The Minor Prophets were particularly concerned about this (Isaiah 1:17, Micah 6:8), condemning the privileged who were insensitive or even callous toward those who were oppressed. Jesus picked up the theme: *"The Spirit of the Lord is on Me . . . to set free the oppressed"* (Luke 4:18).

EVERY true Christ-follower should be concerned about and even grieve when injustice occurs. To passively sit by because we're not personally suffering injustice is to place ourselves in the crosshairs of the prophets—and to betray the heart of Jesus for the weak and oppressed.

Recently my kids marched in a peaceful, police-friendly protest against injustice. I was proud of them. For years I've been rethinking my attitude and perspective on these matters, and recently, it's happening at warp speed. Join me.

God, forgive me for my callous indifference to injustice. Change my heart. Amen

I WOULD HAVE DIED
August 26

"I would have died unless the Lord had helped me. I cried, 'I'm slipping, Lord!'
and He was kind and saved me. When doubts fill my mind and my heart is in turmoil,
quiet me and give me renewed hope and cheer."
Psalm 94:17-19 (LB)

In the summer of 1962, my family moved from one part of Tulsa to a neighborhood that was literally on the edge of the city. Across the street from our house, there was nothing but fields and trees for miles and miles. It was a wonderful playground for a 10-year-old! As that area was being developed, the city began to put in the infrastructure to support more houses. One afternoon, my little brother and I jumped down into a rectangular hole approximately 8' x 10' and about 10' deep.

After a few minutes of exploration, we decided to get out. You guessed it—the walls were too high for us, even with him standing on my shoulders. We would try to crawl out, but the damp clay walls were too slick, and we'd slide back into the hole. We tried and tried but kept slipping back down. For what seemed like hours we yelled and screamed until someone heard us. He lowered a 2 x 4 and we scurried out.

Ten years later, in the summer of 1972, I was working for Shell Oil in downtown Houston. I was all alone and grieving over the breakup of a relationship with someone I thought I was going to marry. I was functional during the day, but at night, I plunged into deep, dark despair. I kept trying to crawl out but kept slipping back down into the darkness. There were evenings I thought I was literally going to die.

But in the darkness, God showed me these verses. They reminded me of that time with my brother in the hole. I memorized them and they kept me alive that summer. Eventually, He lifted me out of the pit of despair—He was kind and saved me. There have been many times since then when I have drawn on the beauty and strength of those words. He has repeatedly given me *'renewed hope and cheer'* in and through my tough and tragic times.

He will do that for you as well.

God, thank You for these words of love and encouragement. Be kind to me. Amen

THE ROCK

August 27

"Come, let us sing to the Lord! Let us shout joyfully to the Rock of our salvation."
Psalm 95:1

Dwayne Johnson is known as The Rock because he has built and honed his body and muscles to look like a rock. If people named me for my physical appearance, I might be called The Roll.

Many times in the Psalms, God is identified as the real Rock (please don't tell Dwayne I said he's not the real Rock), and we see it in this psalm.

Where is the focus right now in your life? It's easy for us to get focused on ourselves, particularly in trial, trouble, or tragedy. We need reminding that our life, and what's happening in it, is ultimately not about us—it's about Him. If our circumstances remain all about us, then there can be no higher purpose for our suffering. Maybe you've heard the saying: "A life wrapped up in itself is a very small package."

The psalmist points us in the right direction. He challenges us to stop looking inside and around and begin looking up. He exhorts us to break into songs of worship and thanksgiving with hearts of joy. He gives a number of reasons. First: God is the source and security of our salvation. *"Rock of our salvation"* refers to the incident in Exodus 17 when the Hebrews were wandering in the Sinai and out of water. God told Moses to strike a rock and out of it would flow life-giving water. Moses responded in faith and obedience and that's exactly what happened. When you think about it, a rock in the desert would be the last place you would think about finding water, right? But that's the way God works at times: He takes the least likely circumstance (finding water in a desert rock) or the least likely person (Moses) to do the least likely thing (strike a rock with a stick) to show His great and glorious power.

He is The Rock; the personal provider and protector of our salvation. The word for *salvation* is *yesha*. The name of God used here is Yahweh, His personal, relational name. Combine these together and you get *Yeshua, Yahweh saves*, aka JESUS! He is the Living Water!

God, You are my Rock and my Redeemer. Bless Your holy name. Amen

THE CREATOR GOD

August 28

"For the Lord is a great God, a great King above all gods. He holds in His hands the depths of the earth and the mightiest mountains. The sea belongs to Him, for He made it. His hands formed the dry land, too."

Psalm 95:3-5

When I went off to college, I learned a lot of stuff—not all of it good! One good thing I learned was how to play spades. In this card game, you and your partner try to figure out how many tricks you're going to get. Occasionally, one of the partners has such a poor hand they bid *nihilo*, which means nothing. If that partner took a trick, they were set and lost a bunch of points.

When you put the prefix *ex* in front of *nihilo*, you get *ex nihilo*, the Latin term for *out of nothing*.

The psalmist is giving us reasons to worship God and he lands on an incredibly important reason: the God of the Bible created everything that is, OUT OF NOTHING! *"In the beginning God created the heavens and the earth"* (Genesis 1:1). We don't know when the beginning began, but whenever it was, God was already. God, who has no beginning, decided to create, and everything we know as the universe came to be.

If God created out of nothing, what are the implications? First, I must exercise faith in the face of a secular insistence otherwise: *"By faith we understand that the entire universe was formed at God's command, that what we now see did not come from anything that can be seen"* (Hebrews 11:3). They'll keep trying to find ways to keep God out of creation, so stand firm in your faith.

Second, if God created the depths of the earth (Grand Canyon) and the mightiest mountains (Mt. Everest), the fathomless oceans and vastness of the continents, He owns them. We don't own, He owns. We are only stewards of His creation. Do I look at myself as a steward of the environment; a steward of the possessions He has entrusted to me?

Third, if God created *ex nihilo*, He is to be worshipped as the Creator God. That's happening right now around His throne. Heaven's residents are worshipping: *"You are worthy, O Lord our God, to receive glory and honor and power. For You created all things, and they exist because You created what You pleased"* (Revelation 4:11).

Let's join them!

THE AWESOME GOD
August 29

"Come, let's worship and bow down; let's kneel before the Lord our Maker."
Psalm 95:6 (CSB)

Sue and I found the series, "The Crown," very interesting. It gave insight into life as Royals in England. When coming into a room where QE is, people bow. After they get to her, they bow and kiss her hand. Upon leaving, they bow and never turn their back to her as they exit. It's got to be a bit socially awkward walking backward for 10-15 steps! This is customary to show reverence for someone of her stature.

The psalmist uses three separate words to accentuate the sovereign, lofty royalty of our God: worship (from a word meaning to lay prostrate), bow, and kneel—as our Maker He is worthy of this awe and reverence.

Have you ever noticed that life is full of tensions and the better you manage those tensions, the better life is? For instance, you may get really frustrated at your job and long to be sitting on a beach somewhere sipping your favorite beverage. But if you release the tension totally, quit your job, you'll have a bigger problem. You have to manage the tension; maintain a balanced perspective.

One of the trends of 21st century American Christianity is the celebration of God as a personal, relatable, interested-in-us God. It's so true! He calls us friend. We call Him Daddy. Jesus gave His life for me, He has my best interest at heart, He's with me no matter what. Much of the contemporary music beautifully captures this dimension. Preaching today tends to follow suit.

But there is another dimension we need to keep in perspective and manage the tension created: God is high and lifted up; He is like us, but different in infinite ways: He is the sovereign, glorious, and Holy One. When Isaiah saw a vision of God, angels hovered and sang, *"Holy, Holy, Holy is the Lord God Almighty,"* and he fell on his face before Him. When the priest would go into the Holy of Holies to make a sacrifice, they tied a rope around his ankle so that if he died in the presence of this awesome, holy God, they could drag him out.

Don't lose your reverence and awe for this holy and transcendent God. He deserves and demands our obedience and worship.

God, show me how to balance reverence with celebration. Amen

THE CARING SHEPHERD
August 30

"For He is our God, and we are the people of His pasture, the sheep under His care."
Psalm 95:7 (CSB)

The psalmist has encouraged us to worship God because He is our Rock (v.1-2), because He is our Creator (vv.3-5), because He is our awesome God (v.6), and now in verse 7 because He is our Shepherd. Psalm 23 comes to mind, right?

Jesus purposely took that title for Himself in John 10:11, *"I am the good shepherd."* A study of John 10 reveals a number of characteristics of the Good Shepherd. First, He gave His life for you: *"I am the good shepherd. The good shepherd sacrifices his life for the sheep"* (v.11). Jesus didn't leave you on your own in this wretched world. He came to rescue you; to redeem you. In doing so, it cost Him His life—His life for mine; His life for yours.

Second, He knows you personally: *"I am the good shepherd; I know My own sheep, and they know Me" (v.14).* In the deepest recesses of every human is the desire to be known. You're not ignored or overlooked—the infinite God knows lil' ol you! He knows you better than you know yourself and knows what you need and what's best for you. And—you can know Him and fall in love with Him!

Third, He gives you direction: *"My sheep listen to My voice; I know them, and they follow Me"* (v.27). He leads us on a path that is so good, so rich, so fulfilling: *"I came that you would have real and abundant life! More and better than you can ever imagine"* (v.10). To experience that life, you need to stick close to Him.

Fourth, He gives you eternal life: *"I give them eternal life"* (v.28). The one common experience of all humans is physical death. Yet the Bible says God has put in us the desire to live forever (Ecclesiastes 3:11). There IS something after this life and Jesus is the only way to gain it.

Finally, if you belong to the Good Shepherd, He owns you and will never abandon you: *"They will never perish. No one can snatch them away from me* (v.28). What great comfort for the believer: NOTHING and NO ONE can separate us from the love of God that is in Christ Jesus! (Romans 8:39).

Jesus, thank You for being my Good Shepherd! Amen

THE WARNING
August 31

"If only you would listen to His voice TODAY! The Lord says, 'Don't harden your hearts as Israel did at Meribah, as they did at Massah in the wilderness.'"

Psalm 95:7-8

I recall a time when I was in high school that my dad kept warning me about keeping my bedroom straightened. I didn't heed the warning and so one day I came home to discover, yet again, the consequences of ignoring his warning. He had emptied the contents of my dresser, desk, and closet, taken off the sheets, piled everything in the middle of the room, and then turned the bed and all the furniture upside down and piled it on top. Lesson learned!

Any loving parent knows the dynamic of having to teach your children to obey and warn them of consequences if they don't. After the psalmist has encouraged us to worship God because He's our Rock, Creator, God, and Shepherd, there is a warning for us: Keep a soft heart toward God and listen for His voice.

This warning is important enough to be repeated three times in the book of Hebrews: *"Listen to His voice today and don't harden your hearts."*

This all points back to the time the Hebrews grumbled against God in the wilderness (Exodus 17; Numbers 20). They didn't have what they wanted when they wanted it. **Whatever worship they offered to God was just lip-service because it didn't result in a deeper trust in Him.** The place of rebellion was named Meribah, which means *"strife"*, and Massah, which means *"testing."* Their hardness of heart led them to contend with the Lord and test His love and patience.

Is there something in your life that you are ungrateful for? When God prompts you to pray, do you—or do you put it off? When He prompts you to turn something you're watching off, do you—or do you continue watching? When He prompts you to ask forgiveness for being selfish, do you—or do you insist on the other to make the first move? When He prompts you to witness for Him in some way, do you—or do you keep your lips sealed?

The hard-hearted Hebrews didn't go into the Rest, the Promise Land—and missed the blessing.

Pray for a Spirit-softened heart—and experience the blessings of His rest—TODAY!

God, forgive me for my hard-heartedness. By Your Spirit, I will listen and respond in faith. Amen

A NEW SONG
September 1

"Sing a new song to the Lord! Let the whole earth sing to the Lord! Sing to the Lord; praise His name. Each day proclaim the good news that He saves. Publish His glorious deeds among the nations. Tell everyone about the amazing things He does."

Psalm 96:1-3

I like the old songs. They touch a part of my personal history and remind me of God's faithfulness at various times of my life. Hymns remind me of when I was a kid sitting with my parents in church and hearing the stories of Jesus for the first time. The earliest contemporary songs by Andre Crouch or Maranatha remind me of my considerable spiritual growth phase as a single in the 1970s. Songs by Sandi Patty and Larnelle Harris remind me of my kids when they were small, Steven Curtis Chapman and Audio Adrenaline when the kids were teens, and so on.

But I love the new songs as well. They are the latest inspirations of the Holy Spirit that prompt my heart to worship God in refreshing and revitalizing ways. My relationship with God can't stay in the past, it must be a circuit of reminding of the past AND refreshing for the day at hand.

The psalmist is challenging us to look for new and refreshing ways to worship God. He calls on the whole earth to get a fresh glimpse of this awesome God that, in turn, prompts us to sing love songs to Him and praise His holy name.

There must be a dailiness to this. My relationship with God can't get stuck in yesterday. Each day I am to get up and look for a new expression, a new insight, a new depth, and experience a new touch from Him.

This will prompt me to proclaim His goodness and redemption: *"Each day proclaim the good news that He saves (and) of the amazing things He does"* (v.3). God doesn't want us to hoard the news, but to declare it by how we live and by what we say to those around us.

If the spring in your heart is bubbling from a fresh and intimate relationship with God, it will spill over into your conversations. It just will.

This all starts with seeking a new encounter with and touch from God each day. That's when we'll sing the new song and talk of this amazing God.

O Lord, I do want to seek You and experience You in a fresh, new way. May it be so.

EVIL

September 2

"You who love the Lord, hate evil!"
Psalm 97:10

Many in our post-modern world resist using the word 'evil.' You won't hear anyone on a newscast describe a horrific crime as evil. One reason is that their worldview contains a notion that humans are essentially good, moral, and only need a little love, encouragement, and education to be ethical and honorable. They lack a biblical view of humanity: that our sinfulness/brokenness, begun in the Garden of Eden and continued by each of us since then, has contaminated us and rendered us wicked and evil in the sight of a holy God.

The only way out of that plight is to confess our personal sinfulness, repent/turn away from it, and place our faith in the Messiah. He then not only redeems us from the penalty of our wickedness, but then, by His indwelling Spirit, begins to restore us back to our pre-Fall

condition; i.e., into His righteous image.

Satan is the personification and chief proponent of evil. Jesus called him *'the evil one'* (Matthew 13:19). Indeed, the entire Bible from Genesis 3 to Revelation 20 speaks of the *evil one*. He is a thief, a liar, a murderer, an accuser; he opposes God, the word of God, the people of God, and the things of God.

Satan and his demons keep coming after us. They can't steal our salvation, but they can steal God's blessings by tempting us and leading us astray. We still have a sin nature that won't go fully away until we are rid of this fleshly, fallen body. It actually wants to cooperate with Satan and participate in evil. They become coconspirators against us. We can fight them by putting on the full armor of God (Ephesians 6), or we can keep letting them pummel us.

We have a choice. The psalmist says, *"If you love God, hate evil."* Not just tolerate it. Not just be glad you're not as wicked as you use to be. Not even just resist it. HATE IT!

We cannot truly love justice without hating injustice. We cannot truly love honesty without hating dishonesty. We cannot truly love purity without hating impurity. Etcetera.

We don't hate people; we hate actions. We don't hate sinners; we hate sin. We cannot say we love God and not love what He loves—and hate what He hates.

God, open my eyes and change my heart to hate what You hate and love what You love. Amen

GLAD WRAP 2
September 3

"Light is sown like seed for the righteous and gladness for the upright in heart.
Be glad in the Lord, you righteous ones, and give thanks to His holy name."
Psalm 97:11-12 (NASB)

I'm old enough to remember when plastic wraps like Glad Wrap were not commonly used. They were developed and marketed in the early 1950s, so growing up, my family used wax paper or tin foil to wrap food in. Because my parents were raised during the Great Depression, we saved the tin foil and used it over and over instead of throwing it away. Sue makes fun of me for using the term 'tin foil' instead of 'aluminum foil' but that's what it was called in those days—and I still call it that. The reason Glad Wrap is preferable to tin foil or wax paper is that you can get a practically air-tight seal that preserves the food much longer.

This psalm is about the Supreme Ruler—Yahweh. He reigns over all creation with power and majesty. Righteousness and justice are the foundation of His throne. All that He has made bows in holy reverence before Him, and fools who refuse will be disgraced and forced to acknowledge His sovereignty.

Knowing all this, the righteous rejoice and are glad.

Remember that to be *righteous* does not require moral perfection, only a relationship with God established by faith, not performance. An upright heart belongs to the one who purposes to honor that relationship with how they live.

Light and gladness are promised for the righteous and upright. In Scripture, light is almost always used in a positive sense.

Light gives direction. Light gives hope. Light reveals truth. Light dispels darkness. Light produces joy and gladness. Who doesn't want more of that?

Are you wrapped in gladness? The brokenness of our world is such a Debbie Downer. People and circumstances can suck the joy and gladness right out of us UNLESS we are wrapped in a gladness that God preserves for those who are upright in heart; who live honorably for Him.

Notice that we have a choice: *"Be glad."* How? *"Be glad in the Lord."* Don't rely on people or circumstance to be the source of your joy; count on this sovereign King to shine light into your soul and wrap you in His gladness.

Yahweh, thank You for all You have done for me in Jesus. Wrap me in Your joy. Amen.

VICTORY IN JESUS
September 4

"Sing a new song to the Lord, for He has done wonderful deeds.
His right hand has won a mighty victory; His holy arm has shown His saving power!"

Psalm 98:1-2

Do you ever feel defeated—like you're not parenting well enough, reading your Bible often enough, praying powerfully enough, witnessing enough, experiencing the joy and abundance of the Christ-life enough? Sure, who doesn't?

This psalm has such encouragement for those who feel defeated. We're exhorted to sing and shout because of the marvelous thing God did by saving us. For sure, the immediate context is the unknown victories God gave Israel over its military/political enemies. But the grander and ultimate expression is in the victories Jesus gives us in salvation. The Hebrew word *'yasha'* can be translated *salvation* or *victory*. **God's salvation is a salvation of victory.**

If you want a quick pick-me-up, read this short psalm through a few times in a row. It breaks into three sections: 1. We're encouraged to sing because of the salvation secured by the Savior (vv1-3), 2. We're encouraged to shout to the Lord because of the universal joy that comes from His salvation (vv.4-6), and 3. We're exhorted to call for all the earth to join in praise of the coming Lord who will consummate His righteous purposes (vv.7-9).

If you're a Christ-follower, think about your own experience of salvation and what the Bible says about it: Jesus died on the cross to pay for your personal brokenness/sin and walked out of the tomb to prove that He had conquered sin and the separation from God it caused. In Christ you were rescued, made right with God, adopted, indwelt by His Spirit, and secured for a destiny that is beyond description when He finally returns.

This great hymn captures the theme:

> *I heard an old, old story, how a Savior came from glory*
> *How He gave His life on Calvary to save a wretch like me*
> *I heard about His groaning, of His precious blood's atoning*
> *Then I repented of my sins and won the victory*
> *Oh victory in Jesus, my Savior forever*
> *He sought me and bought me with His redeeming blood*
> *He loved me 'ere I knew Him and all my love is due Him*
> *He plunged me to victory beneath the cleansing flood*

Jesus, thank You for the salvation I have in You. I'm going to live in the victory of it. Amen!

THE JUST KING
September 5

"Mighty King, lover of justice, You have established fairness.
You have acted with justice and righteousness throughout Israel."
Psalm 99:4

Throughout history, there have been too many kings, princes, popes, potentates, premiers, and presidents who didn't love justice. Sargon II of Assyria had 1000s of Israelites murdered, raped, and enslaved during his land-grab of 721 B.C. Herod the Great had hundreds of babies killed in an attempt to destroy baby Jesus. Vlad Tepes of Romania impaled 20,000 men, women, and children **after** unmentionable torture. Pope Alexander VI was involved in murders, orgies, and even incest with his daughter. The 20th Century saw Mao kill 40+ million, Stalin 20+ million, and Hitler 8+ million. It also saw Richard Nixon create a constitutional crisis by breaking the law and then lying about it, as did Bill Clinton and Donald Trump.

This psalm asserts that our King, King Jesus, is a lover of justice and fairness. Because He is the Maker and Ruler of the universe, He alone gets to decide what justice and fairness are. He asserts that justice and fairness are based on His standard of rightness; i.e., is this right, honest and true?

When God gave Moses the first laws, they weren't just words on a piece of stone that needed to be obeyed. They were expressions of the very nature of God: "I am unique, high, and holy—don't be worshipping other gods. I created you in my image to reflect my glory, and I'm not a murderer, a liar, a thief, or an adulterer," and so on.

The framers of the Constitution didn't dream up the virtues and principles enumerated; they are reflective of the great laws of Scripture that are expressions of who God is and what He insists is right and true. Not all laws in our land have been or are just; e.g., Jim Crow laws, legal abortion laws, same-sex marriage laws. When we stray from His righteous law, we head down an unjust path. MLK righteously orchestrated civil, peaceful disobedience to oppose and finally topple unjust laws; laws not based on the character of God. He was, in fact, upholding God's righteous laws.

When leaders (elected or otherwise) stray from righteous laws and apply their own set of laws, the result is tyranny, injustice, anarchy, and mob rule (e.g., Antifa).

God, give me the wisdom to base my opinions and lifestyle on Your law; Your character. Amen

HOW TO BE THANKFUL
September 6

"For the Lord is good. His unfailing love continues forever,
and his faithfulness continues to each generation."
Psalm 100:5

When I was in grade school, I had a teacher who encouraged us to memorize the 100th Psalm. Each morning we would stand, recite the Pledge of Allegiance (hands over hearts), and then the teacher would read the 100th Psalm or one of us would take a shot at saying it from memory. Then—we would pray. I recall it was such a wonderful way to start the day. The words of this psalm were so comforting. They still are.

The superscription says simply, "A Song for Giving Thanks." Why would this be a psalm for giving thanks?

The whole psalm leads up to the reason we should be thankful, which is found in the last verse:

"For the Lord is good. His unfailing love continues forever, and his faithfulness continues to each generation" (v.5). Four quick reasons to be thankful: 1) Our God is a personal, relational God. **LORD is Yahweh, His personal name**. He is not remote and inaccessible; He seeks a relationship with us; 2) **He is good**. Good carries the idea that He is pleasant and agreeable; 3) **His love is a covenant, enduring love**; not emotional or whimsical; 4) **He is faithful to His word** and promises; always has been and always will be.

Because Yahweh is who He is and does what He does, the psalmist admonishes us to take six actions that result in thanksgiving: 1) *Shout for joy*: this word emphasizes being verbally loud and not holding back when it comes to expressing our joy; 2) *Serve Him with gladness*: not a reluctant, forced action to submit to Him, but a deep-soul desire to please Him in all things; 3) *Come before Him singing*: there is something about singing spiritual songs that brightens the heart and fills it with joy; 4) *Know that He is our Maker and we are His sheep*; that leads to peace (pasture); 5) *Enter into His presence*: the temple worshippers would enter the gates and move into the courts signifying a conscious effort to draw close to God in personal worship; 6) *Give thanks and praise*; identify the blessings He has bestowed on us through His son, Jesus. So much in this short little psalm!

God, thank you for this psalm! As I read it, my heart is filled with thanksgiving! Amen

PORN
September 7

*"I will lead a life of integrity in my own home.
I will refuse to look at anything vile and vulgar."*
Psalm 101:2-3

There was a guy in my church years ago who posted on FB that for his son's 16th birthday, he took him to Hooters as a celebration and rite of passage. They have long since left the church, but I would bet my house and firstborn that his son's life is being ruined by pornography.

A family counselor recently told me that she is working more and more with 8 & 9-year-old children who are addicted to pornography. Some studies place the percentage of adults addicted as high as 86% for men 65% for women. Given what is allowed to come into our homes on the TV just in the commercials, the vile and vulgar are a part of our daily lives.

How do we fight this? It starts with an understanding of integrity. Integrity is a virtue that insists we hold to and stick to our moral principles. Someone has said that integrity is revealed by what we do when no one is looking.

The psalmist declares his intention to lead a life of integrity. He knows that it begins in the privacy of his home. Because this was penned 3000 years ago, one wonders what it was he had to refrain from looking at. Regardless, the psalmist knows that integrity is a private thing that makes its way public; an inner thing that makes its way outward. By extension, what happens in the privacy of our homes will eventually make its way for others to observe.

If parents are not being careful in the home about what they watch, their children will pick up on that and eventually be damaged irreparably. Wise parents today not only limit their personal viewing choices but also utilize tech tools to prohibit the vile and vulgar on their kids' screens. My family uses Covenant Eyes on every device we have—every **Integrity begins with intentionality and is sustained by perseverance.** Parents: don't be a part of what many counselors say is the worst possible addiction a human can have. Put on the mind of Christ and live it in front of your kids.

*God, prick my heart when I watch what is not wholesome and enable me to live a life of integrity.
Amen*

TROUBLE
September 8

"A prayer of one overwhelmed with trouble, pouring out problems before the Lord."
The superscription to Psalm 102

I've been on this earth for seven decades. I don't know if there has been another season in my lifetime filled with more trouble. The only possibility would be during the racial tensions and Vietnam war era of the late 1960s-early 1970s. Having been involved in the ministry of the gospel for almost five decades, I can say unequivocally that the extent of troubles, problems, and trials on the individual level is greater now than I've ever seen.

That's what makes being a student of the Psalms so critically important. They give us an incredible perspective on how the God of the universe relates to us in the midst of our troubles.

As we've discussed before, the superscriptions of the Psalms are titles ascribed either by the author at the time or some editor afterward. It would be difficult to give them the same status as Scripture, but they are certainly informative in helping us understand the psalm.

We're not sure who wrote this psalm or its superscription, but whoever it was wrote it in a time of national and personal trouble. That's what makes this psalm so relevant to our times. It contains some critical perspective as to what's going on in our lives today. Two reminders are embedded in the 13 words of the superscription.

First, people of faith do become overwhelmed with troubles and trials. This is sometimes difficult to rationalize with other realities of the Christ-life: God loves us; Jesus promised abundant life; we are blessed and highly favored. However, our lives are a tapestry woven, not just with bright colors, but with dark, foreboding colors as well. We must accept that God is in control of the colors and the weaving, and trust that He will make all things beautiful at the end.

Second, people of faith can respond to these troubles by praying and pouring out our hearts to God. God desires us to pray; He commands us to pray (Jeremiah 33:3). **Overcoming being overwhelmed begins with calling out to God and pouring our hearts out to Him.**

So when troubled, prayer is our first and best response. He may not fix the problem, but He'll begin fixing us.

God, thank you that I can pray, and You listen. Grant me the grace to be content with that. Amen

LONELINESS
September 9

"I am like an owl in the desert, like a little owl in a far-off wilderness."
Psalm 102:6

Owls are lonely creatures. Even though there are over 200 species WHOO live in every region of the world except the polar ice caps, they are rarely seen. If they are spotted, they are not like other birds that gather in groups.

The psalmist begins his song in a similar fashion as the other psalms: asking God to hear his prayer and deliver him from his distress. But what stands out to me in this psalm is found in v.6.

Owls are mentioned rarely in the Bible but symbolize desolation and tormenting loneliness.

My experience with profound, debilitating loneliness in my early 20s became a turning point in my life. I had just moved to Houston, recently broken up with the love of my life, working for Shell Oil downtown, didn't know anyone, and found it impossible to make friendships that touched the ache.

I'd go to the Galleria on Saturdays just to be around other people. I discovered that you can be incredibly lonely in a crowd. I'd go to church on Sundays hoping to make friends, but it just didn't happen. When everyone left afterward, groups of friends or families would get in their cars with each other; I got in my car—alone.

This went on for a long, long time until I decided I would seek God more passionately than I ever had. I purposed to be content with His companionship. I studied my Bible, memorized Scripture, and cried out to Him. **These disciplines began to deliver me from the life of the owl**. I still remember the night I actually turned down an invitation to go out with some folks so that I could read and study the book of Ephesians. I felt the Lord gave me the choice to test me. By His grace, I passed and slowly He began to add quality and quantity friendships.

From the earliest words of Scripture, it is not good for us to be alone (Genesis 2:18). We desperately need community with each other. But God designed us in a way that human relationships will not be satisfying until our relationship with Him is supreme. Seek Him first and everything else will follow (Matthew 6:33).

God, enable me to be satisfied in You—and to learn what it means to be a good friend. Amen

SELF-TALK
September 10

"Bless the Lord, O my soul, and all that is within me, bless His holy name."
Psalm 103:1 (NASB)

Now we come to one of the most beloved psalms in the Bible. The first five verses are as well-known as any five in Scripture, and this first verse could be included in a small group of verses known by believers and nonbelievers alike (e.g., Genesis 1:1, Psalm 23, John 3:16, Luke 11:2-4).

In these opening verses, David is talking to himself. Self-talk is the internal dialogue we have with ourselves. It can be very powerful, for good or for bad. When used positively, it reinforces healthy perspectives about ourselves and our lives. Whenever we're struggling with negative thoughts, feelings, or circumstances, reminding ourselves of God's truths is absolutely critical.

David begins this self-talk session by telling himself to bless Yahweh. That word *bless* has two distinctive meanings: when God blesses us, He does something good for us; when we bless God, we proclaim how good He is. The N.T. word for *bless* is *eulogia*. If someone does the eulogy at a funeral, they are speaking well of the person. When we bless God, we are praising Him for His beauty, glory, importance, and power.

David is reminding Himself to praise God with all his being. If you know anything about David, you know he was an all-in kind of guy. He commands his soul to praise God. Soul (*nephesh*) is who we are as a person; the life element within us. Sometimes we get caught up in the externals of worship (listening, singing, lifting hands, happy clappies, etc.) and forget that true worship begins deep down inside us. David reinforces this by expanding on his initial self-talk, *"Bless the LORD, O my soul"*, by adding, *"and all that is within me."* This whole-heartedness is what Jesus was talking about in Matthew 22:37, *"Love the Lord with ALL your heart, ALL your soul, ALL your mind."* God wants ALL of me.

Finally, David directs himself to bless, speak well of, God's holy name, Yahweh. His name is who He is: *"I AM."* He is the eternal, omnipotent, high and lifted up One; the Creator of all that is and Redeemer of all that will be. There is none like Him and He is worthy of our all-in praise!

Yahweh, I praise You from the innermost parts of my being. You are worthy of that and more. Amen

FOREWARNING

September 11

"If only you would listen to His voice TODAY! The Lord says, 'Don't harden your hearts as Israel did at Meribah, as they did at Massah in the wilderness.'"

Psalm 95:7-8

In 1968, telephone companies established 3 digits that would become a signal for an emergency, although it took another 20 years before 9-1-1 became nationwide. On September 11, 2001, those 3 digits took emergency and danger to a whole new level. Acting on a well-planned attack formulated by al-Qaeda, 19 terrorists commandeered 4 planes that crashed into the World Trade Center buildings, the Pentagon, and a field in Pennsylvania. It was a wake-up call. Flights ceased for weeks until new safety protocols could be implemented. Barriers were put up around public buildings. Everyone was on edge.

I led a group from Rush Creek up to Manhattan to help start a church that had been scheduled to begin the following spring, but the planters decided to start in October, one month after the attacks. A few weeks later, we arrived to help pass out tracts, take food to fire stations, and offer to pray with passersby. The air still reeked, bicycles were still chained to light posts, and cars were covered with ash 6 inches high—their owners were never found.

New Yorkers were uncharacteristically positive, many stopping to thank us for being there to encourage and pray. There was a mood all over the country that this was a warning; that we needed to collectively and individually reconnect with God. It was the national conversation in the media, in schools, and in offices across the land. Churches were full and God was popular again.

It didn't last.

As a nation, we came off the mat, dusted ourselves off, and tried to get back to normal as best we could. But the more we recovered, the less we turned to God. As a result, there is a whole post 9/11 generation that has no real memory of those days. The "nones," those who indicate no interest in spiritual things, has grown from 8% to 23% nationally; 38% among those born since 9/11.

The only way to turn this around is to seek after God with all our hearts, to raise our families to honor Jesus, and to tell others of His great love for them. He is our only hope.

God, fan the flame of my heart for you so that others will come to know you. Amen

MORE SELF-TALK
September 12

"Bless the Lord, O my soul, and forget none of His benefits."
Psalm 103:2 (NASB)

There have been times in my life when it seems there is very little to feel positive about.

That's when I need to remember how good God has been to me.

David has already directed his soul to praise God for who He is; now he directs his soul to praise God for what He has done. In verses 3-5, he touches on four of the greatest acts of this great God.

First, *"He forgives all my sin"* (v.3). As a pre-Jesus Jew, David certainly had the annual Passover sacrifice in mind. But when Jesus died on the cross, *"With his own blood—not the blood of goats and calves—he entered the Most Holy Place once for all time and secured our redemption forever"* (Hebrews 9:12). I love that phrase, *'once and for all time*'! For the person in Christ, His shed blood covered every sin of the believer, past, present, future. Yahoo!!

Second, He *"heals all my diseases"* (v.3). David included forgiveness and healing in the same breath so the connection cannot be lost. What this CANNOT mean is that confession of sin automatically heals us of any and all diseases. Disease is in the world because of sin and The Fall (Genesis 3) generally, and in our lives specifically—at times—because of our personal sin. For example, if I eat poorly, become overweight, and get diabetes or hypertension, there is a direct correlation. But getting struck with Alzheimer's doesn't correlate to some specific sin— it's a result of the Fall.

So what does David mean? Understanding the entirety of Scripture on the subject, it can only mean that God is the source of all healing, spiritual and physical. There are times that God intercedes and brings physical healing. I've prayed for it and received it. I've seen others healed. God is the source. By His common grace, He orchestrates the discovery of vaccines and medical advances that bring healing. He is the source. But the worst diseases are not physical, they're spiritual: guilt, fear, bitterness, lust, greed, etc. He heals those as well.

With both physical and spiritual healing, there is the now and the not yet. One day all disease will be done away with and we will be forever healed of anything and everything imperfect.

Amen

MORE BENEFITS
September 13

"Who redeems your life from the pit, who crowns you with lovingkindness and compassion;
Who satisfies your years with good things, so that your youth is renewed like the eagle."
Psalm 103:4-5 (NASB)

David has been talking to himself. He's reminding himself of the greatness of God and His many blessings. In v.3 he remembers that God forgives all our sins. In Jesus, God has thrown our sin into the ocean depths (Micah 7:19) and put up a 'No Fishing' sign! Then he recalls that God is the source of all healing, spiritual and physical. We are one sick people and only God can bring healing to body and soul.

David mentions two more benefits. One is that God redeems us. This is really a description of being rescued from the clutches of something dreadful and, by contrast, being put in a place of safety and honor. David had to be thinking of when he was being hunted by King Saul, hiding in caves, always on the run, constantly in the pit of despair. But then God rescued him and placed him in a position of royalty.

Believer, this is a good thing to remember. You may feel troubled by the enemy, but God has placed you in an exalted position: *"You are a chosen people; a royal priesthood, a holy nation, God's very own possession. As a result, you can show others the goodness of God, for He called you out of the darkness into His wonderful light"* (1 Peter 2:9). When you find yourself in the pits, remind yourself that you are a child of the Most High God and He has crowned you with love and compassion.

One more benefit: God satisfies us with good things in a way that gives us a buoyant, resilient strength. Focus on the struggle and feel the strength drain away; focus on God's goodness in your life and sense the strength and courage to carry on. The old song, "Count your blessings, name them one by one" says it well. So does Isaiah 40:31: *"But those who trust in the Lord will find new strength. They will soar high on wings like eagles. They will run and not grow weary. They will walk and not faint."*

God, I bless You from the depths of my soul for who You are and what You have done for me. Amen

FEAR GOD

September 14

"For as high as the heavens are above the earth,
so great is His faithful love toward those who fear Him."
Psalm 103:11 (CSB)

The psalmist highlights the greatness of God's covenant, faithful, enduring love. It's so high and magnificent, we can't even imagine it. To the ancient, the highest unknowable was the heavens. David says that because, *"The Lord is compassionate and merciful, slow to get angry and filled with unfailing love"* (v.8)—it's too high and beyond human ability to grasp. When I think of God's love for me displayed on the cross and demonstrated countless times in my life, I shake my head in disbelief and bewilderment.

But David touches on a prerequisite for experiencing that kind of love: it is for those who fear God. Fear doesn't always mean scared. It depends on context. If someone is outside of Christ, they'd better be scared out of their wits. But if someone is in Christ, there is a different experience.

Let's say that fear is a coin. One side is for unbelievers and the other side is for believers. If you are an unbeliever, fear means dread, terror, fright, and whatever synonyms you can think of: *"It is a terrifying thing to fall into the hands of the living God"* (Hebrews 10:31). God's holiness requires that He hates sin and sees all moral imperfection as wickedness that should be punished by eternal death and separation from Him. Jesus warns, *"But I will show you the one to fear: Fear Him who has authority to throw people into hell after death. Yes, I say to you, this is the One to fear!"* (Luke 12:5).

But if you're a believer, the other side of the fear coin looks completely different. Because you have sued for peace with God, that is, you've confessed your wickedness and sought God's grace and mercy, there is no reason to fear God's judgment. Instead of dread and fright, there is a reverence and awe for the holiness of God: *"Since we are receiving a Kingdom that is unshakable, let us be thankful and please God by worshiping him with holy fear and awe. For our God is a devouring fire"* (Hebrews 12:28-29). Reverence keeps us from being flippant or casual in our conduct and our relationship with Yahweh.

Which side of the coin applies to you?

God, I don't want Your judgment; I want your grace and mercy through Jesus! Amen

TAIL CHASING
September 15

"He has removed our sins as far from us as the east is from the west."
Psalm 103:12

One of the peculiar, yet cute characteristics of many younger dogs is that they chase their tails. They can chase their tails all day long and never catch them.

Reading this verse, the imagery of the dog chasing its tail comes to mind. It's doubtful that David knew the shape of the earth was spherical; apparently Pythagoras was first to pose this in about 600 B.C., 400 years after David. The Holy Spirit sure knew, and He is the real author of all Scripture.

One of the flabbergasting realities of the earth is north and south meet at the poles but east and west never meet—like the dog chasing its tail.

The Spirit undoubtedly prompted David to describe forgiven sin this way. If David had said God had removed sin as far as the north is from the south, that would indicate only temporary forgiveness: north and south eventually meet. But because east and west never meet, it carries the idea of permanent removal. This is no small distinction.

When someone harms us and we forgive them, the offense is still logged into our subconscious and can emerge anytime to be dealt with again; the deeper the offense, the more we have to work at actually forgiving. But not so with God's forgiveness. Hebrews 8:12 says, *"And I will forgive their wickedness, and I will never again remember their sins."* This cannot mean God can't recall our sins, because there will be an accounting at the end of the age for believers to be rewarded for our faithfulness (1 Corinthians 3:14-15, etc.). For that to happen, God must have knowledge of our past lives, good and bad. What it must mean, then, is that once God forgives us, He never has to deal with forgiving us again; there is never any unresolved forgiveness on His part.

This beautiful truth is captured in the awfulness of the cross. When Jesus said, *"It is finished"* (John 19:30), the word He used was *tetelestai*; *"paid in full."* Our debt to God was paid in full with His blood and substitutionary death. When I professed Christ as Lord and believed God raised Him from the dead, that payment was applied to my account. God put my sin as far as the east is from the west. Hallelujah! What a Savior!!

Amen!

HOT WIND

September 16

"As for man, his days are like grass— he blooms like a flower of the field; when the wind passes over it, it vanishes, and its place is no longer known. But from eternity to eternity the Lord's faithful love is toward those who fear Him, and His righteousness toward the grandchildren of those who keep His covenant, who remember to observe His precepts."

Psalm 103:15-18 (CSB)

Here in North Texas, whatever is not watered during the summer probably dies. In the semi-arid climate of Israel, it's even more so. Each spring the showers and snowmelt from the mountains to the north bringing out beautiful dessert flowers and grass. But as the spring melts into summer, hot winds from the east or south put an end to the vegetation that has no deep roots.

This picture of the transient nature of humans is mentioned often in the Bible. The point: we are not here very long. Our lives are like a vapor (James 4:14). On a cold morning when your breath meets frigid air, the vapor is there for a moment, then disappears. Even Methuselah's life (longest living person in recorded history—969 years), was only a vapor compared to eternity.

If my life is a mere vapor, here today, gone tomorrow, what does that say to me about how I should live my life? First, I need to align myself with God and His word. This passage says that God's love is enduring, not just to us, but to our offspring when we revere Him and His word.

My parents lived to see this in me and in my children. I pray Sue and I continue to see this in our children and grandchildren—and for generations after the hot wind brings our demise.

Second, I need to make the moments count. This is key: life is so short that precious little of it needs to be wasted on conflict, bitterness, envy, isolation, self-absorption, or victimization. I have squandered way too many minutes on these. Ugh! Instead, I need to do what is necessary to invest in the lives of people with love, generosity, and presence. The joy and peace that is then produced make life fulfilling, no matter how long it lasts. Grab all that you can get.

God, by Your grace, enable me to make my moments count for You; may Your love capture those who come after me—for generations. Amen

THREAD GOD
September 17

"My soul, bless the Lord! Lord my God, You are very great; You are clothed with majesty and splendor. He wraps himself in light as if it were a robe, spreading out the sky like a canopy."
Psalm 104:1-2 (CSB)

It's not a term used much anymore, but in times past *'thread god'* referred to an individual who was all about the clothes: latest fashions, full closets, expensive outfits, always dressed to the nines. No one has EVER accused me of being a thread god!

Yahweh is the ultimate Thread God. Psalm 104 is a wonderful psalm about God's incredibly beautiful and sophisticated creation.

Here at the beginning of the psalm, the writer makes the point that this gorgeous creation is the natural expression of a gorgeous Creator. Notice the clothing of Yahweh. Splendor and majesty are too closely related to draw distinction. Both carry ideas of honor, weightiness, importance, power, and sovereignty. As God reveals Himself, this imagery helps us understand His essence, His being. He is a God whose splendor and majesty are on display in creation.

He is also clothed in *"light…spreading out the sky like a canopy."* This is an obvious reference to Genesis 1. Light always speaks of purity. Like these other pieces of clothing, light is an expression and image of the Creator God. We can catch glimpses of who He is in the works of His hands.

All of this is intended to solicit awe, wonder, and worship of this magnificent God: "The verse sums up the whole of the creative act in one grand thought. In that act, the invisible God has arrayed Himself in splendor and glory, making visible these inherent attributes. That is the deepest meaning of Creation—**the Universe is the garment of God**" (Alexander Maclaren). One has to wonder how anyone who studies or even just looks upon this creation can do anything but fall in humble reverence and adoration of its Creator.

If splendor, majesty, and light are partial images of Yahweh, we need to remember there is a perfect image of Him: *"Christ is the visible image of the invisible God"* (Colossians 1:15). He said about Himself: *"I am the light of the world. If you follow Me, you won't have to walk in darkness, because you will have the light that leads to life"* (John 8:12).

Follow Him. Worship Him. He is THE Thread God.

Amen!

HIGHLIGHTS

"Give thanks to the Lord, call on His name; proclaim His deeds among the peoples.
Sing to Him, sing praise to Him; tell about all His wondrous works!
Boast in His holy name; let the hearts of those who seek the Lord rejoice.
Seek the Lord and His strength; seek His face always."
Psalm 105:1-4 (CSB)

Psalm 105 is kind of a highlight reel for Israel, recounting God's great deeds for His people starting with the Covenant made with Abraham and finishing with their entrance into the Promised Land. All through this psalm, God is painted as a faithful, promise-making, promise-keeping God whose ways were sometimes mysterious and painful, but always and ultimately for His glory and their good.

The first 15 verses of this psalm are the same as David's song written for the occasion of Israel bringing the Ark of the Covenant into Jerusalem. You'll recall that the Ark was a box with the Ten Commandment tablets inside that had been carried by the Hebrews during their 40-year Sinai wandering. They had been instructed to always keep it well ahead of the wandering tribes signifying the presence, power, and purpose of God. When they came into the Promised Land, as the priests carrying Ark stepped into the floodwaters of the Jordan, the waters receded. It was kept in Shiloh for 400 years until David brought it to Jerusalem and danced the boogaloo.

When I look back over the Lord's dealings with me, it's kind of like a highlight reel. I can't remember every instance but there are certainly instances that stand out and continue to be a source of gratitude and worship for me. Even now as I write this, my mind is flooded with highlights of His faithful and gracious dealings with me. Do yourself a huge favor and take a moment to write down 10 instances of God's loving, sovereign work in your life. You might start dancing too!

I give thanks to Him and call His name with affection. I am prompted to tell others and boast of His wondrous deeds on my behalf. My heart is singing with gladness. I want to seek Him even more knowing that He is the source of peace and joy.

Yahweh, I will seek You always. Thanks and praise to You. Amen

BE CAREFUL WHAT YOU ASK FOR
September 19

"He gave them what they asked for, but sent a wasting disease among them."
Psalm 106:15

If Psalm 105 is a highlight reel of God's good deeds on behalf of His covenant people, Psalm 106 is a lowlight reel of the stiff-necked, wicked, ungrateful actions of His people the 40 years on their way to the Promised Land. These two psalms are flipsides of the same coin: we are rebellious, self-absorbed, deceitful, etc.; on the other side, Yahweh is a faithful, loving, gracious, etc. In Christ, the covenant was struck so that Yahweh and I are fused together forever.

That does not rule out, of course, the discipline of the Lord when we stray from His will. The writer of Hebrews wrote: *"My child, don't make light of the Lord's discipline, and don't give up when He corrects you. For the Lord disciplines those He loves, and He punishes each one He accepts as his child"* (12:5-6).

One of the methods of discipline God uses is to give us what we want. What I mean is, there are times when we keep desiring for things and making decisions based on what we want, not what He wants; times when the Spirit warns us not to do something, but we're so determined that He steps aside and lets us have our way. That never goes well!

The psalmist cites a specific instance in the desert where this happened. You'll find the account in Numbers 11. The Hebrews are in the wilderness after God delivered them from Egypt. They've grown tired of the manna He provided (that's all they had to eat) and began to complain that at least when they were in Egypt, they had a nice variety of spicy foods. They conveniently forgot that they had been enslaved!! So, God gave them what they craved. He sent enough quail for the Hebrews to feast on, but a bunch of them died from it.

Sin always kills. It may not kill you literally, but something in you will die. One translation puts it this way, *"He gave them their request, but sent leanness to their souls"* (KJV). I don't want the discipline of the Lord. I don't want leanness in my soul—I want His fulness. So do you. Be careful want you ask and long for.

God, forgive me for my sinful longings. Shape my desires and will to Yours. Amen

IDOLATRY
September 20

"They exchanged their glory for the image of a grass-eating ox."
Psalm 106:20

Sue and I used to watch American Idol. Simon Cowell was tantalizingly frustrating, Randy Jackson was plain cool, and Paula Abdul—we never knew what was going to pop out of those lovely lips. The show seemed to capture America's penchant for idolizing people with great talent. Indeed, Americans spend at least $3 billion/year worshipping their favorite idol through the celebrity gossip industry and another $25 billion purchasing access to them through what they watch and listen to.

This is nothing new. It's been going on for millennia. The psalmist recalls maybe the most infamous single event of idol worship: they made an idol out of some of the booty Yahweh provided for them as they fled Egypt. What an insult to the Great I AM.

They exchanged their glory for the image of an ox. They didn't reach up, they reached down. They didn't pursue something that would lift, they gave themselves to something that would lower. They didn't worship their Maker; they became the maker of something to worship. Idolatry—who would do that?

We don't have to bow down to a golden ox to be an idolater. Anything can be an idol. In his eye-opening book, *Counterfeit Gods*, Tim Keller writes: "What is an idol? It is anything more important to you than God, anything that absorbs your heart and imagination more than God, anything you seek to give you what only God can give." Word!

It's not the idol that is evil, it is our fallen desire to have another god besides Yahweh that is evil. More likely it is something good, really good in our lives: a spouse, children, a job, travel, or comfort.

Oh yeah, and then there is the idol that Jesus and the New Testament writers mentioned most often: financial security. Our money says, "In God We Trust," but the truth for most of us is we trust the money more than we do God. Remember, a god is anything that captivates your heart and imagination more than Yahweh.

Take a moment to assess where you look to find security, comfort, meaning, purpose, joy, and peace. It's sobering.

God, forgive me of my idol worship of _____. Change my heart, O God. Amen

PARENTING
September 21

"They worshiped their idols, which led to their downfall.
They even sacrificed their sons and their daughters to the demons."
Psalm 106:36-37

Raising our three kids was fun—and a lot of work! In their adolescent years before they could drive, Sue and I would say goodnight on a Friday night with, "See you tomorrow night," because we'd be going different directions taking three kids to different practices or games or contests all day Saturday. It was fun, but also tiring. We tried to balance the benefit of extra-curricular activities with their need to be good students, growing believers, and well-rounded individuals.

There were those parents who had such high expectations for their children that they ended up scheduling activities every evening, all day Saturday, and even Sundays. As their pastor, I tried to gently warn them that such hyperactivity would be counterproductive to their children becoming spiritually, emotionally, and relationally healthy adults. Study after study indicates that over-scheduling kids is a recipe for chronic anxiety and deprives them of certain skills that can only be developed in unscheduled time. I understand the motivation. What parent doesn't want their child to excel? But it's time to take a heart exam: does our motivation include an unwitting kneel before the success god?

In vv.36-37, the psalmist recalls a time in Israel's history when parents made sacrifices to another god. Once the Hebrews hit the Promised Land, they began to take on some of the cultural norms of the Canaanites. One of the norms was to bow the knee to a god known as Molech. Google it and see: the image in a sitting position, arms out in front, with a hole in its midsection. Worshippers would place their child in the arms, head-first into the hole, then build a fire under the arms to sacrifice the child. Unthinkable. But some parents will do what it takes to appease their god.

Christ-following parents must ask and answer the question: is what we are doing with our children shaping them into being maturing believers, or are we overly concerned they won't be successful in our culture?

Parents that I know want the very best for their children. But they also face tremendous cultural pressure. If you're a parent at any stage, take the time to read *Parenting: 14 Gospel Principles That Can Radically Change Your Family* by Paul David Tripp. Do it for Him and them.

God, work in me to parent for Your sake, not mine. Amen

HOARDING
September 22

"Has the Lord redeemed you? Then speak out!
Tell others He has redeemed you from your enemies."
Psalm 107:2

We are a nation of hoarders. We spend over $40 Billion a year to store stuff we can't bear to throw away. Some of us have developed an addiction called, "compulsive hoarding disorder." There's even a show on A&E highlighting those with the disorder as they hoard newspapers, magazines, paper products, household goods, clothing—and sometimes animals.

Most of the Christ-followers I know have a hoarding disorder.

I'm not talking about hoarding stuff—I'm talking about hoarding what is supposed to be given away at every opportunity: the gospel. From the moment it was discovered Jesus had risen from the dead, believers were instructed to *"go and tell"* what had happened (Matthew 28:7, etc.). The early believers kept telling their friends and others that Jesus defeated death and so could they! They were so prolific in the giving away of the gospel that by the end of the 1st century, the gospel message had traveled to every country in the Mediterranean theatre, and by the end of the 2nd century, it's speculated that the gospel had penetrated every province of the Roman Empire! There was no gospel-hoarding going on at all. This was, despite the fact, that during Roman rule, it was illegal to be a Christ-follower and even worse to share the gospel. Some scholars suspect that at least 2 million believers were martyred for their faith from 30-325 A.D.

The psalmist exhorts us: *"Has the Lord redeemed you? Then speak out!"* We may be ignored, rejected, or even cursed, but here in America, we won't die for our faith (at least not yet). 1 Peter 3:15 says, *"Instead, you must worship Christ as Lord of your life. And if someone asks about your hope as a believer, always be ready to explain it."* Are you ready to explain what Jesus did for you on the cross and what He is doing in your life right now?

Do this: write your redemption story on one sheet of paper, i.e., what you were like before you met Jesus, a brief description of your encounter with and surrender to Jesus, and then at least one way that your life has been changed by your relationship with Him. Learn it. Use it. Don't hoard it!

Jesus, forgive me for my hoarding Your love and redemption. Grant me boldness. Amen

YAHWEH RESCUES

September 23

"Some wandered in the wilderness, lost and homeless.
Hungry and thirsty, they nearly died"
Psalm 107:4

Psalm 107 is a psalm of praise for the God who redeems and rescues. The author cites four examples when God physically intervened to rescue His people. God still intervenes in physical, tangible ways—I could fill a book of personal examples. But there are interventions that transcend this physical world when Yahweh rescues from threats that are much more harmful than any physical ones.

The first example is when He delivered some who were lost (vv.4-9). Lostness. The Bible speaks of those who are lost spiritually. Lostness describes the person who is separated from the Father because of their human condition; they've lost their way. That describes every human being: *"For everyone has sinned; we all fall short of God's glorious standard"* (Romans 3:23).

What does it mean to be lost? First, it means to be saddled by the sins of our past. *'Sin'* of course means to miss the mark; to turn away from God and His directives. The result is guilt: a legal guilt before a Just God, and a personal, burdensome, haunting guilt. Humans instinctively know they are morally inadequate. Some try to pretend there is no standard to feel guilty about breaking. Some try to deflect their guilt to others. Some attempt to drown their guilt feelings with work, prosperity, or booze. Others try to be as morally good as they know how. None of this actually works.

Second, it means to be stuck in a state of confusion and emptiness about the purpose of our lives. Some try to find purpose in their careers, others their families, others in altruism. None of this works because it misses the core purpose of humanity. Scripture reveals the lost person is blinded to the truth. They keep wandering and searching, but it's hidden from them until they turn to The Truth.

Third, lostness means to have no genuine hope for the future. The Bible says God has created humanity with a desire to live forever, but most of us don't have a clue how to beat death.

Jesus said, *"For the Son of Man came to seek and save those who are lost"* (Luke 19:10). If you're lost, He came for you. Turn to Him. Trust Him. Let Him rescue you.

Jesus: I accept I'm lost. I trust that You came to save me. Do it! Amen

YAHWEH RESCUES AGAIN

September 24

"Some sat in darkness and deepest gloom, imprisoned in iron chains of misery."
Psalm 107:10

Yesterday we talked about how Psalm 107 is a psalm of praise for the God who redeems and rescues. He cites four physical examples that remind us of greater spiritual instances of God's deliverance. The first example is Yahweh's desire to save the lost (vv.4-9). Jesus came to rescue the lost.

The second is how God rescues those in bondage (vv.10-16). Like lostness, bondage is a condition of the person who is not in Christ. I've been in prison—multiple times. Not for any crimes, but to visit those incarcerated for various reasons. It's a scary place. But prisons today are like resorts compared to those of the ancients. Usually, they were in basements of public buildings, quarries, or even large caves. They had no toilets, no A/C, rancid and meager portions of bread or porridge, and little or no natural light. If you were in prison for very long, your chances of survival were slim.

"Jesus said, 'I tell you the truth, everyone who sins is a slave of sin'" (John 8:34). Until a person is set free from the penalty of their sin by trusting in Jesus and His shed blood to pay for it, they are in and will for eternity remain in bondage.

I'm reminded of a story I heard years ago from a pastor who had a dream that he visited hell. The condition was much like I described above. He saw people in chains, behind bars, writhing in agony. He turned to the dark demon who had escorted him and said, "These people are burning up. Can't you give them some water?" The demon replied: "There ain't no water in hell." The pastor said, "But it's so dark in here. Can't you open up the window and let some light in?" The demon replied, "There ain't no light in hell." Finally in desperation, the pastor said, "Well for God's sake, can't you just end their misery and let 'em die?" The demon said, "There ain't no death in hell."

Fortunately, Jesus can change all that: *"He canceled the record of the charges against us and took it away by nailing it to the cross"* (Colossians 2:14). He paid for your sin. He came to set you free in this life and the life to come.

Jesus—set me free! I trust in You. Amen

DEATH-DEFYING
September 25

"Lord, help!" they cried in their trouble, and He saved them from their distress.
He sent out his word and healed them, snatching them from the door of death."
Psalm 107:19-20

Psalm 107 is a psalm of praise for the God who rescues. He cites four physical examples that remind us of greater spiritual instances of God's deliverance. The first example is Yahweh's desire to save the lost (vv.4-9). The second is how God rescues those in bondage (vv.10-16)

The third example is God's ability to deliver the diseased from death (vv.17-22). The psalmist cites an instance when some people rebelled against God, got sick, and then called out for God to heal them.

Sin is a sickness. In fact, it's humanity's universal and worst disease. It always leads to death.

When Adam and Eve sinned, the result was that all of creation suffered death—and more pointedly, they died, as has every human being since. That curse (Genesis 3) of physical death has not been lifted. Occasionally God intervenes to postpone, but no one escapes it.

Physical disease and death are not the worst of it. The Scripture reveals that spiritual death is much more fearsome: it separates us from God.

Recently, Sue and I were all excited about the arrival of our 10th grandchild, Patton Grant Barksdale. So cute! Yet, because the seed of sin is passed from generation to generation, he was born physically alive but is dead spiritually. The only way he can become alive spiritually and have a relationship with God is to call out by faith and place his trust in Jesus alone: *"You were dead because of your sins and because your sinful nature was not yet cut away. Then God made you alive with Christ, for He forgave all our sins"* (Colossians 2:13).

Jesus called this being *"born again"* (John 3:3, 7). Perhaps you've heard the saying, "Born once, die twice; born twice, die once." Those who are born physically AND spiritually will only taste the physical death—which will give way to a life where: *"He will wipe every tear from their eyes, and there will be no more death or sorrow or crying or pain. All these things are gone forever"* (Revelation 21:4).

If you haven't already, put your trust in this death-defying Jesus who walked out of a tomb, having paid the penalty for your sin. If you have, praise Him for what He did for you.

Jesus, I only want to die once. I surrender to You and ask for life eternal. Amen!

STORM WHISPERER
September 26

*"LORD, help! They cried in their trouble, and He saved them from their distress.
He calmed the storm to a whisper and stilled the waves."*
Psalm 107:28-29

This fourth and final example of God's ability to rescue involves mariners who were caught in a terrible storm and about to drown (vv.23-32). If you've seen, *"The Perfect Storm,"* you can imagine how frightening that would be. They called out to God and He calmed the sea.

I've discovered that there are two storms in life: the outer storm that rages around me, and the inner storm as I battle fear, temptation, despair, anger, etc. So many of my outer tempests have been caused by my own sin and foolishness. Some have been created by the foolishness of others—some by just living in a broken world. Regardless, it's a storm I have to deal with.

If I'm the cause, I can take steps that might quell it: seek forgiveness, make restitution, change a decision, etc. But other storms are beyond my ability to influence. In both cases, I've learned to call on the Storm Whisperer.

Jesus was out with His buds fishing and fell asleep. A storm blew in and they woke Jesus with their screams as the boat was about to capsize. Jesus declared: *"Silence! Be still!"* and the wind and waves were quiet (Mark 4:39). Many times, I have called on the Storm Whisperer and He has stilled the outer storms of my life.

But that inner storm is what He's most interested in, because that is where real faith is tested: will I trust Him, even if the outer storm continues? My outer storms have been so varied: Sue's cancer, mom's Alzheimer's, brother's alcoholism, confronting racism in a former church, mass exodus from and staff mutiny at Rush Creek in 2000—I could go on and on. When those outer storms raged, I called on the Storm Whisperer to quell the fear and bring peace to my weary soul—and He did.

Hours before Jesus' arrest and death and the resulting storm, He promised: *"I have told you these things so that in Me you may have peace. You will have suffering in this world. Be courageous! I have conquered the world"* (John 16:33).

Whatever your storm, find peace IN HIM!

Jesus, be the Storm Whisperer to me, I pray. Amen

BEGIN WITH PRAISE

September 27

"Save with Your right hand and answer me so that those You love may be rescued."
Psalm 108:6 (CSB)

All 10 of our grandchildren live in the Metroplex. Sometimes when they come to our house, they'll run in and immediately start asking to get on the PlayStation or watch something—without hardly saying hello. They rush into our presence without acknowledging who we are.

I find myself doing the same thing when I come into the presence of Yahweh. I start rattling off all my needs and requests without taking the time to acknowledge who He is and what He is about. I forget: prayer time always needs to begin with praise.

We see this in Psalm 108. Verse 6 (above) is the turning point of the psalm. After it, David is laying out his petition for victory over his enemies. But he keeps first things first: he comes into God's presence with praise and adoration.

In v.1, David pledges his faith and trust in Yahweh, prompting him to passionately sing praises to Him: *"My heart is confident in You, O God; no wonder I can sing Your praises with all my heart!"* Our relationship with God is, at its core, a relationship built on trust. We come into God's presence because He is trustworthy, and we believe He will listen and act.

In v.2, David, able to play multiple instruments, indicates that music is a beautiful way to worship Yahweh: *"Wake up, lyre and harp! I will wake the dawn with my song."* I don't play an instrument, but I do listen to praise music during my devotional time. Notice that David's day is begun with this ritual. The wise have always sought God first thing in the morning.

In v.3, the psalmist pledges to not be a closet believer: *"I will thank You, Lord, among all the people. I will sing Your praises among the nations."* True believers realize what we do in public validates what we say in private.

In vv.4-5, David finishes this flurry of praise by extolling God's love, faithfulness, and glory: *"For your unfailing love is higher than the heavens. Your faithfulness reaches to the clouds. Be exalted, O God, above the highest heavens. May Your glory shine over all the earth."*

Begin each day and each prayer with praise. Read over these verses now, out loud as a prayer of praise.

Amen

GOING THE DISTANCE
September 28

"Oh, please help us against our enemies, for all human help is useless.
With God's help we will do mighty things, for He will trample down our foes"
Psalm 108:12-13

In 1989, I was in Las Vegas for the Southern Baptist Convention (!). Word on the street was that we rolled into town with the 10 Commandments and a $20 bill and didn't break either! A wealthy friend contacted me and said he had two tickets to the Sugar Ray Leonard/Hit Man Hearns world championship fight. We met at Caesar's Palace where the fight was staged outside. Each guy was knocked down multiple times and when the last round ended, they were in the middle of the ring, toe to toe, slugging it out, going the distance. What a fight!

That scene is a metaphor for God's people: we're in a fight, our adversary is tough, we get knocked down, but we keep getting up to fight some more because God is with us.

David began Psalm 108 praising Yahweh for His faithfulness, glory, and enduring love (vv.1-5). But then with v. 6, he began to plead with God to give victory to His people over their enemies, specifically, Moab, Philistia, and Edom. From before David and after, these three neighbors were constantly attacking Israel: raiding, pillaging, even capturing families to sell in the slave trade. Yahweh gave Israel victory numerous times, but the enemies never went totally away.

David knew the key to victory was not in human strength, but in the power of Yahweh. Jesus and the New Testament writers built on this theme of fighting the enemy with the strength of the Lord:

> *"I have told you all this so that you may have peace in Me. Here on earth you will have many trials and sorrows. But take heart, because I have overcome the world"* (John 16:33).

> *"No, despite all these things, overwhelming victory is ours through Christ, who loved us"* (Romans 8:37).

> *"For I can do everything through Christ, who gives me strength"* (Philippians 4:13).

You may be knocked down, but if you're a child of God, you're not knocked out. Get up. Arm yourself with the armor of God so that you can *"take your stand"* (Ephesians 6:13) and fight. When you draw your last breath, may you be in the middle of the ring, toe to toe with the enemy, going the distance.

God, be my strength. Amen

ULTIMATE MOTIVES
September 29

"But You, Lord, my Lord, deal kindly with me for Your name's sake;
because Your faithful love is good, rescue me."
Psalm 109:21 (CSB)

A *motive* is a reason for doing something, giving purpose and direction to behavior. Psychologists have determined there are three kinds: biological (to acquire food, water, etc.), social (to achieve, understand, etc.), and personal (a combination of the other two that include goals, habits, etc.). At its core, motive answers the question: Why?

Psalm 109 is maybe the strongest of what are known as the *imprecatory* psalms: A psalm where the psalmist calls for calamity and judgment on a personal enemy or enemy of God. In this psalm, David is using pretty stiff language about what he wants Yahweh to do to his enemy. After he spits out his vitriol and gets it off his chest (vv. 1-20), he cools down and turns to self-examination and reflection. I can identify with that!

In v.21 (read again), David states why God does what He does: His ultimate motives are to glorify Himself and display His love. Not one or the other—both, and in that order.

This is good for us to remember. So many times, I appeal to God based on His love for me: God, because You love me, heal Sue's cancer, grant me success in this endeavor, etc. But upon reflection, that's a pretty selfish prayer: it's all about me and mine. There is another of God's motives that surpasses even His love, and that is His glory and reputation. God always acts in a way that emphasizes the brightness and beauty of His essence.

Knowing this, I need to make sure my own motives in prayer are not just for my desires, my family, my reputation, my, my, my. I first and foremost need to get focused on and caught up in His glory, His desires, His motivations. If that is in the forefront of my heart and mind when I pray, it may just change my prayers!

David said, *"Deal kindly with me—for Your name's sake, because Your faithful love is good."* He asks for God's help, not based on his own merit, but on the basis of doing what's best for God's sake, AND on the basis of God's unmerited and undeserved love. That's a powerful prayer.

God, purify my motives and align them with Yours in my prayers and my living. Amen

CREDIT

"Help me, Lord my God; save me according to Your faithful love so they may know that this is Your hand and that You, Lord, have done it."
Psalm 109:26-27 (CSB)

Perhaps you've had this experience as a parent: your child attempted to do something that they really didn't have the strength to do like open a door stuck in its frame, or push something too big, or lift something too heavy. You slid in beside or behind and encouraged them with, "You can do this!" but the whole time you were the one really doing it.

David understands that he doesn't have what it takes to accomplish what needs to happen in his life. In vv.22-25 he confesses that he is deeply wounded in his soul, gloomy and depressed, weakened considerably from his fasting, and a joke to those who oppose him. Not a great spot to be in!

In his weakened condition, he calls out to Yahweh for help. As he did in v.21, he identifies two reasons for God to respond to his request: God's faithful love and God's glorious reputation. He says, "Help me! I don't deserve your help, your mercy, but I know Your love for me is a covenant love; a love relationship held together by Your will and Your power and Your intentionality to love me no matter what. And God, do this in a way that everyone knows it was not me, but You who did this. I want You to get the praise and glory."

Years ago, I heard a pastor say, "We don't mind God getting the glory as long as we get the praise!" I've never forgotten that. There is something in us that does want people to know God worked in our lives, but there's also something in us that wants to take a good deal of the credit for it. Like the child who thinks she's opening the door, pushing the cart, or lifting the weight, we take way too much credit for what is accomplished in our lives.

Take a moment and list five works God has done in your life in the past year—and then brag on Him about it to His face and to others today.

God, thank You for always working in me and on my behalf. I give You the credit. Amen

THE MESSIAH
October 1

"The Lord said to my Lord, 'Sit in the place of honor at My right hand until I humble your enemies, making them a footstool under Your feet.'"

Psalm 110:1

Throughout the Old Testament, we get glimpses of someone who would eventually appear on the scene, deliver troubled Israel from their enemies, and make all things right: the Messiah (Hebrew), the Christ (Greek) are defined as the Chosen One, the Anointed One.

One of those glimpses is right here in Psalm 110, written by the great King David. Apparently, David received a vision or overheard a discussion between God the Father and God the Son. You'll notice that the word '*Lord*' is mentioned twice. The first LORD is *Yahweh* (*I AM*); the second is *Adonai* (*sovereign, master*). In the discussion, the Father is saying to His Son, "Sit here at My right hand. I'm going to defeat all your enemies." The right hand was always a seat of honor and of authority. Being someone's footstool was a position of humility and subjection.

1000 years later, Jesus is coming to the end of His earthly ministry. He had been wrangling with the Pharisees all day about the authority of His teaching as they peppered Him with their questions. After He had silenced them with His answers, He turned the tables and asked them a question (Matthew 22:41-46):

> *Then, surrounded by the Pharisees, Jesus asked them a question: "What do you think about the Messiah? Whose son is he?" They replied, "He is the son of David."*
>
> *Jesus responded, "Then why does David, speaking under the inspiration of the Spirit, call the Messiah 'my Lord'? For David said,*
>
> > *'The Lord said to my Lord,*
> > *Sit in the place of honor at my right hand*
> > *until I humble your enemies beneath your feet.'*
>
> *Since David called the Messiah 'my Lord,' how can the Messiah be his son?"*
>
> *No one could answer him. And after that, no one dared to ask him any more questions.*

Jesus' question and answer revealed that the Messiah would not just be a physical descendent of David, but an eternal king who would reign and rule forever. The Pharisees were baffled and left to plot this king's assassination.

When Jesus ascended to heaven, He was seated at the right hand of the Father. He is waiting until the Father determines it is time to return, defeat His enemies, and make all things right.

Jesus, I honor You as the Chosen One, the Anointed One. You were sent by the Father, rejected by Your people, offered up as the once and for all sacrifice, ascended into heaven, and will return one day for Your own. Come quickly, Lord Jesus! Amen

REFLECTION
October 2

"The Lord's works are great, studied by all who delight in them. All that He does is splendid and majestic; His righteousness endures forever. He has caused His wondrous works to be remembered. The Lord is gracious and compassionate."

Psalm 111:2-4 (CSB)

The Lord is gracious and compassionate—He wants us to know it and remember it. For the people of God in the Old Testament, there were plenty of examples: the creation account, the establishment of marriage, God's redemption of Adam and Eve after their rebellion, His rescue of humanity through the worldwide flood, the establishment of a covenant with Abraham from which the Jews would emerge as God's chosen people, His provision for them during a great famine through the travails of Joseph, His deliverance from slavery and Egypt through a reluctant leader named Moses, His patience in their desert wanderings and His guidance into the Promised Land. Even after they were exiled to Babylon, God brought them back to reinhabit the land of their forefathers.

The Jews would study these and delight in them. Each one was a cause for reflection, thanksgiving, worship, and celebration. No doubt there were personal stories of Yahweh's grace and compassion as well.

For New Testament believers, we can add the Incarnation: God taking on flesh and blood in a miraculous birth in Bethlehem, all the miracles of Jesus in His three-year public ministry, His voluntary, intentional sacrifice as the Lamb of God to take away sin, His defeat of death by walking out of the tomb that first Easter morning, and His glorious ascension to the right hand of the Father. Add to that the great miracles of the Apostles and the birth and expansion of the church—there is a lot for us to study and delight in.

And then there are the personal examples of God's wondrous works of grace and compassion. One of the reasons I journal every day is to keep track of God's dealings in my life. I spend about 30 minutes writing down what happened the day before, scanning the events and reflecting on what God did or is doing as a result. I keep a list of prayer requests that I mark out when He answers them, noting when and how He did. I delight in them—and Him. You will too!

God, I reflect on Your goodness in my life. I recall those times You worked powerfully in my life. I am grateful for your handiwork in my life. Thank you for Your grace and compassion. Amen

WISDOM
October 3

"The fear of the Lord is the beginning of wisdom;
all who follow His instructions have good insight. His praise endures forever."
Psalm 111:10

When I was growing up, my dad would tell my brother and me to do something or warn us not to do something. If we listened carefully and followed his instruction, life was good. If we didn't—let's just say it didn't go well. One choice was wise, the other choice was foolish.

The writer of this psalm and the writer of Proverbs 1:7 agree: the foundation of genuine wisdom is fearing God and following His instructions and commands. Remember, fear doesn't always mean scared; it depends on context. In this context, it is a reverence and awe for the holiness of God. Reverence prompts us to take seriously His will and word.

Throughout the Bible we are admonished to be students of God's word: *"Be diligent to present yourself to God as one approved, a worker who doesn't need to be ashamed, correctly teaching the word of truth"* (2 Timothy 2:15; CSB). If we claim to be a follower of Jesus but do not take His instructions seriously, it is a grave mistake. In fact, it's extremely foolish.

God's word is *"a lamp to guide my feet and a light for my path"* (Psalm 119:105). Why wouldn't I spend ample amounts of time to study it and know it? To do so gives great wisdom; to treat it with disrespect by ignoring it is profound foolishness.

Wisdom is being able to discern the end result of a present action or circumstance; the ability to judge what is true, right, and lasting. If you want to know how to respond or handle what's going on in your life, dive into the Bible. If you want to know how to live successfully and experience an abundance of joy, peace, and purpose, jump into the Scripture: *"By His divine power, God has given us everything we need for living a godly life"* (2 Peter 1:3).

If you want to get a firm grasp on God's word, hold up your hand and assign one of these five activities to each digit: hear, read, study, meditate, and memorize. Becoming a student of the word will be absolutely life-changing—and wise! My Pathways book can help you become a student. You can order it at www.nextlevelleadership.org

God, thank You for Your word. By Your grace, I pledge to become a student of it. I know that in Your word is the answer to all life's challenges. Thank You for it. Amen

HALLEL

"Hallelujah! Give praise, servants of the Lord; praise the name of the Lord.
Let the name of the Lord be blessed both now and forever.
From the rising of the sun to its setting, let the name of the Lord be praised."
Psalm 113:1-3

The psalmist is obviously excited about something—praising the Most High God!

Psalms 113-118 form the Hallel, a collection of praise songs sung at the great festivals of Israel like Passover and Pentecost. In all likelihood, Jesus and the disciples sang one of these before they left for Gethsemane the night of His arrest. You can guess that *hallel* is the front part of Hallelujah, meaning *'Praise God'*. Hallelujah is an English word that expresses the joining together of two Hebrew words: *'hillel'*, meaning *'praise'*, and *'yah'*, which is the first part of God's personal name, *Yahweh*.

The psalmist then launches into a series of four exhortations to praise God. Notice that LORD is in all caps, signifying this is God's personal name, Yahweh. The King James Bible attempted a transliteration of the name but incorrectly stated it as Jehovah. God is called by other names, *Elohim* (living or creative God), *Adonai* (sovereign God), *El Shaddai* (Almighty God), etc., but Yahweh, I AM, is the one that identifies His personhood.

To praise is to speak well of; to lift up and magnify someone's importance, value, and quality of character. Three of the four times the psalmist exhorts us to praise the <u>name</u> of the LORD. The ancients were given or chose names based on desired character traits or aspired reputations. The name and the person were inextricably joined together. Praise His name, you praise Him. This is why God commanded us to not *"take the name of the LORD your God in vain"* (Genesis 20:7). To misuse His name, to use it as an expletive, to even be casual about it, is an affront to Him.

Those of us who serve this God are to have blessings and praises on our lips from the time we wake up until the time we drop off to sleep, each and every day from now and forevermore.

Spend the first part of your day setting the tone for that: look for ways throughout the day to praise Him for His handiwork in your life. Close the day with a hallelujah!

God, I praise Your holy name. May you be blessed now and forevermore. Fill my heart with praise and adoration for You. What a God You are!!! Hallelujah!!

LOFTY
October 5

"The Lord is exalted above all the nations, His glory above the heavens. Who is like the Lord our God— the one enthroned on high, who stoops down to look on the heavens and the earth?"

Psalm 113:4-6

Have you ever thought about the relationship between high and low? Unless you're playing golf or the Limbo game (how low can you go?), high is preferable to low. People aspire to the highest salary, the highest position, the highest office, the highest power. In creation, with few exceptions like the Grand Canyon, it's the looking up that creates awe: mountains, clouds, sky, sun, moon, stars, etc.

The psalmist reminds us that Yahweh is higher than anything or anyone else; that His throne is above the heavens and the earth. Ancient Jews thought of the heavens in three levels: the sky (clouds & birds), outer space (sun, moon & stars), and the abode of God. So when the psalmist claims that God is exalted and higher than the heavens and earth, he was including all that is. Yahweh is the Most High God; the Exalted One; the Lofty One.

This isn't really about geometry; it's about importance, power, and place. The psalmist insists that Yahweh is higher and more important than any nation; all nations. We who live in the U.S. tend to think that we are the most powerful nation. We probably are. But do you think for a moment that God cowers at our power? He could humble us or exterminate us in the twinkling of an eye. What if He removed His hand of protection and another virus, more devastating than COVID 19 hit us again, and then another again, and then another. Throw in a few natural catastrophes, and we're done. He could do that and more without working up a sweat.

The psalmist says that Yahweh looks far down on the heavens and the earth. This speaks to His transcendence (preeminence beyond our ability to grasp). God is higher, grander, more magnificent, more powerful, and far beyond anything our pea brains can imagine.

This is why we are exhorted in vv.1-3 to praise Him; to lift our hallelujahs to His name. He is the exalted God!

Is Yahweh highest in your life? This is not a geometry question; it's a question of importance, power, and place.

Yahweh—You are lofty and exalted above all nations, above all creation. Take the highest place in my heart. No thing and no one is higher than You. Amen

CONDESCENSION
October 6

"He raises the poor from the dust and lifts the needy from the trash heap in order to seat them with nobles— with the nobles of His people. He gives the childless woman a household, making her the joyful mother of children. Hallelujah!"

Psalm 113:7-9

If you look up the popular definition of condescension, you get something like: patronizing superiority; an "I know better than you" or even "I am better than you" attitude. It's definitely a negative attribute. Why? Because it places one person in a less valuable or desirable position while placing the other person in a superior, more valuable position. I've been around some condescending folks—I pray I am never like that.

But another and more significant usage is the idea of someone with a lofty rank associating with someone of a lesser rank. Rather than staying separated, they initiate togetherness. That idea, the idea of using high rank to help low status, gets closer to who God is and what He has done.

The psalmist has been praising the name of the LORD and His lofty and majestic grandeur. But he doesn't stop there because God didn't stop there. God stoops, He reaches down to touch, then to lift, a fallen humanity.

This condescension is best demonstrated in the incarnation. Since Yahweh is infinitely loftier than anything else or anywhere else, the distance between Him and a weak, frail, temporal, hopelessly broken humanity is incalculable; infinite. What's unimaginable is that He chose to stoop, to condescend, to bridge the gap in order to redeem and rescue.

In the 'kenosis passage' (Greek for *empty*), Philippians 2:5-11, the Bible says that Jesus *"gave up (emptied) His divine privileges; He took the humble position of a slave and was born as a human being. When he appeared in human form, He humbled Himself in obedience to God (the Father) and died a criminal's death on a cross"* (vv.7-8). He left His lofty position, His superior rank, and condescended into our world to be the bridge between heaven and earth by taking on our flesh and becoming one of us: *"The Word became flesh and dwelt among us"* (John 1:14; CSB). Jesus, the one and only God-Man; fully human, fully divine. Fully divine so that He could be the perfect and complete sacrifice for sin; fully human so that He could make that payment for me—and you!

I'm so grateful this exalted God is also a condescending God!

Jesus, I am so grateful that You condescended into this mess to rescue those who would believe. I worship You and say, Hallelujah!! Amen!

FRONT ROW
October 7

"Not to us, O Lord, not to us, but to Your name goes all the glory"
Psalm 115:1

Sue and I had the opportunity years ago to attend a concert by the Four Tops and Four Seasons. The couple who invited us had secured seats on the front row. The way the seating was arranged, we were only a few inches from the stage—so close that during "I Can't Help Myself," the lead singer, Levi Stubbs, handed me the microphone to join in on the song! When I finished, the crowd of 5,000 applauded (that I quit!).

Here is an undeniable fact: God can do what He wants, when He wants, how He wants without our help. But strangely, He almost always chooses to work through people. When I was singing with the Four Tops, they didn't need me to make great music—promise! But I had a front-row seat and got to be a part of something that was awesome.

If you're a Christ-follower, God has given you a front-row seat to be a part of something that is miraculous and life-giving. It begins with the radical changes He begins to make in your life when you surrender to Him and invite Him in to take control. You can't change yourself very much, nor can I. Self-help, self-confidence, self-improvement can change some behavior, but it doesn't change the very nature of who we are. It's window dressing that makes us look better from the outside, but our inside is still cluttered, confusing, and empty. Remember, Jesus didn't come to make good people better; He came to make dead people alive! When we cooperate with Him, we get a front-row seat to the miracle of regeneration (death to life) and transformation (being remade into the image of Jesus).

But it's not just about us. We also become an instrument in His hands to bring the same regeneration and transformation to others in our circles of influence. He bids us to be a part of the eternal! When we choose to join Him, the Christian student, parent, teacher, shop owner, salesperson, or cop is invited by God to a front-row seat to be a part of the miraculous!

But we should take no pride in it: *"Not to us, but to His name goes all the glory."*

God, I want that front-row seat. I surrender my all to You. Change me from the inside out. But don't stop there—use me in the lives of those around me. Let me see You do mighty things. Amen

SOVEREIGN
October 8

"Why should the nations say, 'Where is their God?'
Our God is in heaven and does whatever He pleases."
Psalms 115:2-3 (CSB)

Humans have always felt more comfortable worshipping what they can see. The ancients worshipped the sun, the moon, the stars, etc., or they created images of deities they honored and worshipped. Israel, on the other hand, was forbidden to make any image of a deity, even that of Yahweh. This prompted scorn and ridicule from their image-worshipping pagan neighbors, "Where is your God? We don't see any evidence of Him like we do ours." The psalmist responds, "Well, He's in heaven and He does whatever He wants to do, when He wants to do it."

This assertion by the psalmist is a nod to the sovereignty of Yahweh. Sovereignty has to do with power and authority over something or someone. Yahweh's sovereignty is based on the fact that He created all that is, and as Creator, He is sovereign over all that is. Everything that happens is according to *"the kind intention of His will"* (Ephesians 1:5, 9-11). Authority means that His will is to be obeyed; to refuse brings adverse consequences.

Fortunately, this sovereign God is not an inanimate force, but a personal, caring God. His love and faithfulness are enduring and unfailing (v.1), but He's still God and runs the universe as He sees fit. He doesn't ask our opinion, nor does He require it. This notion of a sovereign God is repugnant to our culture. The post-modern doctrine of self-autonomy has taken a true and healthy principle (humans endowed with choice) and turned it into a god; it's turned humans into gods.

To be certain, God did create humans with volition: the desire and ability to make their own moral decisions. But the person is best served when he/she employs self-determination to resist taking God's role and choose God's will. When we set ourselves up as the final moral authority, the result is identical to when Adam and Eve first made that mistake: pain and suffering.

Chevy Chase used to begin his Saturday Night Live routine with, "Good evening. I'm Chevy Chase, and you're not!" In the same way, Yahweh says, "I'm God, you're not! Don't think you can even try without messing up your life. Follow Me. I know My stuff and I know the way."

Yahweh, I bow before You as my sovereign. Forgive me for being self-determining apart from Your will. Be God in my life in every way. Amen

UNSEEN
October 9

"Why should the nations say, 'Where is their God?'
Our God is in heaven and does whatever He pleases."
Psalms 115:2-3 (CSB)

Humans have always felt more comfortable worshipping the visible. The ancients worshipped celestial bodies or created images of deities they honored and worshipped. Yahweh prohibited idol worship (Exodus 20:4) which prompted scorn and ridicule from their image-worshipping pagan neighbors, "Where is your God?"

Unbelievers still do the same. When chaos erupts in the world, natural catastrophes devastate, and wickedness abounds—many will ask with clinched fists and wagging heads: "Where is your God?" When someone they love is beset with cancer or ALS, when they see reports of mass murders, when racism continues to raise its ugly head, they'll demand: "Where is your God?"

The answer is simple: He's still in heaven, on His throne, conducting the universe as He sees fit. The implications are not so simple: if He's in control, how could this loving God let this happen? God gets the blame for everything wrong in our world. But does He deserve it? He would if He didn't create us with volition and a self-determining nature. But because He did, the wrong in this world is not His fault—it's ours. We live in a fallen, broken world because we are fallen and broken. The original, catastrophic fall was early in the history of humanity with Adam and Eve. Since then, we all have followed the path of determining that we know better than God.

God didn't cause the disease of your loved one. He doesn't cause murders, or racism, or homelessness, or child abuse. We do. Stop blaming God.

Instead, look to Him for hope and real help in the midst of this mess. He hasn't abandoned us—He became one of us in part to let us know that He is with us (*Immanuel*). His blood-bought gift offers us a plan of escape from the despair of this world and the promise of a better life here and in the age to come.

Where is your God? Many make their own gods: careers, possessions, comfort, security, etc. These gods offer hope and purpose, but in the end, they only give emptiness and pain.

My God is in heaven and He does whatever He pleases. It pleases Him to favor me as His child.

God, I can't see You, but I love and trust You. I praise You that Your reign in heaven and reign over the earth. Reign in my heart. Amen

GUNSMOKE
October 10

"And those who make idols are just like them, as are all who trust in them."
Psalm 115:8

When I was a kid, I wanted to be like Matt Dillon, the U.S. Marshall in Dodge City, Kansas. He was the star on 'Gunsmoke,' my favorite western tv show. Each episode began with him and some outlaw in a duel, standing 50' apart, staring at each other, seeing who would be the fastest. Dillon was always faster. I would practice drawing my little cap gun out of the holster as quick as I could, easily shooting my little brother before he shot me.

There is a principle in life that many don't realize: we take on the characteristics of what or who we idolize. Vocalists may imitate Mariah Carey; basketball players imitate MJ. Some of this is fairly harmless assuming the person grows beyond that stage. If I still wore my cap gun at my side, you'd be right to worry about me!

What is not healthy nor right is to foster the worship of idols. When we worship the Creator, it lifts us up; when we worship created things, it lowers us down. **When we make gods after our own image, we end up being made in their image—then they own us.** A person wants what alcohol offers, but if it becomes an idol, it is a wicked master. If someone wants what sex offers, if not careful, it becomes a horrific slave owner.

Jesus warned most of all about idolizing and worshipping the worst god—wealth and possessions: *"No one can serve two masters. For you will hate one and love the other; you will be devoted to one and despise the other. You cannot serve God and be enslaved to money"* (Matthew 6:24). The word for money, *mammon*, means more than just coins and bills; it means all that money can buy; i.e., comfort, toys, privilege, security, etc. By worshipping *mammon*, we are reduced to what it can do for us; secure for us. Consciously or not, we have sunk to being some transactional *thing*; defined by what we purchase and possess. We will become like what we worship.

God said, "Don't have any other gods but Me; love Me with all your heart, soul, and mind." When we worship Him, we become like Him: more loving, patient, gracious, merciful, forgiving, pure, generous—Godly.

Yahweh, show me what gods I worship—and rid me of them! I am resolved to have no other gods but the One True God—YOU! Amen

TRUST OR BUST
October 11

"O Israel, trust the Lord! He is your helper and your shield.
O priests, descendants of Aaron, trust the Lord! He is your helper and your shield.
All you who fear the Lord, trust the Lord! He is your helper and your shield."
Psalm 115:9-11

The stock market crash of October 1929 is legendary for its catastrophic impact on the U.S.

The market fell 24.9% that month and 90% over the next four years. Rumors of brokers jumping out of windows to their deaths prevailed. In a more recent story, Aubrey McClendon, CEO of Chesapeake Energy, saw his company stock plummet and died in a one-car accident the day after he was charged with conspiring to rig bids for oil and gas leases.

When the god you trust can't deliver what was promised, the shock can be overwhelming.

In vv. 4-7, the psalmist has been ridiculing the gods humans make: they have eyes, but can't see; ears, but can't hear; feet, but can't walk, etc. In fact, when we serve them, they draw us down to their level and we take on characteristics of inanimate objects (v.8).

But now the psalmist pivots and contrasts Yahweh with these idols. He calls on three groups to trust Yahweh: the covenant people, Israel; the priesthood who served in the tabernacle and temple; and anyone else who has the wisdom to turn from their idols.

Remember, an idol, a false god, is anything or anyone we look to meet a need more than we look to Yahweh; anything that captivates our hearts and imagination more than Him. It can even be a good thing becomes a supreme thing. We stake our happiness or fulfillment on it; we are crushed when we don't get it.

Trusting a false god will always let us down and disappoint. Trusting in Yahweh will always lift us up and encourage. Life is hard and full of trials and tragedies. Who will you trust to get you through? Trust in Yahweh—trust or bust.

I'm reminded of a millionaire who lost everything in the '29 crash. He was known for his generosity with his church and other ministries. A friend asked the former millionaire, "I'll bet you wish you had all that money you gave away now, don't you?" "No," he said, "I've sent it all up ahead and it's waiting for me!"

God, pry the grips of my idols from around my heart. I confess my tendency to trust in other things and other people to fill and please. Forgive me, I pray. I again assert that I trust in You! Amen

THE NEW ISRAEL
October 12

"The Lord remembers us and will bless us. He will bless the people of Israel
and bless the priests, the descendants of Aaron."
Psalm 115:12

The Psalms, of course, were poem-songs written to be used by the nation of Israel in worship. Inside these psalms are words of encouragement, general wisdom principles, and promises—all aimed at the nation of Israel and its people.

The question arises: if this book and its contents are for the nation and people of Israel, do they apply to Christ-followers? The answer is: absolutely!

Oceans of ink have been spilled trying to sort out the relationship between the ancient nation of Israel and its descendants (Jews)—and the Church. Contrasting terms and frameworks have emerged: dispensationalism, replacement theology, covenant theology, etc. Ugh!

What is critical to know is that the promises and exhortations made to Israel and its people in the Old Testament, can apply to us in a general sense, and many times in a specific sense. How do I know? Because a nation is less determined by geographical boundaries than it is by the people in it. The promises God made with Abraham in Genesis 12 &15 were about land he and his people would possess, but the substantive promises were not about land, they were about blessing, descendants, and the Messiah. The land was the location where most of this would play out, but the promises were still true when Abe's descendants were in Egypt, the Sinai, and in Babylonian captivity.

Many British believers in the 1600s believed that England was the new Israel. Similarly, the early Pilgrims, persecuted by the official church of England, came to America to establish a new Israel. Some evangelicals still consider the U.S. as God's physical representation of the Kingdom.

I, for one, believe God's Kingdom is less about a place and more about a people—the people of faith. Abraham believed God and was made righteous in God's sight. Throughout Scripture, the focus has been on the heart of faith, not a physical place. We who are believers are recipients of the promises of God. We're even priests (1 Peter 2:9)!

Read these psalms as straight from the heart of God to you personally. Interpretation does include context, but don't think for a moment that because you're not a Jew or living in Israel, these don't apply to you.

God, thank you for blessing me as a descendant of Abraham. Your promise to him was fulfilled in Jesus. By Your grace, enable me to live in Your immense and immeasurable promises. Amen

THE ONE CONSTANT

October 13

"It is not the dead who praise the Lord, nor any of those descending into the silence of death. But we will bless the Lord, both now and forever. Hallelujah!"

Psalm 115:17-18

When I was taking algebra, trig, and calculus in high school, I learned there was something called a constant (C) in math problems and science experiments. For instance, in math, Pi is a constant. In science, gravity is a constant. As a parent, a poopy diaper at the worst times is a constant.

Interestingly, some scientists are hypothesizing that certain constants, like the speed of light, are not necessarily constant. Who knew? There is, however, one constant that rises above all other constants and will never, ever change: the praise of Yahweh.

Not everyone will participate: "Though the dead cannot, and the wicked will not, and the careless do not praise God, yet we will shout 'Hallelujah' for ever and ever. Amen" (Spurgeon).

So here's the question: if you don't really esteem praise now, if you don't get caught up in praise now, if those around you in corporate worship seem to get carried away with their praise, what makes you think you will enjoy it more in heaven? C.S. Lewis conjectured that what we yearn for here will be intensified in heaven, but we're likely to recognize more clearly what is truly valuable. If praising God leaves you non-plussed here, how much more non-plussed will you be in heaven?

The desire to praise God is directly proportionate to the level of two realizations. We would do well to get these firmly fixed in our hearts and minds. First, the realization that God is so amazing, so transcendent, so magnificent that He could and did create all that is. All that is! How incredibly smart, powerful, creative, and wise must He be? I worship my Creator and praise His stunning creative ability. The second realization that establishes my level of praise is my thanksgiving for His redemption. He rescued me! I didn't deserve anything but His judgment but because of His great mercy, He saved me through faith in Christ!

Revelation 4 & 5 speak to this dual motivation:

"You are worthy, O Lord our God, to receive glory and honor and power.

For you created all things" (4:11).

"Worthy is the Lamb who was slaughtered— to receive power and riches and wisdom and strength and honor and glory and blessing" (5:12).

AMEN!

THE LISTENING GOD
October 14

"I love the Lord because He hears my voice and my prayer for mercy.
Because He bends down to listen, I will pray as long as I have breath!"
Psalm 116:1-2

As a pastor, I've had countless numbers of people come to me for counsel on various issues from marriage, to parenting, finances, business, depression, addictions, bitterness, or questions about God. Every once in a while, I would offer an insight of wisdom, but most of the time I would just listen. That's all. Many times at the end of the appointed time, they'd stand up and say something like, "Thank you, Pastor. I knew you could help me. I feel so much better now!"

There is something incredibly therapeutic about knowing someone is listening to us. Hearing is not always listening. Listening means you enter into their words, their story, their heart.

The Scripture asserts over and over again that God listens to believers: to our prayers, our cries, our pain. He is not removed from us nor disinterested in our conversations. He enters into our words, our stories, our heart in the matter. A few verses:

"In those days when you pray, I will listen. If you look for Me wholeheartedly, you will find Me" (Jeremiah 29:12-13).

"We know that God doesn't listen to sinners, but He is ready to hear those who worship Him and do His will" (John 9:31).

"The eyes of the Lord watch over those who do right, and His ears are open to their prayers" (1 Peter 3:12).

"And we are confident that He hears us whenever we ask for anything that pleases Him" (1 John 5:14).

Unlike my pastoral counseling situations, God not only listens, but He has the power to answer and act on our requests.

The psalmist identifies this as a key motivation for His prayers: he knows God is listening. I remember when I was first growing in Christ, there were times I felt like my prayers were bouncing off the ceiling. Someone said, "Well, praise God we serve a God who can get below the ceiling!" Don't lose heart in your prayers. God is listening. He will answer. Stay at it. Then have the wisdom to see His answers in your life, even when it is different than what you expected.

God, thank you for listening with a loving, caring heart. By faith, I'll keep praying and trusting You for the answers. Enable me to see those answers when they arrive. Amen

LET GO
October 15

*"Death wrapped its ropes around me; the terrors of the grave overtook me.
I saw only trouble and sorrow."*

Psalm 116:3

Years ago, I was teaching one of my kids to water ski. When the skier was ready, I'd hit the throttle and off we'd go. The skis, if held at the right angle, would thrust the skier on top of the water. More than once, the skis would come off, removing any chance of skiing. Sometimes the novice held on to the rope after the skis were off. The longer they held on, the deeper they went! At that point, the only thing to do was let go and float to the surface.

The psalmist is undoubtedly talking about a physical, deadly threat. He was deceived (v.11) and in deep trouble, convinced that he was about to die. In desperation, he cried out to Yahweh for deliverance—and God answered.

I've mentioned before that I've had a few life experiences where I would've died physically if God didn't rescue me. However, they didn't compare to the two times in my 20s when the threat was not physical, but mental and emotional. During those times, I wanted to die. The terror of being dragged under without any prospect of escape was absolutely overwhelming. The harder I tried, the deeper I went. I felt I couldn't escape. Death seemed like the only option.

But like the psalmist, I kept calling out to God and trusting that He would deliver me: *"Then I called on the name of the Lord: 'Please, Lord, save me!'"* (v.4)—and eventually He did. I NEVER want to go back to that darkness again. Yet, I have to say that I am who I am BECAUSE of those experiences. I discovered the more I let go of my self-determination, the less power that fear and darkness had over me. I repeated over and over again, "God, I'm Yours. Do in me and with me what You want." Miraculously, I begin to head to the surface and breathe.

There's a good chance Jesus sang this song on the night He was betrayed knowing that in just a few hours, grave clothes would be wrapped around Him in death. He didn't fight it. He let go and trusted the Father knowing that a resurrection awaited Him.

Father, feel like the harder I try, the deeper in despair and failure I go. I release all of this to You. Give me air to breathe until I hit the surface again. I am trusting You for a resurrection. Amen

WHEN DEATH KNOCKS
October 16

"Precious in the sight of the Lord is the death of His godly ones."
Psalm 116:15 (NASB)

I pray multiple times daily that my family will be spared an untimely death. In the previous verses, the psalmist is making that same petition (vv.4 &11). I also pray for friends who have terminal diseases that God will touch and heal them. I'm familiar with the death of loved ones: it has been so painful; so grievous.

Although this psalm celebrates deliverance from death, the psalmist knows that death is unavoidable; it's a part of life. When that day comes for the saint, for the one who is in Christ, it may be grievous to loved ones, but to Yahweh, it is a precious thing.

That word, *precious*, carries the idea of value and importance. The death of a saint is no slight occurrence in the eyes of God because each saint is so valuable and precious to Him. So treasured, it appears that He sends angels to attend us at that moment to care for us and transport our souls into His presence (Luke 16:22); *"To be away from the body is to be at home with the Lord"* (2 Corinthians 5:8).

Death is inevitable, but it is a part of God's plan to finally deliver us from the curse of human flesh (Genesis 3). Jesus took the sting out of death when He walked out of the tomb that first Easter morning.

Charles Spurgeon relates a pertinent story about one of his associates:

> When Baxter lay a dying, and his friends came to see him, almost the last word he said was in answer to the question, 'Dear Mr. Baxter, how are you?' 'Almost well,' said he, and so it is. Death cures; it is the best medicine, for they who die are not only almost well, but healed forever.

There is no such thing as an untimely death—it is too valuable to be squandered. We who have chosen the blood of Jesus to protect us from God's judgment, have no reason to fear it. We have an opportunity to bear witness of His care—and to echo the Scripture: *"Death, where is your sting; grave where is your victory? But thank God, who gives us the victory through our Lord and Savior, Jesus the Christ!"* (1 Corinthians 15:55, 57).

Lord Jesus, thank you for conquering sin and death! Enable me not to fear death as those who have no hope. Keep my eyes on You—that will be enough. Thank You for removing the sting. Amen

IS THAT ALL YOU GOT?

October 17

"The Lord is for me; I will not be afraid. What can a mere mortal do to me?"
Psalm 118:6 (CSB)

Toby Keith's song about a woman who broke up with him goes, "Is that all you got, is that all there is? All you can hit me with?" The phase is an idiom that expresses perfectly what the psalmist is saying here about his enemies: "Is that all you got? God is for me, so who are you? God is for me, so what do you think you can do to me? God is for me—that's what I got!!"

The psalmist begins by giving praise to God for His faithful, enduring love and goodness: *"Give thanks to the Lord, for He is good! His faithful love endures forever"* (Psalm 118:1). He repeats the phrase, *"His faithful love endures forever"* four times in the first four verses. He's making a point: he wants all who will listen to know that God's love and goodness are on display in the life of the one who walks with Yahweh.

The specific example he gives is when he was terribly distressed; outmanned and outnumbered. His despair was palpable. He called to the Lord and God set him free. We don't know what form freedom took. But it's obvious that He came to the realization once again that no matter the attack, no matter the setback, no matter the circumstance, God is good, God is faithful, God is loving, and God was for him.

The Apostle Paul picks up on this theme in Romans 8, one of my favorite chapters in all Scripture. Despite the great upheaval, challenges, and even persecution of the early believers, he reminded, *"If God is for us, who can be against us?"* (Romans 8:31). In the face of adversity, trials, and tragedy that life throws us, we can say, "Is that all you got?" Paul finishes the argument that *"in all things, we are more than conquerors through Him who loved us"* (v.37).

Martin Luther held this psalm especially close to his heart. Chased, hounded, threatened with being burned at the stake, when emperors and kings and popes came against him, he did not waive or wilt, standing against them all with the courage of this truth: *"The Lord is for me—what can mere mortals do?"*

God, Your love endures forever. When I feel as if I'm losing or too weak to carry on, remind me that since You are for me, nothing else really matters. Amen

ENEMIES
October 18

"My enemies did their best to kill me, but the Lord rescued me.
The Lord is my strength and my song; He has given me victory."
Psalm 118:13-14

This psalm is the last of the Hallel psalms (113-118); psalms used by the faithful on their way to the temple to make sacrifices and give praise and thanksgiving to Yahweh. The psalmist gives a reason for such jubilation: God had delivered them from their enemies.

Enemies. What constitutes an enemy for God's people? Certainly, there are physical enemies. Israel's entire existence has been characterized by surrounding nations trying to destroy it. Believers all over the world are being physically threatened, persecuted, tortured, and even martyred for their faith.

Although physical threats are rare for American believers, there is a growing persecution for Christ-followers who declare salvation in Jesus alone and strive to live for Him. Abortion and LGBTQ+ issues are bringing great hatred and vitriol on believers who hold to biblical standards. Freedom of thought, speech, and religion are under attack like never before in our country.

But then there are more personal enemies that threaten believers: fear, anxiety, depression, guilt, shame, dysfunctional relationships, crumbling marriages, and sin habits too numerous to mention. Human brokenness seems to become more profound with each generation.

We have an enemy that exploits all of this. We know him as Satan. He has other names or titles: Beelzebub, the Accuser, the Adversary, the Devil. His one objective is to oppose God, the word of God, the things of God, and the people of God. We are warned to know how he works and what his schemes are—he wants to ruin your life! *"Stay alert! Watch out for your great enemy, the devil. He prowls around like a roaring lion, looking for someone to devour"* (1 Peter 5:8).

How are our enemies overcome and defeated? By growing in our relationship with, love for, and trust in Yahweh. He is the One who rescues and gives victory. He gives us the strength to endure. He puts melodies of joy in our hearts that persist even in trial and tragedy. And He gives us hope: *"I have told you all this so that you may have peace in Me. Here on earth you will have many trials and sorrows. But take heart, because I have overcome the world"* (John 16:33).

Jesus, draw me closer to You so that I might gain more strength, joy, and hope to endure and overcome. I know I will have many trials in this world. I take heart that you have overcome the world. Amen

THE CORNERSTONE
October 19

*"The stone that the builders rejected has now become the cornerstone.
This is the Lord's doing, and it is wonderful to see."*
Psalm 118:22-23

If you've ever been to Israel (if you haven't, why not??), hopefully you were able to take a walking tour of the foundations of the ancient temple. The temple was torn down by the Romans in 70 A.D., but below the temple mount, underground tunnels have been carved out running parallel to the foundation. Huge limestone blocks laid on one another (some weighing 160,000 pounds!) are there to marvel at. The foundation is still there 2000 years later!

In any masonry structure, the cornerstone is most important because it is the first stone laid and therefore determines the positioning of all other stones while giving the edifice structural integrity. The psalmist applies this reality to his and Israel's own experience: abandoned, rejected, seemingly weak and defenseless—yet God chose to grant victory and exaltation.

The prophets later used this in predicting the nature of the promised Messiah: He would be ignored, even abandoned, appearing weak, yet later exalted and victorious. Isaiah saw it this way: *"Look! I am placing a foundation stone in Jerusalem, a firm and tested stone. It is a precious cornerstone that is safe to build on. Whoever believes need never be shaken"* (28:16).

Toward the end of His earthly ministry, Jesus was duking it out with the Pharisees (religious leaders) who continued to reject His teaching and Messiahship. He told a couple of parables about how they were going to be judged by His Father, but they didn't seem to get it (Matthew 21:42). So, He quoted Psalm 118:22-23 and combined it with another Isaiah passage: *"But to Israel and Judah He will be a stone that makes people stumble, a rock that makes them fall"* (8:14). Then they got it—and began plotting how to kill Him (Matthew 28:46).

Don't miss this: Jesus is the Cornerstone—He is the foundation for all truth and ultimate reality. Build your life on Him: surrender to and trust in Him. Love and follow Him with all your heart.

Your life will be full, sturdy, overcoming, and able to withstand the storms.

Reject Him and decide to build your life on your own truths and realities, and it won't go well for you here—and in the life to come.

Jesus, I love the fact that You are the Cornerstone! Be my Cornerstone and, by Your grace, enable me to build my life on You. I surrender to You! Amen

ONE DAY AT A TIME
October 20

"This is the day the Lord has made.
We will rejoice and be glad in it."
Psalm 118:24

One of the biggest lessons a person can learn is to live one day at a time. We had learned the truth of that through the years, but when we were going through Sue's cancer diagnosis and treatment, we had to take our game up a level. We knew that if we started trying to live in tomorrow, wondering what would happen in the future, fear would eat us up. **Fear of tomorrow can rob us of the blessing of the present day.**

I love the story of the Hebrews in the wilderness when they had run out of food after their escape from Egypt (Exodus 16). They prayed and God answered. He told them that the next morning, He would do something that would meet their need and bring Him glory. As the sun came up, they wandered to the edge of the camp, and there on the plants and floor of the desert, was some white flakey stuff. Someone picked it up and began to eat it. Others back in the crowd said, "What is it?" "Well," they responded, "it tastes like nuts and honey and…it's good, very good!" "What is it?" they repeated. But the Hebrews didn't know what to call it. So they just called it the *manna*, which means, *"what is it?"* in Hebrew. The What Is It, the mystery bread that came from heaven.

God told them they could gather all they needed for that day, but they couldn't save it for the next day. If they tried, it would turn to worms—except on Sabbath. A whole generation of Hebrews ate practically nothing but manna. Whatever they needed was in the manna. They didn't need anything else; they didn't get anything else. They had to depend on God's provision each day; one day at a time.

Living one day at a time is only possible when we trust God's faithfulness to take care of tomorrow's need. If we try to take today's provision into tomorrow's need, worms will crawl into your life in the form of worry, fear, and anxiety.

So each day, exclaim and confirm: "THIS is the day God has given me to live. I WILL rejoice and be glad in it." If you do, incredible peace and joy will be yours no matter what.

Lord, I accept and confess that each day is something You make; an opportunity to see You more clearly and trust You more firmly. I WILL rejoice and be glad in it—one day at a time. Amen!

THE WORD OF THE LORD
October 21

"Joyful are people of integrity, who follow the instructions of the Lord."
Psalm 119:1

Psalm 119, a meditation on the Word of God, is the longest of the Psalms (176 verses). Since this psalm is the longest among the Psalms, and the Book of Psalms is the longest of the Bible, we can see just how important God's Word is to God! To the casual reader, this psalm can seem redundant and uninteresting. But inside are nuggets of gold to help foster an appetite and respect for God and His Word.

Your Bible probably has the Hebrew word *Aleph* right before verse 1. This psalm is arranged as an acrostic. There are 22 letters in the Hebrew alphabet, the first being *Aleph*, then *Beth*, and so on, so that the psalm is broken into 22 sections, each one beginning with a Hebrew letter and containing eight verses. Each of the eight verses begins with a word starting with the corresponding Hebrew letter. For example, the first 8 verses begin with an *Aleph*.

The psalmist employs nine Hebrew words that can be understood in five main categories (English words italicized):

Word, Words, or *Promises* (dabar & imrāh): divine speech; what God Himself has spoken directly (e.g., to Abraham, Moses, the prophets, John the Baptist, etc).

Laws (mišpāt) and *Statutes* (ēdāh): direction to make decisions, right from wrong, based on the nature and righteousness of God.

Decrees (hōq): the enduring significance of God's Word; like something carved into a rock for permanence.

Law (torāh): teaching or instruction; like a caring father gives his child, yet from a position of authority.

Commands, Commandments (miswāh), *Precepts* (piqqud) and *Ways* (derek): practical application in the small details of life.

There are common themes that run throughout this psalm: a love for God's Word, the commitment to obey His Word, strength and hope in times of difficulty, and guidance for life's decisions.

Charles Spurgeon put it best about Psalm 119: "Its variety is that of a kaleidoscope: from a few objects a boundless variation is produced. In the kaleidoscope you look once, and there is a strangely beautiful form. You shift the glass a very little, and another shape, equally delicate and beautiful, is before your eyes. So it is here."

God, show me the beauty of Your Word. Amen!

BE BLESSED!
October 22

"How blessed are those whose way is blameless, who walk in the law of the Lord. How blessed are those who observe His testimonies, who seek Him with all their heart."

Psalm 119:1-2 (NASB)

In the movie, *The Princess Bride*, Vizzini uses the word "Inconceivable" about events that could not conceivably happen, yet one by one they do. After uttering it yet again, Inigo Montoya says, "You keep using that word. I do not think it means what you think it means!"

I've been hearing a lot of people use the phrase, "I'm blessed." It's being uttered by movie stars, pro athletes, work colleagues, or friends who in many cases, don't appear to really understand what it means.

The word *'blessed'* (*esher*) carries the idea of being happy, joyful, and favored. Who doesn't want to be happy and joyful? Who doesn't want the favor of God in their lives?

Yet not everyone actually has His favor. Only those who have surrendered their lives to Jesus and placed their trust in Him alone can truly say they are blessed of God. His grace and love, demonstrated on the cross, is the basis for being blessed by God. But it's not a one-time decision: if you want to live a life that is full of the favor of God, make sure you build your life on the Word of God.

The first two verses in Psalm 119 look backward and forward to emphasize the blessedness of those who build their lives on God's Word. Looking backward, the psalm echoes Psalm 1: *"How blessed is the man who . . . delight(s) is in the law of the Lord"* (vv.1-2; NASB).

Looking forward, Jesus opened His great Sermon on the Mount with this same phrase: *"Blessed are the…"* (Matthew 5:2) as He outlined the values and ethics of His Kingdom. His closing illustration was about the person whose life is built on the Word: *"And the rain fell, and the floods came, and the winds blew and slammed against that house; and yet it did not fall, for it had been founded on the rock"* (Matthew 7:25 NASB).

The Word of God is the ultimate resource for how to live this life well; day by day with the favor of God. THAT life is a life of joy, purpose, and peace. That's Psalm 119 in a nutshell.

Be blessed!

God, I want all of Your blessing I can get! Draw me to Your word and reveal to me the depth and breadth of Your favor! Amen

YES SIR!

October 23

"You have commanded that Your precepts be diligently kept."
Psalm 119:4 (CSB)

In the military, when an officer gives an order, the soldier is required to say, "Yes sir!" It's an appropriate response from a subordinate that recognizes the authority of someone with higher rank. The order is not up for debate, nor can the soldier vacillate whether or not he or she is going to obey it.

Right at the beginning of Psalm 119, God makes sure we get two things straight: we are blessed and favored when we follow His Word (v.1), and following His Word is not optional (v.4). The Hebrew word for *'command'* is from *miswah*, meaning to give an order. It may sound a bit harsh, but God has ordered us to obey His commands. Two reasons emerge. First, He is God and we're not! Chevy Chase used to open his 'Tonight's Top News' segment on Saturday Night Live, with, "Good Evening. I'm Chevy Chase, and you're not!" As Creator, He gets to decide how the universe is run. We don't.

When Job questioned the fairness of Yahweh, He responded with: *"Where were you when I laid the foundations of the earth? Tell me, if you know so much"* (Job 38:4). When Israel was complaining about God's handling of certain things, God told his prophet Jeremiah to go observe a potter working the clay. His point: the potter gets to decide how to handle his creation. God has decided what is right and wrong, good and evil, helpful and unhelpful, healthy and unhealthy, satisfying and unsatisfying, true and false. So when we come to the Word of God, we should come with the attitude, "Yes Sir! I will do what you want. Now, what is it that You want?"

The second reason God orders us to obey His word is because He knows what is best for us. He created us and He knows us better than we know ourselves. We THINK we know what is best, but we don't really. God ALWAYS KNOWS what is best for us and He has deposited that knowledge in His Word, the Bible.

If you want to live a life that is joyful and in the favor of God, get to know God's Word and obey God's Word. Be blessed!

God, I do want Your blessing. Teach me Your ways that I might walk in them. I understand that my response is to obey. Enable me to do so, Holy Spirit. Amen

MORAL PURITY
October 24

"How can a young person stay pure? By obeying your word.
I have hidden your word in my heart, that I might not sin against you."
Psalm 119:9 & 11

These two verses are critical to the person who struggles with sexual purity. Many believers have memorized these verses and have latched on to them in desperation. Others in society have given up on or mocked the idea of sexual purity. But God's Word never abandons the importance of a person striving for moral purity.

Moral purity was a constant issue in the 1st-century church. The churches in Athens, Corinth, and other cities were right in the middle of some of the most licentious places on earth. Worshippers of Aphrodite would go to their temple and engage in sexual activity with temple prostitutes as a form of worship. The Greco-Roman world cared little for sexual purity.

I'm not sure it's any better today. A recent survey of evangelical millennials revealed that the majority of them (54%) believe there is nothing morally wrong with living together. Commercials today are as bawdy as R-rated movies of 30 years ago. Pornography has grabbed the souls of most Americans, even as young as 8-year-old girls and boys. Don't think for a moment that the aging process removes the temptation. The story is told about an aged seminary professor who was teaching on these verses and moral purity. One young man raised his hand and said, "Professor, when is it that a man finally stops lusting after women?" The octogenarian replied, "I don't know, son. You'll have to ask somebody else!" On a down note, I know of multiple persons in their 70s who have recently had affairs on their life-long spouses.

The psalmist gives us a golden key to purity: hide God's Word in our hearts. Memorizing and meditating on God's Word brings a mysterious and miraculous strengthening to our resolve to obey God, particularly in this area. These two verses and many others (1 Corinthians 6:18-20, Philippians 4:8, 2 Timothy 2:22, etc.) can make an incredible difference if bound to your heart.

If you desire to have a pure heart, begin by memorizing these verses and praying them daily.

God, I do want my thought life to be honoring and pleasing to You. It's not easy these days. I call out to You to work mightily in my heart. Purify me, I pray. Amen

WONDER
October 25

"Open my eyes to see the wonderful truths in your instructions."
Psalm 119:18

I have been fortunate to travel the world. I've seen the wonder of the Grand Canyon in Arizona, the glacier shelves in Alaska, the Alps in Europe—and then there are those incredible pics from the Hubble Spacecraft of galaxies far away with breath-taking splendor on display. Recently we were blessed with our 10th grandchild and were overwhelmed again by the wonder and sophistication of the human body and the life element breathed by God into each baby.

Wonder is defined as "a feeling of surprise mingled with admiration, caused by something beautiful, unexpected, unfamiliar, or inexplicable." I have pics of the places I've been to and all my children and grandchildren—and certainly, they have impacted me. But **nothing** can match the power and effect of God's word on my life. Seriously. What I have experienced in my 50 years of being a student of the Bible has been jaw-dropping, life-changing. Wúnderbar!

The psalmist references this awe-inspiring wonder of God's word. He uses

torah, which you'll remember is teaching or instruction like a careful father gives to a loved child. God has such loving guidance for us in His word. But we can't really discern it with our mind—in fact, Jesus mentioned that its deeper truths are hidden and can only be understood by a work of the Spirit (Matthew 11:25; John 6:63). This is why the psalmist asks that God open his eyes to see something that is not ho-hum, but truly wonderful, meaningful, and life-changing.

Not everyone sees the treasure. A casual reading doesn't generally capture the beauty. Here's what I've learned:

1. I begin with the psalmist prayer: Holy Spirit, open the eyes of my heart to see.
2. I come with an attitude of submission: God, I will seek the truth that I might live the truth.
3. Like a jeweler admiring an expensive diamond, I examine the passage from different angles so that I can fully understand its meaning and beauty.
4. I write down what the Spirit has revealed to me. Sometimes I need to repent. Other times I need to praise or give thanks, or decide, or grant grace.

This will work for you too. His glorious word awaits. Be filled with wonder.

God, draw me to Your word and open my eyes to see the wonder of You and understand how Your word applies in every instance to my life. Amen

ALIENS
October 26

"I am a resident alien on earth; do not hide Your commands from me."
Psalm 119:19 (CSB)

In 1986, the science fiction movie, *Aliens* hit the box office. If you were old enough to see it in the theatre, you'll never forget the scene when the alien comes busting out of that guy's chest!

There's a popular notion that we are not alone in the cosmos; other life forms exist. The rationale: the universe is so vast that the odds of us being the only life forms are infinitesimal. But if God is infinitely powerful and intelligent, it was no big deal for Him to speak what is into reality. The universe is a backdrop and the world a stage upon which God is seeking a relationship with the one part of creation that is made in His image.

There are, however, aliens amongst us. The psalmist confesses he is an alien, and elsewhere the Bible assesses true believers as aliens and immigrants. Here is a sampling:

> *"I think it is right, as long as I am in this bodily* **tent***, to wake you up with a reminder, since I know that I will soon lay aside my* **tent***, as our Lord Jesus Christ has indeed made clear to me"* (2 Peter 1:13-14; CSB). Our bodies are tents; not cabins, houses, or mansions; we are nomads.

> *"Dear friends, I warn you as temporary residents and foreigners"* (1 Timothy 2:11). America is truly the land of the immigrant (Russian, Irish, Mexican, etc.). But the ultimate immigrant is the believer; we are in a foreign land.

> *"They were foreigners and temporary residents on the earth. Now those who say such things make it clear that they are seeking a homeland"* (Hebrews 11:13-14). This world is NOT our home.

There is a world system dominated by *"the god of this world,"* i.e., Satan (2 Corinthians 4:4). He opposes God, the word of God, the things of God, and the people of God. He dominates every fiber of this fallen world: politics, business, education, etc. He is leading the world the wrong direction, the direction of God's judgment.

If you feel like you're swimming against the current in this world, that's a good thing! The only way to keep from getting swept away by worldly notions is to keep your nose in the word of God. If you do, you'll be blessed!

God, thank You for Your word that guides me along the path of life. Remind me that this world is not my home—that what awaits is far grander than anything here. Amen

COUNSELING

October 27

"Your decrees are my delight and my counselors."
Psalm 119:24 (CSB)

Early on as a pastor, I decided I wasn't all that good as a counselor. So, I began a counseling center at Rush Creek staffed by loving, godly, trained folks who could give long-term help to those in need. Years later, thousands have been helped through grief, marital problems, etc.

Having said that, no human counselor can give you the wisdom and insight into your problems like the word of God. I remember hearing a guy say, "The key to success in life is being able to go to the word with your problems and coming away with solutions." That's great advice.

The psalmist uses the word *edah*, which is direction to make decisions, right from wrong, based on the nature and truth of God. If you want to live wisely, if you want to walk the path of peace and joy, if you want success in your relationships, then delight in His *edah*, His decrees, His word.

This is why becoming a student of the Bible is so critical to our mental and emotional health. Since God created us, He knows exactly what we need. He knows the problems and He knows the solutions. He has embedded the insights and understanding we need in His word. If we spend time in His word, gain His wisdom about life and the struggles we face, then we can handle them when they come along.

Delighting in His Word will help you know what grief is and how to deal with it, how to handle a struggling marriage, how to overcome shame and guilt—whatever the issue is, God's Word will speak deep into your soul like no one else can.

If you're dulled, not delighted, by His word, then one or more of four realities are true:

1. You're an unbeliever so you don't have the Spirit to open your eyes;
2. You're a believer but not surrendered to the Spirit's leading, which inhibits revelation;
3. You're not really spending time in the Word each day;
4. You're not taking the time to think through what it's saying and writing it down.

Don't get discouraged. There are online resources (also my Pathways book found at www.nextlevelleadership.org) that can help you. What is fundamentally true is that the more time you spend in the word, the hungrier you get for it.

God, I know I need to get serious about my reading and studying of Scripture. Grant me the ability and desire to delight in Your word. Amen

HYDRATE
October 28

"I lie in the dust; revive me by Your word."
Psalm 119:25

A lesson I've learned late in life is the value of hydration. It regulates body temp, keeps joints lubricated, helps prevent infections, delivers nutrients to cells, keeps organs functioning properly, and improves sleep, mood, and cognition. Here's another benefit: it revives me. I've noticed that if my water intake has been low, I start feeling listless, lethargic—and start looking for a place to lie down! But drinking a big glass of water changes everything in about 10-15 minutes. Energy drinks may give a temporary surge in energy, but they are actually counterproductive because the caffeine in them dehydrates us.

The psalmist has identified something that doesn't just revive the body, but the soul as well: the word of God. When I'm down, discouraged, and struggling to meet the challenge, I know that the key is for me to get in the word of God. There is something energizing, stimulating, life-renewing about God's word. It's like drinking that glass of water I mentioned—10-15 minutes in the word changes everything. I gain God's perspective on things, I gain a more positive outlook, and I'm energized to take on the challenge of the moment. It is truly miraculous!

The Hebrew word used for *'word'* in this verse is *dabar*, signaling divine speech; *direct words from the mouth and heart of God.* Like a coach on the sideline admonishing his fatigued players to give it their best, God's words to us renew and energize us like nothing else. You can try some cultural energy drinks like shopping, TV, activity—but they won't energize your soul. In fact, they make things worse because they keep you from discovering the deep well of soul hydration that is in the word of God.

If you're struggling with energy to meet the challenges God has orchestrated in your life, then double down on your time in the word. Find verses that encourage you and make them your 'go-to' energy drink! I've got quite a few: Jeremiah 29:11, John 1:5; John 3:16, John 16:33, Romans 5:8, Romans 8:1, 31-39, Philippians 4:13, 1 John 4:10 to name a few. I've memorized them so that I can call on them whenever I need reviving. Like a huge glass of water, they penetrate the sinews of my soul and infuse life and vitality into my being.

God, thank You for Your word that renews my soul. I pledge to stop looking to cultural energy drinks and instead, drink from Your word. Amen

GRIEF
October 29

"I am weary from grief; strengthen me through Your word."
Psalm 119:28 (CSB)

"No one ever told me that grief felt so like fear."
C.S. Lewis, A Grief Observed

Of all the human experiences, grief may be the most terrifying. Grief is what we feel when we experience loss: loss of a job, loss of a relationship, loss of health, loss of a loved one. It comes to us when the brokenness of this world shows up at our doorstep.

News flash—grief is God-given. It's His provision for us to deal with the void; a merciful outlet to express the pain of loss.

Some view grief as a sign of weakness or a lack of faith. Nothing could be farther from the truth. David wept and grieved over the loss of his son, Absalom. Habakkuk grieved over the ruin of Jerusalem.

And then there is Jesus. At His good friend Lazarus's funeral, Scripture says, *"When Jesus saw her weeping, and the Jews who had come with her also weeping, He was deeply moved in His spirit and greatly troubled"* (John 11:33). Notice those last words. Deeply moved. Greatly troubled. This indicates a deep, visceral emotion with volcanic motion. Sure enough, what followed was the shortest verse in the Bible: *"Jesus wept."* Jesus experienced grief. No weakness or lack of faith there!

Jesus, more than any single person, grasped the trauma and tragedy of human brokenness. He was on earth to deal with the cause and curse. So when He looked around and saw the pain and felt the loss, His deep grief made its way to the surface—and He wept.

But He didn't get stuck in His grief. Why? He knew how the story is going to end; that He would suffer and die for the brokenness and create a way to overcome it in this life and escape it in the life to come.

The psalmist knew that the word of God would strengthen and encourage him. All through Scripture, we are given words of hope and peace to bring healing in our grief. Jesus identifies with us in our grief (Isaiah 53:3), He comforts us in our grief (2 Corinthians 1:3-5), and He promises that grief won't have the last say (1 Thessalonians 4:13f).

If you are grieving, Google Bible verses on grief. Read them, post them on your mirror, memorize them—and be blessed!

God, I am grieving a loss. Soothe the grief of my heart with Your Spirit and Your word. I find comfort in knowing that You grieve too. Amen

SELF-DECEPTION
October 30

"Keep me from lying to myself; give me the privilege of knowing Your instructions."
Psalm 119:29

I love this verse! Such honesty: *"Keep me from lying to myself!"* We do it all the time. Self-deception is the process of denying or rationalizing away evidence or logic that is contrary to our perceptions or beliefs. The range of examples go from the humorous—the guy who thinks he's a good basketball player even though no one chooses him in a pick-up game, to the tragic—the alcoholic who thinks his drinking is not a big deal.

Self-deception is a big deal. It keeps us from understanding reality and if we can't discern what is real and unreal, what is truth and lie, then we're left wandering around in the dark without finding the path that can lead us to the light.

Self-deception begins in the heart. Jeremiah 17:9 says, *"The human heart is the most deceitful of all things, and desperately wicked. Who really knows how bad it is?"* In our fallen state (Genesis 3), the heart is filled with pride (the worst kind of self-deception) and misperceptions. When a person confesses this to God and stops relying on themselves for truth (repentance), then surrendering to The Truth (Jesus), God's Spirit enters and begins reorienting that person to God's realities. The word of God is indispensable to this process. It keeps orienting us toward the truth.

Self-deception also occurs because we listen to the wrong voices. Some of those voices are the people we choose to receive counsel from. As an example, many a marriage has been destroyed because a spouse listened to bad counsel from friends or workmates. Some of those voices are from lying spirits; envoys of Satan who whisper lies meant to draw us away from God and His truths.

Keeping our noses in the word is critical. But that's not all we need to do—we need to obey the word as well: *"But don't just listen to God's word. You must do what it says. Otherwise, you are only fooling yourselves"* (James 1:22). So many believers listen to or read God's word, but then don't apply it to their lives and obey it—talk about self-deception!

Get your nose into the word and get serious about rooting out the self-deception in your heart and mind.

God, draw me to Your word. Keep me from lying to myself and lead me to the path of true, purposeful living. Amen

DISORDERED DESIRES
October 31

*"Give me an eagerness for Your laws rather than a love for money!
Turn my eyes from worthless things, and give me life through Your word."*
Psalm 119:36-37

Augustine explained that sin is, "disordered love", i.e., loving something more than we should. We tend to focus on sin as something that we do, but after careful thought, we can see that our behaviors spring out of the desires of our hearts. He then gave us a proper, biblical order for our love: to love God first and foremost, then others, and finally ourselves.

This idea of disordered desires is helpful to understand why the world is in such a mess. It began in Eden when our parents desired a fruit basket over pleasing God—and we've been doing it ever since. Since then, the human soul has been tragically marred, scrambling our desires in a way that, without Jesus, we cannot get them in proper order.

The psalmist hits this reality. He confesses he has a penchant for focusing on worthless things, hoping to find life and meaning in them. He recognizes his disordered desires. That's the first step in getting things straight: to comprehend that our desires are terribly disordered. He then calls on God to give, grant an eagerness, a desire, a love for His word. Desires for God and the things of God are not natural to us; we don't possess them innately—God grants them through His indwelling Spirit.

Our affections drift toward things that are so temporal: money, popularity, power, comfort, etc.

Only God's word can reorient us to what is truly valuable. It gives us what we are really, down-deep searching for—LIFE! Jesus concurred with the psalmist, *"The Spirit alone gives eternal life. Human effort accomplishes nothing. And the very words I have spoken to you are spirit and life"* (John 6:63).

God's Spirit takes God's word and reorders the disordered desires in God's people. What is disordered in your life right now? What do you find yourself loving more than God and His word? Take a moment and list the top three, confess them as sin, and call out to God to do what only He can do: change you from the inside out through the power of His word and Spirit.

God, give me an eagerness for Your word rather than a love for _____. Turn my eyes from worthless things and give me life through Your word. Amen!

REVERENCE
November 1

"Establish Your word to Your servant, as that which produces reverence for You."
Psalm 119:38 (NASB)

Any parent knows the insanity of trying to get their small child to obey. Even if they do what you say at the moment, chances are they'll forget it or ignore it in just a few seconds. It's maddening, right? The reason they do this: your word is not established in their mind and heart. Something has to happen to get them to remember and obey. Good parents figure out ways for their children to respect them and what they say.

The psalmist is calling on his Heavenly Father to establish His Word in his life. The Hebrew word for *establish* is *quwm*, meaning to *rise up, get up, endure, stay fixed*. He knows that getting the word established in his heart and mind will produce reverence for God. How so? The Word reveals who God is: His essence and character. Let's examine a few of His 20+ attributes.

1. Eternal. No beginning, no end. He created time, so He is outside of time. Before time began, He was. *"Holy, holy, holy is the LORD, who was, who is, and who is to come"* (Revelation 4:8).
2. Love. Not that He is loving, but He is love. *"God is love"* (1 John 4:18). The word *agape* means *unconquerable benevolence*; does not depend on the object of its love for its continuance.
3. Just. The treatment of each person without partiality and also the proper administration of His moral code resulting in punishment or reward. *"For I Yahweh love justice; I hate robbery and injustice"* (Isaiah 61:8).
4. All-Powerful. While He grants limited power to His creation, His power is infinite and never depleted in any way. *"Yahweh does whatever He pleases in heaven and on earth, in the seas and all the depths"* (Psalm 135:6).
5. Holy. The word *'holy'* means *"set apart."* God is different from anything and everything else. No matter how much something in creation may resemble God, it does not make it God. *"Be holy, because I am holy"* (1 Peter 1:14-16).

As God's word gets established in our hearts, we see more clearly who He is and what He's up to. The end result is a reverence for Him and a desire to worship Him.

God, I do want to know more of who You are. I want to see You more clearly that I might worship You more passionately. Amen.

PITIED
November 2

"Remember Your promise to me; it is my only hope."
Psalm 119:49

Have you ever heard the phrase, "My word is my bond"? Apparently, it goes back to the 1500s and was adopted as the motto of the London Stock Exchange in 1801, enabling deals to be struck without immediate documentation or written pledges.

The psalmist is repeating a recurring theme throughout the psalms: God is faithful to what He says; He's the God of His word; His Word is His bond.

This indispensable character trait of God is our only hope. If He is not good for His word, if what He says is not what He does, if we can't count on Him to follow through on His promises, we're not only terribly deceived—we are fools above all other fools. The psalmist knows this and exclaims: "God, if Your word, your promises are not true—I'm doomed!"

It's proper to say that we have faith in the promises of God, but the *'it'* in this verse points not to the promise itself, but to the Promise Maker. The psalmist is counting on God remembering and following through on the promise. The promise is no good unless the one making it is willing and able to deliver.

Counting on the Promise Maker and claiming His promises is one of the keys to victorious living. Do you have some of God's promises bound around your heart; promises from Yahweh that are enabling you, encouraging you, strengthening you, reviving you? If not, Google the promises of God and start memorizing these 'protein pills' of spiritual growth.

Counting on the promises of God sets us up for victory if they're true—or pity if they're not. Paul makes this argument about the reality of Christ's resurrection and the promise of our resurrection in Him:

> *For if there is no resurrection of the dead, then Christ has not been raised either. And if Christ has not been raised, then your faith is useless and you are still guilty of your sins. In that case, all who have died believing in Christ are lost! And if our hope in Christ is only for this life, we are more to be pitied than anyone in the world* (1 Corinthians 15:13, 17-19).

I'm not counting on being pitied—I'm counting on God's faithfulness!!

God, I believe You, I trust You. You and Your faithfulness are my only hope! Amen

SONGS
November 3

"Your statutes are the theme of my song during my earthly life."
Psalm 119:54 (CSB)

Have you ever been singing in church and someone around you is singing real loud, but they can't sing on key? Maybe YOU are the one who can't carry a tune! It doesn't really make any difference, does it? The Scripture says, "Make a joyful noise," right? No matter that our voices may be more noise than melody!! It's all about the heart.

More important than the song we sing with our voices is the song we sing with our lives. Our psalmist touches on this reality when he identifies the theme of his life song is the Word of God. The Hebrew word used for statutes is *'hōq'* referring to the enduring significance of God's Word; like something carved into a rock for permanence.

The permanent, rock-solid theme of the entire Bible is the glory of God. In the Old Testament, the Hebrew word for *glory* is *'kabod,'* carrying with it the idea of importance, honor, fame, weightiness, and majesty. In the New Testament, the Greek word is *doxa*, meaning fame, splendor, brightness, and beauty. The glory of God is all about the beauty and fame of God.

Everything we do as believers is to enhance His fame: *"So whether you eat or drink, or whatever you do, do it all for the glory of God"* (1 Corinthians 10:31). To use the analogy, our life song is to be on key; a melodious tune that highlights the glory, the fame of our God.

When things are going well in our lives, we are to sing/live on key. There's not a good thing in our lives that is not from God: *"Whatever is good and perfect is a gift coming down to us from God our Father"* (James 1:17; NLT). If there is good in our lives, God is the source and the reason, not us.

But of course, life is not always easy. In those times too, we must sing His praises. Paul and Silas were in prison, yet they were singing praises to God (Acts 16:25). In good times and in bad, our lives are to sing the tune that our God is amazing, kind, generous, gracious, and faithful.

What song are you singing? Is your life song in tune and on key? If so, you'll be blessed!

God, enable me to sing a song with my life that shines the light on Your fame. I pray that the tune is in key with Yours. Amen

PORTIONS
November 4

"The Lord is my portion."
Psalm 119:57

My dad, born in 1923, grew up in a family of six children during the Great Depression. I remember stories of them making a meal for all eight family members out of one chicken or a couple of squirrels they shot. Needless to say, when they sat down for dinner, their portion was pretty small. Recently I've noticed that the portions at restaurants have increased significantly. I ordered lasagna the other evening and I couldn't eat the whole thing—there was way more than I needed.

The Christians I've known tend to land in one of those two groups: God is a part of their lives, but not everything, or, He is everything to them. The first group would call themselves Christ-followers, but in reality, they're not following Him that close. They're not in the word every day, not trying to memorize His word, don't keep a prayer journal, not committed to a small group, not serving, casual about church attendance, etc. Their portion is pretty small. The second group of Christ-followers is all-in: Bible study is daily for them, they've learned to pray effectively, they're burdened for their lost friends, committed to their church, etc. Their portion is huge.

The first group is always hungry—for more of the wrong stuff! They keep tasting what the world offers to satisfy, but money, popularity, power, and comfort don't satisfy the hunger. Just look at the celebrities in our country that have all that but are empty, messed up, and suicidal. The second group is always hungry—for more of God! When a need arises, they access their portion by getting in the word and through prayer.

The psalmist makes the point that no less than Yahweh Himself was his portion. Whatever he needed, God was enough. If he was afraid and needed courage, God was enough. If he was lonely and needed companionship, God was enough. If He felt empty and needed fulfillment, God was enough. If he was depressed and needed joy, God was enough. Yahweh was his portion.

Is God enough for you? Or are you still looking to the stuff of this world to meet the deficit in your life? By the way, if the infinite God is not enough for you, no thing and no one, will be.

God, be my portion. Direct my heart to You. I want You to be more than enough. When I start looking to the things of this world as my portion, remind me I have much more in You. Amen

ANCHORED
November 5

"Evil people try to drag me into sin, but I am firmly anchored to Your instructions"
Psalm 119:61 (CSB)

Boats and ships come equipped with anchors. The smallest may weigh 10 pounds while the heaviest on record is 75 tons! The purpose is the same regardless of size: to keep the boat or ship from drifting into the rocks because of currents and/or winds.

The psalmist uses this imagery to talk about God's word. He's saying that when the people around him and circumstances are trying to influence him away from Yahweh, God's word anchors him and keeps him from drifting that way.

There are so many influences in our lives that try to blow us into the rocks. The most powerful is Satan himself. He is constantly tempting us to make decisions that are harmful and get in the way of our relationship with God. Then there are those around us who don't have a biblical worldview. God is not central in their lives which means their lives are wrapped around them and theirs. It is a worldly outlook and value system.

The Apostle John warns us against such a view: *"Do not love this world nor the things it offers you, for when you love the world, you do not have the love of the Father in you. For the world offers only a craving for physical pleasure, a craving for everything we see, and pride in our achievements and possessions. These are not from the Father, but are from this world. And this world is fading away, along with everything that people crave. But anyone who does what pleases God will live forever"* (1 John 2:15-17).

Paul talked about this as well: *"Then we will no longer be immature like children. We won't be tossed and blown about by every wind of new teaching. We will not be influenced when people try to trick us with lies so clever they sound like the truth"* (Ephesians 4:14).

The only way to avoid being blown into false doctrine or a worldly perspective and lifestyle (and crashing on the rocks) is to get grounded, anchored in the word of God. His instructions, His directions are time-tested guides to keep us moored to the truth; living a life for His glory and our good. Get anchored in God's word—and be blessed!

God, thank You for Your instructions. By Your grace, I will anchor my life to Your word so that I don't get blown off course by the philosophies of this world. Amen.

EASY WAY OR HARD WAY?
November 6

"Before I was afflicted I went astray, but now I keep Your word.
You are good, and You do what is good; teach me Your statutes."
Psalm 119:67-68 (CSB)

My dad was a gentle, good-humored man who loved to tell corny jokes and get down on the floor and play with my brother and me in whatever game we were playing. But when he gave us a command, we could choose the easy way or the hard way. The hard way was painful. He loved us too much to let us get away with our disobedience.

The psalmist asserts Yahweh is good. His goodness means that He is benevolent toward all people (it rains on the just and unjust), has offered salvation to all people, and is particularly benevolent and loving to those who receive His invitation. God's goodness means that He is not evil, abhors all evil, and because He is also just, will either discipline or judge evil depending on who He's dealing with.

Discipline and judgment are two different actions. Judgment has to do with penalty and punishment. Fortunately, true believers will avoid the judgment of God because they're trusting in Jesus' blood and death on the cross to atone and pay for, their wickedness. Those who are outside of Christ will have no way to avoid the just wrath of a holy God.

For believers, our loving and good Father has given us commands and guidance to live a life that is pleasing to Him and will be pleasurable and fulfilling to us. When we wander, He loves us too much to let us stray too far, so He will discipline us.

This discipline can come to us in many forms: our secrets becoming public; the consequences of our sin being experienced in a painful way; etc. One of the worst afflictions is administered by the Holy Spirit who grieves when we sin and creates an unrest in our souls as a result.

I have experienced the discipline of the Lord countless times. By His grace, it has prompted me to turn to and delve into His word more ardently and passionately so that I will be strengthened not to repeat my sin. Given the choice between the easy way or the hard way—I want the easy way.

God, thank You for Your afflictions in my life! Use them to draw me closer to You. I definitely want to avoid the hard way when possible. Amen

THE SCHOOL OF AFFLICTION
November 7

"It was good for me to be afflicted so that I could learn Your statutes."
Psalm 119:71

If you were to ask me the times I grew the most spiritually, became less worldly, hungered for God and His word more passionately, sensed God's presence more closely—it would be the times I went through great affliction. Those times have been the great turning points of my life.

Martin Luther said, "I never knew the meaning of God's word until I came into affliction. I have always found it one of my best schoolmasters." Why is that? How is it that afflictions can be such a positive influence in our lives? Because trials and suffering remind us how weak and frail we are, and how much we need God to get through them.

In those seasons of suffering, I become desperate to dive into God's word to find perspective, promises, and hope. In the process, though my faith is being tested, I come out of the affliction stronger in my faith and more resilient in adversity. The psalmist uses the word *decrees* (hōq): which is the enduring significance of God's Word; like something carved into a rock for permanence. When the sands are shifting under my feet; when everything around me and in me feels upside down and chaotic, God's word is constant; it's the rock Jesus talked about:

"Anyone who listens to My teaching and follows it is wise, like a person who builds a house on solid rock. Though the rain comes in torrents and the floodwaters rise and the winds beat against that house, it won't collapse because it is built on bedrock" (Matthew 7:24-25).

God uses pain and suffering to our advantage—IF we cooperate with Him in the process. To be certain, many people become bitter, hardened, cynical as a result of their affliction. When affliction arrives at your door, how do you respond? Do you find it as an opportunity to draw close to God through His word, or to push Him away in disgust and disappointment? Do you want to leverage the moment or discard the opportunity?

Don't waste the pain!

God, I know I am to be thankful in all matters, so thank You for what You're wanting to do in my life through this trial. Grant me the grace to cooperate with You. Amen

CLOUDED VISION
November 8

"Your hands made me and formed me;
give me understanding so that I can learn Your commands."
Psalm 119:73

Elon Musk is the CEO and product architect of Tesla. To say he is the brains behind the fastest growing plug-in battery-electric car line in the world is an understatement.

When I was a kid, at the bottom of every cereal box was a toy of some kind. One was a small plastic submarine with a tiny compartment to put baking soda in. A hole in the lid of the compartment let water in slowly to interact with the soda, creating movement.

What if I had an audience with Elon Musk and told him that he had it all wrong; that he needed to switch to baking soda as his mode of propulsion? That would be laughable if not so pitiful.

The maker of something knows the purpose of that thing, how it is to behave, and what its value is. Since Yahweh is the Maker and Creator of humanity, His knowledge of our purpose and being is unapproachable by puny little human brains. Yet, we have the arrogance to walk into His office and tell Him that we know better our purpose, value, and how to live. It's no laughing matter.

The psalmist reaches back to Genesis: *"Then God said, "Let us make man in Our image, according to Our likeness"* (1:26; CSB). *"Then the Lord God formed the man out of the dust from the ground and breathed the breath of life into his nostrils"* (2:7; CSB). It's interesting that in the creation account, the verb *'create'* (*bara*) is used for light, water, stars, etc. But in 1:26 it is *'make'* (*asah*), and in 2:7 it is *'formed'* (*yatsar*). The imagery seems to be that the rest of creation God spoke into existence. But with humans, He got down on His knees in the dirt to form and fashion us—very personal; very intimate.

God made you. He knows what's best for you. His instruction manual is the Bible. If you want to know what your purpose is, what makes you tick, how to squeeze the best out of this life, then gain that understanding by learning His word. If not, you'll have a clouded vision of what your purpose is and why you're here—and you'll miss out on so, so much.

God, You made me and shaped me. Enable me to understand Your purpose for my life and cooperate with You in shaping me more like Jesus. Amen

COMFORT
November 9

"O may Your lovingkindness comfort me, according to Your word to Your servant."
Psalm 119:76 (NASB)

When one of our children was hurt or felt afraid, they would come running to us looking for words of comfort. When they didn't do well in sports or school or relationships, they would come to us for words of comfort—that's what parents do!

Because Yahweh is our Heavenly Father, He too welcomes us to come to Him for words of comfort. In fact, *'word'* in the text is the Hebrew word, *imrāh*, which is divine speech; what God Himself has spoken. The psalmist is saying that he knows that God loves him, and that love is poured out and spoken to him through God's written word. We can see the love of God on display in the word of God. The result is a comforted heart.

I can't tell you how many times I've been troubled, hurt, slandered, struggling, failing, fearful—and I've gone to the Scripture and found great comfort in the word of God. When you are experiencing those emotions, who or what do you turn to for comfort? Some folks turn to alcohol or other drugs, others turn to shopping and purchasing, some turn to activity and busyness, some turn to entertainment or amusement. These may comfort for a while, but not for long.

God's word is so powerful and adequate for the task. Here's a sampling:

Fear: *"Don't be afraid, for I am with you. Don't be discouraged, for I am your God. I will strengthen you and help you. I will hold you up with my victorious right hand."*
Isaiah 41:10

Uncertainty: *"Trust in the Lord with all your heart; do not depend on your own understanding. Seek His will in all you do, and He will show you which path to take."*
Proverbs 3:5-6

Grief: *"And now, dear brothers and sisters, we want you to know what will happen to the believers who have died so you will not grieve like people who have no hope."*
1 Thessalonians 4:13

Failure: *"The godly may trip seven times, but they will get up again."*
Proverbs 24:16

Rejection: *"You are coming to Christ, who is the living cornerstone of God's temple. He was rejected by people, but He was chosen by God for great honor."*
1 Peter 2:4

Now, those are words of comfort!!

God, thank You that Your Scripture is FULL of words of comfort. I love You! Amen

MERCY, MERCY, MERCY
November 10

"Surround me with Your tender mercies so I may live, for Your instructions are my delight."
Psalm 119:77

In 1966, Joe Zawinul wrote a song for Julian "Cannonball" Adderley and his jazz group called Mercy, Mercy, Mercy, rising to #2 on the soul chart. It was later covered by The Buckinghams in 1967, who took it to #5 on the pop chart. To be fair, the song is about a girlfriend who "knocks me off my feet—have mercy on me!" It ends with the vocalist saying, "Mercy, Mercy, Mercy!" But when I think about the love and mercy Yahweh has shown me in my life, I sometimes want to shout, "Mercy, Mercy, Mercy!" It's the idea of "O my—this is—You are—Incredible!!"

Mercy in the Old Testament is the idea of compassion; that God has compassion on us in times of suffering. Someone has said that compassion is your pain in my heart. True compassion enters into the pain and suffering of the other. That's our compassionate God. He is not aloof; not detached—the incarnation is the ultimate proof of that. He took our pain and agony on Himself and suffered it for our sake.

In this psalm, the writer asks that God would surround him with His tender mercies. Then he points to a great source of those mercies: the word of God. On the pages of Scripture, we see God displaying mercy on behalf of His people again and again. He saw Adam and Eve awkward and ashamed, then provided clothing and protection for them. When Elijah was running from Jezebel, He provided food and water. When Jesus saw the multitudes, *"He had compassion on them because they were confused and helpless, like sheep without a shepherd"* (Matthew 9:36), healing the sick and lame.

Pain and suffering can come unexpectantly and for unknown reasons. What is certain is that God's Spirit, author of the Scripture, has and continues to dole out volumes of mercy and compassion when we seek Him and His word. This is why the psalmist says, *"Your instructions are my delight."*

Dig deep into the word. Make it a discipline that sustains you every morning, every day, every trial, every joy. As you delight in His word, you will more and more exclaim: "Mercy, Mercy, Mercy!"

God, by Your Holy Spirit, draw me to Your word that I might delight more and more in it—and You! Amen

THE SHAME CULTURE
November 11

"Bring disgrace upon the arrogant people who lied about me;
meanwhile, I will concentrate on Your commandments.
May I be blameless in keeping Your decrees; then I will never be ashamed."
Psalm 119:78, 80

We live in a unique time for many, many reasons. One of the trademarks recently is to shame people or groups of people whose thoughts, opinions, speech, or behavior are considered reprehensible. In some countries, the shame culture elicits harsh responses like throwing acid on one's face or even killing them because they shamed their family. In our country, it's not about family, it's about ideology. If you say something that is outside their worldview, the result is a relentless assault with sometimes ruinous consequences; your opinion is not just wrong—you are a bad person.

It's interesting that the psalmist mentions being shamed by someone who was slandering him. He calls on Yahweh to settle the score. His main concern is that he does not speak or act in a shameful way. He recognizes that it's God's business to take care of the arrogant; his business is to get focused on God's word.

Concentrating on the word of God keeps us from shame. It does so by guiding us to live in a way that brings honor, not shame. For instance, it shows us the value and the way to moral purity so that we can avoid being ashamed because of adultery or pornography. It shows us the way to self-control so that we can avoid the shame of being drunk or otherwise out of control. It shows us how to love our spouse so that we can avoid the shame of destroying our marriage out of self-centeredness. This applies to all conduct and all relationships.

Should Christians experience shame? Shame is a popular topic in Scripture, used 227 times! Many times it applies to the believer who has wandered from God's way, as our psalmist who wants to avoid experiencing shame.

Truth is, I have a history of shameful acts. Fortunately, I have a Savior who died for my sin and shame. Hallelujah! I have repented of those shameful acts and when they surface in my consciousness, I gladly recall that the blood of Jesus has paid to exonerate me with His precious blood!

Jesus, I praise You for Your rescue from a shameful life, Your blood that covers my shameful acts, and Your word that guides me on the honorable path. Amen

SETTLED

November 12

"Lord, Your word is forever; it is firmly fixed in heaven."
Psalm 119:89 (CSB)

I was taught in school that Christopher Columbus was the first European to land in the Americas in 1492. Now it's widely held that Leif Erickson, the Viking explorer, landed in Newfoundland, Canada in about 1,000 A.D. Turns out neither actually set foot in the land called the United States of America. What will they say next? The moon is not made of cream cheese? Sheesh!

There is not much in our world that is settled. Long-time-held laws of the land can be overturned by the Supreme Court. Centuries-old mores can disintegrate in a generation or two.

But there is one thing that is settled and will never change or be proven untrue: the word of God!

Isaiah put it succinctly, *"The grass withers and the flowers fade, but the word of our God stands forever."* (40:8) The stuff of this world is in constant flux, but God's word is not. It's settled.

The wise believer approaches the Bible with the conviction that it is true. The reader is not the final authority on truth; God and His word is. God is the real author of the Scripture: *"All Scripture is inspired by God and is useful to teach us what is true and to make us realize what is wrong in our lives. It corrects us when we are wrong and teaches us to do what is right"* (2 Timothy 3:16). *'Inspired'* means *"God-breathed."* The words we read on the page are fixed and held firmly in heaven.

There is a worldly notion that the Bible is antiquated, conflicting, and untrustworthy. But when a skeptic takes the challenge seriously to study it from beginning to end, including the disciplines of textual, philological, literary, and form criticism—the word of God withstands the scrutiny. Here's a good statement of faith taken from the Baptist Faith and Message (2000):

> The Holy Bible was written by men divinely inspired and is God's revelation of Himself to man. It is a perfect treasure of divine instruction. It has God for its author, salvation for its end, and truth, without any mixture of error, for its matter.

God's word is settled in heaven. I pray it is settled in your heart.

Yahweh, enable me to build my life on Your settled, unchanging word. Everything else may change or be uncertain, but not You and Your word. Amen!

THE ULTIMATE WEAPON
November 13

"The wicked hope to destroy me, but I contemplate Your decrees."
Psalm 119:95

A study of war and weapons (military science) is an interesting education. Early in human development, our ancestors used sticks and clubs. With the advent of the iron age, body armor, shields, swords, and spears emerged. Each time a weapon was developed by a people, their enemy would develop some kind of counter weapon. This has gone on for ages. Examples in modern times would include the development of tanks and anti-tank artillery, missiles and anti-ballistic missiles, etc.

The psalmist recognized this concept with regard to his enemies and the word of God. They were intent on destroying him, but his counter weapon was the word. *'Decrees'* (ēdāh) means to give direction in order to make decisions, right from wrong, based on the nature and truth of God. The implication of this verse is that his enemies were not out to physically destroy him necessarily, but to lead him down a path that would be ruinous. The way he could avoid that was to contemplate and meditate on God's word in order to stay on the right path.

At the onset of Jesus' earthly ministry, the Spirit led him into the wilderness for 40 days of prayer and fasting (Matthew 4). At the end of that period, Satan came to Him to tempt Him; to lure Him down a path that would be ruinous. Three times Satan tempted Jesus with hedonism (*"make these stones to bread"*), egoism (*"go ahead and jump—You won't die"*), and materialism (*I'll give you the kingdoms"*). If Jesus had succumbed to even one of those, we would still be dead in our sin.

But three times, Jesus countered with the word of God. All three times He responded, *"But the Scriptures say . . ."* (Notice the present, not past tense—God's word is alive! Hebrews 4:12). Finally, Satan left Him alone.

In a very real way, Satan learned an important lesson that day: when it comes to the word of God, he has no counter weapon. His strategy, then, is to create doubt in the word or tempt you to ignore it!

Don't fall for Satan's temptations. Know God's word and meditate on it. When the Enemy comes, quote Scripture and watch its power lead you to victory!!

God, thank You for this powerful counter weapon. I will learn to use it effectively so that I can live victoriously. Amen

LIGHT
November 14

"Your word is a lamp to guide my feet and a light for my path."
Psalm 119:105

In 1990, Amy Grant and Michael W. Smith wrote a song that is still one of my favorites. Google it and listen to the original recording of "Thy Word" by Amy. If you listen to the words carefully, you'll notice that God's word and God's presence are synonymous.

The psalmist uses the Hebrew word *dabar* when he refers to God's *word*: divine speech; what God Himself has spoken. It emphasizes the vocalization of God's speech (e.g., "Let there be light"). So here we have the idea that God speaks to us in a manner that gives us direction for the moment; as it were, from the very lips of God.

What an amazing reality: God speaks to us as we trod this path called life! It's easy to get turned around, confused, discouraged, fearful, and unsure. But when we're well-acquainted with His word, He speaks to us to give us what we need to stay on the right path.

To the ancients, a lamp was absolutely necessary to avoid stumbling, falling, injury, or worse. If you've ever been trying to make your way in considerable darkness, a light is absolutely necessary. Darkness hides reality; it conceals the truth. Light dispels the darkness and reveals reality and truth.

This is a major characteristic of the word of God. He is not trying to hide the right path from us, He wants us to discover and follow it: the path to genuine life, fulfilling life, victorious life, eternal life. However, we live in a dark world—and it seems to be getting darker. The only way is to listen for His directions as we study His word.

When I was a kid, I recall my dad wanting to go fishing at night. To get from our camping spot to the boat, we had to walk across some uneven rocks that led by some cliffs at the edge of the lake. As I trailed him, he would shine the flashlight just in front of me, speaking directions like, "Step here. Be careful here. Jump here."

That's the nature of God's word. He has spoken to us through His word and He uses it in our lives to speak truth, reality, direction, courage, hope, and perspective.

God, I desire to walk the right path. Use Your word in my life to be my light and direct me. Thank You! Amen

MILK
November 15

"Your word is completely pure, and Your servant loves it."
Psalm 119:140 (CSB)

I've mentioned we have 10 grandchildren: five girls and five boys!! They are all as good looking and brilliant as their Nana!

According to WebMD and about every other reputable site I visited, breastfeeding is the preferred method of getting the nutrition a baby needs. The American Academy of Pediatrics recommends breastfeeding exclusively for the first six months. Some mothers have difficulty with this method and need to utilize baby formula as a healthy alternative, but au naturel is still the preferred way.

The Apostle Peter captures this process and this verse in Psalms to talk about spiritual growth:

> *"Like newborn infants, desire the pure milk of the word, so that by it you may grow up into your salvation, if you have tasted that the Lord is good"* (1 Peter 2:2; CSB).

Two words are used in both verses: word and pure, which are two distinguishing characteristics. First, it is God's word. Not Moses', not Abraham's, not David's, not Paul's or Peter's—it is God's word, *imrāh, divine speech.* God is the author of Scripture. Second, it is pure; i.e., there are no contaminants or impurities in it. Don't get caught up in the heresy that the Bible is flawed because those who wrote it were flawed. As 2 Peter 1:21-22 claims, men were moved by the Holy Spirit to utter or eventually write the Scriptures: 40 authors over 1500 years with one message—Yahweh is a glorious, redemptive, loving God.

When my new grandson gets a little older, his parents will begin to feed him some of that nasty baby food—and generally, he'll like it. It's natural for someone to feed a small child. But if he were 25 years old and still needing someone to feed him, something would be terribly wrong.

That's the spiritual condition of most Christians I know: they have been believers for years but still need someone to feed them. They depend on their pastor to feed them deep truths (meat) instead of being able to feed themselves. That's tragic.

Are you mature enough to feed yourself? Fall in love with God's word: read it, study it, memorize it, meditate on it—and sense the power of a changed life!

God, grant me the desire to feed on Your word and I pledge to respond to it. Amen

DESPISED

"I am insignificant and despised, but I don't forget your commandments."
Psalm 119:141

For much of my adult life I've tried to live the Christ-life and tell others about Him. In college, there were those who despised my unwillingness to participate in their revelry—to the point they gathered as a group and threatened to beat me. In the oil business, I found real resentment from my colleagues when I shared the gospel. A friend of mine was attacked and beaten to the point of brain injury just for sharing the gospel. I've had scores of students (Jr., Sr. High, & college) tell me stories of being taunted and berated by their classmates, teachers, and professors for their faith. A dear friend who is presently in his last year at West Point has experienced criticism, pressure, even threats from his superiors for being bold about his faith.

There is the notion some have in our country that Christians are not persecuted. The Oxford Dictionary defines it as: "hostility and ill-treatment, especially because of race or political or religious beliefs." To be sure, it does not begin to compare to what is going on in other parts of the world—yet. But it is no less real to those who are despised for their faith. It appears that those who deny persecution here in America do not live in a way that elicits ill-treatment. The writer of Hebrews called us to be *'strangers and exiles'* (11:13). We are to live in a way that makes us strange, even despised.

The psalmist and Martin Luther held that in common. In 1521, Luther stood before the Holy Roman Emperor, Charles V, at the Diet of Worms, defending himself from the charge of heresy. If he lost, he would have been burned at the stake. His heresy? Sola Scriptura: The Bible alone is our source for faith and practice. His last word of defense was:

> *Unless I am convicted by Scripture and plain reason—I do not accept the authority of popes and councils, for they have contradicted each other—my conscience is captive to the Word of God. I cannot and I will not recant anything, for to go against conscience is neither right nor safe. Here I stand, I cannot do otherwise. God help me. Amen*

He then sat down. Miraculously, he avoided execution—though he was greatly despised throughout the Empire the rest of his life.

The Greats for Christ always are.

God, I pray that I will seek Your approval more than anyone else's. Grant me boldness to live and proclaim Your word. May it be so!

THE KEY
November 17

"I rise early, before the sun is up; I cry out for help and put my hope in Your words."
Psalm 119:147

Our garage is in the back of the house, so we never come through the front door. Recently I went looking for a front door key on a key chain with 5-6 keys. None of them worked! I finally found the right key to accomplish what I needed.

I've had zillions of people ask me through the years: "What's the key to establishing a consistent time with Jesus?" My answer is always the same: "Begin your day with God in prayer and reading His word." The psalmist reinforces that in the verse for today: he's learned to get up early, lay his concerns before the Lord, and get in the word.

Jesus did the same: "*Before daybreak the next morning, Jesus got up and went out to an isolated place to pray*" (Mark 1:35). I've always figured if the Son of God needed to get up early and seek God, guess I'd better too! I remember when I was struggling with establishing this discipline decades ago—I was NOT a morning person, so I kept trying to get with Him later in the day. I struggled with consistency. About then I heard someone say, "When does an orchestra tune its instruments, before or after the concert?"

To build consistency, set your alarm 15 minutes before you normally do. Fix a cup of java, head to a quiet place, pick up your Bible, read a psalm, and then pray. Your body and the Adversary will fight you on this so it may take months before it is engrained. But neuroscience validates that new habits can be established after repetition. That's the way God wired our brains.

The most powerful praying is praying God's word. Praying Scripture is the most hope-filled praying we can do. It reminds us of who God is and what He's up to. In that Quiet Time, we can listen for His voice and receive whatever is needed for the day.

If you're not seeking Him early and daily, decide NOW that tomorrow you will. Mature believers I know spend 45-60 minutes a morning. They started with 5-10 minutes and grew to where they are today. You can do it too!

God, get me up early to seek Your face, Your will, and Your word. Amen

REVIVAL
November 18

"Revive me according to Your word."
Psalm 119:154 (NASB)

I grew up in a faith tradition that held nightly church meetings for one or two weeks every year called revivals. We invited our friends who may have been far from God, hoping to see them come to Christ. We prayed and sang and repented. An 'evangelist' would come into town who was particularly gifted to preach the word effectively. It was a wonderful time.

Through the millennia, revival has broken out when there has been a renewed interest in the Bible. King Josiah in the Old Testament stressed the reading of God's word and revival broke out. In the New Testament, the preaching of God's word was the first action the minutes-old Church took: 3,000 people were saved, and revival broke out all through the Mediterranean world. In the 14th-16th centuries, Wycliffe, Huss, and Luther focused on the word and revival broke out across Europe. In the 18th century, revival broke out in America (1st Great Awakening) from the powerful preaching of Scripture. Many other examples exist—point is, when one person, group, or nation focuses attention on the word of God, revival occurs.

The word *'revive'* shows up all through the Psalms, most dramatically in the 119th Psalm. It's basic meaning is 'to restore life; restore health.' Our world is so chaotic and so challenging that it sucks the life out of us every day, doesn't it? We are broken, those around us are broken, the world is broken. That brokenness depletes healthy attitudes, actions, feelings, relationships, etc. From my view, it's getting increasingly difficult to live to the fullest.

That's why I MUST spend time in God's word every day. It's the only way I keep my sanity!! When I'm discouraged, disheartened, or depressed, I turn to the word and the recovery process begins again.

If life is extracting vibrancy from you, draining the life out of you, get into the word. Nothing renews and revives like it.

God, thank You for Your word. Speak words of life to me. Enable me to see it as a lifeline for constant renewal. Amen

PEACE
November 19

"Those who love Your instructions have great peace."
Psalm 119:165 (NLT)

In the movie, *Miss Congeniality*, Sandra Bullock plays an FBI agent undercover as a contestant in a beauty pageant. When the finalists were interviewed, the host asked, "What is the one most important thing our society needs?" All said, "World peace." When Bullock was asked, she replied, "That would be harsher punishment for parole violators, Stan." The audience was stunned—and silent. Realizing the awkwardness, she added, "And world peace!"—to thunderous applause.

Everyone wants world peace, peace in their relationships, peace in their souls. Truth is, no genuine peace comes just because we want it. As the psalmist says, genuine peace comes when there is an alignment with the Word of God.

There will never be world peace (until Jesus comes) because the world is fallen and out of alignment with God's word. In our relationships, there is no peace until those in the relationship align with biblical values. That's not to say non-believers can't have harmonious relationships, but if they are, it is because they align with God's values: selfless love, trusted fidelity, willing sacrifice, humble confession, and gracious forgiveness.

And then there is the human soul. We're a country that can't find rest for our souls: 50 million Americans take medication to help them deal with despair, anxiety, and depression. We think we'll find peace in activity, so we hyperactivate which makes it worse. We think it will come with achievement or accumulation, but that doesn't work either. The world's way is not the way of inner peace.

Biblical peace is the idea of rest, of shalom, of wholeness. Only in Christ does that begin to occur in the soul. Only when believers align with the Word does that rest, shalom, flood the human soul.

Jesus talked about this: *"Come to Me, all of you who are weary and carry heavy burdens, and I will give you rest. Take My yoke upon you . . . and you will find rest for your soul"* (Matthew 11:28-29; NLT). Seeking Jesus, the Living Word, through His written word, is the pathway to soul-peace. Instead of running about trying to find peace in every bush or furrow, let His Word act as a yoke to direct you down the path to inner rest, wholeness—and be blessed!

Jesus, show me in Your word what's not in alignment in my life that I might find peace. Amen

UPWARD STEPS
November 20
The Songs of Ascent

Psalms 120-134 are called '*Songs of Ascent*,' with each one containing the superscription, "A Song of Ascent." Most likely they were used by Jewish pilgrims as they ascended to Jerusalem for Passover (one of the three required feasts for all Jewish men) and as they ascended to the Temple via the southern steps.

A study of the first verses of each psalm can give us interesting insight as to what they were thinking, saying, and singing as they ascended to the "City of God" and into, as they believed, the presence of God.

1st Song

Yahweh Hears Our Prayers

"I took my troubles to the Lord; I cried out to Him, and He answered my prayer."
Psalm 120:1

In this psalm, the writer is describing treacherous adversaries who will stop at nothing to slander and malign him. The picture the psalm gives us is of a person who is wounded by the lies and deceit, praying and counting on God to hear his prayer. The situation seems impossible, *"I search for peace; but when I speak of peace, they want war!"* (v.7), but he will keep on praying.

Persistent praying is very productive.

Jesus encouraged us to keep praying, even when we grow tired: *"One day Jesus told his disciples a story to show that they should always pray and never give up"* (Luke 18:1). We are commanded to pray: *"Call to me and I will answer you and tell you great and incomprehensible things you do not know"* (Jeremiah 33:3; CSB). '*Call*' is not a suggestion, it is a summons, a decree. Prayer should be our first response to our needs, but unfortunately, sometimes it is the last resort.

The psalmist knows where to take his troubles. He cried out to Yahweh and experienced the handiwork of God. As we travel through life, it's important to remember that conversation with God is the best and most important thing we can do—particularly when the road gets rough.

Yahweh, thank You for wanting me to pray, waiting for me to pray, and answering me when I pray. Teach me to be a more effective pray-er. Amen

UPWARD STEPS

November 21
The Songs of Ascent
2nd Song, Part 1

I'm Lookin'

"I look up to the mountains— does my help come from there?
My help comes from the Lord, who made heaven and earth!
Psalm 121:1-2

To the ancients, mountains were more than just scenery: they were reminders of God's awesome power. The travelers would normally avoid routes that would take them up high hills or mountains (no electric bicycles!), but instead would follow roads or paths that were lower and more level. Looking up to the mountains as they walked by, their gaze would naturally continue beyond the peaks to the sky and space beyond.

Ancient Hebrews reckoned there were three heavens. The first heaven was where the birds flew, i.e., the sky. The second heaven was where the celestials were placed, i.e., outer space. The third heaven was the abode of God. Depending on the context, when you read the word 'heaven' in the Old Testament, it could refer to one of these three. Here it probably refers to the first and/or second usage.

The psalmist is aware of his weaknesses and knows he needs help—divine help. Ultimately, the strength and guidance to carry on come only from Yahweh. We cannot save ourselves and we cannot fix ourselves. Human pride insists: "I can handle this. I can do this. I can fix this." I, I, I. The truth is we are absolutely helpless to fix our brokenness. That's why Jesus came and conquered.

We travel a path that is difficult and challenging; a path that has steep climbs that cannot be made with human effort and ingenuity.

This psalm is a reminder that along life's journey, God tirelessly and relentlessly guards His faithful ones. Life can be hard, painful, even tragic, but the believer can count on the awesome power, love, and mercy of God along the way: *"The Lord keeps watch over you as you come and go, both now and forever"* (v.8). His eyes are on you—always.

Yahweh, thank You for being ever-present and all-powerful to watch over me. Amen

UPWARD STEPS
November 22
The Songs of Ascent
2nd Song, Part 2

He's Lookin'

"The Lord keeps watch over you as you come and go, both now and forever."
Psalm 121:8

When we lived in Mississippi, our house was one block from the grade school. We could see the entrance from our kitchen table window. When Ben (firstborn child) headed to his very first day of school, we watched from that window as he walked along the sidewalk to the school, notebook and lunch pail in hand. He walked up the steps, opened the door, turned and waved at the window, knowing we would be watching. Then he disappeared inside. I get choked up all over again thinking about that seminal day in our lives. When school was out that day, we were stationed at the window watching as he came home.

The Psalmist touches on this dynamic as the pilgrims are making their way to Jerusalem for one of the three required feasts. God's watch care was not limited to those wayfarers; it is a reality for every person who is a child of God. Remember, not everyone is a child of God—only those who have placed their trust in Jesus alone to save them. This is a stated truth throughout the New Testament, most clearly in John 1:12, *"But to all who believed Him and accepted Him, He gave the right to become children of God."*

For we who are His children, there are few realizations more comforting than the fact that God watches over us in our coming and our going. The word *shamar (keep, preserve, watch)* is used to emphasize God's attentiveness toward us. Like Sue and me at the window, our heavenly Father watches over us throughout the days AND the nights; through the wonderful times AND the awful times.

Did you notice that the psalm begins with the admonition to keep our eyes on God? It finishes with the affirmation that God keeps His eyes on us.

This psalm is a reminder that along life's journey, God tirelessly and relentlessly guards His faithful ones. Life can be hard, painful, even tragic, but the believer can count on the awesome power, love, and mercy of God along the way: *"The Lord keeps watch over you as you come and go, both now and forever."* (v.8) His eyes are on you—always.

Yahweh, thank You for being ever-present and all-powerful to watch over me. It gives me great comfort. Amen

UPWARD STEPS
November 23
The Songs of Ascent
3rd Song

The City of The Great King

"I was glad when they said to me, "Let us go to the house of the Lord."
And now here we are, standing inside your gates, O Jerusalem."
Psalm 122:1-2

Finally, the pilgrims would have arrived at Jerusalem, also known as the City of David, because David captured it, made it the capital, and moved the Ark of the Covenant there.

Jerusalem is one of the oldest cities in the world. In all likelihood, the first reference of it in Scripture is when Abraham, returning from war, stopped by Salem where the high priest Melchizedek gave him wine and bread. In gratitude to Yahweh, Abraham gave him one-tenth of the spoils of war (Genesis 14:20). Salem, a derivative of *'shalom,'* means *"peace; to be made complete or whole."* Jeru, from *'yara,'* means *"established or revered."* So together Jerusalem is the place established and revered for the purpose of completion and wholeness. This certainly speaks of the temple, where sacrifices were made on behalf of the people to make them whole before Yahweh.

But the greater significance is found in the cross, where on a hill He created, just outside the city walls of Jerusalem, Jesus was sacrificed to make whole any and all who place their trust in Him alone: *"For this is how God loved the world: He gave his one and only Son, so that everyone who believes in Him will not perish but have eternal life"* (John 3:16).

Jesus called Jerusalem, *"The city of the Great King"* (Matthew 5:35), quoting Psalm 48:2. The King refers not to any earthly king, but to the King of Kings. Jerusalem will be the place that Jesus will return to and reign from in the age to come. John writes of the New Jerusalem (heaven) where all believers will reside. One day, our journey will be complete, and we'll be able to say, *"Here we are, standing inside your gates, O Jerusalem!"*

Jesus, thank You for coming to Jerusalem and dying on the cross to make me whole! I love You for it. I can't wait to be in the New Jerusalem with You! Amen

UPWARD STEPS

November 24
The Songs of Ascent
4th Song, Part 1

Fine Dining

"I lift my eyes to you, O God, enthroned in heaven. We keep looking to the Lord our God for His mercy, just as servants keep their eyes on their master, as a slave girl watches her mistress for the slightest signal."

Psalm 123:1-2

Occasionally, Sue and I will go with friends to a really nice restaurant. Fine dining is quite an experience. It's not just about the food, it's also about the service. The servers are trained to look for half-empty glasses to fill, vacant bread baskets to replenish, and even respond to the facial expressions of the guests. When I eat, they are constantly using one of those little scrapers to clean up the crumbs and mess around my plate!

The psalmist touches on this dynamic of a servant who keeps his/her eyes on the eyes of the master for the slightest signal. God is the master; we are the servants. We have other facets of our relationship with Jesus: brother/sister, friend, co-hear, etc.

But there is one New Testament word that identifies a different aspect to our relationship with Jesus: *doulos*. It's translated bondservant in most English translations, but in actuality, it refers to a certain class of slave (see Acts 4:29, Romans 1:1, Philippians 1:1, 2 Peter 1:1, et al—all use *doulas*/slave). This slave-master relationship is sometimes underrepresented when talking about the Christ-life. But Romans 10:9 says, *"If you confess Jesus as Lord…"*. Philippians 2:11 says *"every knee will bow, every tongue will confess that Jesus is Lord."* The word I, *kurios*, means owner or master. *Kurios* and *doulos* go together. A *doulos* never really attained freedom but was transferred from one master to another. For those in Christ, that means that we WERE slaves to sin, but now WE ARE slaves to Christ. He went into the slave market and redeemed us; bought us. He didn't pay with dollars or bitcoin. He paid with His own precious blood.

As slaves to Jesus, we marvel that He would call us friends, Kingdom citizens, even co-heirs to reign with Him. But He is still our Master. We look to Him for guidance, for instruction, and as in this psalm, mercy. Look intently for even the slightest signal of His love for you. It should be enough for the slave.

Jesus, thank you for purchasing me with Your blood. You are my master and I purpose to please You in all things. I am needy. I look to You for mercy. Amen

UPWARD STEPS

Contempt Fatigue

"Have mercy on us, Lord, have mercy, for we have had our fill of contempt.
We have had more than our fill of the scoffing of the proud and the contempt of the arrogant."
Psalm 123:3-4

If you try to live for Jesus in this world, contempt will come your way more than you'd like. Many in our own country here in the U.S.A. consider Jesus' followers to be fanatics who are out of touch with contemporary culture.

Actually, it's just the opposite. The teachings of Jesus and about Jesus are as relevant today as any time in history. They speak to all the issues of contemporary culture. They point the way to a life that is full of joy, peace, fulfillment, and all the abundance God offers. Those who follow Him know how to sort through the milieu of conflicting and confusing values and circumstances our world has to offer.

It's not complicated. Respect every human being (preborn or born) because they are created in the image of God. Treat others in the same way you want to be treated. Don't take the high position of judging other people—let God do that. Forgive others who have injured you because God has forgiven you much more. Meet, fall in love with, and stay married to someone of the opposite gender because marriage is the beautiful metaphor of Christ and His church. Yet such simple teachings invoke contempt and even rage from others.

The psalmist is calling on God to grant mercy because he and others have had to put up with the scoffing and contempt of unbelievers. He's fed up with it; he can't take it anymore! He knows the only way to endure it is by God's touch in his heart.

He's begging for mercy and looking intently to God for it: *"We keep looking to the Lord our God for his mercy, just as servants keep their eyes on their master, as a slave girl watches her mistress for the slightest signal"* (v.2). If you've ever been to a nice restaurant where the wait staff is very attentive, you've noticed they keep the water glasses full, the crumbs removed, and watch for your eye to attend to whatever needs you have. The psalmist is doing the same: looking intently to God to supply his need of mercy in trying times. We can too.

God, grant me mercy to not only put up with the contempt but love scoffers as You do. You are my supply of mercy. Amen

UPWARD STEPS
November 26
The Songs of Ascent
5th Song, Part 1

Rescue Me!

"What if the Lord had not been on our side when people attacked us?"

Psalm 124:2

One of the certainties of life is adversity. We can't avoid it—until finally we go to be with Jesus. Until then, we are not left defenseless against adversity. God allows it and uses it for His own good purposes.

As the pilgrims made their way to Jerusalem and eventually into the temple complex, one of the songs they would sing was written by King David. He recounts graphically how the enemies of Israel were stronger and mightier than Israel was: *"They would have swallowed us alive; the raging waters would have swept over us"* (vv.3, 5). There was no hope for them if it hadn't been for Yahweh.

One of the benefits of growing in the Lord is that we can look back over our life with Him and see how He has delivered us again and again from what could have destroyed us. The mature believer can take heart in present adversities because he/she has experienced God's strength and deliverance over and over again.

What or who is attacking you at this stage in your life? Know three truths are present in every challenge:

First, our enemies are not flesh and blood. You may think your enemy is your spouse, friend, workmate, or neighbor. Not true. The real adversary is Satan himself: *"Your adversary, the devil, prowls about like a roaring lion seeking whom he may devour"* (1 Peter 5:18). *"For we are not fighting against flesh-and-blood enemies, but against evil rulers and authorities of the unseen world"* (Ephesians 6:12).

Second, we will be defeated if we meet the challenge in our own strength. We're admonished to take up spiritual weapons for this spiritual warfare: *"Therefore, put on every piece of God's armor so you will be able to resist the enemy in the time of evil. Then after the battle you will still be standing firm"* (Ephesians 6:13).

Third, the path to victory is the path of faith in Yahweh. Our enemy is stronger than us, but *"if God is for us, who can be against us?"* (Romans 8:31). Take up the armor and trust in Him. The battle belongs to the Lord! It may not be easy. You may get overwhelmed at times—but you can stand with the bloodied and bruised victors of Christ.

God, I confess, if it weren't for You, I'd live in defeat. Fight for me today!! I want to live in victory. Amen

UPWARD STEPS

Trump

"Our help is from the Lord, who made heaven and earth."

Psalm 124:8

If you're a bridge or spade player, you understand the concept of playing a trump card. The suit that is the trump suit outranks the other three suits. In the game of spades, the deuce of spades outranks even the aces of hearts, diamonds, and clubs. It wins the trick, no contest. The weakest in the trump suit is more powerful than the strongest in the other suits.

The Psalmist has been proclaiming that if God had not been for Israel, they would have been overcome and defeated many times by the Philistines and other enemies: they would have been swallowed up like an earthquake (v.3), drowned like in a flood (v.4 &5), torn apart as like a wild lion (v.6), and ensnared like a bird in a trap (v.7).

The Psalmist employed these images to describe the perilous and weak position and strength of Israel. As he says in vv.1-2, *"What if the Lord had not been on our side? Let all Israel repeat: What if the Lord had not been on our side when people attacked us?"* It's a question that begs an answer. The answer is: "Well, we were weak, overwhelmed, swallowed up, surrounded, trapped, and doomed. But—we had a trump card!"

Yahweh is the ultimate trump card: *"Our help is from the Lord, who made heaven and earth."(v.8).* Maybe we sense some confidence here, as the player who holds the high trump; maybe a little defiance that is reminiscent of young David when he goes up against Goliath: *"You come to me with sword, spear, and javelin, but I come to you in the name of the Lord of Heaven's Armies—the God of the armies of Israel, whom you have defied."* (1 Samuel 17:45)

When we are weak, overwhelmed, swallowed up, surrounded, and a sense of doom and gloom hangs over us, remember this: what comes against us doesn't even been to compare to the God of the universe; this God made heaven and earth, for crying out loud! Stick your chin out, and puff your chest up: you have THE Trump Card! He outranks all things, all persons, and all powers that come against you. Let your faith be encouraged and built up by that truth.

God, I enable me to walk with boldness, confidence, and faith that YOU are in control and all-powerful. You are the maker of heaven and earth. I worship You. Amen.

UPWARD STEPS

Stability

*"Those who trust in the Lord are as secure as Mount Zion;
they will not be defeated but will endure forever."*

Psalm 125:1

The movie, *The Man Who Went Up a Hill but Came Down a Mountain*, is a delightful tale, supposedly true, about two English cartographers who discovered a Welch mountain was a few feet short of the required 1000 feet and reclassified it as a hill. In the end, they helped the townspeople carry dirt up to the top to make it a mountain again.

In ancient times, geological structures that rose significantly above a plain or a valley were called mountains. Biblical writers had never seen Mt. Everest or Pikes Peak—or they'd probably have used the word 'hill' instead. Regardless, hills and mountains are known for their prominence, permanence, and stability.

As these pilgrims ascended to Jerusalem, the topography would have stood out. Many would have traveled along the side of the Mediterranean Sea. Others along the Jordan River, which is 1000' below sea level as it flows adjacent to Jerusalem. Jerusalem's elevation is about 2,500' above sea level—that's a 3,500' climb! It sits on or in between a series of mountains, including Mt. Scopus, Mt. Moriah, and Mt. Zion.

The psalmist declares that those who trust in Yahweh are as secure and stable as Mt. Zion. Jesus talked about this in Matthew 7:24-27, contrasting the life built on His word with the life built on sand:

> *Anyone who listens to my teaching and follows it is wise, like a person who builds a house on solid rock. Though the rain comes in torrents and the floodwaters rise and the winds beat against that house, it won't collapse because it is built on bedrock. But anyone who hears my teaching and doesn't obey it is foolish, like a person who builds a house on sand. When the rains and floods come and the winds beat against that house, it will collapse with a mighty crash.*

The psalmist adds something more to his metaphor: *"Just as the mountains surround Jerusalem, so the Lord surrounds His people, both now and forever"* (v.2). We may be stable because we build our lives on His word, but our stability doesn't compare to His. He is unmovable and unshakable—and He surrounds us with His love and strength. In unstable times, hold to these truths and you WILL endure!

God, I do hold to You and Your word. Surround me with Your love and power. Amen

UPWARD STEPS

November 29
The Songs of Ascent
7th Song, Part 1

Restoration

"Yes, the Lord has done amazing things for us!
What joy! Restore our fortunes, Lord, as streams renew the desert."
Psalm 126:3-4

If you ever are blessed to visit Israel, one of the interesting aspects of the topography is that there are dry river and stream beds all through the country called wadis. A wadi remains dry most of the time unless there is rain that feeds it. Interestingly, the water that fills them comes from somewhere else. What I mean is that when it rains in the higher elevations, the water runs into these wadi beds and tumbles down to the lower, dryer elevations. Streams in the desert!

The Psalmist calls for God to restore what had been lost. In all likelihood, this Psalm was written after Israel's return from captivity. They were exiled to Babylon and when Persia conquered Babylon, they ended up there. From there, under Ezra and Nehemiah, they were repatriated to their homeland after 70 years, just as God had promised.

But of course, their indifference and disobedience led Yahweh to exile them in the first place. Upon their return, they were strangers in their own land and totally disenfranchised. Yet through God's mercy and providence, their land was once again restored to them.

God is the God of restoration! He restores what we have lost, given up, or has been taken from us. As in the case of salvation, restoration is a work of grace. It's not a self-improvement project. Just as the lower, dryer regions need rain from somewhere else to make its way to them, so we need refreshment from the only Source that can restore the soul.

The Holy Spirit in you is the resident Source of Restoration. Time in His word and time with Him in prayer starts the precipitation. Faith and trust in Him, even when it seems dry and hopeless, turn sprinkles into cloud bursts. Broken relationships begin to mend. Broken hearts begin to heal. Shame and guilt turn to shouts of gratitude. Mayhem and confusion turn into calm and confidence. This is our God. The restoring God. He will do amazing things for you and, like the pilgrims and Psalmist, you will sing songs of praise and gratitude.

God, thank You for being so good, so restorative, so merciful. I need You—and I need You to restore what I've lost. Hear my cry! Amen

UPWARD STEPS

November 30
The Songs of Ascent
7th Song, Part 2

From Sorrow to Singing

"Those who plant in tears will harvest with shouts of joy.
They weep as they go to plant their seed, but they sing as they return with the harvest."

Psalm 126:5-6

It is a phenomenon of the human experience that the greater the sacrifice, the greater the reward; the greater the test, the more satisfying the success; the greater the setback, the sweeter the victory.

Because of Israel's disobedience to God, He raised up Babylon to sack Jerusalem and cart off thousands to Babylonia. Seventy years later, God returned them to the Promise Land in ecstatic celebration: *"We were filled with laughter, and we sang for joy. And the other nations said, 'What amazing things the Lord has done for them'"* (v.2).

But there was still work to be done: the restoration of the temple and the city walls that had been torn down. The psalmist appeals for Yahweh's redemptive nature to come front and center: *"Restore our fortunes, Lord, as streams renew the desert"* (v.4).

Think for a moment of the more painful events of your life: loss of a loved one, termination of a job, the failure of a marriage, the estrangement from a family member. These may have occurred because of your poor choices or the poor choices of others. Regardless, the pain of such trauma was/is likely to generate many tears. Yet Yahweh has a miraculous way of turning those tears into joy when we call on His redemptive nature to restore what has been lost. The key is to look to Him for the restoration—not relationships, not substances, not our own effort, not accumulation. Only He can bring streams of refreshment to our dry and parched souls.

In the great trials and tests of life, know that God is looking for us to trust Him and be faithful. Sow those seeds of faith, even in the midst of tears, and know that God will someday turn your weeping into gladness with a harvest of joyful singing.

Yahweh, I know You make gardens out of ashes and singing out of sorrow. I trust that You will turn my dirges of sorrow into songs of joy. I look to You. Amen

UPWARD STEPS
December 1
The Songs of Ascent
8th Song, Part 1

Frustration

"Unless the Lord builds a house, the work of the builders is wasted.
Unless the Lord protects a city, guarding it with sentries will do no good."
Psalm 127:1

If you've never been to Edinburgh, Scotland, you've missed a great city. Sitting high on a hill at the edge of the North Sea, its castle is the most often besieged castle in Europe. The city motto, written in Latin and taken from Psalm 127:1, appears on its crest and is affixed to all official documents: "Nisi Dominus Frusta," meaning, "Without the Lord, Frustration."

It's interesting that this psalm is ascribed to Solomon. You'll recall that he also penned the Book of Ecclesiastes. The primary theme of that book is, "Vanity, Vanity—all is vanity. Life is futile. Accomplishments are meaningless." Solomon had built ports, gardens, fortresses, palaces, a standing army—even the Temple. Yet as he looked back over his accomplishments and achievements, he was left with a deep sense of futility because he had drifted away from Yahweh in those pursuits, and his heart was far away from God.

In time, everything he built succumbed to decay and ruin. Without the Lord, Frustration.

God created human beings with the desire to create, to build, to achieve. But because of the Fall, this ambition is warped and broken. We create, we build, we achieve—but in the end, if what we accomplish is not done in cooperation with Yahweh, it doesn't last and it doesn't fulfill. Without the Lord, Frustration!

This principle doesn't just apply to our nicely decorated houses, our well-manicured yards, our carefully chosen and developed careers—it applies to EVERYTHING in this life: hobbies, savings and retirement accounts, travel, even family.

Accomplishment without Jesus is empty. Without the Lord, Frustration.

What parts of your life are not under the Lordship of Christ? What are you pursuing that He is not integrally a part of? Repent of your independence and ask Him to fill your ambition with a joy to do it all for Him. Accomplishment without Jesus is empty. Without the Lord, Frustration.

God, I recognize the principle that without You, life is not the same. I do want to invest my money and moments in concert with Your will and desire. Work that out in me, I pray. Amen

UPWARD STEPS

Legacy

"Unless the Lord builds a house, the work of the builders is wasted.
Unless the Lord protects a city, guarding it with sentries will do no good."

Psalm 127:1

The American family is in trouble. There are so many reasons we couldn't possibly discuss them all in a page or even an entire book. But let's identify just a few of the more significant ones.

One reason is the urbanization and isolation of nuclear families. For most of human history, families grew up around aunts, uncles, grandparents, cousins, etc. Divorce was rare. Family traditions and family experiences were interwoven into each life, creating a strong sense of family. Extended family members could step in and help, encourage, and even chide if necessary. Chasing jobs and careers in other regions/cities broke down the extended family and the result has not been pretty.

That touches on another reason: material accumulation/career accomplishment. Until the late 20th century, there was always a parent or grandparent at home with the children, particularly in the formative years. With the migration away from extended family and the pursuit of affluence, the advent of both parents working left the children to be raised by hirelings (daycare, schools, etc.). Those best suited to raise their child abandoned the task to others.

Most importantly, the number of parents who actually, factually walk with Jesus and seek His pleasure above all else is shrinking drastically. Survey after survey indicates that, even amongst evangelicals, very few families make church a serious priority, read the Bible, have devotions, or pray together.

This psalm is primarily about the family unit: we can't build a home and establish a lasting legacy without the Lord. If you are a parent, your highest responsibility is NOT to provide Xboxes, TVs, vacations, or college. God made you a parent to disciple and nurture your child(ren) in the ways and teachings of Jesus—and do it in a way that they pass it to their children and so on. That's a legacy that will last—for eternity. All others will burn away.

No matter the age of your children, begin to pray together. Read the Bible with or to them. Tell of the marvelous things He has done and is doing in your life. Build a legacy. There is nothing more rewarding—or important.

God, I desire to be a better parent/grandparent. Show me how. Grant me courage and follow-through. I don't have a more important purpose in life. Amen

338

UPWARD STEPS
December 3
The Songs of Ascent
8th Song, Part 3

Family

"Children are a gift from the Lord; they are a reward from Him."
Psalm 127:3

Miranda Lambert wrote and sang, "The House that Built Me." In the song she goes back to the house she was raised in, bringing back fond memories of her childhood—and the love her parents showed her in that house.

The house that built me. Yesterday v.1 reminded us that *"Unless the Lord builds a house, the work of the builders is wasted."* We build the house, but then the house builds us. Of course, it's not really the house that does the building, it's the parents. We need to make sure that God is integrally involved in the construction.

The Scripture says that children are a reward! That's good to remember when they're keeping you up all night as a newborn, or the diaper doesn't hold the poop, or they get obstinate as a two-year old, or flat out rebellious as a teenager. It's good to remember when they say mean things or act in ways that cause you to think: "I must be the worst parent in the world!"

Children are a gift, a blessing directly from Yahweh! They will cause untold anxiety, fear, frustration, anger, guilt, hurt, and suffering. What other gift does that? NOTHING!

But despite all the pain and hardship they bring, there is real potential for joy and satisfaction like no other endeavor in life. That's why we need to keep remembering that each child is a gift from God. How so? In parenting, we get glimpses of our Heavenly Father's love for us. In parenting, we get hints of how our rebellion against Him must hurt and disappoint. In parenting, we are drawn closer to Him for strength, patience, and wisdom. And sometimes, when a child makes horrible choices and even disowns us, we gain some understanding of God's broken heart for people who are lost and far away from Him.

Don't try to parent one millisecond without the Lord. It's difficult enough with Him; impossible without Him. No matter the relationship with your child(ren), pause and thank God for the blessing and gift He gave you.

God, I do thank You for each of my children. What a gift. May I be the parent who creates fond memories for them—and me. Build (or rebuild) my home, for your honor and my their good. Amen

UPWARD STEPS
December 4
The Songs of Ascent
8th Song, Part 4

Reward

"Children born to a young man are like arrows in a warrior's hands. How joyful is the man whose quiver is full of them! He will not be put to shame when he confronts his accusers at the city gates."

Psalm 127:4-5

Nature or Nurture? There has been an ongoing debate about the essence of human beings: is who we are a matter of genetics and heredity or is it determined by environmental variables like childhood experiences, how we were raised, social interactions, etc.?

While the debate rages on amongst secularists, the Bible is clear that it's not an either/or—it's both. On the genetic/hereditary side, we know that a child's nature is impacted by the fall of humanity (Genesis 3). Every aware parent can testify that a 2-year-old possesses a sin nature: demanding, selfish, defiant, etc. Proverbs 22:6 says, *"Start a youth out on his way; even when he grows old he will not depart from it"* (CSB). The Hebrew word for *'his way'* means *'to bend the bow.'* Each child has a particular bend. One is quiet, one is loud. One is more compliant, one more defiant. The variables are endless. It is important as a parent to fully grasp and understand your child's bend. Each child will be different, so you'll want to parent them with their differences, their bend, in mind. To do otherwise is harmful and even dangerous.

But the Scripture focuses mostly on nurture. Despite the bend of each child, the Scripture teaches over and over that the parent needs to nurture each child toward godliness: *"Listen, O Israel! The Lord is our God, the Lord alone. And you must love the Lord your God with all your heart, all your soul, and all your strength. And you must commit yourselves wholeheartedly to these commands that I am giving you today. Repeat them again and again to your children. Talk about them when you are at home and when you are on the road, when you are going to bed and when you are getting up"* (Deuteronomy 6:4-7), *"Listen, my son, to your father's instruction, and don't reject your mother's teaching"* (Proverbs 1:8), *"Bring them (children) up with the discipline and instruction that comes from the Lord"* (Ephesians 6:4).

The psalmist understands this. He likens children to arrows: they must be carefully shaped and guided with skill and care. He finishes this great psalm with the declaration that a house well-built and children well-raised brings the great reward of joy, along with deep satisfaction and honor, not shame, as others observe the character and behavior of their children.

God, give me wisdom, understanding, and favor as I endeavor to raise my children in the discipline and instruction from You. Enable me to fashion them and guide them as You would have me. Amen

UPWARD STEPS

December 5
The Songs of Ascent
9th Song, Part 1

Fear + Follow = Favor

"How joyful are those who fear the Lord— all who follow His ways!"
Psalm 128:1

The Amazing Race is a reality show that pits 11 teams against each other to see who can get to the destination first. The prize for first place is $1,000,000, second place $25,000, and 3rd $10,000. To be able to win some money, you have to find the clues, properly decipher them, and successfully make your way to the next clue. There are multiple clues that take the contestants to multiple countries and eventually the finish line.

Our psalmist is emphasizing that if we fear Him and follow His ways, there are multiple rewards and benefits. Remember, fearing God in this context means to respect and revere Him—after all, He is the Ruler of the Universe!

When we examine the benefits of fearing and following, we find that they are much more valuable than mere money. First, we will be able to see fruitfulness in our work and, more importantly, find joy in our work: *"You will surely eat what your hands have worked for. You will be happy, and it will go well for you"* (v.2; CSB). So many of us trudge through our day at a job that brings little fulfillment or satisfaction. Beyond that, what we earn doesn't seem to take care of all our needs. Not so the person who fears and follows God.

Second, your family life will flourish: *"Your wife will be like a fruitful vine within your house, your children, like young olive trees around your table"* (v.3; CSB). This is an obvious reference to childbearing, but it applies even to marriages who struggle to get pregnant. The big, abiding principle is that when we fear and follow, our marriages will be incredibly fruitful with love. And if God grants us children, they will want to follow our example when they grow up and experience a flourishing family as well.

Finally, there is the overall sense of God's favor in our lives when we fear and follow: *"In this very way the man who fears the Lord will be blessed"* (v.4; CSB).

The clues and directions for a blessed life in God's Word. Find and follow them. Do it because God deserves our respect and obedience. Then begin to experience His wonderful favor.

God, teach me Your ways so that I may please You and experience Your favor. I want every part of my life to flourish! Amen

UPWARD STEPS

December 6
The Songs of Ascent
9th Song, Part 2

Fruity Hands

"You will enjoy the fruit of your labor. How joyful and prosperous you will be!"
Psalm 128:2

Most caring Americans see the need for a social safety net for those who are temporarily displaced or out of work. The Bible speaks to this often through the Torah (Moses' Five Books of the Law), the history books like Ruth (each owner of a field was to leave the edge of it unharvested for the immigrants or needy), the prophets (who condemned the privileged for splurging on themselves and neglecting the poor and disenfranchised), and the teachings of Jesus who was constantly speaking to and ministering to the poor and neglected.

But the Bible is clear: human beings were created to work, to build, to improve, to cultivate. When God created humanity, He charged them with purpose and fulfillment: *"Then God blessed them and said, 'Be fruitful and multiply. Fill the earth and govern it. Reign over the fish in the sea, the birds in the sky, and all the animals that scurry along the ground'"* (Genesis 1:28). This was before the fall of humanity in Chapter 3 of Genesis. That means work is not a result of the fall but a privilege and purpose of humanity. Work is a gift from God. However, as a result of the fall, it is clear that pain was added to the pleasure of work (Genesis 3:17-19).

As the nation of Israel emerged (after it escaped from Egypt), penalties were levied for those who refused to work. In Proverbs we see the worst possible penalty: to be called a *'sluggard.'* A sluggard is someone who won't take responsibility for their life. Their lives are marked by inactivity, moving from one job to the other, laziness, relying on someone else to provide, etc. Proverbs in particular heaps condemnation and ridicule on the sluggard: *"Despite their desires, the lazy will come to ruin, for their hands refuse to work"* (Proverbs 21:25).

In the New Testament, Jesus told parables condemning the lazy and sluggardly (Matthew 25:26-30). The Apostle Paul was typically blunt: *"If anyone isn't willing to work, he should not eat"* (2 Thessalonians 3:10).

The Bible doesn't indicate what work we should do, whether it is as a doctor, admin, entrepreneur, parent, construction worker, etc. It only requires that we: *"Work willingly at whatever you do, as though you were working for the Lord rather than for people"* (Colossians 3:23). The psalmist makes the point: a good work ethic brings a fruitful, joy-filled life.

God, thank you for the job you've given me. By Your grace, I purpose to do it whole-heartedly, as if I'm working for You. Actually—I am. Amen

UPWARD STEPS

December 7
The Songs of Ascent
9th Song, Part 3

Fruity Marriage

"Your wife will be like a fruitful grapevine, flourishing within your home."
Psalm 128:3

I often say that Sue and I have been happily married for 38 years. Problem is, we've been married for over 40 years!! We've certainly had our troubles and challenges. We've said and done things that have deeply hurt each other. There have been many times, particularly earlier in our marriage, where we weren't sure if or how we could go on.

The reason that we did go on and push through is that we both knew that our marriage was NOT as much about our happiness as it was/is about honoring the Lord. This psalm begins with how good life is when we fear the Lord. As I mentioned a couple of days ago, fearing God in this context means to respect and revere Him. As Christ-followers, we knew our marriage had a greater purpose than our happiness.

Most marriages today start out with the notion of falling in love and living happily ever after. Let me just say, that's a dirty lie! Marriage is hard work—VERY hard work. Most importantly though, we need to understand that marriage is not a human construct. It was created and established by God, so He alone gets to decide what it is-- and what its purpose is.

Marriage is THE central human relationship to help us understand the gospel--plain and simple. Marriage helps us understand the gospel and the gospel helps us understand marriage. The gospel (*good news*) of course is that even though human beings are hopelessly warped and broken, God did not abandon us in our brokenness but came after us. That's gospel. When Sue loves me even when I am unlovable, that's gospel. When I work through my frustration with her and choose to serve her, that's gospel.

Despite our flaws, we love each other—just as Jesus loves us.

Instructing the church on marriage, Paul mentions in Ephesians 5:32, "*This mystery is profound, but I am talking about Christ and the church.*" Tim Keller, in his book, "The Meaning of Marriage," is the best book I know on the topic. He makes the point that marriage is so painful and so wonderful. It's a mystery. The gospel is so painful and so wonderful. It's a mystery.

The secret to a great marriage? Do for your spouse what God did for you through Jesus. If you do, as the psalmist said, your marriage will flourish.

Sue and I have persevered through all the trials and pain because we understand that marriage is not about our happiness; it's about honoring and living for Jesus.

God, forgive me for the selfishness and pride that is tainting my marriage. Enable me to love my spouse as You have loved me. Amen

UPWARD STEPS
December 8
The Songs of Ascent
10th Song

Survival

"The Lord is righteous; He has cut the ropes of the wicked."
Psalm 129:4

Rob Konrad and Lauren Conner have one thing in common: both found themselves knocked out of a boat miles offshore—and survived. Konrad ended up in the water for 16 hours and swam an estimated 27 miles until he touched the Florida shore. Conner was thrown off a boat in the middle of Chesapeake Bay, swimming all night until she reached the shore. Both of them knew the key to survival was what Dory said in the movie, *Finding Nemo*: "Just keep swimming!"

Life is tough. There are times when the waves just roll us over and knock us down—or out of the boat. We find ourselves in a sea of failure, doubt, confusion, fear, and even panic. There's no grandiose expectation of success—only gritty, gutsy survival.

The 129th Psalm is a psalm about how God had delivered Israel in times past and how they needed to trust Him to do the same in the future. For the present, they were primarily interested in survival. That's why the psalmist exclaims: *"He has cut the ropes of the wicked."*

In other words, "I was about to go under, but Yahweh has delivered me—and I will survive."

The Apostle Paul penned the same message in 2 Corinthians 4:8-9, *"We are pressed on every side by troubles, but we are not crushed. We are perplexed, but not driven to despair. We are hunted down, but never abandoned by God. We get knocked down, but we are not destroyed."*

Sometimes survival is all we can achieve. The key is putting one foot in front of the other and trusting God to get us through; to not give in to the panic and despair, but to just keep swimming.

Both Konrad and Conner were able to survive because they kept thinking of their families. There was something worth persevering for: i.e., being able to hold their loved ones again.

If you've been knocked out of the boat by some waves of misfortune, don't give up! What are some things that you can focus on as rewards that will keep you going? Call out to Yahweh; He will give you strength. He will enable You to persevere. He will cut the ropes that tie you down.

Yahweh—I need You. I do feel adrift; sometimes even that I'm drowning. Grant me the strength to just keep swimming. Amen

UPWARD STEPS
December 9
The Songs of Ascent
11th Song

Love that Rescues
Psalm 130

"From the depths of despair, O Lord, I call for Your help."
> Are you struggling today? Are you experiencing a measure of discouragement?
> Call on Yahweh.

"Hear my cry, O Lord. Pay attention to my prayer."
> When you pray, don't just offer up a few words. Pray passionately. Pray persistently.
> Cry out to Him.

"Lord, if You kept a record of our sins, who, O Lord, could ever survive?"
> For the unredeemed, there is a record book of sin, amounting to millions of entries over
> a lifetime. For the redeemed, God wipes the entries clean by the blood of Jesus.

"But you offer forgiveness, that we might learn to fear You."
> God's forgiveness should never be taken for granted but should always invoke a healthy
> fear and respect.

"I am counting on the Lord; yes, I am counting on Him. I have put my hope in His word. I long for the Lord more than sentries long for the dawn, yes, more than sentries long for the dawn."
> The wise don't put their trust in themselves or the advice of others; they have learned to
> put their trust in God and what He says. After a night standing duty, sentries can't wait
> until the sun peeps above the horizon. So it is for those who love and trust Yahweh,
> particularly in despair: we want and need Him and His presence to peer into our
> darkened lives.

"O Israel, hope in the Lord; for with the Lord there is unfailing love. His redemption overflows. He Himself will redeem Israel from every kind of sin."
> Just as ancient Israel put their hope in Yahweh, so the New Israel, made up of Christ-
> followers, puts our hope and confidence in God and His incredible, overflowing love and
> redemption. We are great sinners, but Christ is a GREAT SAVIOR!

God, I praise You for your redemptive mercy and love. Thank You for rescuing me. I love You! Amen

UPWARD STEPS
December 10
The Songs of Ascent
12th Song

Childlike Faith

"Lord, my heart is not proud; my eyes are not haughty. I don't concern myself with matters too great or too awesome for me to grasp. Instead, I have calmed and quieted myself, like a weaned child who no longer cries for its mother's milk. Yes, like a weaned child is my soul within me.

O Israel, put your hope in the Lord— now and always."

Psalm 131

Children have a number of advantages over adults. One is their natural tendency to trust. They haven't grown jaded like the rest of us. I remember a time my young daughter crawled up in a tree and couldn't figure out how to get down. I walked up and said, "Go ahead and jump. I'll catch you." She didn't think a moment about it. She leapt out of the tree into my waiting arms.

This psalm is credited to David, although we're not sure of the circumstances. One theory is he wrote it as a response to his wife, Michal, when she accused him of being unsophisticated and undignified as he danced, barely covered, in front of the Ark of the Covenant as they brought it into Jerusalem.

If so, David was insisting that he was not too proud or haughty to worry about what people thought. His motto might have been: "I don't take myself too seriously." The result was that he threw off his royal robe and elite attire so that he could dance happily and unrestrained before the Lord.

As a matter of fact, David was determined to become more like a child, unconcerned with the expectations of others and disinterested in complicated relationships. For him, it was all about Yahweh—the simplicity of loving Him and the ease in trusting Him.

That's good advice for all of us. Stop taking ourselves too seriously. Kick back more. Allow ourselves to get overcome, even giddy, in the presence of God. So what if we look foolish? Children don't worry about stuff like that. They trust that others will accept them for who they are, and trust that Jesus loves them—this they know.

God, enable me to become more childlike in my faith and in my relationship with You. You are worthy of my trust. Amen

UPWARD STEPS

December 11
The Songs of Ascent
13th Song, Part 1

Unfulfilled Expectations

"Lord, remember David and all that he suffered."

Psalm 132:1

If you're normal, your life has been dotted with numerous disappointments, trials, and unfulfilled expectations. It's a part of the human experience.

King David ruled Israel for 40 years from 1010-970 B.C. His reign is known as Israel's 'Golden Age.' Among the stories of this heroic figure are his fight with Goliath, his struggle with Saul, his battles with the Philistines, and his capture of Jerusalem to make it the capital.

But David was far from perfect. He foolishly had at least eight wives (!) who gave him at least 19 sons. This was a recipe for disaster later in life. He slept with another man's wife and then had her husband killed when she got pregnant. He was not a good parent, and his lack of control over his family led to many sorrows, including, rape, murder, and insurrection.

He experienced other hardships: as a young man, he was despised by his family, he was a hunted fugitive for years, his wife despised him, he was betrayed by his own son, and his family was in constant conflict.

Still, David was known as a *"man after God's own heart,"* meaning that He desired a deeply intimate relationship with God. This is evident in many of the psalms he wrote.

His greatest desire was to build a permanent structure (Temple) for the Ark of the Covenant, which had been the symbol of God's presence and power since the days of Moses. Since entering the Promise Land, it had always been housed in a tent called The Tabernacle. Unfortunately, in the end, God wouldn't let him build the Temple.

Even kings can't get everything they want! David was, however, able to find and secure the place for the Temple to be built, collect the funds to build it, and continued doing other things that prepared the way for his son, Solomon, to get the job done after his death.

What do you do when your expectations go unfulfilled? If you believe it is from the Lord, keep finding ways to bring it to pass, trusting that the ultimate fulfillment is on God, not you.

Lord, enable me to deal with my disappointments in a godly way, and to be faithful to what You have laid on my heart. Amen

UPWARD STEPS

December 12
The Songs of Ascent
13th Song, Part 2

Ancestry.com

"The Lord swore an oath to David with a promise he will never take back: 'I will place one of your descendants on your throne. If your descendants obey the terms of my covenant and the laws that I teach them, then your royal line will continue forever and ever.'"

Psalm 132:11-12

It seems that for the last decade or two, there has been an unprecedented interest in discovering family ancestors. For many, there is a deep desire to know where we came from, who we came from, and discover the stories of our family tree.

The importance of lineage is a constant theme throughout the Bible. You'll find lots of entries about who begat who; so-in-so is the son of so-in-so so who is the son of so-in-so. This was definitely a big part of ancient Hebrew custom, but none more important than the line of King David.

Why? This passage tells us why: God made a promise to David (2 Samuel 7:12-16) that through his bloodline, He would raise up someone who would reign on His throne forever, an obvious reference to the Messiah. This line of thinking is found in almost all of the books of the prophets. This passage is quoted by the Apostles in the book of Acts as evidence that Jesus was that man. Gospel writers, Matthew and Luke, went out of their way to trace Jesus back to David—a necessity for anyone claiming to be the Messiah.

From 1000 B.C. until 4 B.C. (approximate date of Jesus' birth), Israel kept looking for this man who would deliver them from the oppression of their enemies and return them to the Golden Age of David. When He did appear, many of them refused to accept Him as the Davidite king because He didn't fit the mold of a political and military figure that they had assumed the Messiah would be.

As a believer, YOU are a part of the lineage of David since you are a son or daughter of God through faith in Jesus. YOU are the new Jew and a part of the new Israel. One day Jesus will return and YOU will reign with Him forever and ever. That's YOUR lineage; that's YOUR future!

God, help me to fully grasp my heritage in You and live each day knowing that I am in the line of David and born of You into Your family. Amen

UPWARD STEPS

December 13
The Songs of Ascent
13th Song, Part 3

What's the Score?

"There I will make a horn grow for David; I have prepared a lamp for My anointed One.
I will clothe His enemies with shame, but the crown He wears will be glorious."

Psalm 132:17-18

In any contest, there is some sort of metric to indicate who is ahead and ultimately decide who won. In scavenger hunts, it's who finishes first, in elections it is votes, and in kids sports, it's the number of participation trophies . . .

At any one time, an assessment of the struggle between good and evil can be pretty discouraging. Biblical values including the need for salvation, Jesus as the only way, integrity, compassion, justice (see Minor Prophets and Sermon on the Mount), sanctity of human life, monogamous (opposite gender) marriage for life, right to worship, right to speak, right to personal conscience, and right to personal determination are being overrun by notions that are more akin to the French Enlightenment (if you want to see the result of that, study the French Revolution) than the Bible.

Beyond that, since at least as early as Genesis 11 and the Tower of Babel, there has been a rise in a coordinated effort, known as 'the world system,' that has increasingly opposed God and His kingdom and His people. It is a mindset and an interlocking set of structures that dominate politics, education, finance, industry, and commerce. Ultimately, Satan is behind it and empowering it.

Looking at the scoreboard right now, it would be easy to conclude that the world system is winning—and probably is. But a note of caution is in order: this game ain't over by a long shot!

Our psalmist quotes Yahweh as saying that He will make the Messiah's power increase (horn is a euphemism for power) and that eventually all His enemies will be put to shame. Bible believers look to the day that Jesus returns and does away with all who opposed Him and His kingdom.

When the final tick of the stadium clock occurs in this age, the worldly notions of this age and all the systems and structures that have been placed on that foundation, will be radiated into nothingness by the infinitely beautiful and powerful light of Christ.

So don't lose heart, pilgrims. Just pray, *"Come quickly, Lord Jesus—Come!"* Amen

UPWARD STEPS

December 14
The Songs of Ascent
14th Song

Row, Row, Row Your Boat

"How wonderful and pleasant it is when brothers live together in harmony!"
Psalm 133:1

Do you know what an octuple scull is? It is the long, slender rowboat that competes in various events that have eight rowers, each with two oars. It cuts across the water, propelled by the power of the arms, legs, and torsos of those in the boat. If one of them gets out of sync or fails to meet the same power as the other seven, bad things begin to happen.

That's a pretty good picture of a group working in harmony with one another. The psalmist makes the point that harmony amongst believers is something that is delightful and satisfying.

The Bible talks a lot about harmony and unity. Jesus identified it as a critical component of the gospel when He prayed in the Garden: *"I pray that they will all be one, just as You and I are one—as You are in Me, Father, and I am in You. And may they be in Us so that the world will believe You sent Me"* (John 17:21). The early church demonstrated that quality: *"All the believers were united in heart and mind"* (Acts 4:32). The Apostle Paul gave additional insight, *"Above all, **put on love**, which is the perfect bond of unity"* (Colossians 3:14).

Unity and harmony are not options for those in Christ. We have a common God, a common faith, a common baptism, a common mission, and a common destiny. **What binds us together is far more than anything that tries to tear us apart.**

Notice the Colossians verse above. The key to unity is not agreeing with each other. That will NEVER happen this side of heaven. The key is love—agape love. Love that looks beyond fault and sees need. Love that reaches out. Love that bridges the gap.

Every octuple scull has a coxswain: someone in the back of the boat who calls the pace and directions out to the rowers. Our coxswain is Jesus. He has called us to live in unity. Not an option. Is there someone you need to reach out to, maybe for the umpteenth time, to try to make amends and restore unity? Do it!

God, give me the love and grace to live in unity with fellow believers; to listen for and follow Your voice. Amen

UPWARD STEPS

December 15
The Songs of Ascent
15th Song

Show Time

*"Oh, praise the Lord, all you servants of the Lord, you who serve at night
in the house of the Lord. Lift your hands toward the sanctuary, and praise the Lord.
May the Lord, who made heaven and earth, bless you from Jerusalem."*

Psalm 134:2-3

The actors in a Broadway play practice as many as eight weeks before opening night. I read where the actors for Hamilton only had four weeks and were a hot mess on opening night! When the curtain went up, it was showtime. In sports, it's the same thing. When the whistle blows, all the prep and talk are over—it's showtime!

This psalm is the last of the Ascent Psalms (120-134). You'll recall that they were sung by the Jewish pilgrims as they ascended to Jerusalem for Passover (one of the three required feasts for all Jewish men) and as they ascended to the Temple via the southern steps. Once in the Temple complex, singing, offering sacrifices, pledging their devotion and worship to Yahweh were all conducted.

But after Passover, after all the emotion and religious fervor, it was time to head back home.

This last Ascent Psalm gives us the sense that the pilgrims might be doing just that: encouraging the Temple priests to carry on faithfully, blessing the Lord exuberantly, calling on the Maker of Heaven and earth to bless them—and heading home; heading back to their normal lives.

These Pilgrims made quite a trek to the Temple. The activities during Passover week must have been meaningful and thrilling. But when it was all said and done and when they returned home, it was time to live out what they had celebrated in Jerusalem.

Contemporary believers need to remember that at the conclusion of each worship service we attend. We need to know that one purpose of worship is to prepare us for reentering our normal lives. I attended a church once that had this over the exits of the worship center: "You're now entering the mission field!" Another well-known and relevant quip was often repeated after student camps or revivals: "It doesn't matter how high you jump—it matters how straight you walk when you come down."

Showtime is not the hour+ worship service on Sunday morning, nor the Bible group we attend. All that is preparation for living out our faith where we live, work, and play. Take this with you each week and when you walk out of the gathering, say to yourself and Yahweh: "It's showtime!"

O God, don't let me leave my passion for You inside the four walls of the church! I want to live the way You called me to live. Amen

WHO'S BOSS?

December 16

"The Lord does whatever pleases Him throughout all heaven and earth,
and on the seas and in their depths."
Psalm 135:6

I remember clearly sitting in the audience in 1973 when a local Christian businessman brought a message at a Vespers service on the Lordship of Christ. It made such an impact I bought the cassette tape (!) and listened to it so many times I still have the whole talk memorized to this day. He began by asking, "Who's Boss? Is Jesus Christ really the Lord of your life?"

Whenever we talk about the Lordship of Christ, we're talking about letting God be God in our lives. Lordship speaks of authority, control, and rule—His sovereignty—over all things. The sovereignty of God combines three other attributes into this one overarching essence: His omniscience (having knowledge of all things at all times), His omnipresence (having presence in all places at all times), and His omnipotence (having power over all things at all times).

The psalmist says it right: *"The Lord does whatever pleases Him throughout all heaven and earth, and on the seas and in their depths."* He does what He wants, when He wants, how He wants. He does what He pleases. He is sovereign.

But there is a wrinkle in this. As the man said that evening: "Of all creation, we have the right of choice. You take the birds of the air; they make their flight of migration every year. You take our planets coursing in their orbits, and you have yet to see one of them go off and do their own thing. You take our physical laws, and the only way we can go into outer space is that they never change; they always stay the same. But we as men and women can decide for ourselves."

Here is a conundrum: how can humans have choice if God is sovereign? To be honest, I've never heard a completely satisfying explanation of this, yet I do believe that both are found in Scripture. The distance between my limited understanding and the full knowledge of God is so vast, I will never be able to grasp it on this side of heaven.

What I can grasp is Jesus' call to follow Him, to make His will my will, His command my joy—and to fully submit to His authority in every area of my life. When He said, *"If anyone wants to follow after Me, let him deny himself, take up his cross daily, and follow Me"* (Luke 9:23; CSB), He was calling us to a life of complete dominance and submission.

The mystery of it all is that despite how all this sounds, my life is more joyful, more peaceful, and more fulfilling when I exercise my choice to do what He pleases, not what pleases me. He's a much better boss than I am!

Who's boss? Is Jesus Christ really the Lord of your life?

Jesus, I do now submit every area of my life to You. Do what pleases You in and through me. Be my Lord, my Boss, my Sovereign. Amen

IMPOTENCE

December 17

"The idols of the nations are merely things of silver and gold, shaped by human hands.
They have mouths but cannot speak, and eyes but cannot see.
They have ears but cannot hear, and mouths but cannot breathe.
And those who make idols are just like them, as are all who trust in them."
Psalm 135:16-18

No, this is not about that!

Our psalmist now moves from a discussion of power and sovereignty (yesterday) to one of impotence and incapacity. The focus shifts from Yahweh, the one true God, to the handmade gods of the pagan nations. This is quite a contrast.

If you've ever been to Mexico or Central America, you've had a good chance to see idols of the ancient Mayans. They sit mute and motionless in a sealed case—a testament to their impotence.

There are many religions that practice idol worship, the largest being Hindus and Buddhists. The great preacher of the 19th century, Charles Spurgeon, told the following story:

> The Rev. John Thomas, a missionary in India, was one day traveling alone through the country, when he saw a great number of people waiting near an idol temple. He went up to them, and as soon as the doors were opened, he walked into the temple. Seeing an idol raised above the people, he walked boldly up to it, held up his hand, and asked for silence. He then put his fingers on its eyes, and said, 'It has eyes, but it cannot see! It has ears, but it cannot hear! It has a nose, but it cannot smell! It has hands, but it cannot handle! It has a mouth, but it cannot speak! Neither is there any breath in it!' Instead of doing injury to him for affronting their god and themselves, the natives were all surprised; and an old Brahmin was so convinced of his folly by what Mr. Thomas said, that he also cried out, 'It has feet, but cannot run away!' The people raised a shout, and being ashamed of their stupidity, they left the temple, and went to their homes.

'Ashamed of their stupidity'—interesting. As Tim Keller pointed out in "Counterfeit Gods," the human heart is an idol-making factory. An idol is anything that we love more than Yahweh. It isn't necessarily bad. In fact, the most dangerous idols are good things; good things that we desire in our hearts more than Yahweh: family, health, income, career, etc. Yahweh warned us to not worship idols (Exodus 20:4-6). That sin will be a chain to us and a burden passed down for generations.

Do you recognize the idols in your life? If so, the 'ashamed of their stupidity' thing ought to kick in and lead you to repentance. I know mine and marvel at my foolish stupidity. God help me!

God, these are the areas of my life that I desire more than You. I'm ashamed of my stupidity. Forgive me and change me!! Amen

THE ENERGIZER GOD
December 18

"Give thanks to the Lord, for He is good. His faithful love endures forever."
Psalm 136:1

You've probably noticed the commercial on television about the Energizer Bunny. When all the other brands of batteries have quit, the Energizer Bunny keeps on pounding his drum and moving around.

Psalm 136 is quite an interesting psalm. It is divided into 26 verses, each one extolling some attribute, act of deliverance, or redemptive work of God in Israel's history, from creation to deliverance from Egypt and the stroll through the Red Sea to the defeat of kings that opposed them on the way to the Promise Land.

At the end of each verse, the psalmist exclaimed: *"Give thanks to the Lord, for He is good. His faithful love endures forever."* Each of the 26 verses identifies something to give thanks for and attaches that to God's goodness and faithful love; His covenant love (*chesed*). Over and over again he proclaims that this Energizer God never runs out of power to do good on behalf of His people; the reservoir of His faithful love never runs dry.

To be sure, the lives of the Hebrews were not easy. Most of this psalm is recounting the travails of being enslaved in Egypt, the power of Pharoah, the fear and panic of the Egyptian army behind and the Red Sea in front, the conflict with two kings, and their constant supply chain problems with food and water.

But looking back, the psalmist proclaimed that the goodness and faithful love of God endured.

What a great practice to foster. Take a moment and list at least five instances when you were up against it, and God came through for you in one way or another. After each one, say, *"Give thanks to the Lord, for He is good. His faithful love endures forever."*

Then list five issues going on in your life right now that are quite challenging, and by faith, say, *"Give thanks to the Lord, for He is good. His faithful love endures forever."*

Our God is THE GOD who never slumbers or sleeps, who always watches over us, whose goodness and faithful love are always working for our personal good and for His glory!

God, I praise You that Your love and goodness never run dry. Enable me to see and experience this in the midst of my challenges. Amen

WELCOME TO BABYLON
December 19

"But how can we sing the songs of the Lord while in a pagan land?"
Psalm 137:4

A delightful video is that of Steve Martin and friends singing, "Atheists Don't Have No Songs." It is worth googling. Martin speaks before they sing: "You know, religious people have such beautiful art and music. Atheists have really nothing." Then they get into the song—a couple of excerpts: "For atheists, there is no good news, they'll never sing a song of faith. In their songs, they have a rule: the he is always lower case;" "Baptists have the rock of ages; atheists just sing the blues." It's hilarious.

Christians do have such songs of joy and hope. But like our psalmist, we don't always feel like singing. A little background: after God raised up Nebuchadnezzar to discipline His people, they were carted off to Babylon. Separated from their homeland, their great city, and the Temple, they were in deep grief: *"Beside the rivers of Babylon, we sat and wept as we thought of Jerusalem"* (v.1). Their captors taunted them in their grief, *"Sing us one of those joyful songs of Jerusalem!"* (v.3). Even in a casual reading of this psalm, one feels the gloom and despair.

When life is good and going well, it's easy to sing songs of joy. But what about when times are not good and things are not going well. Will you still sing songs of joy?

A few points to remember:

1. We too live in Babylon. This world is not our home. *"For this world is not our permanent home; we are looking forward to a home yet to come"* (Hebrews 13:14).
2. We don't belong here. *"Dear friends, I warn you as temporary residents and foreigners—strangers and exiles"* (1 Peter 2:11). Pilgrims. Immigrants. Our citizenship is with another kingdom.
3. We're just passing through. Don't get too settled here. The Apostle Peter often uses the word 'tent' to describe his own body. *"I think it is right, as long as I am in this bodily tent, to wake you up with a reminder, since I know that I will soon lay aside my tent, as our Lord Jesus Christ has indeed made clear to me"* (2 Peter 1:13-14). A tent. Not a log cabin. Not a house. Not a mansion. Not a structure with wood, brick, and mortar. A tent. What's the main feature of a tent? It's portable, not permanent.

This Christmas season, no matter how gloomy and dark you feel, begin to sing the songs of joy like Silent Night, O Little Town of Bethlehem, Hark the Herald Angels Sing, and Joy to the World. Pray that, by God's grace, you will be able to lift your voice and thereby lift your spirits.

God, help me to see how brief this difficult time really is—and fill my heart with peace and joy. Amen

INTIMATE
December 20

"O Lord, You have examined my heart and know everything about me. You know when I sit down or stand up. You know my thoughts even when I'm far away. You see me when I travel and when I rest at home. You know everything I do. You know what I am going to say even before I say it, Lord. You go before me and follow me. You place your hand of blessing on my head. Such knowledge is too wonderful for me, too great for me to understand!"

Psalm 139:1-6

Psalm 139 is one of my favorite psalms for so many different reasons. If David was known as the 'sweetest psalmist,' then this is the sweetest of his psalms. I never tire of reading it and experiencing a deeper intimacy with God as I do. The psalm itself breaks down into four sonnets; four movements. As we drink from it the next four days, I pray it will bless you as it has me.

This section is all about the omniscience of God—that's a fancy word for an attribute of God that He sees and knows everything. He knows everything about Himself, everything about His creation, everything that's ever happened or will happen anywhere in that creation. David marvels at three aspects of God's universal knowledge and how it intersects our lives:

He knows me. It's not just that He knows all things, it's that He knows ME!

He knows little ol' me! It's personal; it's intimate. This Being that is so high, so exalted, so glorious—actually takes notice of me. He doesn't just take notice, He has full knowledge of who I am. Jesus said that He even knows the number of hairs on my head—which is diminishing each year! He really knows us, knows us better than ourselves. He knows what is in our hearts—yikes! He knows what we think, what we desire, what we fear, what we hide. He knows everything about us. In any relationship, knowledge and understanding are the building blocks of intimacy. He knows me. Wow!

He sees me. It's not just that He sees all things, it's that He sees ME!

This is another aspect of God's all-knowingness. He not only knows my insides, but He knows my outside stuff too. He keeps up with all that I do. He sees our activity, our inactivity, our travel—everything down to the minutest detail. He is the all-seeing and all-knowing God. There is nothing going on in my life that He doesn't see and have knowledge of. Nothing surprises Him or catches Him off guard. That's good to know that He isn't when I am!

He cares for me. It's not just that He cares about His creation, He cares about ME!

Important dignitaries have a detail of agents that go before and behind to care for them. The psalmist paints the picture that God goes before and behind us to illustrate God's care for us.

David mentions God's hand on his head. It's the idea of God placing His hand over us to protect us.

All of this, David says, is too wonderful to even grasp. I agree!

God, I marvel at Your knowledge and care for me. Thank You. Draw me closer to You. Amen

CLOSE

"I can never escape from Your Spirit! I can never get away from Your presence! If I go up to heaven, You are there; if I go down to the grave, You are there. If I ride the wings of the morning, if I dwell by the farthest oceans, even there Your hand will guide me, and Your strength will support me. I could ask the darkness to hide me and the light around me to become night— but even in darkness I cannot hide from You. To You the night shines as bright as day.
Darkness and light are the same to You.
Psalm 139:7-12

This section is all about the omnipresence of God—a fancy word for that attribute of God that He is ever-present in every place at every time; not just any time, but at every time whenever time is, was, or will be. Remember, time is a created thing and God is outside of time in the sense that He is not bound by our concept of it or the reality of it. Let's just put it this way: He's everywhere, He's everywhere! David points out three realities about God's universal presence and how it interconnects with our lives.

He's always with me. It's not just that He's with others, it's that He's with ME!

This is one of the great realities and promises of God we can count on: He will never leave us or forsake us. This is repeated scores of times throughout Scripture from Genesis to Revelation.

David says it right: there is no place I can go, no situation I can be in that God is not there with us. Others may abandon us—parents, spouses, friends—but God will never desert us. If we feel He is not close, it's because we've moved. It's not that He's not there, we just can't sense His presence. That's when we need to rely on His promise that He'll always be with us. **It may seem dark and gloomy to us, but it's never that way to Him.**

He always strengthens me. It's not just that He strengthens others, He strengthens ME!
One of the many verses in the Bible that reinforces this is Isaiah 41:10, *"Don't be afraid, for I am with you. Don't be discouraged, for I am your God. I will strengthen you and help you. I will hold you up with My victorious right hand."* We are weak and feeble, aren't we? But with God's strength, *"we are more than conquerors"* (Romans 8:37). Do you feel overwhelmed, unable to meet the challenge? Memorize this verse and call on the Lord for HIS strength to get through.

He will always guide me. It's not just that He guides others, it's that He guides ME!

David speaks of God's guidance in his life. Again, Scripture is replete with evidence of God's guidance when called upon: *"Trust in the Lord with all your heart; do not depend on your own understanding. Seek His will in all you do, and He will show you which path to take"* (Proverbs 3:5-6); *"Your own ears will hear Him. Right behind you a voice will say, 'This is the way you should go,' whether to the right or to the left"* (Isaiah 30:21). Feel lost or confused? Count on the Lord to direct Your steps and step out in faith.

No matter where I am or what's going on in my life, God is close to me. Amazing!

God, thank you for never leaving me and always being near. Keep me close!! Amen

CREATED

December 22

"You made all the delicate, inner parts of my body and knit me together in my mother's womb. Thank you for making me so wonderfully complex! Your workmanship is marvelous—how well I know it. You watched me as I was being formed in utter seclusion, as I was woven together in the dark of the womb. You saw me before I was born. Every day of my life was recorded in your book. Every moment was laid out before a single day had passed. How precious are your thoughts about me, O God. They cannot be numbered! I can't even count them; they outnumber the grains of sand! And when I wake up, you are still with me!"

Psalm 139:7-13-18

This section is all about God's most important sacred creation: US! Humans are unique in all of creation because only humans are created in the image of God. Biblical Christians reject any notion of modern evolutionary theory. We did not emerge and evolve over millions of years—we were intentionally and instantly created by the Master Designer. This is foundational to the faith: *"Then God said, 'Let Us make human beings in Our image, to be like Us'...So God created human beings in His own image. In the image of God He created them; male and female He created them"* (Genesis 1:26-27). David draws our attention to three features of God's creation:

He fashioned me. It's not just that He created me, He did so with great care.

David uses the imagery of a piece of cloth being knit together; his delicate parts carefully placed.

He mentions the complexity of the human body—it far exceeds the rest of creation. In the creation account of Genesis 1 and 2, God merely speaks the various aspects of the universe into existence. But with us it's different. Genesis 2:7 says that God *'formed'* Adam out of the dust. *'Formed'* is the Hebrew word meaning *to fashion*. It's as if when it came to creating humans, God got down on His hands and knees in the dirt and fashioned us into what we are. He didn't command us to become as other creations, He personally, intimately fashioned us with His hands.

He purposed me. It's not just that He created me, He did so with great purpose.

David points out that every moment of his life was laid out and recorded even before He was born. Our lives can feel disjointed, random, even chaotic. But Scripture demonstrates that God is constantly orchestrating events that lead us to the grand purpose of knowing Him, loving Him, and glorifying Him. Every person is created for that great purpose.

He delights in me. It's not just that He created me, He did so for His own pleasure.

David makes this remarkable claim: *"How precious are Your thoughts about me, O God."*

Like a father watching his child learn to walk or playing sports or walking across the graduation stage—our Heavenly Father watches us and delights in us. Inconceivable!

To read this section and to see how God personally and carefully knits us in our mother's womb and knows us and our future even before we are born, makes us even more committed to protecting the pre-born child.

God, I am overwhelmed at how personal the fashioning of me was to You. I worship You. Amen

HOLY

"O God, if only You would destroy the wicked! Get out of my life, you murderers! They blaspheme You; your enemies misuse Your name. O Lord, shouldn't I hate those who hate You? Shouldn't I despise those who oppose You? Yes, I hate them with total hatred, for Your enemies are my enemies. Search me, O God, and know my heart; test me and know my anxious thoughts. Point out anything in me that offends You, and lead me along the path of everlasting life."

Psalm 139:19-24

This final section of this great psalm is all about God's holiness. It might seem odd at first glance that David would finish the beautiful, intimate psalm with harsh, scathing words. David had many faults, but disloyalty wasn't one of them. Believing that God was holy, he desired to be holy and was willing to take on anyone who wasn't. Front and center here is the reality that some people are evil. As a matter of fact, the Bible says that all humans are innately wicked and evil. That doesn't mean that everyone is an ax murderer, it only means that outside of Christ, our moral depravity leaves us helpless, hopeless, isolated from God and worthy of His eternal judgment. So what are the intersections with this passage and our relationship with Jesus?

I should identify with Him.

David is, at the same time, commanding the evil ones to get out of his life AND calling on God to destroy them! This simply illustrates that David is so extremely loyal to Yahweh that he is frustrated and offended that these folks would oppose the Lover of his soul. He is staking the claim that He is a Yahweh man. That's a good word for us to remember as we work and live alongside people who are outside of Christ. They need to know that we are one of God's people and we are loyal to Him. Do the people in your life know of your love and loyalty for Jesus?

I should hate what He hates.

David doesn't mince words: *"O Lord, shouldn't I hate those who hate You? Shouldn't I despise those who oppose You? Yes, I hate them with total hatred, for Your enemies are my enemies."* David at other times had a softer tone with those who didn't know God, but here he is riled up. What this does for us is to remind us that we need to hate what God hates. God hates sin. He hates what sin does to people. He hates anything that opposes Him, His word, or His people. We are warned not to be too friendly with the things of this world—we are aliens! (1 Peter 2:11). Jesus is worth our undivided loyalty.

I should desire to please Him.

Notice how David finishes, not only this section, but the entire psalm: *"Search me, O God, and know my heart; test me and know my anxious thoughts. Point out anything in me that offends You, and lead me along the path of everlasting life."* As he was railing against those who were offensive to God and him, he was also conscious of the fact that he was far from perfect. He called on God to shine His spotlight on his heart and mind to see what sin was lurking and needed to be repented of. He wanted to please God above all else. So do I. Do you?

Search me, O God, and know my heart; test me and know my anxious thoughts. Point out anything in me that offends You, and lead me along the path of everlasting life. Amen

FILTERS
December 24

"Take control of what I say, O Lord, and guard my lips."
Psalm 141:3

One of the real challenges in our world today is finding entertainment on television that's not spoiled with filthy language and expletives. I don't know who writes this stuff, but it appears their own personal language is pretty foul, and they assume their characters should speak the same way. We have started watching programs on Netflix and Prime through a filtering service called VidAngel. They are the ones who streamed The Chosen, a wonderful and fresh expose' on the life of Jesus. You can set the filters to screen out filthy language and bawdy scenes. I highly recommend it.

It's not just on the TV. I am astounded at the coarse and vulgar language people use in public. I hear words and phrases out of the mouths of adolescents and adults that are shocking. My grandma used to say that people who use curse words indicate their lack of intelligence to express themselves otherwise.

My problem is not vulgarity, it's foolishness. I find myself making comments at the expense of others just to get a laugh. I say things that make me seem better at something than I really am. I over-exaggerate (get it? over + exaggerate!) all the time (get it?). All of this and more is foolish and sinful.

And then there are the times that I enter into gossip: sharing information with someone who is neither a part of the problem or solution; sharing information that demeans, belittles, or casts someone in a poor light.

The Bible speaks to the power of the tongue. The 9th Commandment warns us against lying. Ephesians 4:29 says, *"Don't use foul or abusive language. Let everything you say be good and helpful, so that your words will be an encouragement to those who hear them."* James, the half-brother of Jesus informed us that the tongue is so powerful that it can be used to move many people in the right direction, or it can be used to set people aflame with wickedness. James warns us that the tongue leads us into blunders: *"Indeed, we all make many mistakes. For if we could control our tongues, we would be perfect and could also control ourselves in every other way"* (3:2). Ultimately, the tongue reveals what is in our hearts: *"What you say flows from what is in your heart"* (Jesus in Luke 6:45).

Our psalmist appeals to God to set a filter, a guard over his mouth. I make the same prayer so very often. But I also need to pray that He changes my heart so that a filter is rarely needed.

God, change my heart and fill it with good things. Set a guard over my lips that all I say will be honoring to You and helpful to those around me. Amen

ADVENT
December 25
Selected Psalms

Today we celebrate Christ's coming. Some believers call it Advent. The word 'advent' comes from the word *'adventus,'* a Latin translation of the Greek New Testament word, *'parousia.'* Both words mean presence, arrival, coming, or official visit.

The observance of Advent began probably in the 3rd-4th Centuries A.D. and was originally all about the 2nd Advent, that is the 2nd coming of Jesus. Among His last words on earth, Jesus promised His return: John 14:3 *"If I go away and prepare a place for you, I will come back and receive you to Myself, so that where I am you may be also."*

More recently, in the past few centuries, those who observe Advent focus on the 1st Advent, the 1st coming, that we call Christmas. Those who observe Advent do so to help them get their eyes off the secularization of Christmas and focus on the real meaning of Christ's first advent.

The Psalms contain a number of prophecies about the first coming/advent of the Messiah, all of them written hundreds of years before His appearing.

Psalm 2:7-8 *"The king proclaims the Lord's decree: The Lord said to me, 'You are my son. Today I have become your Father. Only ask, and I will give you the nations as your inheritance, the whole earth as your possession.'"* The immediate application was God's adoption of David and his lineage—but is ultimately fulfilled by the birth of Jesus and His eventual reign over all nations.

Psalm 89:4 *"I will establish your offspring forever and build up your throne for all generations."* This verse extends the Messiah's reign for all of eternity.

Psalm 110:1 *"The Lord says to my Lord: 'Sit at My right hand Until I make Your enemies a footstool for Your feet'"* (NASB). *'Sit at My right hand'* indicates that the Messiah will sit on a throne; the *'right hand'* signifies not only a place of honor but also the participation in power. Jesus mentioned this verse in Matthew 22:44 to make the point that with the Pharisees, the Messiah would be more than just a human son of David—and that He was it!

Psalm 110:4 *"The Lord has taken an oath and will not break His vow: 'You are a priest forever in the order of Melchizedek.'"* Melchizedek was the king of Salem (later named Jerusalem) and the high priest of the Most High God. He makes a brief appearance in the book of Genesis—and seems to have no beginning or end. The psalmist is letting us know that the Messiah will be like Mr. M. The writer of Hebrews compares Jesus with Melchizedek: a king and priest who literally has no beginning or end.

This morning, rejoice in the incarnation: that God condescended to this earth in the form of a man. As God/Man He fulfilled every prophecy pertaining to the Messiah.

Joy to the world, the Lord has come!! Amen!

REVEILLE
December 26

"Let me hear of your unfailing love each morning, for I am trusting you.
Show me where to walk, for I give myself to you."

Psalm 143:8

On any morning on just about any U.S. military base or ship, a bugle will sound out the staccato notes to a tune called reveille. The word comes from the French word, *reveiller*, meaning *"to wake up."* It appears there is no known composer of the tune and it is used by the military of at least six countries. The U.S. military adopted it in 1812 to muster service members for roll call and to begin the day.

Once again David is in trouble. Because he was often in so much of it, we can't really attach this psalm to any one incident or danger. In the first part of the psalm (vv.1-7), he is pleading with God to hear his prayer and not judge him. Instead, he proposes, he hopes that God will listen because He is faithful and just. It's the 'just' part of God's nature that David calls on because the forces that would do him harm are hounding him. In the latter part of the psalm (vv.9-12) he pleads with God to rescue him from distress and danger.

But right in the middle, David plays reveille to muster God's attention and affirmation each morning: *"Let me hear of Your unfailing love each morning."* Bottom line, what David needed most was to hear from the Lord: "If I can just hear from You each morning, I'll get through this."

The saints for centuries have made the same claim: when life is tough, even tragic, when challenges seem too high and emotions seem too low—they want to meet with God and hear His voice. They know how important it is to rendezvous with Him each morning. Do you? Time with God each morning makes ALL. THE. DIFFERENCE. IN. THE. WORLD!!

Blow reveille tomorrow morning, and each morning, seeking the Lord and listening for His voice. He'll show you where to walk and how to get through.

God, thank You that I can meet with the Creator of all that is each morning! Wake me with thoughts of You. Praise You.!! Amen

GENTLE ON HIS MIND

December 27

"O Lord, what are human beings that you should notice them,
mere mortals that You should think about them?"

Psalm 144:3

In 1967, Glenn Campbell released the song, "Gentle On My Mind." It was an instant hit with its down-home, folksy melody and words. The lyrics paint a picture of a man who seemed to have his lover constantly in his thoughts. Images of her settled gently on his mind.

David is the writer of this psalm and we believe that he wrote it after finally being placed on the throne following a protracted scuffle with Saul. There were still battles to be fought and enemies to be defeated (i.e., the Philistines), but he pauses to bless Yahweh for His favor and the resulting victory:

> *Praise the Lord, who is my rock. He trains my hands for war and gives my fingers skill for battle. He is my loving ally and my fortress, my tower of safety, my rescuer. He is my shield, and I take refuge in him. He makes the nations submit to me (vv.1-2).*

If you've studied the life of David, you know that he was chosen by God to be king while still a 15-year-old teenager. He was despised by his older brothers, even more so after he came against and killed Goliath a few years later. He served in King Saul's court afterward and was the object of abuse and death threats. Eventually, he had to flee for his life while Saul tried to hunt him down and kill him. This continued until he was 30 years old. Tough life.

So now as he sits on his newly acquired throne reflecting on the handiwork of God in his life, he is overwhelmed with the humble thought: what am I, who am I that You, Creator of the Universe, would think about me or even notice me?

There is this realization that must come to every person eventually, either this side or the other side of death: I deserve God's judgment. As a morally depraved and wicked individual, the only attention I should get from God is His wrath and fury. When we accept that perspective in this life, we repent and turn to Jesus who offers us The Way, The Truth, and The Life with the Father, avoiding His judgment. What we deserve was placed on Jesus at the cross and by faith, we take that to be true for us individually. For those who refuse this perspective, they will be forced to acknowledge it in the life to come: *"at the name of Jesus every knee should bow, in heaven and on earth and under the earth, and every tongue declare that Jesus Christ is Lord, to the glory of God the Father"* (Philippians 2:10-11).

The glorious thing about recognizing this truth now is that we are flooded with gratitude and amazement that God would stoop to save us; that as great and awesome as He is, that He would think of me or even notice me!! Yet, He does. We are constantly gentle on His mind!

God, thank You for thinking of me with warmth and affection! I love You!! Amen

SLOW
December 28

"The Lord is gracious and compassionate, slow to anger and great in faithful love."
Psalm 145:8 (CSB)

Have you ever known someone who had a hair-trigger? I'm not talking about a gun; I'm talking about anger; a temper. I've known people who, with the slightest provocation, are ready to get into a fight, either verbally or physically. In all honesty, I would characterize myself that way at times. I am so impatient that, sadly, I can feel frustration and anger well up in me pretty quickly—especially when I drive! I don't defend it but only identify it as a part of my fallen nature. However, by God's grace, He has granted me a growing amount of self-control (a fruit of the Spirit) and I find that His indwelling Spirit is transforming my nature to be more like that of God's.

God's nature doesn't need transforming. He is who He is: always has been and always will be. He is, among other glorious attributes, morally pure and perfect. He is a just God who demands that His creation obey and worship Him. Fortunately, He is also gracious and compassionate. His justice and righteousness are balanced with mercy and kind-heartedness.

That doesn't mean that He is all teddy bears and lollipops. He does experience anger. And in His infinite wisdom, He displays His displeasure on whomever He wants, how He wants, when He wants.

Our psalmist here, King David, certainly experienced and wrote about the discipline of Yahweh in his life in other psalms. But in this psalm, David focuses on the fact that God doesn't have a hair-trigger with those with whom He has a covenant relationship. About Yahweh, David writes, He is *"slow to anger and great in faithful love."* That last phrase, *faithful love,* is the Hebrew word, *chesed,* meaning covenant love. It's not a sentimental love as we know it, it carries with it the idea of strength, faithfulness, devotion, and loyalty. If you are in a covenant relationship with God through faith in Christ, He has that love for you.

As I've learned to love Sue more, I've more understood the *chesed* of God. It's not that I don't FEEL love for her—I do now more than ever. But it's beyond that. I have this deep-seated devotion and loyalty to her that is incredibly powerful. One of the effects of it is that I am more patient, less trigger-happy, more kind, less frustrated. I am becoming *'slow to anger'* as I grow in my faithful, *chesed* love.

How about you? Are you seeing more and more how patient God is with you; how kind and compassionate He is with you? Do you thank and praise Him for that every chance you get?

And does His *chesed* toward you prompt *chesed* toward those around you? I pray so.

God, thank You for being so patient and kind with me. I praise You. Enable me to be a conduit of that love to those around me, particularly my family and close friends. Amen

DUPLICITOUS
December 29

"The Lord is close to all who call on Him, yes, to all who call on Him in truth."
Psalm 145:18

Do you know who Eddie Haskell was? He was a character on the "Leave It To Beaver Show" back in the 1950s and 60s. One moment he was all gentlemanly and proper with adults, and the next moment, when no parent was around, he was a devilish scoundrel. Google a clip and you'll see what I mean.

Have you ever known someone who said or acted one way in front of one group, but another way in front of another? We use various terms to describe them: hypocrite, double-dealing, two-faced, or duplicitous. No one really respects someone like that.

Neither does God. Notice the verse for today. The writer is David and he knows full well that God doesn't respond to people who are dishonest because he was guilty of asking God for something while his heart wasn't really aligned with God.

The phrase, *"God is close to all who call on Him"* refers to the fact that God wants us to pray to Him, to call on Him. In fact, He commands us to: *"Call to Me and I will answer you, and I will tell you great and mighty things, which you do not know"* (Jeremiah 33:3; NASB). He's close, He's leaning in, He's all ears when we call on Him.

That is, if we call on Him in truth. What that means is that God responds to us when our hearts are in line with His. It does no good to pray for your spouse to love you more if you're treating him/her with disrespect. It does no good to pray for a certain job if you have no intention of using that job for His glory. It does no good to pray for financial success if you have no intention of tithing or more on the money you get. Psalm 66:18 (NASB) puts it this way, *"If I regard wickedness in my heart, The Lord will not hear."*

When we come before the Lord in prayer, it is incumbent upon us to first search our hearts to see if our hearts align with His heart. In areas where that is not true, we need to confess, and if necessary, reconcile and make restitution.

Don't be like Eddie: all holy when you come before God and then after you've thrown your request at Him, leave with the intention of living the way you want. You wouldn't let your child get away with that. Neither does our Father. He loves you too much to let that happen.

God, purify my motives when I pray. Enable me to pray for Your will in all things. Amen

SCARS
December 30

"He heals the brokenhearted and bandages their wounds."
Psalm 147:3

As I begin my eighth decade on this earth, I can honestly say two things: first, either by my own doing or the doing of others, I have suffered many, many wounds, some of them deep; second, God has faithfully brought healing to me in ways that are difficult to explain, yet undeniable.

I'm not naïve nor possess a pollyannish outlook on life. Severe emotional trauma as an adolescent, debilitating depression with suicidal tendencies as a young adult, along with a guilt and shame-ridden wandering, the loss of both of my parents and only brother—all wracked my heart with great pain. Add to that the wounds of ministry (people will say and do the cruelest of things to a pastor) including guile, hatred, subterfuge, and betrayal—and you get part of the picture. Then there is Sue's cancer along with the 5 months of chemo and month of radiation where I dealt with the very real fear and possibility that she would not survive.

Yet I can honestly say, without any equivocation, that God has been good to me. He has healed me in so many ways. Yes, there is still some scarring, but those scars only serve to remind me of His grace, mercy, and healing power. So it is no problem for me to give praise to my God. In fact, as this psalm says in v.1, *"Praise is pleasant, delightful, and fitting."* It's a pleasant and delightful experience to praise God. And it certainly is fitting given all that He has done for me.

The most important act of His kindness is evident on the cross: *"But God demonstrates His own love toward us in that while we were yet sinners, Christ died for us"* (Romans 5:8; NASB). The biggest wound of any of us was caused by sin. It's an eternally fatal wound unless we invite Jesus to bring healing to our souls.

Are you brokenhearted? Do you have wounds that need healing? Whether they were caused by someone else or self-inflicted, there is no limit to His love, His mercy and grace, and His healing power. Here's how the Apostle Paul put it:

> *"And may you have the power to understand, as all God's people should, how wide, how long, how high, and how deep His love is. May you experience the love of Christ, though it is too great to understand fully"* (Ephesians 3:18-19).

There is no heart He can't mend, no brokenness He can't fix, no wound He can't heal. Trust Him. Depend on Him. Call on Him. Praise Him.

God, I have some wounds that are not healed. I ask that You show me how to cooperate with You to experience your restoration in my life. Amen

THE BEGINNING
December 31

"Praise the Lord! Praise God in His sanctuary; praise Him in His mighty heaven! Praise Him for his mighty works; praise His unequaled greatness! Praise Him with a blast of the ram's horn; praise Him with the lyre and harp! Praise Him with the tambourine and dancing; praise Him with strings and flutes! Praise Him with a clash of cymbals; praise Him with loud clanging cymbals. Let everything that breathes sing praises to the Lord! Praise the Lord!"

Psalm 150

Here we are at the conclusion of our journey through the Book of Psalms. It is divided into five sections, each concluding with a doxology, an expression of praise. At the end of this fifth section, Psalm 150 serves as a doxology for the entire Book of Psalms.

It begins with *"Praise the Lord!"* In Hebrew, it's just one word made up of two parts: *hillel*, meaning to praise, and *Yah*, the first syllable in God's name, Yahweh. In the English, it is Hallelujah. This *"Praise the Lord!"* actually begins and ends each of the last five psalms.

Psalm 150 is different than almost all the other psalms: there is no appeal to God, there is no discussion of adversity, there is no admonishment to walk the correct path, there is no conversation about enemies and victory. It is a passionate appeal for creation to let it all out and praise the Creator. There is no spatial limit to where we should praise God—here on earth as in the Temple, or as high as the heavens (v.1). Wherever we are, we can and should praise God. There is no rational limit to our praise of God—He has demonstrated His unequaled power and greatness in our lives (v.2) and has given us every reason to praise Him. By whatever means necessary, we should praise Him (vv. 3-5). The psalmist lists a variety of musical instruments to use, but the most important one listed over and over in the Psalms is the instrument of our voice.

He concludes with the clear and compelling admonition: *"Let everything that breathes sing praises to the Lord!"* This last psalm has one point, a point reinforced from the very beginning: let every creature that God has breathed life into, praise the Lord.

That is exactly what is going to happen at the end of this age:

> *And then I heard every creature in heaven and on earth and under the earth and in the sea. They sang: "Blessing and honor and glory and power belong to the One sitting on the throne and to the Lamb forever and ever."*

When we get to heaven, will be singing and shouting praises to the Lamb forever. If you don't enjoy it for 20 minutes now, how will you feel when it's part of what we do FOREVER? Begin today, and continue it this coming year, praying for and developing a heart of praise. If it's in your heart, it will find its way to your lips!! Hallelujah!!

Yahweh, grant me a heart of praise that compels me to sing and live a life of praise. Amen!

BE BLESSED

Made in the USA
Columbia, SC
28 November 2021